DATE DUE FOR RETURN

FORGING REVOLUTION

Metalworkers, Managers, and the State
in St. Petersburg, 1890–1914

HEATHER HOGAN

INDIANA UNIVERSITY PRESS

Bloomington and Indianapolis

The paper used in this publication meets the minimum requirements of American
National Standard for Information Sciences—Permanence of Paper for Printed
Library Materials, ANSI Z39.48-1984.

Manufactured in the United States of America

Library of Congress Cataloging-in-Publication Data

Hogan, Heather, date
    Forging revolution : metalworkers, managers, and the state in St. Petersburg,
1890–1914 / Heather Hogan.
    p. cm. — (Indiana-Michigan series in Russian and East European studies)
(Studies of the Harriman Institute)
    Includes bibliographical references and index.
    ISBN 0-253-32837-3
    1. Metalworkers—Russia—St. Petersburg—History. 2. Industrial relations—
Russia—Saint Petersburg—History. I. Title. II. Series. III. Series: Studies of the
Harriman Institute.
HD8039.M5H64   1993
331.7'669'0947453—dc20   93-12364

1 2 3 4 5 97 96 95 94 93

To Chris

CONTENTS

ACKNOWLEDGMENTS

I have been fortunate in receiving the help of many friends, colleagues, teachers, and institutions over the years and it is now a pleasure to acknowledge my gratitude.

The librarians of the University of Michigan, the Hoover Institution, the New York Public Library, the Library of Congress, and Oberlin College Library helped in countless ways. I am also grateful for the assistance of many *sotrudnitsy* in the archives and libraries of Moscow and Leningrad, especially S. I. Gmelina of TsGIA, and Lidiia A. Nikulina and Elena A. Suntsova of LGIA. Special thanks go to Professor Boris V. Anan'ich, my adviser during the 1978–79 academic year.

Among the institutions whose support made possible the research and writing of this book, I would like to thank the International Research and Exchanges Board, the Charles E. Culpeper Foundation, the American Council of Learned Societies, the National Endowment for the Humanities, the W. Averell Harriman Institute for Advanced Study of the Soviet Union at Columbia University, the Russian Research Institute of Harvard University, and Oberlin College.

I am most grateful to my colleagues in the History Department of Oberlin College who have provided a supportive and intellectually challenging environment in which to teach and to learn. Special thanks go to Gary Kornblith who has critiqued portions of this manuscript in various states of completion.

Many people have read conference papers and discussed drafts of this manuscript; I appreciate their time and thought, and wish to acknowledge in this way just how much scholarship is a collective enterprise. I wish to thank especially Barbara Engel, Laura Engelstein, Daniel Field, Ziva Galili, Esther Kingston-Mann, Diane Koenker, Timothy Mixter, David Montgomery, William Sewell, Ron Suny, Gerald Surh, Frank Wcislo, and Allan Wildman. I have been privileged to have Reginald Zelnik read my work over the years; I've learned a great deal about Russian labor history from Reggie and wish to thank him most sincerely for the enormous care with which he read this manuscript. I believe he has strengthened it in many ways. I owe a special debt to Leopold Haimson who has generously shared his magisterial studies on the late Imperial period with me, as well as his insights into the special militance of Petersburg workers. He has influenced my thinking in many important ways, while offering much support.

William Rosenberg has guided this project from its inception as a doctoral dissertation; by now he has read more drafts than I am able to recall. He has helped in countless ways, all the while challenging, teaching, and encouraging me tirelessly. As teacher, scholar, mentor, and friend, I wish to thank Bill very much.

Finally, my family deserves mention. My grandmother, Agnes Budge Peerless, insured that the intellectual interests of her two grandchildren were carefully nurtured. My brother, Richard Hogan, has provided an inspiring example of excellence in teaching, rigor in scholarly pursuits, and boundless curiosity about the world. My daughter Katie has grown up with this book and has been enormously forgiving of all the time it has taken to complete. I hope she knows just how much her hugs, pictures, and words of encouragement have meant. My husband Chris has contributed far more than I can adequately express. I am deeply grateful for his patience, humor, self-sacrifice, and even, at times, his anger with a project that seemed never-ending. Despite the long hours this book required, I trust that Chris and Katie realize that my first love resides with my family.

LIST OF ABBREVIATIONS

d.: delo (file)

f.: fond (collection)

IRL: *Istoriia rabochikh Leningrada. Tom pervyi. 1703-fevral' 1917.* Leningrad, 1972.

l., ll.: list, listy (folio, folios)

LGIA: Leningradskii Gosudarstvennyi Istoricheskii Arkhiv

MVD: Ministerstvo vnutrennykh del

1909 survey: Soiuz rabochikh po metallu, St. Petersburg. *Materialy ob ekonomicheskom polozhenii i professional'noi organizatsii peterburgskikh rabochikh po metallu.* St. Petersburg, 1909.

* NPRR: *Nachalo pervoi russkoi revoliutsii. Ianvar'-mart 1905 g.* Edited by N. S. Trusova et al. Moscow, 1955.

ODR: *Obshchestvennoe dvizhenie v Rossii v nachale XX-go veka.* Edited by L. Martov, P. Maslov, and A. Potresov. 4 vols. St. Petersburg, 1909–14.

OIL: *Ocherki istorii Leningrada.* 4 vols. Edited by V. M. Kochakov et al. Moscow-Leningrad, 1955–64.

op.: opis' (inventory)

Petersburg Industrial Society: *Obshchestvo dlia sodeistviia uluchsheniiu i razvitiiu fabrichno-zavodskoi promyshlennosti*

PSMFO: Petersburg Society of Mill and Factory Owners (*Peterburgskoe obshchestvo zavodchikov i fabrikantov*)

* RDVL: *Revoliutsionnoe dvizhenie v Rossii vesnoi i letom 1905 g., aprel'-sentiabr'. Chast' pervaia.* Edited by N. S. Trusova et al. Moscow, 1957.

RSDRP: Rossiiskaia Sotsialdemokraticheskaia Rabochaia Partiia

TsGAOR: Tsentral'nyi Gosudarstvennyi Arkhiv Oktiabr'skoi Revoliutsii

TsGIA: Tsentral'nyi Gosudarstvennyi Istoricheskii Arkhiv

TsGVIA: Tsentral'nyi Gosudarstvennyi Voenno-istoricheskii Arkhiv

* VPR: *Vysshii pod"em revoliutsii 1905–1907 gg. Vooruzhennye vosstaniia, noiabr'-dekabr' 1905 g. Chast' pervaia.* Edited by A. L. Sidorov et al. Moscow, 1955.

* VPRIA: *Vtoroi period revoliutsii, 1906–1907 gg. Chast' pervaia. Ianvar'-aprel' 1906 g.* Moscow, 1961.

* VPRII: *Vtoroi period revoliutsii, 1906–1907 gg. Ianvar'-iiun' 1907 g.* Edited by N. S. Trusova et al. Moscow, 1963.

* VPRMS: *Vtoroi period revoliutsii, 1906–1907 gg. Chast' vtoraia. Mai-sentiabr' 1906 g. Kniga 1.* Edited by G. M. Derenkovskii et al. Moscow, 1961.

* VPROD: *Vtoroi period revoliutsii, 1906–1907 gg. Oktiabr'-dekabr' 1906 g.* Edited by M. S. Simonov et al. Moscow, 1963.

* VPSO: *Vserossiiskaia politicheskaia stachka v oktiabre 1905 g. Chast' pervaia.* Edited by L. M. Ivanov et al. Moscow-Leningrad, 1955.
ZIRTO: *Zapiski imperatorskogo russkogo tekhnicheskogo obshchestva*

*A volume in the series *Revoliutsiia 1905–1907 gg. v Rossii. Dokumenty i materialy.*

FORGING REVOLUTION

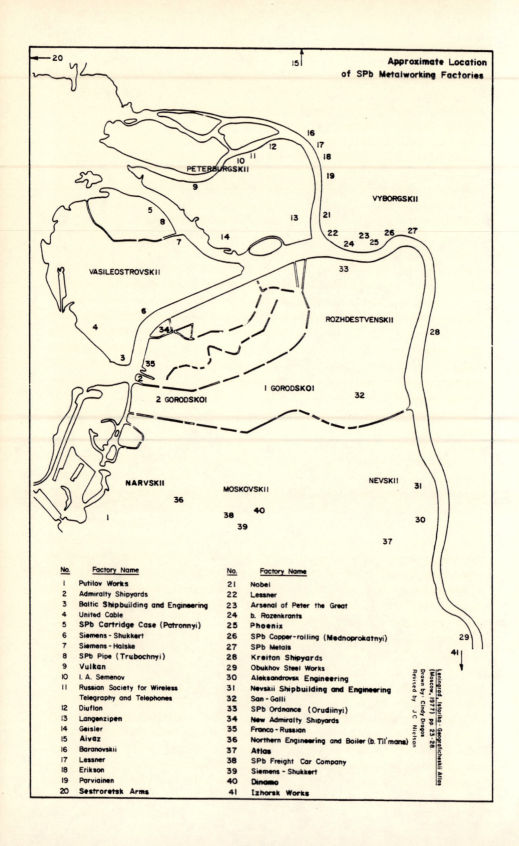

Approximate Location of SPb Metalworking Factories

No.	Factory Name	No.	Factory Name
1	Putilov Works	21	Nobel
2	Admiralty Shipyards	22	Lessner
3	Baltic Shipbuilding and Engineering	23	Arsenal of Peter the Great
4	United Cable	24	b. Rozenkrants
5	SPb Cartridge Case (Patronnyi)	25	Phoenix
6	Siemens - Shukkert	26	SPb Copper-rolling (Mednoprokatnyi)
7	Siemens - Halske	27	SPb Metals
8	SPb Pipe (Trubochnyi)	28	Kreiton Shipyards
9	Vulkan	29	Obukhov Steel Works
10	I. A. Semenov	30	Aleksandrovsk Engineering
11	Russian Society for Wireless Telegraphy and Telephones	31	Nevskii Shipbuilding and Engineering
12	Diuflon	32	San - Galli
13	Langenzipen	33	SPb Ordnance (Orudiinyi)
14	Geisler	34	New Admiralty Shipyards
15	Aivaz	35	Franco - Russian
16	Baranovskii	36	Northern Engineering and Boiler (b. Til'mans)
17	Lessner	37	Atlas
18	Erikson	38	SPb Freight Car Company
19	Parviainen	39	Siemens - Shukkert
20	Sestroretsk Arms	40	Dinamo
		41	Izhorsk Works

Leningrad, Istoriko - Geograficheskii Atlas (Moscow, 1977) pp. 23-28.
Drawn by: Cindy Dragos
Revised by J.C. Nielson

INTRODUCTION

Many of the grand themes of Russian history have reemerged with particular force in recent years, reminding us of important continuities even as polity and society appear to be changing rapidly. Such "cursed" questions as Russia's relationship to the West and the issue of overcoming "backwardness" loom large now, as does the relationship between state and society. This study looks closely at an earlier attempt to "modernize" authoritarian institutions and "catch up" with an economically more powerful West from the vantage point of the metalworking industry of St. Petersburg in the late Imperial period.

The tsarist regime's drive to industrialize Russia at the end of the nineteenth century led to the growth of an urban working class and an expanding cadre of professionals and managers; the beginnings of new organizational structures (and values) to nurture emergent capitalist forms; and a host of troubling questions about the place of "modern" industry in a still largely agrarian and autocratic polity. The Petersburg metals industry was central to this process of economic development, as well as crucial to the military security of the tsarist state. It was led by a powerful group of entrepreneurs and financiers who pursued a vision of an economically more vital and socially more productive nation and who came, with the passage of time, to employ Imperial Russia's most militant workers. In the evolving relationship of labor and management in the all-important heavy industry of the capital, the upheaval experienced by key segments of urban Russia in its struggle with "modernity" may be perceived.

For the metalworking industry of the capital, the confrontation between tradition and modernity was shaped by two important phenomena in the first years of the twentieth century. At the turn of the century, a serious economic downturn undercut demand and forced the industry to come to terms with the problem of excess capacity: the costs of the chaotic growth of the 1890s now had to be faced—economic crisis impelled financial, organizational, and technological reorganization. During 1905, industrialists encountered a different order of problem: intense strike conflict over the course of the revolutionary year revealed a crisis of labor discipline, forcing industrialists to rethink supervision of the shop floor and encour-

1

aging them to move away from older, more overtly coercive methods of labor control.

Recognizing that extant managerial approaches were no longer effective, Petersburg heavy industrialists set out to "modernize" their methods of labor discipline and recoup the economic losses of the recent past. They were encouraged in these efforts by some of Russia's leading engineers, who had begun to advance a technocratic and productivist vision of the future Russia which hinged on the "rationalization" of its dominant institutions. Like so many other members of the emergent professional middle class in Europe and America at this time, Russia's engineers forwarded their claims to leadership on the basis of a positivist faith in the prerogatives of experts and with a boundless confidence in their ability to utilize science and technology for the benefit of all. Dismissive of the "backwardness" of those who embraced a different way of seeing, the technical intelligentsia soon found itself enmeshed in a growing crisis of authority in urban-industrial Russia.

The upheaval experienced by the metalworking industry in the first years of the century proved central to the social and political conflict which came to shape life in the capital city in the years before the outbreak of World War I. Important here is the fate of the democratic project in Imperial Russia and the reasons why the St. Petersburg entrepreneurial elite abandoned emergent parliamentary institutions and moved instead toward a type of corporatist politics which characterized German and Italian industrial magnates in the post–World War I period. Just as significant are the reasons why the new institutional approaches which emerged over the course of 1905–1906 for the resolution of labor-management conflict and which in other countries developed in the direction of a reformist trade unionism were instead deployed in the Petersburg metalworking industry in a highly confrontational manner. In this case, liberal forms proved unable to transcend autocratic context.

Western historians of Russian labor have offered a variety of explanations for the labor radicalism that came to shape the late Imperial period. In their studies of 1905, for example, both Laura Engelstein and Gerald Surh have focused on the particularities of the urban environment and distinctive workplace settings as factors which fostered working class militancy. Moreover, Surh in particular has emphasized the centrality of the experience of participation in militant strike struggles in shaping worker attitudes.[1] Further, while most Western scholars have found the interaction between workers and socialist intelligentsia important in shaping working class politics, none would accept the wooden, one-dimensional view of orthodox Soviet historiography that posits a militant working class walking hand in hand with the Bolsheviks to the inevitable triumph of October. My study accepts these recent findings and seeks to extend them into a later period, but it also focuses attention on politics at the point of production and the particularities of labor radicalism when examined through the prism of an evolving relationship between labor and management. In endeavoring to bring the mentalité of employers and engineers more clearly into view, and in investigating closely the changing structure of an industry that was vital to the national economy, my investigation seeks to broaden the range of factors taken into consideration when assessing the nature of the crisis besetting state and society in the late Imperial period.

While this study largely centers on that prototypical Marxist proletarian—the "militant" metalworker of the early twentieth century—I argue against the dominant Soviet paradigm that sees in the activism of metalworkers the ineluctable unfolding of revolutionary class consciousness. As Reginald Zelnik reminds us, the life course of a Russian worker was never a linear progression from "darkness" to "consciousness," but rather was marked by all sorts of ambiguity and conflict.[2] And while I find that a consciousness of class did develop in the post-1905 period, I judge it to arise from contingent phenomena which included the "lived experience" of metalworkers in the factory and within their communities; the interaction between metalworkers and their radical intelligentsia patrons; the keen involvement of metalworkers in the political and economic struggles of 1905 and their exhilarating if brief experience of "freedom" following the issuance of the October Manifesto; and, especially, the bitter reality of political repression and managerial counteroffensive over the 1907–1914 period. Both structural and historically contingent phenomena shaped the perceptions and activism of metalworkers.

From these perspectives on the nature of labor radicalism, I have come to question some of the conclusions advanced in the literature. Thus, contrary to the recent findings of Robert McKean, I argue that increasing numbers of metalworkers were attracted to Bolshevism because the uncompromising critique of polity and society that it offered "made sense" to them on the basis of their lived experience. Viewed from below, Bolshevik ways of seeing were very much gaining ground by the eve of World War I; viewed from above, Bolshevism remained extraordinarily fractious and organizationally weak.[3] Contrary to the researches of Victoria Bonnell and Geoffrey Swain, I find metalworkers rejecting on a grass-roots level the cautious trade unionism espoused by most Mensheviks because the changing structure of the industry made such an approach hopelessly ineffective. Metalworkers thus emerge as active agents in the rejection of a reformist trade unionism, rather than passive recipients of the repressive policies of employers and state officials who refused to allow such organizations to develop.[4]

Many of the questions raised in this study about the particular militance of metalworkers and the problems of class formation have been asked by American and European labor historians; so, too, questions concerning the organizational and technological development of the industry will be familiar to historians of the "second" industrial revolution (ca. 1880–1920), as will the conflicts surrounding the introduction of the "science" of management.[5] But it is my hope that the view from St. Petersburg will expand this ongoing discussion by looking closely at the ways in which the politics of modernization in an autocratic state influenced working class formation and consciousness, the strategies adopted by business elites, as well as the specific

and particular ways in which the industry "rationalized" in the early twentieth century.

In the end, Western-inspired models took on radically different valences
in the Russian context. "Amerikanizm" did not overcome "backwardness"
in the early twentieth century, but rather challenged in an often threatening
and offensive manner the dominant cultural norms. Both metalworkers and
their employers struck out in their own directions, ultimately frustrating the
vision of Russia's small and fragile liberal intelligentsia.

I

PETERSBURG'S METALWORKING INDUSTRY IN THE POST-EMANCIPATION ERA

The Growth of the Industry

Founded with a keen eye for the military needs of the state by Peter the Great in the first years of the eighteenth century, St. Petersburg by mid-nineteenth century remained nonetheless a predominantly commercial and administrative center. Despite its long history of shipbuilding and arms manufacture, on the eve of Emancipation the heavy industry of the capital was relatively stagnant and very largely state owned. It was only at the time of the Crimean War (1853–1856) that a private industry of importance began to emerge.

Government orders for military materiel rather than the needs of the private sector led to the establishment of such firms as Siemens-Halske (later a leader in electrical engineering), San-Galli, Lessner, St. Petersburg Metals (destined to become the largest machine-building factory in the capital), and Carr and MacPherson (later the Baltic Shipbuilding and Engineering Works). And although the end of the Crimean War led to a sharp decline in government demand, the industry again began to advance in the 1860s. Such future giants of Petersburg heavy industry as the Ludwig Nobel Machine Construction Factory (1862), the Obukhov Steel Mill (1863), the Semiannikov and Poletika Works (1863)—later known as the Nevskii Shipbuilding and Engineering Works—and the Putilov Factory (1868) were established, in large part, as a result of the government's heightened interest in military modernization. Equally important was the regime's new concern for railroad construction, which generated significant demand for rail, rolling stock, and a vast array of goods associated with the development of a complex transportation network. By the mid-1870s, however, the economy as a whole experienced the effects of a European financial crisis which tightened credit generally in Russia; and while heavy industry was pulled out of its financial difficulties, temporarily and in part, by the outbreak of the Russo-Turkish War in 1877, the boom of the late 1870s was short-lived.

By the winter of 1880–81 the first signs of a serious economic downturn appeared. Within a year, Russia joined Europe in a severe depression which lasted until 1887. Meantime, the Ekaterinoslav railroad was completed, opening the mineral wealth of the Donbass to extensive exploitation and laying the foundation for the emergence of a vast metallurgical complex in the Ukraine. Both developments seriously affected the capital's heavy industry: some of the firms established during the earlier boom period went under, some were reorganized as joint-stock corporations, some were acquired by the state. Still others were forced to alter their product line substantially in response to the opening of the South.[1]

Shaped by the boom-bust cycles of the post-Emancipation decades and the mercurial demands of the state, the metalworking industry bore the scars of an uneven process of development. Consider, for example, the experience of the Putilov Works.

In late 1867, Nikolai I. Putilov, an engineer, mathematician, and former official in the Naval Ministry, secured a government contract to manufacture rails for the Nikolaev railroad. The contract was paid in advance, with prices set at generous rates. With the infusion of these monies, he immediately acquired the old State Iron Works and by the end of January 1868 was successfully producing rails. The factory grew rapidly. By mid-1870, Putilov and his 2,500 workers celebrated the rolling of their four millionth pood of rail. Still, the factory soon experienced serious financial difficulties. By 1873, Putilov was forced to give up sole ownership of the firm and reorganize his holdings into a joint-stock corporation; but this effort soon faltered as well due to the financial crisis sweeping Europe. Putilov was forced to curtail production and fire a third of his work force. His attempt to relieve the financial pressure by entering into the production of rolling stock also failed, and through the end of the decade the factory's debt continued to grow.

Putilov's death in 1880 did not alter the financial fortunes of the firm. Debts continued to mount through the early 1880s, until the factory was acquired in 1883 by the Briansk-Warsaw syndicate of metallurgical firms, located in the rapidly developing Southern region, for the express purpose of eliminating competition in the rail market. (While the Southern firms could produce rails more cheaply, the Putilov works had important ministerial connections which provided it with the lion's share of the market.) Once the Briansk-Warsaw group had accomplished its goal, the Petersburg firm was again put up for sale. By the end of the decade the majority shareholder was N. N. Antsyferov, the chairman of the board of the St. Petersburg International Bank.[2]

The Baltic factory highlights somewhat different patterns. In the mid-1850s two Englishmen, A. A. Carr and Mark MacPherson, established a small foundry and machine shop at the southern tip of Vasil'evskii Island, principally for the repair of steamships. Weathering the difficult economic times of the late 1850s, the factory expanded significantly in 1863 and began to produce not only war ships and nautical equipment, but locomotives as well. But Carr and MacPherson also fell into debt and were forced to sell. The plant was purchased by a London-based concern in the early 1870s, which renamed the company the Baltic Shipbuilding and Engineering Works and expanded into rolling stock. Despite lucrative government orders and a work force of just over 1,000, however, the insolvency of the firm led to its reorganization in 1877 as a Russian-held corporation in which the Naval Ministry became a principal shareholder. Still unable to retire its debt, the company went into receivership in 1884. Over the course of the next decade, the financial situation of the works was substantially improved, while the factory and yards were rebuilt and expanded. By 1894 the Naval Ministry made formal its decades-long interest in the factory and acquired the Baltic works in sole ownership. Beginning as a product of private entrepreneurship, dire financial problems had transformed the Baltic works into a leading state-owned firm before the end of the century.[3]

The early history of the Nevskii Shipbuilding and Engineering Works illustrates still other aspects of the development of the capital's metalworking industry. In 1857, P. V. Semiannikov and Vasilii Poletika, both mining engineers, acquired the iron foundry of John Thomson; subsequently they purchased an additional parcel of land on the Shlissel'burg tract and significantly expanded the factory in 1863. With an eye to the program of military modernization then being pursued by the War and Naval Ministries, Semiannikov and Poletika sought government orders for new ironclad ships, building three such vessels between 1863 and 1868. When the government curtailed further orders for ironclads, the factory retooled to produce locomotives and rolling stock, but to finance this rebuilding reorganized as a joint-stock corporation. Despite major loans and stock issues, mounting indebtedness and poor management plagued the firm through the latter of the 1870s. Receipt of new orders for ironclads in conjunction with the Russo-Turkish War failed to compensate for the sharp decline in government contracts for Russian-made locomotives between 1877 and 1880. Repeated government loans did not prevent the dismissal of hundreds of workers or the continuing fiscal instability of the factory, but merely postponed bankruptcy until 1886. In 1890, V. A. Titov acquired the factory at auction and, aided by the Mamontov family of Moscow, established a joint-stock corporation. With the resources and connections of Savva Mamontov, Nevskii seemed well positioned to profit from the boom of the 1890s.[4]

As these case histories indicate, the metalworking industry of the capital was fundamentally shaped by the virtual absence of a private market in heavy goods and by the changing demands of the state. But the state's involvement in the industry went considerably beyond that of consumer: through loans, subsidies, inflated prices and guaranteed orders, the state emerged as the industry's chief creditor. At the same time, the state's need for dependable suppliers of military goods often impelled it to acquire outright financially troubled private plants. Sometimes banker, sometimes entrepreneur, always consumer and competitor, the involvement of the state was both extensive and problematic. Its presence often provided a disincentive to fiscally sound, technically rational methods of production and fostered instead haphazard, even chaotic growth. Its intervention often destabilized the finances of a firm, while its mercurial shifts in the procurement of military materiel and railroad goods made possible the ruinous tendency of some factories to junk valuable equipment and extant plant in order to retool hastily to secure new contracts. The industry's great dependence on government orders, state financing, and ministerial connections thus tied its growth to the vagaries of diplomacy, budgetary constraints, and, all too often, influence peddling in the higher reaches of government.

Russia's increasing participation in the European economy also shaped the native metals industry. The boom-bust cycles of the capitalist West tended to last longer and run deeper in Russia's still primitive industrial sector and this too contributed to financial instability. Linkages with Europe were important in other ways as well. Foreigners played a leading role in the development of the capital's heavy industry, first as private entrepreneurs—as, for example, John Thomson, Carr and MacPherson, the Nobel family, and F. K. San-Galli—second and increasingly with the passage of time, as organizers and financial backers of joint-stock corporations, and finally as directors of Russian subsidiaries of foreign firms—as in the case of Siemens-Halske. Moreover, given the absence of a sufficient number of native professional engineers before the turn of the century, Europeans occupied important managerial and technical positions. And this helped Petersburg heavy industry to become more technologically sophisticated, in many cases, than metalworking plants elsewhere in the Empire.

Other equally important and characteristic features of Petersburg industry also took shape in the decades following Emancipation. Most striking was a conspicuous tendency to large factory size and hence to a highly concentrated work force. By 1891, the Putilov works employed 3,500 workers, the Nevskii factory 3,000, the Baltic works 2,200, the Obukhov plant some 1,500, and the Franco-Russian works 1,840. These five factories alone accounted for approximately one half of the work force in heavy industry, which by 1890 numbered 24,841.[5] At the same time, certain patterns of ownership emerged: in addition to the large role of state-owned factories in the capital, which employed perhaps one third of the work force in the industry, joint-stock corporations soon came to occupy a significant and expanding place as compared with individually owned concerns, which proved increasingly unable to generate the capital required in metal processing. Further, there was a pronounced universalism in production, due primarily to the vagaries of government contracting and the largely inelastic demand for heavy industrial goods on the private market. And finally, several major divisions were articulated within the industry which focused on specific product lines. These included armaments, shipbuilding, railroad construction, machine-building, and electrical engineering and, as will be seen below, created divisions that would prove of some importance with the passage of time. Still, despite these peculiarities, there can be no question that heavy industry had become a vital and visible part of St. Petersburg's economy by 1890.[6]

The Entrepreneurial Elite: An Overview

Few of the pioneers of Petersburg's heavy industry survived to witness the great expansion of 1890s. Like the industry they founded, Petersburg's early entrepreneurial elite proved highly vulnerable to the vagaries of the market and heavily dependent on foreign sources of capital and expertise. So too, the generations that followed reflected the patterns which defined the further evolution of the industry: a continuing instability in the ownership of leading firms; intimate contacts with the government and with foreign industrial and financial circles; an increasing interdependence between the leaders of the industry and the capital's major financial institutions; and a proclivity for technical and managerial innovation.[7]

The first generation of entrepreneurs included such well-known figures as Nikolai Putilov and P. M. Obukhov. Both were trained engineers from the gentry who had a flair for invention and technical detail, and both had strong ministerial connections which proved crucial in the establishment of their enterprises. But within a decade of the founding of the Putilov and Obukhov works, both men had lost their factories: the former was reorganized as a joint-stock corporation, while the latter passed to the Naval Ministry. So too, Vasilii Poletika, an engineer of noble origin and co-founder of the giant Nevskii works, was forced to relinquish control of his factory to a joint-stock corporation in the 1870s. For a time he left industry altogether, but at the time of his death in 1887 was again at the Nevskii works, employed by the board of directors as its chief executive officer.

Equally characteristic of the first generation was the prominence of foreigners as developers, managers, or principal stockholders. But here, too, few of the early leaders survived as sole owners of their firms and many became quite Russified. Carr and MacPherson sold out to the Naval Ministry; Lessner early on formed a joint-stock corporation; and during the 1890s the sons of James Moorehead reorganized as a share partnership. Atypical of the Petersburg metalworking industry was the Ludwig Nobel factory, which remained a private family holding from its founding in the 1860s to the end of the Imperial period.

One can identify a second generation of Petersburg's presumptive industrial elite among the managers and directors of the joint-stock corporations and Russian-based subsidiaries of foreign firms. While little is known of the top executives of foreign-controlled firms, men like P. A. Bartmer of the Ludwig Nobel factory and B. A. Efron of Siemens-Halske would emerge as important figures in the capital's industrial community and active participants in the Petersburg Society of Mill and Factory Owners (*Peterburgskoe obshchestvo zavodchikov i fabrikantov*). Also representative of the further evolution of the industry was N. I. Danilevskii. A leading expert in locomotive design and construction, with important contacts in the Ministry of Ways of Communication, Danilevskii was hired by the board of directors of the Putilov works in the early 1890s. Like Nikolai Putilov before him, he was an energetic and inventive man who preferred work on the shop floor to paperwork in the office. But unlike Putilov, who was the owner and chief executive officer of his own firm, Danilevskii served at the pleasure of a board of directors and exerted no independent control over the factory. Moreover, and indicative of a developing specialization in industrial management, Danilevskii was largely uninvolved in the financial administration of the factory, which was the province of A. I. Liaskii, a member of the board and a well-known financier.[8]

In the aftermath of the economic crisis at the turn of the century, but more clearly in the wake of the 1905 revolution, the next generation of Petersburg entrepreneurs emerged: directors of major banking houses and leaders of the capital's financial oligarchy. Typical was Aleksei I. Putilov, who regained control of his father's firm not through inheritance and not by assuming the day-to-day management of the factory, but as the chairman of the board of the Russian-Asiatic Bank. Aleksei had little of his father's interest in engineering and technology; his expertise was in the area of finance and banking. Like A. I. Vyshnegradskii, the director of the Petersburg International Bank from 1906 to 1917, Putilov came to control a remarkable array of industrial concerns by the prewar period.[9]

Through much of the late Imperial period, Petersburg's heavy industrial community witnessed great instability and flux. Few individual owners were able to maneuver between the unpredictability of state demand and the boom-bust cycles that periodically rocked the industry; nor were many able to generate regularly the huge amounts of capital required by the large size of the enterprise and the sophisticated technologies employed in machine construction and metal processing. In consequence, there was little stable leadership in the industry.

The peculiarities of the metalworking industry also influenced the social makeup of Petersburg's industrial elite: a significant number of foreign nationals, as well as the representatives of diverse estate (soslovie) and ethnic groupings came to make up Petersburg's nascent bourgeoisie. Since the needs of heavy industry for capital and technical expertise could not be satisfied by Russian banking and educational systems before the turn of the century, foreign participation was inevitable, particularly given the capital's geographic proximity to the West and the lucrative contracts the government was willing to offer. Also contributing to the social diversity of this elite were the engineers and military men, nobles and state officials, whose profitable contacts with influential bureaucrats catapulted them into successful business careers.

The overwhelming dependence of heavy industry on the state also fostered an exchange of personnel with the government that had social as well as political ramifications. With increasing frequency high state officials sat on the board of directors of leading firms; and following 1905, representatives of the state-owned military factories regularly attended the sessions of the Petersburg Society of Mill and Factory Owners. Most leaders of the industrial community were in regular professional contact with the military and bureaucratic establishment, and generally shared their social values.

All of this helped to retard the emergence of a stable community of industrialists in St. Petersburg able to influence the culture and politics of the surrounding urban milieu. In this and many other important respects, the industrialists of the capital differed from their counterparts in Moscow. In the old capital a more coherent industrial community had begun to emerge by the turn of the century, based in large measure on the fortunes made in textiles and transmitted through family owned firms to successive generations. Requiring considerably less capital than heavy industry, the Moscow textile barons did not have to seek outside investors or turn to joint-stock forms of ownership; relying on the private, domestic market, they did not need to depend on the more volatile state market for their livelihood. Moreover, the profits made in textiles were consistently higher than those enjoyed by the Petersburg metalworking industrialists, and in contrast to the latter, the Muscovites were not forced to send their profits abroad in the form of dividends and interest payments. The greater stability that textiles afforded the Muscovite elite found reflection in their support for the arts and in the aspiration of some of their numbers to political leadership in the late Imperial period.[10]

The socioeconomic conditions which structured the experience of the capital's industrial elite made their search for political definition and employer unity a difficult one. Prior to the turn of the century, the participation of all but a few of Petersburg's industrial leaders in national or even local affairs was modest and episodic. And even when engaged in public life, their focus was on particularistic, preeminently economic issues of direct relevance to industry.

Of the first generation of Petersburg entrepreneurs, only Poletika, Nobel, and to a lesser extent Putilov and San-Galli spoke out on issues of great moment to the industry. The overwhelming majority of their colleagues remained silent, unwilling to organize or even participate in associations sympathetic to the needs of their industry. Speaking at the 1870 industrial congress, Poletika noted in frustration that manufacturers and industrialists had distinguished themselves by their absence. Unable to explain their disinterest, he wondered aloud whether it was "the result of our usual indifference and apathy; or does the fault lie in our everlasting slumber?"[11]

If such general silence was striking, so too was the way in which the few vocal spokesmen of Petersburg heavy industry presented their case. Typically, Petersburg's leading industrialists argued their views in the public forums sponsored by the Imperial Russian Technical Society (*Imperatorskoe Russkoe tekhnicheskoe obshchestvo*) and the Russian Industrial Society (*Obshchestvo dlia sodeistviia razvitiiu promyshlennosti i torgovli*). These organizations, founded in 1866 and 1867 respectively, as well as the Industrial Congresses of 1870 and 1875 they actively sponsored, provided a setting in which those concerned with the development of native industry might comfortably express their concerns. These societies, however, had not been established at the initiative of Petersburg industrialists, nor did they attract a large membership from the capital's manufacturers. Rather, they were the creation of professionals and technical specialists who felt themselves better qualified to speak for the interests of industrialists than industrialists themselves. And the passivity of most manufacturers appeared to confirm this view. Moreover, the leaders of Petersburg industry seemed content to air their grievances, gather material in support of their positions, draft recommendations, and follow the time-honored tradition of humbly petitioning the government and waiting for it to act. Slow to organize as an autonomous, citywide interest group, Petersburg manufacturers tended instead to lobby the bureaucracy about their needs while faithfully serving the state on various governmental commissions.

It was not until 1897 that the industrialists of the capital were able to secure legal recognition for a permanent organization representative of their interests. Many felt the need to mobilize in response to a variety of government initiatives of direct practical consequence to them; others were reacting to the first serious outbreak of labor protest in the capital. Characteristically, particularistic concerns provided the essential motivation. Textile industrialists, suffering from overproduction and the strikes of 1896–97, spearheaded the effort to organize the Petersburg Industrial Society (*Obshchestvo dlia sodeistviia uluchsheniiu i razvitiu fabrichno-zavodskoi promyshlennosti*, which was reorganized in 1906 as the Petersburg Society of Mill and Factory Owners). The large metalworking firms played a decidedly secondary role. Initiative and leadership was provided by Karl Pal', a leading textile industrialist, and S. P. Glezmer, an important figure in the capital's dyeing industry, while the membership of the society as a whole reflected not only the dominance of light industry, but the larger presence of factories working for the private market as compared with those producing for the state.[12]

By the end of the century, then, an important segment of the Petersburg industrial community had been able to build an organizational structure through which the interests of the various sectors of the capital's industry could be articulated. But in this early period, the majority of metalworking industrialists played a modest role, most choosing not to participate in an organized expression of common economic concerns. Apparently the largess of the government toward heavy industry, the intimate contacts between the industry and the bureaucracy, and the solicitude of the Ministry of Finance for big business lessened the need heavy industrialists felt to unite in an autonomous association.

Petersburg Metalworkers and the Question of Class Formation, 1861–1890

At the time of Emancipation in 1861, perhaps 10,000 metalworkers labored in the heavy industry of the capital. Most were so-called "freely hired" workers, privately owned serfs earning wages in urban industry to pay quitrent fees to their rural masters; and state peasants whose families had for generations been attached to the state-owned military factories of St. Petersburg and its environs. Over the course of the next several decades, the ranks of Petersburg metallists would be filled from much the same stock: peasant migrants from the countryside, the children of metalworkers, and others from the city itself.

The absence of adequate data makes it impossible to define precisely the weight of each social group in the capital's metalworking industry or to measure changes in their relative proportions over time. It is therefore impossible to describe quantitatively the complex and often contradictory process of proletarianization among Petersburg metalworkers in the post-Emancipation era, much less correlate objective indicators with subjective dispositions. Moreover, quantitative measures and presumptions about the emergence of an hereditary working class can obscure the fact that movement from village to urban industry, or from a peasant to a proletarian identity, was rarely a unilinear or unequivocal phenomenon.[13]

It may be more useful to think about class formation as occurring (or failing to occur) on a variety of levels, each at a different pace and at different points in time. Thus we may observe "the making of a working class" within the context of the heavy industry of the capital and as a result of the particularities that defined that industry at specific points in time. Similarly, we may observe the construction of a working class through the discursive categories of the radical, but especially the Marxist intelligentsia. And we may also understand class formation in those cases and places where workers acted in a collective way as a class; and in those attitudes and dispositions which workers adopted in relationship to other actors who were perceived to be acting in their own class interests, e.g., in relationship to employers and the state.[14] With due emphasis on contingency and ambiguity, we can delineate some of the ways in which a distinctive process of class formation may have occurred among Petersburg metalworkers in the late Imperial period.

The capital and its heavy industry grew very largely on the basis of peasant in-migration. A city of more than one-half million in the first years of the 1860s, some 35% of the population belonged to the peasant *soslovie*. By the turn of the century peasant numbers had swelled dramatically: in a city of over 1.4 million inhabitants, they comprised almost two-thirds of the total. Most of this in-migration fed the burgeoning worker community and was concentrated in the industrial districts that ringed the central city (i.e., Narvskii, Nevskii, Vyborg, Petersburg), or in the immediately adjacent suburbs (i.e., Lesnoi, Poliustrov, Shlissel'burg, Petergof).[15]

Many of these migrants came from relatively distant provinces, while comparatively few came from Petersburg guberniia or other, nearby areas. According to 1869 city census data, for example, among metalworkers from the peasantry, 37.1% were migrants from Tver and Iaroslavl' province, while only 12.4% were from Petersburg province. This pattern persisted through the end of the Imperial period: membership data on the Metalworkers' Union from 1907 indicate that the largest percentage of members (34.8%) came from the Central Industrial Region, and of these, 16.5% from Tver province.[16] While the point should not be overemphasized, the relatively long trip home tended to attenuate ties to the land and to the village.

Peasant migrants were very often leaving infertile soil and overcrowded conditions, especially so with the passage of time. Some had long since abandoned agricultural pursuits and taken up handicrafts instead; some therefore brought to Petersburg the firm knowledge of a trade and the much needed skills of blacksmithing, metal crafting, or carpentry. And although the greater share of Petersburg metalworkers were drawn from the peasantry to fill the gangs performing manual labor, a certain percentage could assume considerably more prestigious and demanding skilled positions, sometimes displaying wholly "rural" attitudes while on the shop floor.[17]

Children of workers in the factories constituted a second and, with the passage of time, increasingly important source of labor for the St. Petersburg metalworking industry.[18] While probably still formally ascribed to the peasant *soslovie*, these workers maintained only marginal ties to the land and to village ways.[19] Typical, then, for many of Petersburg's older factories was the following description of the Putilov works.

> At the beginning of the 1890s, the basic mass of workers at the factory were cadre Putilovtsy-*metallisty*. From generation to generation whole families of fitters, lathe operators, and rolling mill hands worked at the Putilov factory. These were the descendants of enserfed workers at state factories and the Tula *kustars* brought by Putilov, [and were now] native inhabitants of the Narvskii Gate [district]. They did not have allotments, they were not connected to the countryside, even though many continued to be counted as peasants according to their passports.[20]

If a core of hereditary workers was apparent in heavy industry, so too, however, was the sharp demographic imbalance between the male and female population of Petersburg and the implications of such an imbalance for marital and child-raising patterns. Again, precise statistics are lacking, but an investigation by Reginald Zelnik of the two most heavily industrial districts of the city in 1869—the Aleksandro-Nevskii and the Narvskii—is broadly suggestive. Among those employed in manufacturing, the proportion of males to females was extremely high, about 4:1; still more skewed was the ratio between men and women aged 15 to 20, and only slightly less so among those aged 20 to 30. In short, men of prime marital age greatly outnumbered women in the city's two leading industrial districts, although a significant number of men were married and lived in the city without their families.[21] One of the most striking characteristics of the lower-class population in the post-Emancipation period was thus the absence of a settled family life, a pattern that pertained for decades: by 1897, of those metalworkers who married, only 31% lived with their families in St. Petersburg.[22]

A third source fueling the growth of Petersburg's working-class population came from the lower urban social groups (*sosloviia*)—petty townsmen and urban artisans (*meshchane* and *tsekhovye*). Constituting 16.7% of the population in 1862, their relative weight in the city grew to 19% by 1900; in absolute terms, an increase from 89,585 to 275,122.[23] Without ties to the land, already familiar with the urban environment, sometimes possessing skills vital to industry, this segment of the population also provided an important source of workers for heavy industry. A survey of Baltic workers in 1901 indicated that about 17% were petty townsmen or artisans (*remeslenniki*) at this time.[24] But however acclimatized to the city workers from the lower urban estates may have been, there is no need to assume they held a particular cluster of attitudes or possessed a certain type of skill; their discipline, sobriety, or mobility could be just as "pre-industrial" as that of their co-workers from other parts of the Empire or other social groups.

Because Petersburg city and province lacked an adequate pool of trained workers, heavy industrialists were forced to pay comparatively high wages and to provide relatively good working conditions to attract and retain the workers they needed. By necessity and by design, the conditions at the big factories acted as a magnet for potential recruits and at the same time fostered a longer typical length of service (*stazh*). This in turn reflected the fact that employment in this sector was more than a temporary or seasonal occupation for its work force. By the same token, the capital-intensive technology utilized in metalworking required continuous operation and hence a stable work force. By 1893, for example, year round employment in Petersburg industry as a whole stood at nearly 90%, while the all-Russian figure was just 71.75%; similarly, the all-Russian figure for metalworking was 88.9%, while the average for all sectors was 70.9%.[25]

These various patterns of population growth, in conjunction with the specific needs of heavy industry, contributed to the emergence of a more permanent working class. The journey home was long and expensive and discouraged the pursuit of seasonal work in urban industry, which in turn attenuated the peasant-cum-worker's ties to the land. For the peasant craftsman or urban artisan, the relatively good conditions offered by the big factories attracted and kept them in heavy industry. By the early 1890s, year-round employment in Petersburg industry had become the norm. And for the children of long time workers in the factories, few other occupational choices were available: return to the village was already unthinkable and opportunities to emerge out of Russia's rigid *soslovie* structure were virtually absent.

Yet there were important, countervailing pressures on this worker milieu; the transition from peasant to proletarian was scarcely the unambiguous, seemingly ineluctable process depicted by older schools of Soviet historiography. Many metalworkers retained significant material and affective ties to the village. At any given point, workers could be found at quite different stages in what was clearly a complex and confusing process of social development, while any number of experiences could rekindle vital memories of the village and reinforce elements of a peasant *mentalité*: the sending of wages home, the renewal of a passport, the arrival of a family member or *zemliak* (fellow countryman) in the city, the celebration of certain holidays. Even as a cadre of hereditary metalworkers was in the making, its group identity remained fluid. At the same time, the relative weight of this core group in Petersburg generally and in heavy industry particularly fluctuated constantly, depending on the vagaries of the economic cycle and on the periodic waves of peasants who flooded into the city, fleeing either famine and pestilence in the countryside or seeking better wages and a different life in the city.[26] Thus, the particular needs of the metalworking industry produced a core of hereditary proletarians tied to the city in important ways, but periodically submerged this cadre in a sea of new recruits utterly unfamiliar with the urban-industrial environment. The interaction, often the tension, between metalworkers who had begun to identify with their new surroundings and those still distant from the "imperatives" of Petersburg's giant factories was to have important implications for labor mobilization throughout the late Imperial period.

Although Petersburg metalworkers engaged in a process of transition common to most of Russia's industrial labor force, metalworkers were nonetheless distinguished from workers in other sectors by a number of characteristics. Among the most important were literacy, income, skill, and as noted, a degree of permanence in the city that was greater at any given time than most other segments of the capital's laboring population. Generally speaking, only printers rivaled metalworkers in these ways, but the work environment of the printing industry differed radically from that of heavy industry.

The metalworking industry (and most especially the machine construction sector) required a relatively large number of literate workers able to read drafts, interpret shop drawings, and carry out basic arithmetical calculations. According to one estimate, Petersburg metalworkers already had a 49% rate of literacy in 1862, as compared with 38% for Petersburg workers generally. By 1897, the percentage of literate metalworkers had climbed to 73%, indeed higher, since workers of the small shops and smithies of Petersburg were included in these figures.[27] Reflecting in particular the increase of literacy among younger people, by 1897, 84% of male metalworkers aged 17–19 were able to read, while the rate fell to 74.6% for ages 20–39; and to 63% for those between 40 and 59.[28] The literacy of Petersburg metalworkers was especially impressive given an overall rate of 54% for urban males, and just 21.2% for the population as a whole.[29]

Wage data are scattered and unsystematic, particularly so for the years following Emancipation; and gaining an accurate sense of metalworkers' income is made still more difficult by the fact that average monthly or annual wage data tend to conceal substantial differences between skill levels, as well as between factories.[30] Nonetheless, two broad generalizations can be drawn with certainty: wages of workers in St. Petersburg were typically higher than wages paid in other parts of the Empire and wages of Petersburg metalworkers typically exceeded those received by workers in other industries in the capital. The higher wages of Petersburg metalworkers in turn reflected both the generally high level of skill and literacy required by the heavy industry of the capital and a work force that contained virtually no females and comparatively few children.[31]

These generally higher rates of literacy, income, and skill among metalworkers had important functional consequences. Heavy industrialists were perforce concerned about improving the educational opportunities available to workers, given their great dependence on trained cadres. The more farsighted employers therefore opened schools at their factories, or encouraged the efforts of philanthropists in the early 1860s to establish Sunday schools, or supported the Russian Technical Society in its efforts from the mid-1870s on to develop vocational schools for workers. And while primary schools for the urban poor were all too slow to develop in late nineteenth century Petersburg, independent efforts had some, albeit modest, success: by the mid-1890s, the Technical Society had organized 35 schools, most attached to major factories, while approximately 36 Sunday schools and evening courses functioned as well.[32] The industry's need for literate workers, however, contributed not only to the workers' search for vocational education, but to a thirst for knowledge more generally; in turn, workers began to acquire the intellectual tools with which to perceive and to criticize the world around them.

By the same token, the absence of a qualified labor pool, as well as the capital-intensive technologies that demanded year-round operation, dictated the comparatively high wage levels which pertained in the metalworking industry. This permitted a modest expenditure on items not directly related to subsistence, e.g., books and periodicals, better clothing and housing, various forms of entertainment. The discretionary income enjoyed by some metalworkers thus allowed the development of certain tastes and aspirations which could ultimately prove threatening to the established regime within and outside the factory, and at the same time served to distinguish metalworkers from workers in other industries.

These various characteristics informed a developing discourse among the progressive intelligentsia as they sought to interpret differences within Petersburg's working population. Most apparent was the broad categorization of workers as *zavodskie* as distinct from *fabrichnye*.[33] Members of the Populist Chaikovskii Circle in the first years of the 1870s and the "father" of Russian Marxism, Georgii Plekhanov, some years later left rich descriptive accounts which suggest the emerging perspectives of the radical intelligentsia. In the early 1870s, for example, A. V. Nizovkin wrote:

> I must say that the *zavodskie* bore on themselves, so to speak, the imprint of the city civilization; they dressed very well, lived not in masses, not in artels, but separately, especially the workers of the machine plants; they did not drink scandalously and in general had an excellent appearance; the *fabrichnye*, on the contrary, dressed like peasants, lived untidily and always in groups, and drank scandalously.

Nizovkin went on to remark that *"zavodskie* considered it demeaning and confusing for one to have business with a *fabrichnyi*, and the *fabrichnyi* considered himself on the contrary flattered if a *zavodskii* spoke to him."[34] In his memoirs, Peter Kropotkin noted the same differences, not only commenting that the *zavodskie* had become continuous city dwellers and acquired a definite trade, but perceiving also the contempt with which they treated the mass of factory operatives.[35]

A more detailed picture of these distinctions is found in the reflections of Plekhanov, who lived in Petersburg during the second half of the 1870s and who wrote from the vantage point of the early 1890s. Undoubtedly wishing to identify an emergent working class ready to assume the liberating mission outlined by Marx, Plekhanov stressed a cluster of characteristics found among the *zavodskie*: "The more I became acquainted with Petersburg workers, the more I became astounded by their *kul'turnost'*. Witty and articulate, able to stand up for themselves and relate critically to their surroundings, they were *city dwellers* in the best sense of the word."[36]

Plekhanov went on to stress—perhaps underlining the break from his own Populist past—the great distance of these workers from the countryside, as well as their condescension toward the village person who was contemptuously dubbed a "gray" (*seryi*) type, that is, ignorant or dull-witted. This layer of urbanized workers was distinguished by a level of intellectual development and a set of daily needs which, in Plekhanov's judgment, even placed them above some students. The *fabrichnye*, in contrast, worked longer hours and earned less money, were unable to rent apartments individually and thus lived collectively in overcrowded rooms; they "knew and read less" and in general retained more solid ties with the countryside. And precisely these ties to the land meant that their already meager earnings were reduced still further by the obligation to send money home to pay taxes and redemption dues.[37]

Reflective of his Marxist contempt for the "idiocy of rural life," Plekhanov drew the lines sharply in his discussion of the process of transition from village to city.

> It seems that the *fabrichnyi* who has only just left the village remains for some time a real peasant. He complains not about the oppressions of the boss, but about the heavy taxes and the peasant's lack of land. A stay in the city seems to him a temporary and very unpleasant necessity. But little by little, urban life subjects him to its influence; imperceptibly he acquires the habits and views of a townsman. Working in the city for a few years, he already feels ill at ease in the country and does not willingly return there, especially if he has come into contact with "intellectual" people and has become interested in books. I knew such *fabrichnyi*, who when forced to return home for a time went there as if in exile and returned like the *zavodskii* worker B—n, a convinced enemy of the *derevenshchiny* (the village types). The cause was always the same: rural customs and ways became unbearable for a person whose personality had begun to develop somewhat. And the more talented the worker, the more he thought and studied in the city, the faster and more decisively he broke with the village.[38]

But seeking to explain the apolitical or openly destructive forms of working-class life, Plekhanov also noted the alienation and loss of moral bearings experienced by workers in the city:

> I do not intend to idealize the conditions of contemporary urban life. . . . Landing in the city from the village a worker sometimes does, in fact, begin "to indulge himself" [*balovat'sia*]. In the village he lived according to the precepts of his father, without argument subordinating himself to long established customs. In the city these customs immediately lose their meaning. So that man is not deprived of all moral standards, these necessarily must be replaced by new habits, by new views on things. Such a replacement gradually occurs in actuality, since the unavoidable daily struggle with the boss already imposes on workers mutual moral obligations. But "in the meantime" the new worker nevertheless experiences a moral crisis, which is sometimes expressed in rather ugly conduct.[39]

Projecting their attitudes and observations back onto the 1870s, Plekhanov and others probably exaggerated the differences between *zavodskie* and *fabrichnye*; certainly there were many "dark" metalworkers laboring in the big factories year after year and living shoulder to shoulder with the "downtrodden" in the capital's overcrowded slums. And yet with the passage of time, as well as the expanding interaction of workers with the radical intelligentsia, some metalworkers began to adopt the discursive categories validated by their would-be mentors. It was surely the case that some workers who eventually found their moorings in the city became engaged in a quest for knowledge and a more "civilized" life, and began to find the filth, ignorance, and brutality that defined the working-class districts unbearable. Newly acquired aspirations, both material and intellectual, undoubtedly fostered among some workers a sense of dignity and individuality that clashed quite violently with the pervasive "darkness" of the slums. At the same time, however, the degrading and seemingly endless cycles of drunkenness, debauchery, wife-beating and brawls, followed by ritualized supplications to a distant and unknowable God, could produce a revulsion and alienation in "developed" *zavodskie* that undercut a perception of common class interests.

For those *zavodskie* fitting this sort of profile, education and the different life it opened to them provided a means of escape: alienated from their wretched surroundings, the study circle (*kruzhok*), rather than the shop or the tavern or the corner that passed for home, became the focus of their lives. But this focus meant isolation from family life and other workers, as well as detachment from the struggles developing on the shop floor. Moreover, even the *kruzhki* could be sharply distinguished according to the predominance of *fabrichnye* or *zavodskie*. According to one observer, the *fabrichnye* sought basic literacy, while the *zavodskie* were already eager for more advanced study: "*Zavodskie* workers, i.e., workers of engineering factories, fitters, metal turners, founders, and the like, were in general significantly beyond the *fabrichnyi*, and for them [the *zavodskie*] systematic lectures on politics, economics, history, the European labor movement, and so on, were established."[40]

Such different levels of educational attainment could be productive of different attitudes and capacities in other areas as well. Some *zavodskie*, L. E. Shisko noted, had already organized group funds and libraries by the mid-1870s and this in turn contributed to the greater independence these workers displayed in their relations with the revolutionary intelligentsia as compared with the *fabrichnye*.[41]

Another painful reflection of the social isolation of some *zavodskie* were the relations that typically pertained with women. Compounding the extreme demographic imbalance between males and females was the absence of literate and urbanized women, a situation which left "developed" workers without suitable mates. It was therefore to the male camaraderie of the *kruzhok*, rather than to a settled family life, that many *zavodskie* were drawn. Plekhanov recorded the derisive comments of some of the workers he encountered: "Our women are complete fools, but female *intelligenty* won't go for our lads; they give themselves up to the students."[42] Thus many remained single, disdainful of the downtrodden women workers they met in the city and contemptuously superior to the "village types."[43]

While collectively metalworkers were typically identified as *zavodskie* by their intelligentsia patrons, they were, in fact, far from a homogeneous mass. Their ranks were highly stratified and in important ways the distance between skilled and unskilled metalworkers, as well as between "hot" and "cold shop" workers, could be as great as that between the *fabrichnye* and *zavodskie* in the working-class population as a whole. These distinctions were rooted, at least in part, in the nature of work in heavy industry, which included, on the one hand, the hot and heavy labor of metal founding and on the other, the clean and precise work of machine construction. Skill distinctions were also influenced by the vastly differing levels of technology that were employed in basic metallurgy, metal processing, weapons manufacture, electrical engineering, and industrial and transport machine construction.

Commenting in the early twentieth century on life in a major metalworking factory, P. Timofeev noted that workers could be divided into two broad groups:

> there are the so-called skilled or specialist workers [*masterovye*] and common laborers [*chernorabochie*]. The words "skilled worker" [*masterovoi*] and "worker" [*rabochii*] are now used completely without distinction. But within labor's ranks, the word "worker" [*rabochii*] as it is understood by the intelligentsia has penetrated only recently. In the not too distant past, to call a skilled worker a "worker" was a brutal insult, for this worker possessed skills that required three to six years of training.[44]

If years of specialized training were one important attribute of the *masterovoi*, so too were a cluster of other characteristics. Master of a trade, he was typically master of his own work life. Indispensable to the process of production, fully literate and able to earn a decent income, his skills gave him an autonomy and a sense of self-worth that was not shared by the unskilled laborer who could be replaced at the whim of an employer. And yet, this "ideal type" must be treated cautiously, for there were exceptions to the easy equation that skill equaled a particular type of self-awareness.[45]

Because the Petersburg metalworking industry was characterized by a significant diversity in production, the skilled metalworker had to be able to move from one complex task to another:

> The chaotic shifting of orders promoted their [the newly arrived workers at the Putilov Plant] versatile skills. They were thrown back and forth between the production of a 3-pound bushing and a complex casting of 3–4,000 poods; from the manufacture of a mobile kitchen on wheels to the production of electric turret fittings for a dreadnought.[46]

The specific nature of work thus promoted the development of a multi-competent worker, not a narrowly specialized one—a worker able to conceptualize a variety of processes and relationships, to generalize on the basis of a mastery of skills, to carry out a significant variety of non-routine tasks, and to exercise judgment regularly in the course of work. Very often, a "cold shop" worker was engaged in the construction of an entire machine: the interpretation of a shop drawing, the materials and tools to be used for the task, the speed and depth of the cuts, the finishing and polishing of the work. All these decisions would very largely be at his discretion. So too the founder would need to know the various properties of metals to carry out the heat, the charge, and the pour.

But even while sharing an important set of common characteristics, crucial distinctions remained between the skilled workers of the "hot" and "cold shops." The memoir of Aleksei Buzinov, a metalworker at the Nevskii factory, captures not only the general differences between metalworkers and others, but the significant distinctions within the major plants:

> Metalworkers felt themselves to be the aristocrats among workers. Their profession required great skill, and therefore toward others, weavers and the rest, they looked [as if from on high], [as if] on a lower category or on [some sort of] country bumpkin; today, he is at the factory, tomorrow he goes to peck the land with an ancient wooden plow. The superiority of the metalworker, with all the advantages that flow from it, is recognized by all.
>
> ... However, the more I became rooted in the factory family, the more clearly I saw the heterogeneity within the limits of even a single enterprise. Soon I felt that workers of the machine shops—fitters [*slesaria*] and turners—also looked at me from above. After this I clearly distinguished the humble position of workers in the hot shops: the foundry, rolling, and blacksmith shops. Among them I saw a more uncouth and clumsy sort of people, both in step and speech. In each individual face, through the strong fiery sunburn, the crude features

showed through clearly, which said that in their work strength predominated
and not a quickness of wit. I also saw that beside an experienced founder, even
a shabby fitter seemed to be an educated and thinking person. The fitter held
his head higher, was sharper and keener in his speech. He was able to fit in a
dozen words with a bit of irony, while the founder found time for only one,
"yes and well," something very simple. With the fitter, one was automatically
inclined to talk about something in general and not only about wages. In a
word, the worker of the machine shop was already not that semi-raw material
of the foundry and blacksmith shops, but seemed to have passed through the
exacting, shaping action of the machine tools and instruments.[47]

Thus while a founder or blacksmith possessed a valuable skill and earned
a respectable income, his hot and physically taxing labor seemed to shape a
more limited set of mental faculties. Other characteristics of his work environment shaped him as well. A relatively primitive level of technology obtained in the hot shops, so the basic tasks of lifting, hauling, and loading
materials in and out of the furnaces were performed by men not machines.
Peasant Russia provided such workers in abundance, for what was required
was not literacy or skill or mental acuity, but physical strength.[48] And since
recruitment typically proceeded on the basis of *zemliak* ties, bonds to the
peasant past were regularly reinforced.[49] Moreover, precisely because hiring
so often proceeded on the basis of village ties, parochial affinities, rather than
broadly based associations, were fostered.[50] Life in the metallurgical shops,
therefore, bore the strong imprint of rural ways, while workers here shared
many of the attributes of the *fabrichnyi*: religious values remained strong, as
did the self-destructive bouts of drinking. Attachment to the city was tenuous.
Next to the skilled "cold shop" worker, most of those who labored in the "hot
shops" seemed to be the archetypal uncultured "peasant type."[51]

Technology was important in another way: work at the furnace was a
continuous operation, usually conducted on two twelve-hour shifts. When the
process was arbitrarily interrupted, the furnace could be seriously damaged.
Rooted in the nature of work, then, was an obstacle to labor solidarity: hot
shop workers could not just walk off the job and leave the furnaces without
causing substantial losses to the entire factory and its work force.[52] Moreover,
skilled and unskilled alike worked a longer, more debilitating workday and
therefore had correspondingly less time to pursue other interests.

The ratio of skilled to unskilled altered substantially in the cold shops,
hence creating a markedly different social environment. Here work was
considerably cleaner, more precise, and less physically taxing. It rested more
clearly on the individual skills of the craftsman utilizing hand or machine
tools than on the collective strength of a work gang moving materials around
the furnace. As noted by Buzinov, the shaping action of the instruments
honed a finer set of mental faculties for the fitter or turner, and produced a
worker more likely to engage critically with the world around him. Located
here, in short, was the archetypal *zavodskii*—a skilled, literate, and comparatively well paid worker, adapted to the urban-industrial environment.

Of course, not all Petersburg metalworking factories contained such huge masses of workers or possessed their own metallurgical departments; hence the social diversity that characterized the mixed-production giants like Putilov, Nevskii, Obukhov, or Baltic was less apparent at more specialized plants like Nobel or Lessner. Nonetheless, the division of factories into departments and departments into specialized shops contributed still further to differentiation according to "shop" (*tsekhovshchina*): "Each branch of production, and even each shop, infects workers with a professional and shop patriotism, which sings of the glorification of its own trade and spits through its lips on everything else."[53]

As we shall see, the phenomenon of *tsekhovshchina*, variously translated as shop particularism or craft orientation, would remain a concern of labor activists seeking broader industrial or class solidarities throughout the Imperial period.

There were, finally, differences between "old-timers" and younger workers; frequently, the former had been given special privileges by the factory administration in the form of good housing or bonuses, or kept on the payroll in hard times. "Old-timers" formed a stable and typically conservative stratum, and were able to provide a modest education and access to a job for their children. Especially in such state-owned plants as Obukhov and Izhorsk, they formed a constituent part of the patriarchal order and often played a key role in the hiring process.[54]

The patterns of working-class life that began to emerge in the post-Emancipation decades were shaped by these various lines of stratification. Sharp differences in skill and income, literacy and degree of urbanization helped to keep workers isolated and alienated from one another. "Developed" *zavodskie* might sometimes recoil from the "stultifying ignorance" and "complete spiritual darkness" of the "peasant types," and retreat to the *kruzhok* for solace. Mutual distrust, even contempt, far more readily than a shared perception of class or common interest, defined the relations between skilled and unskilled metalworkers, "hot" and "cold shop" workers, young workers and old-timers, urban dandies and worker-*intelligenty*. But these various differences should not be congealed into rigid ideal types; the lines were fluid and the cluster of characteristics defining any single individual were, of course, infinitely diverse. Nor should the influence of intelligentsia perceptions be exaggerated: the interactions between Marxist intellectuals and worker activists that would come to shape the Russian labor movement by the early twentieth century were mostly chance encounters in the two or three decades following Emancipation.

But the many differing experiences of workers had important implications for labor mobilization. The impermanence of the unskilled in urban industry and their continuing ties with the countryside meant that a return home in hard times or periods of strike conflict remained a viable option: those who stayed behind felt left in the breach, forced to rely on their own resources without the support of a unified mass.[55] Just as important, the grievances of

many new recruits and unskilled laborers centered more readily on the problems of the village commune (*mir*) than on the oppressions of the foreman.
But at the same time, the unskilled were often envious of the better wages
earned by the skilled metalworker, and in the latter's view undermined the
collective good by laboring overtime to the point of utter exhaustion to make
up the difference. On the other side, however, the involvement of workers in
the world of the *kruzhki* and in the more cultured, refined life of the mind
pulled many a worker away from the factory and the concerns of the shop
floor. So too, long-time workers in industry were often oblivious to their less
accomplished comrades: enjoying relatively good wages, perhaps a home
and garden, the promise of a job for their children, as well as a secure if
subservient relationship with the boss, many old-timers had little incentive
to join in a common assault on the old factory regime. Prior to the early
twentieth century, a lack of empathy for fellow workers was one typical
product of the better education, discretionary income, and greater familiarity
with the urban-industrial environment that was enjoyed by the skilled
metalworker; and the successive waves of labor migrants only tended to
exacerbate tensions within the ranks of the work force.

II

THE INDUSTRIALIZATION
OF THE 1890s

An Industry in Upheaval

Sergei Witte came to the Ministry of Finance in the aftermath of the disastrous famine of 1891–1892, a catastrophe which like the Crimean debacle before it revealed both the inability of the government to cope with a national emergency and the continuing inadequacies of the economy. It now appeared that the fiscal stringency practiced by successive ministers of finance since the death of Alexander II in 1881 had bled the peasantry white. And so it would be the mass suffering of a hungry and infirm peasantry that would again rekindle the social and political ferment of "society" that had subsided during the years of political reaction and economic depression following Alexander's assassination. In this atmosphere of heightened public concern with the viability of Russia's autocratic institutions, the new minister of finance pressed the further industrialization of the Empire. Yet, as we shall observe, Witte's policies brought enormous upheaval to Russia's social and economic institutions, challenging the prerogatives of established agrarian elites, while leaving uncertain the place of newly emergent urban-industrial interests in the autocratic polity.

Witte's developmental strategy hinged on the twofold policy of state-sponsored railroad construction and monetary reform. The former was to stimulate the growth of indigenous heavy industry and at the same time open new markets for Russian goods. The latter, by providing a stable and convertible currency, would attract foreign capital and expertise. And so, the construction of the Trans-Siberian railroad, approved by Alexander III in 1891, went forward with a feverish burst of building activity in 1893. Between 1893 and 1900, the state made available extraordinary sums for its development; by 1899 almost 18,000 versts of new track had been laid across the Empire.[1] The Trans-Siberian, built almost entirely of Russian materials, created a huge demand for rails, rolling stock, and bridge structures. So too, the opening of new towns and industrial areas required a vast array of construction materials, from pipes and pumps for water and sewer lines to cable and transformers to illuminate the streets and power the trams.

To secure foreign capital, Witte aggressively pursued the monetary reforms begun by his predecessors and was able, by 1897, to convert to the gold standard. At the same time he mounted a skillful public relations campaign to boost investor confidence. His efforts were largely successful. With the lure of guaranteed orders, substantial profits, an extensive market, and a stable currency, foreigners flocked to Russia. And with the protection afforded by the nearly prohibitive tariff of 1891, foreign involvement in Russian industry came either in the form of a massive influx of investment capital or in the establishment of subsidiaries of foreign firms, rather than in the export of raw materials or finished goods.

The "boom" decade of the 1890s was thus a time of tumultuous socioeco-nomic change, with St. Petersburg emerging as a highly visible and crucially important participant in this process of accelerated urban and industrial de-velopment. The city experienced an extraordinary period of demographic upheaval, in large measure due to the immigration of peasants fleeing the hungry countryside. City census data reveal that the population of St. Peters-burg exclusive of the industrial suburbs increased by 30.7% between 1890 and 1900, while the working-class population expanded by 60% in the same period. Paralleling the growth of the population was the expansion of the city's industrial base: approximately one-third of the factories existing in the capital by 1900 were founded during the last decade of the nineteenth century.[2]

Particularly dramatic was the growth of the metalworking industry. New factories were built; older plants were significantly expanded and refitted. Employment in metalworking and machine construction more than doubled, from about 31,400 in 1881 to 79,800 in 1900. By the turn of the century, the labor force in metalworking constituted some 24.5% of the capital's industrial employment.[3] Much of this growth was concentrated in a relatively few factories and therefore the already established tendency toward a highly concentrated work force in the industry was reinforced: according to one estimate, in 1894–95 some 77% of Petersburg metalworkers labored in plants with more than 500 workers.[4] Table 2.1 illustrates the dimensions of change for a characteristic cross-section of metal factories.

Just as important as this quantitative change was the qualitative develop-ment underway. With the increased competition of the newly opened Donbass region, the heavy industry of St. Petersburg began to shift from basic metalworking (e.g., the production of rails) to more complex types of metal processing and machine construction. The capital's heavy industry began to focus especially on locomotive and freight car manufacture, which became the city's leading branch of industrial machine construction. By the turn of the century, this sector was even beginning to adapt to serial production.[5] In other areas of machine construction, however, development lagged. With few exceptions (e.g., diesel engines), Russian machine construction could not compete with foreign firms, this being especially true in the manufacture of textile and complex agricultural machinery. As in the past, the capital's ma-chine construction factories manufactured a bewildering array of goods, sometimes fabricating single machines from scratch to suit individual orders.

TABLE 2.1
Work Force Size in Selected Metalworking Factories, 1891 and 1901

Factory	1891	1901	% Increase
Putilov	3,506	12,441	255%
Nevskii	3,000	5,359	78%
Franco-Russian	1,840	2,000	9%
Baltic	2,200	4,557	107%
SPb Metals	870	1,546	78%
Rozenkrantz	400	800	100%
SPb Pipe (Trubochnyi)	1,700	4,000	135%
Lessner	300	597	99%
Langenzipen	590	950	61%
Izhorsk	2,331	4,544	95%
Obukhov	1,562	3,696	137%
SPb Nail (Gvozdil'nyi)	900	1,242	38%
Rechkin	500	2,208	342%
Nobel	600	800	33%
Aleksandrovsk	1,200	1,428	19%
SPb Iron Rolling Mill (Zhelezopro.)	420	860	105%
Totals	21,919	47,028	115%

Source: Bulkin, "Ekonomicheskoe polozhenie rabochikh metallov do 1905 goda," table following p. 91. (Note: figures for 1901 probably understate the change, given the onset of depression. See Shuster, *Peterburgskie rabochie 1905–1907 gg.* p. 16.)

During the 1890s, the capital emerged as the Empire's leading center for electrical engineering. In this sector, the presence of German capital and expertise was particularly marked, as was the tendency for Russian-based subsidiaries of foreign firms to assemble parts rather than manufacture the entire product.[6] These firms were among the most technologically sophisticated in the capital and, to a degree atypical of the rest of the industry, were not as heavily dependent on state demand.

Always a leader in armaments and shipbuilding, Petersburg's significance as a prime defense contractor also continued to grow, although a major share of this market remained in the hands of state-owned rather than private factories. But at both state and private plants important technological advances were made in the 1890s, among them the introduction of interchangeable parts for some weaponry.

While important sectoral differences could be noted in the capital's heavy industry, perhaps the most striking contrast lay in the varying levels of technology employed in metal founding and machine construction. Most of the large factories had at least small forging capabilities—some had major mills and rolling shops—but these tended to be the most primitive departments in the factory. Poorly mechanized, operating on physical labor, these so-called "hot shops" were often the chief bottleneck in the production process.[7]

Equally notable was the haphazard, even chaotic development of some of the capital's metalworking factories. At least in part this was due to the continuing dependence of heavy industry on the government market. According to one estimate, for example, government expenditures for the railways during the 1890s totaled 116 million rubles, almost half of the 259 million ruble output of the entire metallurgical and machine building industry in 1897 (exclusive of agricultural machinery).[8] According to another, in 1903, 85 privately owned Petersburg factories produced goods valued at 73 million rubles, of which 59.4 million rubles went to the state.[9]

Such an overwhelming reliance on state-generated demand reinforced the tendency, indeed the need, of the industry to respond to the erratic shifts in state orders by altering the composition of its output. Thus many of the plants founded decades earlier for diverse metallurgical products shifted to the manufacture of rolling stock, trying to take advantage of the new market for these goods. But perhaps more to the point, inflated government contracts, often paid in advance of fulfillment, permitted industrialists to ignore careful cost controls. With profits guaranteed by a government concerned with rapid industrialization and foreign competition largely eliminated in the production of heavy industrial goods, employers had little incentive to economize and could absorb the costs of high overhead by passing them on to the state. And given the general absence of trained production engineers and accountants who might be more concerned with rational organization and cost-benefit ratios, disorderly production and financial operations were all too often tolerated.[10]

Just as precarious was the financial situation of many metalworking factories. Some firms opened without first securing the requisite resources, counting instead on government contracts paid in advance to cover operating expenses. Others sought to generate capital by reorganizing as joint-stock corporations: over the course of the 1890s, the number of joint-stock corporations increased in the capital's heavy industry and as a result stock offerings in this sector rose dramatically on European and Petersburg exchanges. Credit was easy through the decade and vast sums of capital were generated, but by the end of the century the increasingly speculative character of this investment had become apparent.[11]

Not surprisingly, then, many Petersburg plants found themselves in tough technical and financial situations when the boomtime conditions of the 1890s began to wane. Consider, for example, the experience of the Putilov and Nevskii works.

On the eve of the industrial upsurge of the 1890s, much of the vast territory

TABLE 2.2
Putilov Works 1885–1886 and 1899–1900,
Annual Value of Production by Department

Department	1885–1886		1889–1900	
Metallurgical	4,668,060 r.	77.1%	5,178,279 r.	26.8%
Locomotive	——		5,609,348 r.	29.0%
Freight car	490,907 r.	8.1%	4,670,153 r.	24.2%
Engineering	695,753 r.	11.4%	1,008,879 r.	5.2%
Artillery	106,605 r.	3.4%	2,823,309 r.	14.8%
Totals	6,061,225 r.		19,289,868 r.	

Source: 1909 survey, p. 17.

owned by Putilov remained undeveloped, with buildings separated by groves of trees and large parcels of land inundated with water. The factory complex consisted of twelve rather far-flung shops employing 3,000 workers and retained a somewhat semi-rural appearance. By the turn of the century a remarkable expansion had occurred. The groves had been cleared and new drainage channels had been dug to provide for the twenty-seven shops that now covered the factory grounds and the more than 12,000 persons who worked in them. A fundamental shift had also taken place in the range of goods manufactured. In contrast to a production profile in the 1880s in which metalworking predominated, by the end of the next decade more than half the output of the factory was in transport machine construction. (See Table 2.2.)

In 1892, the factory received its first order for locomotives, a government contract for the production of twenty-eight over the course of two years. On the successful completion of these, the factory was awarded another contract in 1894 for eight engines a month. Within just six years and with the addition of orders from private railway companies, Putilov was turning out 160 locomotives annually. Freight car construction, begun at the factory in 1874, also expanded significantly with the addition of passenger and specialty-car manufacture (e.g., cattle cars, restaurant, even church cars). New locomotive and freight car assembly shops were added to the factory complex and in 1895 a special shop for bridge structures and boilers was constructed; the pattern shop, the wood-finishing shop and several others were also expanded and retooled.

In the latter part of the 1880s, Putilov largely abandoned the production of rails due to the opening of the Southern metallurgical complex. But in 1894 the factory again sought a major government contract, arguing that the iron deposits of the Northern region which would supply Putilov's production of rails should be developed in the national interest. Winning the case, Putilov received a multimillion-pood order for rail at the highly inflated price of 1.68 kopecks per pood (the market price was 85 kopecks). In the event, the Northern deposits proved inadequate: the factory ceased the production of rails in 1898 and its metalworking shops were directed instead to the manufacture of structural beams.[12]

But what amounted to the government's extraordinarily generous subsidy of the factory was not lost in a futile exploration of the Northern mineral deposits. Rather, the monies were very largely diverted into the development of artillery production. Over the course of the decade, the factory emerged as a major defense contractor, and to support the new line of production several new shops and offices were added. A design office, a laboratory, and a firing range substantially augmented the technical capabilities of the factory, while a new gun-carriage shop and a crucible steel shop greatly enhanced its productive capacities.

The shift to military contracting also fostered the development of multifaceted contacts between Putilov and the leading arms manufacturers of the West. At the outset, the Russian firm worked off Western designs for artillery pieces, but soon it began to design and produce its own models. Throughout the 1890s, however, the factory remained heavily dependent on European manufacturers, not least because Putilov's artillery shops were equipped with the best machine tools available for purchase in the West.

In addition to Putilov's production of rolling stock and military hardware, the factory began to manufacture industrial machinery. In 1897, a new machine shop was opened for the construction of steam engines, cranes, and machine tools. And while most of the output of this shop went to the factory's own needs, a small percentage found its way onto the private market.

The extraordinary development of the Putilov works was reflected in its overall output, the value of which increased fivefold from 4,079,718 rubles in 1890 to 19,492,883 rubles in 1900. But the rapidity and the enormity of the change was apparent in other ways as well:

> Turning out such diverse products, the Putilov factory developed in a disorderly, planless, chaotic [manner]. In expectation of orders, the board [of directors] frequently expended huge sums on the construction of new shops and on the purchase of equipment. Depending on advantageous orders, the equipment of the factory was supplemented.[13]

Especially problematic was the factory's own service sector: the hundred or so low capacity boilers failed to produce the requisite steam; the poorly laid out internal railway system did not connect some of the outlying shops; the maze of water and sewer lines apparently remained a complete unknown as the appropriate mapping had not been undertaken; most shops were not properly equipped with electric light. Soviet historians have concluded that "the cheap work force covered all the losses of the destructive organization of production at the factory."[14]

Despite this, the high overhead costs were not sufficiently pressing in the

1890s to compel management to reorganize. The long hours and low wages of labor on the one hand, and the inflated prices of goods sold to the government on the other, permitted lax controls over factory operations to persist. Overall, the impression given by the various production processes utilized at Putilov during the 1890s was that of an anarchic commingling of old and new in industrial plant.[15]

The Nevskii works experienced a similar expansion, supplementing existing facilities with new shops and machinery in the early 1890s and hiring almost 2,500 additional workers over the course of the decade. A substantially new, almost exclusively foreign staff of technical and administrative personnel was also recruited. The value of production grew from one million rubles in 1891–92 to four million rubles in 1895 and to 5.8 million rubles in 1898. In addition to locomotive construction, the factory also advanced as a shipbuilder, winning major contracts from the Naval Ministry for torpedo boats.

Yet hints of the future difficulties to be experienced by the plant were already apparent in factory inspectorate documents from mid-decade. An 1895 report noted the dangerous conditions created by the overcrowding of several shops as new machine tools were added without a corresponding removal of old equipment. The inspector also contrasted the more modern structures in the factory complex to other shops housed in decrepit old buildings with cracked and slanted walls. Still more disquieting were the liquidity problems of the factory and its reputation for delays in issuing workers' wages. Among the relatively few labor protests to occur in the metalworking industry of the capital during the 1890s was the upheaval at the Nevskii plant in late 1894, when workers ran riot through the factory offices protesting the gross delays in the payment of wages on the eve of the Christmas holidays.

More shocking was the revelation of the fraudulent dealings of Savva Mamontov, Nevskii's principal shareholder and a man with vast industrial holdings. Inappropriately transfering huge sums between his various enterprises and grossly mismanaging the financial operations of the Nevskii works, Mamontov's behavior brought the factory to the point of financial collapse. Moreover, Mamontov's questionable dealings and his subsequent bankruptcy contributed to an already panicky stock market and helped to precipitate the crash of September 1899. But over the course of the decade the importance of the Nevskii works as a contractor for the Naval Ministry had become so great that the state would not permit the factory to close. In August 1899 the State Bank became the major stockholder of the Nevskii factory, although formally the firm remained a private, joint-stock corporation.[16]

As the Putilov and Nevskii examples indicate, the development of the capital's metalworking industry over the 1890s was thus both extensive and chaotic. In many cases, old plant and auxiliary services remained without fundamental change and coexisted anachronistically with new equipment and shops. Plant layout was often ill-conceived, electrical and mechanical power limited, connecting track between shops inadequate and poorly laid out, and as new machinery was added, floor plan was ignored and shops became congested. Because labor was comparatively cheap and in abundant supply, much of the movement of materials was done by common laborers, which postponed the laying of internal track and the mechanization of many aspects of the metallurgical process that had traditionally been performed by physical labor. All too often, the huge capital outlays for expansion and retooling were undertaken without requisite attention to future markets and careful cost controls. Thus the pattern of fiscal instability characteristic of the industry in the post-Emancipation era continued to define the development of the industry at the turn of the century.

Shop Management

The great expansion of physical plant and work force size in the 1890s contributed to a greater distancing between factory owners and the rank and file. In the earlier period, employers like Putilov and Poletika had prided themselves on their paternalistic concern for their workers. Putilov was known for the factory-wide celebrations he held for the pouring of each millionth pood of rail, his walks through the shops at holiday time, and his "sermonettes" following prayers. Indeed, throughout the pre-1905 period, most factories tried to promote "appropriate" behavior by supporting religious devotion: icons hung in many shops, prayers often began the workday, lectures on religious themes were sometimes arranged. And especially at state-owned plants like Obukhov and Izhorsk, the patriarchal order was buttressed by the building of churches, cottages, and bathhouses for workers on factory grounds.[17]

There were less subtle means of enforcing labor discipline, however. In virtually all the major factories, workers were routinely searched on exit from the grounds to prevent theft, while upon hire and also at holiday time workers were subjected to a humiliating medical examination. Yet prior to the turn of the century, such crude encroachments on the person of the worker and such transparent forms of intimidation rarely led workers to protest.[18] Moreover, work was sometimes organized in ways that explicitly built on the traditions of serf bondage: Putilov, for example, recruited on the basis of artels[19] composed of relatives and zemliaki, in the hopes of utilizing the mutual responsibility (krugovaia poruka) enforced by the artel as a means of control.[20]

Meanwhile, the tremendous expansion of physical plant necessarily altered established personnel hierarchies and challenged the capabilities of technical and supervisory staff. The most acute problem was the shortage of trained foremen and department heads able to manage the shops efficiently.[21] Typically, these positions were filled either by skilled workers promoted from the bench or by foreigners, since Petersburg heavy industry suffered from a serious shortage of native engineers.

The foreman of the 1890s was an exceptionally powerful person in the life of the worker and exercised a substantial degree of discretion over both the work process and the human relations pertaining on the shop floor. Typically he hired his own men, determined their rates and wages, judged the quality of the work performed, set the amount of overtime, assigned machine tools, and allocated the work. As one worker stated, the foreman was "tsar and god" in his shop.[22]

Contemporary reports leave little doubt that many Petersburg foremen exercised their authority in an arbitrary, often brutal manner. Searches, fines, coerced overtime hours, sometimes beatings and the constant use of abusive language were the routine methods of enforcing labor discipline; so too were unexplained rate cuts, arbitrary promotions or abrupt dismissals, and the constant surveillance of the lavatory and shop for the smallest violation of the rules. Bribes played a key role in the daily routine of the factory and were often necessary to get hired on, to procure decent materials and tools, or to insure that work was accepted at the full rate. Favoritism flourished, reinforced by the steady stream of newly arrived peasants seeking out a foreman from the same village or region. And doubtless shaping the daily exercise of a foreman's power was the pressure he himself felt from upper management to get the work out and maintain order in the shops.[23]

Not surprisingly, tension frequently marked the relations between rank and file workers and foremen just promoted from the bench. Such workers often made exceedingly hard task masters; often they had gotten their promotion—and kept it—only by currying favor with the boss.[24] Little better were relations with foreign foremen, for conflict was scarcely avoidable between Russian workers and foreign supervisory personnel who could not speak the same language, especially when many viewed the Russian worker as culturally backward, technically incompetent, and morally dissolute. Typical was the comment of the factory inspector of the Shlissel'burg road area who remarked that "foreign foremen and factory managers (English and especially German) are, in the majority of cases, extremely rude with workers."[25] Indicative, too, was the habit of foreign administrators at the Nevskii plant to contemptuously call every worker "Ivan."[26]

It was often the case, moreover, that lower level staff was not technically competent or was simply overwhelmed by the enormous expansion of plant and equipment. The result was disorganization on the shop floor. Some machine tools stood idle for want of people who knew how to run them; tools and materials were not stocked in sufficient quantities; primitive conditions in some shops slowed the work in others.[27] "I didn't like the shop," recalled A. Svirskii on his first day of work at the Putilov factory; "there one felt the complete absence of order." Looking at the broken windows and the dirty, damp floor he could only exclaim: "Such a wealthy factory and such loathsomeness." He also observed that workers not so much worked as "bustled about," not because they slacked off, but because the shop was poorly organized. Running here for a file and there for a bit of iron, waiting in line to heat a piece of work, nothing was properly at hand.[28]

The cost of such disorder was often borne directly by the labor force. Delays in the work process cut heavily into piece rate earnings; low productivity meant long hours of overtime; filthy shops and sloppy layout inevitably contributed to an appalling accident rate. Ignorance of the work process itself often bred worker contempt for managerial personnel and undercut their authority. "Our engineers only wear fine frock coats, but don't know their business."[29]

There were, however, many factors that conditioned social relations on the shop floor. Precisely because of "looseness" in the shop, workers could exercise a certain amount of control over the work process and often bend it to their needs. A clearly defined hierarchy of command did not yet exist, nor were workers fixed to a single task performed monotonously hour after hour. Indeed, the very fluidity of staffing patterns and job assignments and the great shortage of skilled personnel at all levels meant significant horizontal and vertical mobility.

Nor did the foreman's authority rest exclusively on the use of force; it was shaped by the attitudes of the workers themselves. Most workers respected skill, and insofar as a foreman demonstrated knowledge of his craft and an ability to organize work properly, his authority was accepted. Equally to the point, as the acute observer Timofeev tells us, what mattered to many workers in the years before 1905 was not that a foreman treated them humanely but that he let them make a living. "The more a foreman let them earn, the more they respected him."[30] So too, a certain informality pertained in these early years which rested in part on the common social origins of many workers and foremen, in part on the absence of strictly defined rights and responsibilities to be exercised by foremen, and in part on the absence of any generally recognized set of qualifications or credentials for the occupants of that position.

Also shaping shop management was the uncertain position occupied by the Russian engineer. While significant social distance and educational difference defined the relationship between the Russian engineer and those "beneath" him, the nature of his schooling and his tenuous grasp of the production process undercut his authority and made his importance to upper management rather problematic.

Until the very end of the nineteenth century, Russia possessed only a handful of higher technical institutes. These were elite institutions, graduating only some 250 engineers a year during the 1880s. Not only were the number of graduates clearly inadequate to the needs of the developing economy, but the curriculum offered by these schools was heavily oriented toward theory and in most cases inappropriate to the practical requirements of industry.[31] In contrast, most foreign engineers were educated in polytechnic institutes and gained valuable "hands-on" experience working directly in industry. Thus most Russian engineers found themselves ill prepared to meet the challenges of the 1890s. They were expected to assimilate a vast array of new technology and called on to oversee a radical expansion of physical plant, but lacking adequate training they could not compete with foreign specialists, nor could they usually match the expertise of "self-taught" technicians and skilled workers. Many native engineers, then, must have experienced a peculiar isolation on the shop floor:

> If you consider that foremen almost always came from former workers, people without any training [*vospitanie*] and education, then the above-mentioned examples [of abuses in hiring] are not surprising. If even among shop managers, people standing at the head of business, there were almost illiterate people to be found, then what could be expected of their subordinates. Such a shop manager would not tolerate a cultured man around him, [a man] standing above him, so as not to lower himself in the eyes of the workers.[32]

Feeling the sting of foreign condescension on the one hand, graduate engineers could not but feel highly conflicted in regard to the "self-taught" on the other, whose practical expertise they were forced to respect, but whose lack of "culture" was offensive. Moreover, some who worked in manufacturing retained a sharp disdain for manual labor—typified in the wearing of white gloves—which was in part a reflection of their academic, highly theoretical education, and in part a residual effect of their *soslovie* origin. Many more, especially those working at the state factories, bore the marks of a military-engineering education and years in the army or navy, which found expression in a pronounced sense of rank and a proclivity for hierarchical command structures.[33]

There were, then, many ambiguities and much upheaval in shop floor relations. Foremen wielded an enormous amount of power, often in a highly dictatorial manner, not least because upper management often lacked a sophisticated understanding of the production processes in use. Native engineers cast about for a more secure professional identity, unable to firmly anchor claims to authority in a detailed knowledge of the work process. Yet, it was precisely at the level of shop management that workers and employers met: the typical flare-point of industrial conflict.

For the most part, though, labor discipline held over the course of the 1890s because of a combination of intimidation and arbitrariness, worker deference to authority, and the safety valve provided by significant horizontal and vertical mobility. During these years of great expansion, workers silently accepted the abuse and indignity heaped upon them, and when anger took on overt forms, it typically appeared as an exercise in summary justice—the carting out of an offending foreman in a wheelbarrow, the dispatch of a threatening, anonymous letter to a hated supervisor, even the delivery of a coffin to the home of an oppressor.[34]

Working-Class Districts in the 1890s

The great expansion of the work force in heavy industry naturally led in the 1890s to changes in St. Petersburg's industrial physiognomy. During this decade, the Vyborg district grew by 69.6% and developed into the capital's leading center for machine construction, where such important firms as Nobel, Lessner, Baranovskii, Erikson, St. Petersburg Metals, Phoenix, and Rozenkrants were located.

Like Vyborg, the Petersburg and Vasileostrov districts were situated close to the city center and also contained a number of important metalworking and machine construction firms. Vasileostrov was dominated by the state-owned Baltic shipyards and the St. Petersburg Pipe Factory (Trubochnyi), but also contained several major private firms, among them the Siemens-Halske electrical engineering factory and one of two Siemens-Shukkert plants. A number of leading machine construction factories were located on the Petersburg side, a district composed of a series of islands situated between Vyborg to the northeast and Vasileostrov to the southwest. These included the I. A. Semenov factory, the Geisler and Diuflon firms, both in electrical engineering, the Tiudor Works, and one of two Langenzipen factories, which was concerned with engineering and metal processing.[35]

Approximately one-third of Petersburg metalworkers were employed in plants situated in the near suburbs of the city. To the southwest of the city just beyond the Narvskii district was the Putilov works (located in the Petergofskii *uchastok*), the largest and most famous of the mixed-production metalworking factories.[36] In the southeastern sector of the city in the Nevskii district and just beyond along the Shlissel'burg road (*Za Nevskoi Zastavoi*) were such similarly large and important factories as the Nevskii Shipbuilding and Engineering Works, the Aleksandrovsk Engineering Works, and the machine shops for the Nikolaev railroad, as well as the state-owned Obukhov Steel Works. Growth in this district and along the Shlissel'burg road had been especially tumultuous.[37] Still farther to the southeast of the city in the village of Kolpino was the Izhorsk Works of the Naval Ministry, while to the northwest of the city in the village of Sestroretsk was the Sestroretsk Arms complex, also state owned.[38]

As the industrial structure of the city began to emerge more clearly, so too did the distinctive characteristics of these districts. In part this was shaped by the microgeography of the area; in part, by its emerging social composition, that is, the relative predominance of metal or textile workers, printers or leatherworkers, artisans or shopkeepers, as well as the proportion of workers to persons of other *sosloviia*. Sometimes what gave particular form to a district was the "weight" of an especially large factory, such as Baltic in Vasileostrov; or the availability of cultural and educational opportunities for the "lower classes"; or the presence of numerous higher educational institutes or the barracks of the Tsar's Guards.

In the 1890s, these distinctive characteristics seemed to retard the emergence of a common working-class culture and to foster instead a series of "special worlds" inhabited by isolated groups of workers. Thus Iulii Martov described the Putilov workers:

> Occupying a gigantic area on the outskirts of the city, beyond the strict police order and decorum imposed on the capital during the time of reaction, the

> Putilovtsy lived in their own world, within a sphere of autonomous factory interests, penetrated by the corporative spirit of the factory's freemen. [T]hey dominated the surrounding worker population in the villages of Volynkina, Tentelevka and the others, which were covered with chemical, tannery, textile, and other such industrial enterprises.[39]

Martov surmised that workers at the Baltic plant were even more "culturally developed" than the Putilovtsy given that Vasileostrov district was "populated primarily by students and long overcrowded by 'Germans' and foreigners [who] promoted the 'Europeanization' of their cultural outlook."[40]

Particularly distinctive was the Nevskii district, home to the Nevskii, Obukhov, and Aleksandrovsk metalworkers and described in 1906 by Petr Garvi:

> the Nevskii region stretched out for many versts along a narrow strip of land compressed between the Neva River and the Nikolaevsk railroad. On this narrow strip between water and railroad arteries giant plants were scattered one after another. . . . This was a special world, a proletarian kingdom, cut off from Petersburg by the broad expanse of the Aleksandr Nevskii Monastery and the vacant lands adjacent to it.[41]

Martov, noting the libraries, reading rooms, and Sunday and evening classes available in this district and the "Europeanized" workers these opportunities apparently produced, remarked that

> [i]n these circumstances, that type of Obukhovets so characteristic of the times evolved—absolutely an urban dweller, sometimes, as we ascertained with amazement, one that could scarcely be distinguished in his general bearing from a student. But there were no revolutionary traditions at the plant, [for] the relative security and privileged position of the workers at a state plant, indeed the plant most favored by the government, had an impact; and among the most advanced proletarians of other districts, the reputation of the Obukhovtsy was [marked by a certain] duality: "the lads are conscious, but are more notable for their dandyism, their attraction to the ladies and to amateur theatricals."[42]

There were indeed many attractions in the Nevskii district. In the late 1880s, for example, an amusement park was underwritten by a local factory owner and philanthropist. Vena, as it was commonly called, was frequented by many "old-timers" who enjoyed the music, vaudeville and sentimental dramas performed there. And while many young "dandies" also enjoyed strolling around Vena, other working-class youth preferred the Sunday and evening classes, especially those held at the Kornilov school, the largest and most important school for Petersburg workers in the 1890s.[43]

A variety of subcultures thus coexisted in turn of the century Petersburg, rather than any very coherent working-class community. Indeed, the organized fistfights which pitted factory against factory and street against street violently demonstrated the lack of community.[44] While identities based on the district or the factory or the craft or the *kruzhok* may have provided some sense of worker stability, and while *zemliak* ties may have softened the wrenching change from village to city, the tumultuous process of urban-industrial development taking place in the capital in the 1890s still had the consequence of magnifying the sense of alienation already apparent for some time within the ranks of metalworkers. Because of the speed and scope of this expansion, the overcrowded industrial districts became still more congested and seemed to be overtaken by a downtrodden mass, while life on the shop floor turned equally chaotic, with established hierarchies and work structures shifting rapidly in response to the enormous expansion of physical plant and work force size. Thus many, perhaps a majority, of metalworkers experienced the 1890s as profoundly "disorganizing."

Worker-Intelligentsia Relations

And yet, for some, there was the very real exhilaration of mastering a trade or acquiring an education; and while the demographic upheaval had an enormously disruptive impact on the life of the Petersburg working class, other developments were underway that would ultimately mold a greater solidarity. One such factor was the evolving relationship between workers and the intelligentsia, a relationship shaped by the fact that the Empire's capital city possessed distinguished educational institutions and stood at the very center of Russian intellectual life. Petersburg workers had opportunities for interaction with the intelligentsia and exposure to cultural trends that were comparatively rare for workers elsewhere in the Empire. By the same token, Petersburg's teeming factory districts opened an alluring arena of activity to the radical intelligentsia. Both social groups would seek out the other for their own purposes; each would be shaped by the encounter.[45]

Sustained contact between workers and radical *intelligenty* had begun with the efforts of the Chaikovskii circle in the early 1870s and continued from the mid-1880s under the influence of a few isolated Marxist groups. Over the same period of time a somewhat broader-based contact between workers and the intelligentsia developed as well, especially so in the late 1880s and early 1890s when the number of Sunday and evening schools for workers expanded significantly.

While touching the lives of comparatively few workers, the educational activities of the intelligentsia nonetheless had a stunning impact. At the evening courses, wrote one observer, "conscious life began." Workers from across Petersburg became acquainted at these lessons, thereby "preparing the soil for future solidarity." And as this participant further explained, "it was as if a previously unknown world instantly opened up; everything seemed strange and miraculous, one wanted to know and understand everything."[46]

The long-term effect of such encounters was to facilitate the emergence of a self-conscious stratum of educated, politicized working-class leaders linked by a set of common experiences and attitudes, a network of contacts across the city, and conversant in a particular sort of discourse. The short-term consequence was the painful isolation of this worker elite from the "gray" mass. Ironically, study of socialist doctrine and the lessons of the European labor movement under the guidance of the radical intelligentsia tended to distance the "conscious" elite from the experience of the overwhelming majority of Petersburg workers and foster disunity rather than solidarity.

Until the famine of 1891–92, both the educative and the more explicitly politicizing activities of the intelligentsia remained modest. But at this juncture social activism was rekindled among reformist and radical elements alike, who were appalled by the failure of the government to respond to the emergency: political quiescence and the "small deeds" psychology of the era of counter reforms was now broken. Equally important to future developments was the failure of the peasantry to rise up in response to the horrors of famine and epidemic disease and, consequently, the push this apparent passivity gave the radical intelligentsia to abandon its Populist faith. As well, the further progress of industry and the clear emergence of an industrial proletariat living in appalling squalor helped the Marxist position capture the field of radical discourse until the end of the century.

Over the course of the 1890s, worker-intelligentsia contact not only expanded, but took on qualitatively new forms. Circle study and teaching in the Sunday and evening schools continued and attracted a growing number of skilled and literate workers from the major metalworking factories.[47] But a more activist approach was developing as well. During the spring of 1895, Kremer's pamphlet "On Agitation" began to circulate in St. Petersburg and by the fall, following the formation of the Union of Struggle for the Liberation of the Working Class (*Soiuz bor'by za osvobozhdenie rabochego klassa*), its tactical line was fully adopted. The new approach hinged on the writing and distribution of agitational leaflets which documented the specific grievances of workers at a particular factory and presented them in a readily accessible language.[48]

Central to this new sort of contact between socialists and the rank and file was the cultivation of a cadre of politicized workers willing to gather information about daily life on the shop floor and assume the risks of getting the broadsheets into the factory. At the outset, many "advanced" workers who had come to value the camaraderie of the study circle and to disdain the *fabrichnye* felt abandoned by the *intelligenty* and resented the new line.[49] But Martov, writing in 1895, began to perceive that "there were worker youths who strained to get beyond the narrow limits of circle study" and who sometimes "made attempts to address the gray mass directly."[50]

Martov's observation highlighted a crucial development which the Union of Struggle soon seized upon: a new generation of worker youths was apparent in the factories, a generation hungry for education and yearning for greater activism, curious about the life of a more diverse segment of the working class, frustrated by the evident passivity of their elders and the exclusivity of circle study, and at times eager to reach beyond the programmatic prescriptions of the radical *intelligenty*. This was the generation shaped by the rapidity of Petersburg's industrialization, by exposure to the complexity and diversity of urban life, and by the increasing opportunities for contact with the radical intelligentsia.

The biographies of several Union of Struggle agitators illustrate the common characteristics which defined this new but still tiny stratum of working-class activists. Some, like Alexander Shotman (b. 1880) or B. Zinov'ev (b. 1874), were the sons of long time Petersburg workers and artisans; as adolescents they were apprenticed at a major metalworking factory and came into contact with Social Democratic ideas through study circles or Sunday and evening classes. Others, like Ivan Babushkin (b. 1873) or B. Zhukov (b. 1877), were sons of poor peasants and had come to the capital in search of wages. Both Babushkin and Zhukov found work in the Nevskii works, became skilled metal fitters, and attended the Sunday school for workers in the Nevskii district. All four were united by their youth, skill, and a thirst for knowledge which led them toward radicalism.

Their histories suggested another common experience as well: each worked at several major metalworking plants over the course of the decade. Sometimes they changed jobs to avoid dismissal for their organizing activities, or to set up worker circles in different plants, or to look for better wages and conditions. But all demonstrated a remarkable mobility which rested on the value of their skills to a rapidly expanding industry, and which also contributed to a growing sense of independence and self-worth based on their mastery of a trade.[51]

The conditions that shaped this new cadre of young activists facilitated the spread of socialist ideas. Each new job offered the opportunity to join a local circle or to create one; each dismissal threatened the collapse of revolutionary work at a particular plant but left behind lasting traces of organizational activity. Over the course of the 1890s, increasing numbers of workers gained at least a passing familiarity with radical ideas, while activists began to build a network of associations across the city. Thus Sil'vin recalled the impact of agitational leafletings around Putilov:

> The leaflet usually touched on some sort of particular instance: an abuse, a violation of law, the lowering of pay without notification, etc. A factory inspector would arrive, an investigation would begin, the police would conduct their own inquest. All this was an event in the monotonous life of the factory; it gave rise to talk; it provoked interest.[52]

Martov observed that at leading metalworking plants like Putilov, Aleksandrovsk, and Obukhov "there was already a certain milieu under the direct or indirect influence of the members of worker circles, and our proletarians did not feel themselves to be some sort of alien element in the shop." The task of distributing the pamphlets at these factories came down to technical finesse, for the rank and file here understood that however the pamphlet appeared, it "came from a certain, well-known group of comrades, [and] they [the masses] would never disclose their conjectures [about who these comrades were] to the plant administration or police."[53]

The attention of a few young activists soon began to turn to the factories. Babushkin wrote of donning the garb of a textile worker in order to visit the teeming factory barracks. Life here was a complete unknown, "a different world," which he set out to explore "for his own edification." He would soon return to gather materials on the grievances of this mass.[54] Others, like B. Zinov'ev, took up the task of distributing agitational leaflets with particular zeal, passing out broadsheets on the streets, in the taverns, and through the slums surrounding the *fabriki*.[55]

Of course, it was not only the appearance of a handful of young metalworkers in the world of the *fabrichnyi* that was important, but the specific content of the ideas that they spread. The Union of Struggle's agitational work conveyed the concepts, values, and theoretical constructs worked out by the Marxist intelligentsia since the 1880s; their efforts pursued a particular type of political socialization that aimed to inject a certain set of attitudes and discursive categories into the still embryonic labor movement. As Allan Wildman has demonstrated convincingly on the basis of an analysis of SD leaflets, a generation of workers was now exposed to a variety of Marxist propositions laid out in a simple and persuasive manner. At the outset, the broadsheets dwelled on the values of worker solidarity, collective action, and peaceful, non-violent protest; next, the linkage between the workers' economic plight and their lack of political rights was drawn; finally, concepts of class struggle and the inevitability of a political confrontation with the autocracy were explicitly articulated. Thus the centrality of political struggle was the underlying principle injected into the agitational literature almost from the outset; as such, this emphasis represented a shift away from the essentially anarchist teachings propagated by many adherents of the Populist movement. And given the fact that in the mid-1890s the Marxist position was virtually uncontested by competing radical groups in the factories, the ideological vision of the Union of Struggle was able to exert a powerful influence on the developing workers' movement.[56]

At least in part because of the Union of Struggle's efforts, workers in the capital's textile mills rose in a dramatic series of strikes in 1896 and 1897: the first major outbreak of strikes in Imperial Russian history. Perhaps 16,000 workers struck repeatedly in coordinated fashion in May and June 1896 and again went out in smaller numbers in January 1897. The experience of collective action and the eventual success in securing national legislation shortening the workday stimulated an important change in attitude among many of those "gray" types heretofore untouched by oppositional activity.[57]

K. M. Takhtarev noted that the clash of workers with the government "produced a real revolution in the minds of even the least conscious and most oppressed workers," and that, influenced by the events surrounding the strike, "the attitudes of broad layers of workers toward socialists and agitators

and to illegal socialist literature changed."[58] A reporter from *Nashe vremia*
observed an equally important change:

> Whoever was in Petersburg in the summer of 1897, whoever saw and heard
> what was happening and what was being said in the streets of our capital
> during the general strike of the textile workers, will probably agree with us.
> Those alert, excited faces, that heightened tone in the conversations of people
> accustomed to silent labor. . . . Everyone speaking loudly, asserting that they
> would not yield until they won. And you felt that within the most ordinary,
> most average member of this crowd a man had awakened. Amidst the total
> and age-old silence, you heard a single protesting voice, the voice of the
> worker. His speech was still incoherent, still primitive, still expressed only
> immediate needs and "crude" material interests. But it was the speech of men,
> not slaves! The cause of freedom had been born and was growing. And the
> effect of such events on other social groups could also be observed in the
> streets.[59]

That the strikes influenced the attitudes of other segments of the work force
is suggested by the reactions of the young metalworker Semen Kanatchikov,
then an apprentice patternmaker in a Moscow machine construction factory.
As recounted by Zelnik, news of the strike led Kanatchikov to his first
significant act of solidarity with fellow workers—a contribution to the textile
workers' strike fund—and then, when his employer shortened the workday,
promoted the conception in Kanatchikov's mind that managerial authority
could be successfully challenged.[60]

If this first strike wave marked a decisive turning point on the road to
political activism for many workers, it was no less a decisive moment in the
evolution of the Marxist movement. For the strikes led to a devastating wave
of arrests among the Social Democratic intelligentsia of the capital, the dis-
ruption of the work of the Union of Struggle, and the collapse of effective
ties with other centers of Social Democracy in Russia and in the emigration.
By the spring of 1898, a number of groups all competing for leadership of the
labor movement had emerged, each espousing its own brand of Marxism.
Between 1898 and 1903—with agitational work made exceptionally difficult
by the tsarist police, with the attention of the Marxist intelligentsia riveted
on the struggle to combat "heresies" at home and the threat of Bernsteinian
revisionism abroad, and with signs of a new socioeconomic and political
conjuncture reflected in an "awakening of society"—the paths of the labor
and Social Democratic movements in Russia largely diverged.[61]

Repression and Politicization

The repression following the 1897 strikes thus seemed to usher in a period
of quiescence. But appearances could be deceptive. While strike activity
declined, tension in the factories did not. In a revealing report dated May 17,

1899, the senior factory inspector, S. A. Lebedev, discussed a work stoppage at the St. Petersburg Freight Car Company brought about by an apparently minor change in rules governing Saturday work and payment for it. He concluded that it was an exceptionally poor time to change rules for little reason, since "the agitation conducted since 1896 among workers has especially intensified in the current year and each minute one may fear the outbreak of extensive strikes, primarily among workers of the engineering factories." As if to underline the seriousness of the situation, Lebedev closed by noting that "every factory inspector in Petersburg guberniia knew this."[62]

At least in part this unrest was fostered by an intensification of the often indiscriminate repression practiced by the autocracy and the underlying confusion in the government's labor policy that it represented. For in the aftermath of the textile strikes and in the context of the waning influence of Witte in the highest councils of state, the Ministry of Internal Affairs asserted its prerogatives as the guardian of public order. In a famous "secret" memorandum on August 12, 1897, to provincial governors, Minister of Internal Affairs Goremykin insisted that the government expand its surveillance over workers, prevent worker-intelligentsia interaction, and move quickly to arrest and exile any worker suspected of anti-government activity. He further suggested that at times of worker unrest legal norms might be suspended. A year and a half later, in February 1899, special factory police forces were added to the instruments available to the autocracy to monitor working-class behavior.[63]

Goremykin's willingness to suspend legal norms in his fight with worker unrest underlined the validity of a basic Social Democratic proposition, namely, that each time workers rose to protest their abysmal working conditions they would confront the power of the autocracy. If the working class was to improve its position in Russian society, argued the SDs, it would have to struggle for democratic rights. Without freedom of speech, assembly, and association, gains would be lost. In important respects, then, the work of the Union of Struggle since the mid-1890s prepared many workers to interpret the increasing repression in a political way.

Repression also seemed to help politicize workers standing completely outside any organized expression of dissent. The presence of factory police, the sudden disappearance of a fellow worker or apartment mate, the news of an acquaintance's prison term or exile, or the appearance of a gendarme to conduct an investigation could be a disturbing, quite frightening event which gave immediate and concrete expression to the repressive power of the state. Wrote Kanatchikov about his period of detention in 1900:

> The visit of this simple, illiterate woman [his aunt] who surmounted so many obstacles in order to obtain her meeting with me—what better proof of the justice of our cause than when the masses, dimly and unconsciously, begin to show their sympathy! . . . Later . . . it became even clearer that I enjoyed enormous sympathy from both workers who knew me and those who didn't.

> Spotting me from a distance on the street, even my former enemies would
> rush up to me, warmly squeeze my hand, and question me at length about
> my health and about prison, while speaking with disdain about gendarmes,
> spies, and the oppressive and arbitrary conduct of factory administrators.[64]

In often imperceptible ways, then, the working-class milieu receptive to
oppositional ideas noted by Martov and others in the mid-1890s was gradually widening toward the turn of the century. As Wildman and others have
noted, "events educate."

The arrests of 1897–98 also highlighted tensions in worker-intelligentsia
relations. Simply put, many workers resented what they saw as intelligentsia
"tutelage." Many chafed under the overly directive, sometimes arrogant
leadership of "the students" and craved a greater sphere for their own independence. Perhaps the most notable expression of this was the appearance
of the newspaper *Rabochaia mysl'* late in 1897. The paper was the product of
the joint efforts of worker circles at the Obukhov and Izhorsk metal factories.
Its worker editors were able to publish two issues and collect materials for a
third before the police caught up with them. But the paper then passed into
the hands of sympathetic, "workerphile" *intelligenty* who were able to continue publication with a fair degree of regularity until 1902.[65]

The express purpose of *Rabochaia mysl'* was to record the authentic voice
of the rank and file, unvarnished by the ideological constructs of the intelligentsia. In important respects it was remarkably successful. The paper gave
expression to a range of working-class sentiments, from the simple recitation
of shop floor grievances by the "gray" mass to the more sophisticated concerns of the politicized worker elite. On the whole, however, *Rabochaia mysl'*
appealed to the ordinary worker and was dominated by his perceptions. Its
great popularity rested on the opportunity it afforded the average worker to
lay out all his complaints, petty and substantial, for the world at large to see.
As Wildman has noted:

> There is no question but that the possibility of creative self-expression an-
> swered a deeply felt need of this awakened generation of workers for self-def-
> inition and self-assertion. Whereas heretofore the worker was obliged either
> to acquiesce or to allow others to speak for him, he could now speak with his
> own voice, vent his own spleen, define his own values.[66]

Many advanced workers soon tired of the largely apolitical grumblings of
the "gray" worker and turned away from *Rabochaia mysl'* in search of a more
compelling explication of their needs, some to find it on the pages of the more
"political" *Rabochee delo* which began publication in April 1899. The history
of *Rabochaia mysl'*, however, reflected the significant heterogeneity of the St.
Petersburg work force and the continuing absence of a coherent relationship
between the conscious worker elite, the "gray" mass, and all the many and
diverse segments of the working population in between. Nonetheless,
Rabochaia mysl' played an important role: by printing worker correspondence

from scores of factories and by repeating familiar grievances again and again, the paper contributed to the perception of the commonality of labor's oppression. And by publishing worker observations in a format similar to the Petersburg dailies and thereby departing from the traditional style of small, easily concealed underground leaflets, the paper responded to the need felt by many workers to make public, visible, and hence legitimate their life concerns.[67] As reflected in the textile strikes, as well as on the pages of *Rabochaia mysl'*, many ordinary workers began to reject a silent acceptance of their fate, reach out to a larger world, and find appropriate forms for their self-expression. The mundane but corrosive work of *Rabochaia mysl'* doubtless contributed to the "agitation" noted by factory inspector Lebedev.

In sorting out the many changes occurring in the metal factories over the course of the 1890s, it is useful to distinguish between the nature of the politicization underway and the process of class formation. In the major plants an oppositional milieu was in the making. The existence of worker circles over the decade, however fleeting their duration in a particular shop or factory, left lasting traces of such activity; so did periodic leafleting, the textile strikes, and the repression suffered by fellow workers. At the same time, a new generation of metalworkers had begun to emerge, characterized by literacy, mastery of a skill, relatively high wages, and a thirst for knowledge which led to contact with the radical intelligentsia, as well as to a growing identification with the urban-industrial environment. A few of these young, accomplished metalworkers—influenced in particular by the Union of Struggle—began to reach beyond their own immediate world and explore the life of their less developed comrades. They became the key conduit for the spread of agitational leaflets to the factories and plants of the capital and yet their interest in the life and labor of the "gray-types" was scarcely typical of their comrades in metalworking.

As the writing of one sensitive observer suggests though, by 1900 it was no longer appropriate to describe the political development of St. Petersburg labor solely in terms of the polarity between "advanced, conscious" worker and "gray-type"; rather, it was time to appreciate the emergence of an intermediate layer of politically mature workers.[68] These were not yet worker-revolutionaries, not the "eagles" of the labor movement, but they were keenly interested in political issues and already bored by *Rabochaia mysl'*.

> The Dreyfus case, the student movement, the difference between unlimited and constitutional monarchy and republican forms of government, finally the history of the Russian and West European revolutionary movement—these are the themes which this category of worker thinks about; frequently [they] are interested more in questions of political life than in their own immediate economic interests, the connection between [those interests] and general social conditions long since having been understood.[69]

Hence a developing sense of dignity and self-worth based on literacy, skill, relatively high wages, and mobility underlay the receptivity of many metalworkers to the political message of Social Democracy, namely, that the historic absence of political rights for Russian labor and labor's less than full participation in civil society had to be effaced. Many "advanced" workers had come to recognize the central importance of a struggle for civil rights and the need for open and legal organizations of labor. Moreover it seems that by the end of the century the effective collapse of the Union of Struggle had opened the fledgling labor movement to other models of organization and discourse. The dominance of Social Democracy was broken just at a time when economic crisis and "liberationist" sentiment helped to advance a variety of ideological visions, all competing for influence over broad segments of Russian society. So too, labor's own striving for greater public recognition was increasingly in conflict with the current concerns of the SDs, who were focused on conspiratorial work in the deep underground and enmeshed in doctrinal upheavals of little relevance to most workers.

Yet what was just as impressive as the emergence of a politically sensitive layer of workers by the end of the century was the general failure of metalworkers to participate in collective protest or strike action. No wave of strikes enveloped this sector; only a few metalworkers came to the aid of striking textile workers and identified with their cause; a mere handful celebrated May Day. It seems that those very conditions that had facilitated the process of politicization also undercut larger solidarities: precisely because of the rapidity of growth in heavy industry, the formation of stable communities within and outside the factory gates was blocked. The influx of peasant-workers, the cultural chasm dividing the populations of rural and urban Russia, the great instability of established shop hierarchies, and the significant mobility of skilled workers militated against strike actions and seemed to highlight rather than mute the differences that separated one metalworker from another, and metalworkers generally from their putative comrades outside heavy industry.

What one can observe in the waning years of the century, then, was the politicization, in a broadly democratic vein, of a small but growing segment of workers. Political consciousness at this juncture very largely meant an anti-autocratic, not an anti-capitalist or socialist outlook. A coherent notion of class and class conflict did not structure the thinking of most metalworkers. The experience of metalworkers did not support the notion of a united class of capitalists arrayed against them; clashes with management, episodic in any case over the 1890s, remained at the level of the individual enterprise and were fought within its confines. Moreover, there was little in the workplace culture or in the patterns of daily life that would impel a metalworker to identify his cause with that of Petersburg labor as a whole. On the contrary, the material aspirations of some metalworkers and the educational strivings of others could lead to other patterns of identification. Thus the attitudes and experiences of many metalworkers made them receptive to the ideas of a broadly based "liberationist" movement against the autocracy, yet quite distant from any exclusivist struggle pitting labor against "society."[70]

III

THE EMERGING CRISIS, 1900–1904

The crisis that would culminate in the Revolution of 1905 found its first reflection in the last year of the nineteenth century. The outbreak of student protest during 1899 as well as the onset of a severe economic crisis combined to stimulate a broadly based critique of the autocracy. With the new century, three major oppositional political parties emerged, each articulating a competing vision of the future Russia. Thus began the "awakening of society" long awaited by Tsar Nicholas's critics.

With the first signs of unrest in the universities, the attention of radical society turned away from the labor movement. Students suddenly became the standard bearers of the opposition, especially given the decline in strike protest which attended the economic downturn. Although the ferment in the higher educational institutions of the Empire had initially focused on the various restrictions constraining academic freedom, the repressive actions of university officials and the state gradually widened the conflict. Thus, when students at the University of St. Petersburg aired their grievances on February 8, 1899, the day marking the eightieth anniversary of the University's founding, the rector reacted swiftly and called in the police to quell the disturbances. Dispersed by force, the students responded with a call to strike; within days they were joined by some 25,000 students from across the Empire. What had begun as a conflict between students and university officials over issues of academic freedom expanded over the next two years into a far more broadly based movement seeking civil liberties and substantive political change.

Just as threatening to regime stability as the wave of student protests was the onset of a serious economic downturn. During the summer of 1899 a crisis on European financial markets sharply curtailed the capital and credit available to the Russian government and to Russian industry. The State Bank, soon followed by the major commercial banks, began to increase interest rates; financially strapped investors were forced to unload their securities. Panic selling sent the value of stocks plummeting, culminating in the "black days" of September 22 and 23, 1899, on the Petersburg Exchange and in a series of spectacular bankruptcies. But the crisis was hardly confined to the financial markets or the collapse of a few major firms. Falling prices, first in the consumer goods sector and then in producer goods, signaled a more fundamental economic dislocation. As domestic demand for the products of light industry contracted, the underlying weakness of the internal market was revealed: poor harvests in the last years of the century and the pressure of taxes on the peasantry highlighted the constraints Russia's agrarian sector imposed on the economy as a whole.[1]

The social consequences of the economic crisis were everywhere apparent: peasant disturbances began to break out across the Empire, while hungry migrants in search of wages in the cities swelled the ranks of the unemployed. Urban workers experienced the depression through falling rates and wages; the coercive pressure of foremen now further empowered by the threat of dismissal for the smallest infractions of labor discipline; and finally in unemployment.[2]

Equally apparent was the waning influence of Witte: the sharp downturn in the economy called his developmental strategy into question. Agrarian interests, long hostile to the favored position accorded industry, now gained increasing support in the higher spheres of government and helped fuel ministerial conflict over a range of policy issues. Moreover, while Witte was still able to retain control over the factory inspectorate, his authority was steadily eroded by the increasing intervention of the Ministry of Internal Affairs and its police organs in labor-management relations.

Important, too, to the developing instability of the regime were the long term consequences of Russia's penetration into the Far East. The provocative decision to build the Trans-Siberian railway across Manchuria placed Russia at the very center of a host of competing economic and diplomatic interests. When the Chinese Eastern Railroad was ravaged by the Boxers in the summer of 1900, Russian involvement expanded dramatically. By the fall, Imperial troops occupied much of Manchuria, thereby not only contributing to the problems which would eventually topple the Manchus, but challenging Japanese interests in the region as well. St. Petersburg's haughty disregard for the growing power of Tokyo would soon lead to war.

The Impact of the Economic Downturn
on the Metalworking Industry

The economic crisis affected the various sub-branches of the heavy goods sector at different times and with different degrees of intensity; aggregate figures thus tend to disguise the particular experience of specific industries. There is no doubt, however, that the basic metallurgy of the South and the metal processing and machine construction of the capital was severely affected.[3] In general terms, output in the metalworking industry of the Empire fell from 373.5 million rubles in 1900 to 313.3 million rubles in 1902, a decline of 16%. More dramatic was the decline in the output of rails (falling from a 1900 peak of 30.3 million poods to just 20.6 million poods in 1903, a drop of 32%) and in the production of locomotive engines (falling from 1,225 engines in 1901 to 922 in 1903, or a decline of 25%).[4] According to factory inspectorate reports covering private industry in Petersburg, the number of workers declined by 7,704 in 1902, these losses occurring primarily at metalworking factories.[5] And despite the relief afforded by government weapons orders for the Russo-Japanese War, the industry remained depressed for most of the decade.

Archival material studied by A. F. Iakovlev illustrates the fate of several major metalworking plants of the capital. For example, Obukhov's output stood at 3,826,000 rubles in 1901, down from 6,122,000 rubles in 1899; the factory then ran in the red for several years. The Putilov works cut its work force by 23% by the end of 1902, while its output fell by 45% in comparison with 1899–1900. Between 1899 and 1901–1902, Phoenix experienced a 59% drop in output, while St. Petersburg Metals suffered a 31% decline in its financial turnover between 1901 and 1902.[6] In the electrical industry, the sub-branch most severely affected was electrical engineering, especially those plants that had developed rapidly in the 1890s in the expectation of huge orders for the electrical equipment needed by the transport machine-construction sector. V. S. Diakin reports that such important Petersburg firms as Siemens-Halske and Shukkert experienced "major losses" in the 1901–1903 period.[7]

The shocks inflicted by the economic downturn impelled Petersburg industrialists in the first years of the new century to introduce a series of reforms in the financial and marketing structure of their industry; with time and the persistence of economic stagnation, they would be pressed to embark on a series of further changes which affected the organization of production processes in their plants.

As we have seen, the growth of St. Petersburg industry during the 1890s had been intimately tied to massive government orders for rails and rolling stock. The crisis at the turn of the century forced the government to curtail its huge capital outlays for railroad construction and with this the lucrative market for heavy industrial goods largely collapsed. This structure of demand for the products of heavy industry—concentrated in the form of government orders—encouraged producers in the 1890s to enter limited commercial agreements which sought to control the sale and pricing of their goods. By the turn of the century, these agreements developed into a number of syndicates which dominated important sectors of heavy industry. Between 1901 and 1903 syndicates were established in locomotive and freight car construction, bridge construction, iron pipe manufacture, and nail and wire production. Although not yet receiving formal sanction, syndicates were encouraged by the government as a measure of self-help to the ailing industry; between 1902 and 1906 most legal impediments to their existence were gradually eliminated.[8]

The government sought to help in other ways as well. Under the aegis of the Ministry of Ways of Communication, a Committee on Railroad Orders (*Komitet po zhelezhnodorozhnym zakazam*) was created in June 1902, and although it was conceived as a temporary measure authorized to function only until January 1, 1906, it ultimately enjoyed a considerably longer life. The committee was charged with the distribution of orders for locomotive engines, freight cars, rails and ties. It worked closely with the giants of the industry organized in three syndicates in metallurgy and transport machine-construction (i.e., Prodamet, Prodparovoz, and Prodvagon). Jointly, the committee and the syndicates not only dictated the market-share of participating firms, but fixed prices and standards on quality. The result was that the committee provided a small number of major firms with a steady if diminished stream of highly inflated orders. These practices not only helped to moderate market fluctuations, but forced out smaller, less privileged competitors within the industry.[9]

The Witte administration also attempted to help industry by providing interim financing. As the research of I. F. Gindin demonstrates, the State bank in these difficult years pursued a policy of granting irregular loans and long term credits on extremely favorable terms for selected plants of particular importance to the government. These policies were often undertaken without regard for the underlying viability of the enterprise and in contravention of the legislation governing the State bank. The loans were intended to support major firms and did little to protect smaller plants from the ravages of the economic crisis.[10]

The ability of the major industrialists and their syndicates to influence the distribution of state orders, the intervention of the government in bailing out selected plants, and the problems of capitalization brought about by the crisis on European money markets combined to force the closure of many smaller firms. Between 1901 and 1904, sixteen machine-construction factories with a basic capital of 7,254,000 rubles were liquidated, while another ten such companies with a basic capital of 12,455,000 rubles joined this list between 1905 and 1909. One notable consequence of the economic crisis, therefore, was the further concentration of the industry.[11]

The crisis on European financial markets also altered the pattern of foreign investment. By the turn of the century, foreigners were withdrawing from direct participation; they tended instead to establish subsidiaries of foreign-based firms or to invest through the intermediary of Russian banks, whose development they now fostered. The intense capital scarcity of the early twentieth century forced industrialists to reorganize the financial structure of their plants to gain access to foreign investors. Privately owned firms were reconstituted as joint-stock corporations, while the "giants" of heavy industry, already structured in joint-stock corporations in the 1890s, looked to financial reorganization through banking institutions. Typically, debts were consolidated and refinanced, and banks issued new, usually preferred, shares on European exchanges.[12] Reflecting this trend of reorganization and consolidation, the number of joint-stock companies in the metalworking industry of St. Petersburg grew from nineteen to forty-two between 1900 and 1913, while the number of workers employed in these plants rose from 36% to 54% of the total number of metalworkers in the capital.[13]

Equally important in shaping heavy industry in the first decade of the new century was the changing pattern of state entrepreneurship. Witte's developmental strategy had been challenged by the economic crisis, as well as by the recurring incidence of poor harvests and peasant disorders. Many in government and industry now realized that the problems of agriculture had to be addressed in a more systematic manner and that this would doubtless entail a different set of budgetary priorities. Thus the government chose not to resume its massive investment in heavy industry, not only because of the tightening of credit available from European sources, but because of increasing public concern over the fate of rural Russia. In consequence, the metalworking industry was confronted by the severe and immensely costly problem of excess capacity. Given the sharp reduction in state demand, the industry was forced to look to the private, considerably more competitive market to sell its goods.[14] Of course, the turn to this market was modest and halting, and could not be otherwise given the structure of the economy and the weak demand for the products of heavy industry. Thus the preeminent strategy of the leading industrialists was to focus on the formation of syndicates and thereby control access to the now more limited state market. Nonetheless few could escape the reality of the new competitive pressures brought about by the economic crisis and were hence challenged to bring down the high costs of production that were embedded in the cavalier approach to factory organization that had developed in the 1890s.[15]

The economic dislocation of the first years of the new century thus underlay an important series of adjustments in the heavy industry of the capital. The marketing syndicates, the elimination of weaker enterprises, and the ways in which the changing patterns of foreign investment influenced the financial structure of many plants all combined to bring about the first phase in a process of consolidation and concentration in the metalworking industry.

The "Obukhov Defense" and Its Aftermath

Upheaval in the economy spilled over into social conflict in the capital early in 1901. Student protests, now joined with increasing frequency by workers, flared in February and March. As alarming was the assassination of Minister of Education N. P. Bogolepov on February 14, the first major terrorist assault in twenty years. And on March 4, a mass demonstration occurred at the Kazan Cathedral, to be broken up by an unprecedented level of police violence. Appalled by regime brutality, some seventy-five leading literary figures joined in a letter of protest to the government. Again the autocracy reacted with force: noted writers and academics were arrested, journals were censored, and professional associations were closed.

In the tense atmosphere following the Kazan demonstration, workers and Social Democrats in the capital prepared to mark May Day. April 22, the first Sunday after April 18 (May 1 according to the Western calendar), was fixed for an open demonstration on Nevskii Prospekt. But fearful of major disorders, the police carried out a wave of arrests on the night of the 18th. While several thousand workers converged on Nevskii at the appointed time, in the absence of leaders and a clearly defined plan the demonstrators were easily dispersed. Despite the actions of the police and largely deprived of Social Democratic leadership workers agitated for another demonstration on May 1.

On the night of April 30–May 1, strikes broke out in textile factories on the Vyborg side. At the same time, other workers in this district and elsewhere downed their tools. Strikes and demonstrations on May 1 combined to produce a series of violent clashes with the police, as well as the aggressive presentation of a variety of demands, including one for an eight-hour day. Further skirmishes with the police on May 2 led to the construction of barricades along Vyborg's Samsonievskii Prospekt.[16]

Several hundred Obukhovtsy also observed May 1 by not showing up for work. On the following day, learning that management had decided to fire a number of their absent comrades as an example, many protested the arbitrary action and asked to be dismissed as well. Over the next few days, a strike action was considered and demands touching on a variety of grievances were discussed. On the morning of May 7, workers gathered in the factory yard and elected delegates to bring demands to management; and while most workers then returned to their shops to begin work, strike leaders fanned out across the factory grounds to call workers to join in a walkout. Combining violence and persuasion, the militants closed down most of the factory. Many then left the grounds to mobilize workers at neighboring plants and to prepare for the inevitable arrival of the police. Armed with bricks, pieces of iron, and other projectiles, Obukhovtsy were soon engaged in a bloody battle with police units and armed troops. When the violent confrontation was finally over, seven workers lay dead and scores more were wounded.[17]

On the morrow of the "Obukhov defense" unrest spread through the metalworking factories of the capital. At the Baltic Shipbuilding and Engineering Works, Aleksandrovsk Engineering Works, the Nevskii Shipbuilding and Engineering Works and elsewhere metalworkers struck, demanding not only the recognition of May Day as a legal holiday, but wage increases and the introduction of the eight-hour day. Strikes and unrest continued through May and into June, in the end constituting the first major wave of metalworker protest in Imperial Russian history.

For the Obukhovtsy, the politicization of their ranks had been of relatively recent origin. In conjunction with a significant increase in government orders for military goods in 1898, the Obukhov management had expanded and reequipped the factory. Virtually alone among the metalworking factories of the capital at the time, Obukhov worked at full capacity during the first years of the industrial downturn and its work force expanded rather than contracted. In the past, the factory had insured that only fully "trustworthy" workers were hired by relying on recommendations provided by the "old-timers," that stratum of privileged workers patronized by the management. But the factory's demand for labor outstripped its capacity to filter carefully incoming workers and as a result many of the young "conscious" metalworkers recently thrown out of other factories as well as unskilled migrants from the hungry countryside found jobs at the plant.[18]

While these young, skilled workers were not the highest paid or the most skilled in the factory, they tended to hold the more desirable jobs in the "cold shops" where the work was considerably cleaner, more precise, and less physically demanding than in the "hot shops" and where the wages were substantially higher.[19] Considerably less secure were the unskilled, auxiliary workers who were largely migrants from the countryside: hired on a day-to-day basis, never knowing if they would have a permanent job, they earned a daily wage of just 60–80 kopecks, sometimes for the same tasks performed by laborers on the regular staff.[20] It was almost certainly the interaction of these two groups of workers that provided the critical leaven at the plant, for they expanded circle study and disturbed the order that had been maintained by the "old-timers" and their sons.[21] Moreover, it seems likely that the presence of these young activists began to influence those Obukhovtsy described by Martov several years earlier as advanced, fully urbanized proletarians, distinguished, however, more by their dandyism than by their militance.[22]

In the wake of the bloody confrontation with police and troops, Obukhovtsy returned to the factory on May 11 to elect delegates to talk with management and to elaborate a set of demands.[23] In important ways, the demands encapsulated the history of the factory over the past several years and highlighted aspects of labor-management relations that had provoked conflict. Some of the grievances focused on wage issues: workers insisted on increases in piece rates and a 25% rise in the day wages of unskilled laborers. They wanted the rates to be posted in the shops and to remain unchanged for the contract period. Of central concern to Obukhovtsy was the marked pattern of falling rates and wages since 1898, a decline that in part reflected the pressure exerted by the rising unemployment that attended the industrial crisis. Also at issue was the arbitrary lowering of rates that had already been set and the unfair distribution of piece rate earnings by the "seniors" running the work crews. Workers were further angered by the sharp disparity in wages, which some perceived as a deliberate ploy of the administration designed to sow dissension.

A second set of demands were related to disciplinary issues: fines for lateness, conflicts with foremen over dismissal slips, and rules which prevented workers who had taken dismissal from reentering the factory for a three-month period. Other grievances impinged on factory order more generally: workers sought the dismissal of Colonel Ivanov, the assistant director, and several foremen; a report on the size and disposition of the fund accumulated on the basis of fines; provision of support for the widows and children of injured workers; and an end to the rude and impolite address regularly used by supervisory personnel in their dealings with the rank and file. Workers also insisted on regular, annual election of their representatives as a means by which they could legitimately express their grievances. Taken together, workers were protesting the host of oppressions that defined their work life, cut into their earnings, and left their dependents helpless. More particularly, they were responding to the deeply offensive actions of Ivanov, who in their eyes was responsible for many of the strictures imposed over the past several years, and who had precipitated the bloody clash on May 7 by his arbitrary dismissal of workers celebrating May Day.

A third demand—the abolition of overtime work—revealed one of the greatest sources of tension. Over the past several years, overtime had become virtually compulsory and had added several hours to each working day. While long hours permitted workers to compensate for the declining rates and wages, the extra work was clearly exhausting; it was ethically problematic for many workers given the throngs of unemployed at the factory gates; and its compulsory aspects were richly productive of conflict with lower level supervisory personnel. In this context, too, the abuses of managerial authority were made significantly more offensive by the crude, impolite forms of address regularly used by foremen.

A final set of issues reflected the broader processes of politicization taking place in the capital. The demands for an eight-hour day and the recognition of May Day as a legal holiday were doubtless inspired by worker activists and Social Democratic agitation over the past several years. And the insistence that fired and detained workers be liberated and rehired suggested both a questioning of constituted authority and a developing sense of solidarity within labor's ranks.[24] In sum, worker grievances regarding the shop floor relations of labor and management were infused by a perception of injustice and pursued with a sense of solidarity heretofore largely absent in the metal factories of the capital, and thus confronted the forces of order with a new and complex set of problems.

In the event, General G. A. Vlas'ev, director of the Obukhov works, proved initially responsive to the workers' demands, agreeing to act on most of their grievances, and stating that while it was not within his authority to recognize May Day as a legal holiday or to introduce an eight-hour day, he would discuss these issues with the Naval Ministry.[25] On May 29, he instructed all heads of shop to regulate "the earnings of the skilled workers in all shops, equalize them in conformity with the quantity and quality of the work, determine the maximum number of workdays in a month, and in general put in order all that relates to the work force."[26] Apparently, the directive also envisioned the creation of several committees to study these issues.[27]

While the reasons remain obscure, the policy of moderation first adopted by Vlas'ev was abandoned in early July. Suddenly the hated Ivanov returned to the factory after a two-month leave of absence, and just as suddenly Vlas'ev ordered that only those workers who had served for at least five years at the factory and who were no younger than twenty-five years of age could be elected deputies. When workers walked off the job in protest on July 7,

Vlas'ev immediately closed the factory. On the night of July 8–9, a well-planned wave of arrests occurred, taking several hundred activist Obukhovtsy as well as all the elected representatives. Within days, Vlas'ev announced that work would resume under the former conditions; moreover, he informed workers that they would no longer have the right to elect deputies. What had first appeared as an important victory for the Obukhov workers turned into a stunning defeat.[28]

The violence at Obukhov and elsewhere, as well as the substance of the workers' demands, not only called into question the dominant patterns of labor-management relations, but impinged on issues of state security and the future direction of tsarist labor policy. Despite the subsequent repression, worried officials recognized the need for some further action and embarked on detailed investigations of the sources of labor unrest. These studies soon revealed the increasingly divergent assumptions of managers and state officials about the sources of labor conflict; they also provided a detailed description of the social milieu that was producing a growing number of working-class activists.

Naval Ministry officials commissioned one such investigation for their Baltic facility on June 6. Headed by A. N. Chikolev, an assistant to Baltic's board of directors and a man who had worked closely with private industrialists grouped in the St. Petersburg Industrial Society, the study developed data on the wage structure and workday of some 32,000 metalworkers at ten major metal plants in the capital.[29] Chikolev concluded in his investigation that socialist agitation lay behind the recent unrest at the Baltic factory: radicals had gained a sympathetic response to demands for an eight-hour day, an across the board increase in pay with the establishment of a minimum wage, and the abolition of overtime, only by appealing to the "inert mass" of workers on the basis of their purely "local" concerns and by reference to a few particularly vexing aspects of their employment at a given plant.

Asserting that the eight-hour day was inappropriate to Russian conditions and rejecting demands for wage increases and a minimum wage as making "no sense," Chikolev's approach to labor's demands was fundamentally dismissive. He argued, for example, that while the somewhat shorter hours in foreign factories had led to a greater intensity of labor and hence to certain gains in productivity, Russian workers were as yet unable to use their leisure hours wisely. Dissipating their time and money in the taverns, they came to the factory "clouded" by drink, and productivity consequently suffered. Although Chikolev recognized that shorter hours were "desirable," he insisted that any reduction had to be accomplished over a number of years and could only occur after workers had gained the ability to use free time more judiciously.

Chikolev also found demands for a minimum wage of one ruble "arbitrary" and argued more generally that wages had to be based on the overall conditions of supply and demand, as well as on the skill of the worker and his length of service at a particular factory. Finally, Chikolev maintained that there was no reason for Baltic to pay a ruble a day wage when workers were waiting at the gate ready to accept 60 kopecks. In short, Chikolev seemed to join with those employers who found longer hours "beneficial" for Russia's uneducated workers and who believed that wage levels were properly left to "impersonal" market forces.

If the majority of workers had been led astray by socialist demands, what were those particularistic conditions that provided the grounds for mass unrest and how could they be alleviated? Chikolev found the principal cause of the recent disorders in the abolition of overtime work called forth by the industrial crisis at the turn of the century which reduced the amount of work at the factory and hence deprived workers of the supplemental wages they typically earned on overtime. Accustomed to a higher level of earning, workers suddenly found themselves in difficult financial straits. The socialist demand for an abolition of overtime, he argued, was linked to a demand for a general increase in day wages and was thus meant to compensate for the loss of overtime earnings. Chikolev, however, offered no alternative proposals to alleviate the economic plight of the work force; rejecting out of hand a general increase in wages, he apparently felt that workers simply had to adjust to the vagaries of the economic cycle and wait out the hard times.

Chikolev made several specific recommendations. He suggested that the factory start the process of shortening the workday, beginning with a reduction of one-half hour, to a nine and one-half–hour day; that two holidays be added to the regular schedule of free days (not, however, May Day); that piece rates be reexamined with the intention of increasing them "somewhat"; and that the search which workers found so humiliating be abolished. More generally, he advised that state and private factories of similar type work together to standardize conditions of employment and institute uniform rules pertaining to the length of the workday, the schedule of regular holidays, fines, grants for illness, and so on.

Little in Chikolev's report, then, indicated that the demands voiced by workers in the spring of 1901 should be viewed as legitimate; still less suggested that Baltic's workers were capable of independent, purposive action or that managerial assumptions about labor unrest required serious reexamination. Rather, managers should seek to eliminate the apparently minor but offensive conditions which irritated workers at a given factory (e.g., the search, fines for a few minutes' lateness, etc.), and work to establish uniform conditions in the plants. Although these were modest proposals, Chikolev's concluding remarks implied that disorder could well be expected in the future if the economy did not improve and if employers failed to institute timely preventive measures.

Some weeks after Chikolev presented his report to the board of directors of the Baltic factory, the head of the plant, Major-General K. K. Ratnik, submitted a penetrating critique of the findings.[30] Complementing Chikolev's investigation with his own research, Ratnik rejected any simplistic depiction of Baltic's workers as an "inert mass" easily manipulated by socialist propaganda and instead suggested that the recent disorders could best be understood by examining the differing needs, resources, and aspirations of the work force, particularly in light of the recent industrial crisis.

Relying on data from a work force census taken a year prior to the disorders, Ratnik observed that poorly paid skilled workers and common laborers were much more likely to leave the plant in the hard times that attended the recent industrial downturn than were the more highly skilled cadres. Thus, for example, his research revealed that the rigging department, which relied heavily on the unskilled labor of recent migrants, had a remarkably high rate of turnover, while the highly skilled work force in the pattern-making shop remained quite stable. Suspecting that this strong correlation between retention and skill level depended on a variety of factors related to the material situation of his work force, Ratnik investigated more closely the composition of the shops and the degree to which Baltiitsy retained ties to the land.

Ratnik's study revealed that by far the largest segment of his labor force consisted of workers from the peasant *soslovie*, some 80% of the total. Of these, about half retained an allotment in the countryside. These peasant-workers were relatively better off than others at the factory for they often derived a supplemental income from their land and, at the least, could return to their farmstead in times of unemployment, illness, or old age. And while landed workers might spend their adult lives in the city, Ratnik found that their primary identification remained with the land. They typically married in the village or looked for a "country girl" in the city, and endeavored to establish a household which would nurture children in the values of rural Russia. If raised in the city, their children were trained under the watchful eye of a parent or fellow countryman, usually in one of the trades of the "hot shops," that is, those metallurgical processes which relied on manual labor, a relatively short apprenticeship that would not attenuate ties to the land, but that paid a decent wage (e.g., blacksmithing, hammersmithing, etc.). Ratnik concluded that landed workers and their children were the most stable, materially secure, and conservative element at the factory; their ties to the village had not been broken and for this reason, he seemed to argue, they were not among the ranks of the worker militants.

Of those peasant-workers without an allotment, Ratnik found that a significant number lacked even a family farmstead. These were poor, landless peasants whose ties to the countryside were purely formal and who were well on their way to becoming permanent urban dwellers. But the major-general was particularly concerned with the plight of those young people who had been forced to leave the land because their families could no longer feed them, but who were nonetheless obligated to send back part of their earnings to the village. Because these youths had not been raised in the ways of the factory, they were unable to compete with their urban counterparts for the best-paying jobs. They typically worked as assistants to the skilled cadres (machinists, turners, joiners, etc.), but their wages advanced at a slower pace.

Such workers struggled to make ends meet, for they often bore a heavy financial burden for both their rural kin and, as they grew older, their own urban-based families. Workers in this group represented an important transitional element: they had left the land, but had not become fully attached to the city. Ratnik argued that the wages of these workers demanded serious attention and he implied that by improving their economic well-being and by strengthening their bonds to the land, the stability of this group within the factory could be fostered and the influence they exerted over their children enhanced.

Almost 17% of the work force belonged to the petty townsmen and artisanal estates, and these workers, as well as the children of the landless peasantry who had grown up in the city, constituted the most unstable and undisciplined element in the factory according to Ratnik. " . . . in large part literate and in their own way well read," these workers were the "most developed," even "gifted" segments of the labor force and typically occupied those positions that were the best paid and least demanding of physical labor. As pattern-makers and joiners, draftsmen and machinists, as *masterovye*, but never *rabochie*, they received "good wages" which were, however, inadequate to their "broadly developed urban needs." Concerned to provide their children with the best education they could afford and to establish them among the "intelligentsia" of factory labor (draftsmen and clericals), the parents subsequently found themselves in direct conflict with their rebellious offspring, who rejected the authority of the "less developed" older generation. It was this skilled, urbanized youth, argued Ratnik, yet to suffer material hardship or assume responsibility for a family, that provided the workers' movement with its most active and militant elements. Ratnik went on to stress that the material situation of workers from the lower urban estates was extremely unstable, in large part because they would sooner accept poverty if they lost their regular job than take up the position of common laborer which they so disdained. Despite all this, the major-general concluded that "this group of workers from the petty urban bourgeoisie and from the artisans is the most able, providing from its ranks a large part of the intelligent crew leaders (*ukazateli*), assistant foremen, and even foremen, and therefore, the improvement of their daily lives, not only materially but also morally, deserves special attention, as the best technical support of production."

Ratnik's analysis was compelling: he had described the emergence of a significant category of workers who retained no meaningful ties to the countryside, but formed instead the nucleus of an urban proletariat. Literate, technically proficient, with broadly developed urban tastes, at times fulfilling lower level supervisory positions and displaying a keen sense of professional pride, these workers—and most particularly their children—stood at the heart of the developing labor movement. And in what was surely a sobering realization, Ratnik emphasized that Baltic's productive viability rested squarely on their shoulders. As he now recognized, moreover, the core of the activist labor movement resided with those who had already begun their adaptation to urban-industrial life, not those who were just experiencing the trauma of dispossession.

Just as important, the observations of the major-general revealed one of the key underlying causes of the recent protests. Skilled cadres had been profoundly affected by the economic crisis not only because wages had declined sharply, but because young metalworkers had experienced the economic downturn as a blow to their self-esteem. Over the course of the 1890s their sense of self had been built on good wages, the independence fostered by the mastery of a valued skill, and a pride in their accomplishments—a set of characteristics which had encouraged many to seek out further education and to engage in a variety of urban-based pursuits. Now, however, many had been forced to pawn their belongings for a pittance, give up apartments for "corners," accept the degrading work of a common laborer, and ultimately confront poverty and unemployment.[31] In this light, the wage demands voiced in the spring of 1901 emerged as the critical issue for many metalworkers.

Analyses of the strikes at both Obukhov and Baltic thus pinpointed the central role that had been played by the young, skilled, urbanized workers and the young, landless migrants from the countryside. These findings were also supported by the observations of Assistant Minister of Internal Affairs P. D. Sviatopolk-Mirskii, whose study highlighted yet another facet of the social milieu which shaped these young people:

> The inquests of recent years attest that the efforts of the revolutionaries have not been in vain and thanks to their diligence criminal teachings have taken firm root in schools for workers, making them open breeding grounds of propagandists. The majority of worker-agitators and the leaders of various strikes have visited these schools, where, under the leadership of so-called intelligenty, they have adopted an anti-government way of thinking, [and] then spread it with growing success among their comrades.[32]

While according a central role to worker-intelligentsia interaction, Mirskii was mindful as well of the distress caused by the economic downturn and related conditions of urban life: the material insecurity attendant upon disability and old age, the grossly inadequate housing situation, the dissatisfaction caused by inflation, the absence of primary schools for working-class children, and the lack of libraries and sufficient quantities of "appropriate" reading materials. Mirskii thus implicitly identified problems that resulted from rapid urbanization, and at times even seemed vaguely aware that urbanization had created qualitatively new needs and expectations among segments of the working class. Speaking of the lack of social insurance, Mirskii noted that few "simple" Russians were inclined to save, "especially in view of the temptations of the urban setting."[33] Discussing housing conditions, he remarked more generally that "the needs of the worker in the city rapidly increase, especially in the capital."[34]

The reports of both Ratnik and Mirskii reveal, in effect, the expanding world of the worker, particularly the world of the young metalworker, which was the result not only of a specific sort of contact with radical intellectuals, but of a complex range of interactions with the city, made possible, at least in part, by the good wages and literacy enjoyed by skilled workers. Both observers realized that Petersburg's work force could no longer be perceived as an undifferentiated mass; it contained a stratum of workers sufficiently large and sufficiently alienated to replenish regularly the ranks of the activists agitating in the factories.

What these reports also suggest are the ways in which the longer term processes of development shaping the work force in heavy industry intersected with the political and economic conjuncture that occurred at the turn of the century. The civic protests of society, and most particularly the street demonstrations of the students, showed workers a more open and active way to express political grievances. In this now considerably more charged political environment, the first significant collective protests of metalworkers took place. And these actions revealed that the patterns characteristic of metalworker protest in the 1890s had begun to change.

Central to this mobilization of labor protest was the economic downturn at the turn of the century. Falling wages, mounting unemployment, the loss of occupational mobility, and the arbitrariness of foremen combined to impinge on the relatively privileged status of the metalworker and to threaten his self-esteem. For the first time the young, skilled metalworker confronted the poverty and despair that defined the lives of his less accomplished comrades. And this experience helped to turn the attention of these privileged workers, far more clearly than in the past, toward the wages, hours, and conditions that pertained generally in heavy industry.

Prescriptions for Change

The various studies that sought to understand the causes of the recent disorders also shed light on the major assumptions which characterized managerial and bureaucratic thinking around the turn of the century.[35] Thus, for example, Chikolev's fundamentally dismissive attitude toward workers' grievances reflected the belief of some within the Ministry of Finance that the proper role of government in labor-management relations was a modest one and that long term economic development would ultimately benefit Russia's work force. Mirskii's views, in contrast, were consistent with the more interventionist policy pursued since the last years of the nineteenth century by the Ministry of Internal Affairs, while Ratnik's thinking revealed an entirely different sort of perspective at work. The attitudes of key segments of the St. Petersburg industrial community, which defy simplistic characterization, may be gleaned from memoranda they submitted in criticism of the labor legislation proposed by the government in the early years of the twentieth century.

Mirskii's appreciation for the insecurity of workers in the urban setting, his dawning awareness of differentiation within the working class, and his conviction that further disorders would take place because the "evil" of revolutionary propaganda had already sunk deep roots in the capital reflected the realization now shared by many within the MVD that the existence of a working class and a labor problem could no longer be denied.[36] The illusion that strong ties to the land and patriarchal relations in the factory would prevent the emergence of a "rootless, landless proletariat" now gave way to concerns about crafting government policies responsive to the new reality.

Mirskii's recommendations, however, did not depart in any significant way from the basic positions held for several years by the MVD; rather, he asserted the need for a more comprehensive and consistent application of the Ministry's dual policy of repression and "tutelage." Thus, he stressed equally the need for improved police supervision, most especially the subordination of the factory inspectorate to the local organs of the MVD and an expansion of the police units assigned to worker districts, as well as a series of efforts designed to improve the material situation of the laboring population (e.g., the establishment of savings banks and consumer cooperatives; the construction of new housing; provision of primary education for workers' children close to the factories). He also advocated the creation of a national insurance fund for workers with the participation of employers, and legislation permitting workers to elect deputies to communicate their needs to managers and factory inspectors (so-called worker elders [*starosty*]).[37]

These were what might be called "extra-industrial" responses to labor unrest, that is, police supervision coupled with a series of social welfare programs. To the limited degree that he "entered the factory" Mirskii focused on the problematic relations of workers with lower-level supervisory personnel. He was quite concerned to stress that not only foremen and their assistants, but even "seniors" [*starshii*] and crew leaders exercised a most arbitrary power over workers, capriciously assigning jobs, lowering rates, even firing workers who had the temerity to complain. He concluded that "the inadequate supervision of lower level employees both at private and state factories served as a constant source" of worker dissatisfaction and also facilitated agitation. It was in this context that he proposed the election of worker elders (*starosty*).[38]

Importantly, Mirskii did not comment generally on the many demands voiced by workers in regard to wages and hours and thus, in the end, his report revealed the very real limits of governmental intervention into the relations of labor and management. For Mirskii would go no farther than to call for a modest degree of worker representation in the form of "elders"; he was not willing to insist that employers increase wages or reduce hours and therefore he was unable to address adequately those problems which were most pressing from the point of view of labor. At this juncture, the government through Mirskii chose not to challenge the proprietary prerogatives of Russia's entrepreneurs, who had long insisted on their unilateral right to determine the essential conditions of labor within the factory.

There were, though, a few officials within the MVD who were prepared to do so. Sergei Zubatov, chief of the secret police in Moscow, sought to respond to the emergent labor movement by developing a policy later given the name of police socialism. Here was a bold plan indeed, allowed to go forward because of the general inclarity pertaining in ministerial circles over a national labor policy. Zubatov's approach permitted workers to organize under the auspices of the police in order to articulate their economic needs, while a renewed effort to root out oppositional politics in the factories was undertaken by more aggressive attempts to arrest the radicals. While Zubatov's unions succeeded in attracting many workers for a time, strikes soon revealed that the police could not channel labor in the desired direction. The police chief's ambitious project was soon disavowed by the government and roundly attacked by enraged employers.[39] As we shall observe below, the decision by the patrons of Georgii Gapon to allow a similar experiment to go forward would have considerably more dramatic repercussions.

In contrast to these provocative policies, Ratnik's report struck out in a different direction. Particularly interesting were both the fundamental legitimacy he accorded worker demands for better wages and shorter hours and the ways in which he thought about responding to them. Whereas Chikolev flatly asserted that Russia's uneducated workers could not use free time wisely, Ratnik ordered an investigation of labor productivity. Examining the level of mechanization at the factory, Ratnik learned that most of the factory's output depended on the strength and stamina of workers whose productivity was indeed affected by the length of the workday. Ratnik then studied the comparative hourly productivity of piece-rate workers on regular days (ten hours) and Saturdays (seven and one-half hours). On the basis of this evidence, Ratnik determined that an eight and one-half–hour day could be introduced without loss to the factory or to the workers' paychecks. Clearly surprised that this figure closely approximated the "socialist" demand for the eight-hour day, the major-general was at pains to insist that his findings were both completely unexpected and fully justified by the hard data generated by his research. He concluded that Chikolev's recommendation for a nine and one-half–hour day was "arbitrary" and that an eight and one-half–hour day was objectively possible.[40]

In regard to wage issues, Ratnik again criticized Chikolev's superficial judgments and again revealed the insights of a quite different sort of managerial mentalité. For Ratnik, Chikolev's suggestion that piece rates be increased "somewhat" made little sense, since he ignored such basic considerations as the relative advantage of piece rates or shop pay in the final cost of the product, the quality of a product manufactured under the different wage systems, and the level of supervision required to fulfill the work done by the hour or by the piece.[41] Ratnik also registered his opposition to any across-the-board increase in wages because of the "corrupting" influence such a method had on workers.[42] Presumably he believed that such general increases eliminated individual incentives to diligent labor.

Yet just as striking as Ratnik's focus on mechanization and labor productivity was his meshing of such "modern" and "rational" methods of analysis with the more familiar assumptions and arguments of tsarist bureaucrats. Thus when Ratnik sought the "proper" beginning for the eight and one-half–hour day, he considered the marital situation of his workers and the distance traveled to work, and concluded that a startup time of 7:30 or 8:00 in the morning would be most supportive of a stable family life.[43]

> With this schedule there would not be such a difference in the rising time of the family, even taking into consideration the children, and the worker could enjoy morning tea and a meal with his family, which is more profitable for him; he could help the family with morning cleanup and other domestic chores, especially if the wife or elder children were ill, and he would appear at the factory more cheerful, better fed and rested, and in a good mood.[44]

Ratnik was not only interested in issues of cost and profitability; he was concerned about worker welfare and troubled by the erosion of a proper moral climate in the urban-industrial setting.

Taken as a whole, Ratnik's views were suggestive of new trends in managerial thinking. Here was a manager conversant with industrial processes, wage systems, and market forces, and able to undertake studies of comparative labor productivity; and from this point of view, Ratnik was able to question the subjective judgments of his colleagues and offer a new approach to the resolution of labor conflict. Because he viewed worker demands for better wages and shorter hours as legitimate and because he recognized that the productive viability of the factory depended on the skills of the urbanized segments of his work force, Ratnik urged Baltic's board of directors to address seriously the "material and moral" needs of the work force. Most importantly, his attention to issues of productivity suggested that he viewed improvements in this area of the factory's performance as the means by which the material betterment of his work force could be attained.

There was, however, much of the "traditional" bureaucrat revealed in Ratnik's report; there can be little question that he was deeply concerned with the ways in which the recent disorders threatened public order and challenged the authority of state officials. But Ratnik's hope, it seems clear, was to find new ways to foster the stability, morality, and respect for authority that had been undermined by the unsettling conditions of the urban-industrial environment and the disintegration of the peasant economy. As we shall observe in detail below, it would be men like Ratnik—engineers and managers at state-owned factories in the first years of the twentieth century—who emerged as leaders in the area of industrial rationalization and who fostered an interest in the doctrines of scientific management; but it would also be men like Ratnik who believed that the consequent gains in productivity should go to the benefit of labor, not to the maximization of profits.

Years after the fact, Chikolev would complain that the memorandum of 1901 had been lost in the state's cumbersome bureaucratic apparatus.[45] At least in the short term, the views of Mirskii and his superior, D. S. Sipiagin, enjoyed a more sympathetic response. Apparently deeply disturbed by these reports, Nicholas ordered the convocation of an inter-ministerial conference on labor issues. Meeting in March 1902, Ministers Sipiagin, Witte, A. S. Ermolov, and N. V. Murav'ev, and Grand Duke Sergei Aleksandrovich agreed to proceed with the development of a wide range of labor legislation and to reexamine the level of police surveillance over the working population. Included in these discussions were not only a variety of social welfare programs, but reexamination of the punitive regulations regarding strikes and proposals to impose criminal penalties on employers who arbitrarily violated the contract of hire. In the end, however, the several commissions laboring over the course of a year and a half produced little more than a highly restrictive (and completely voluntary) law on factory elders and an equally limited accident insurance scheme.[46]

The St. Petersburg Industrial Society proved a tenacious foe of even these modest projects.[47] For example, the Society opposed any social welfare legislation specifically crafted for workers, because such legislation not only presupposed the existence of a working class, but "artificially isolated" it from the rest of the population. While not opposing social welfare per se, it argued strenuously that such programs be developed for the entire population and be administered within existing institutions (e.g., the zemstva, city dumas, etc.), not new bodies especially established to serve limited aims.[48]

Petersburg employers also argued forcefully against the institution of factory elders. The government had proposed such a measure in the belief that elders would provide workers with an orderly method of airing their legitimate concerns and hence lessen the likelihood of conflict. Employers replied that the danger lay not in the absence of organization but rather in the promotion of any organization whatsoever on the part of workers.[49] In a statement to the State Council, the chairman of the Society, S. P. Glezmer argued that it would be a "great mistake" to believe "the dream" that worker organizations would remain within the prescribed limits. Rather, it would become more difficult "to regulate the powerful will of the organized, [made] strong both by its level of organization and by the exclusivity [zamknutost'] of the worker mass, artificially merged into one whole."[50]

Again, spokesmen for employers argued that workers should be given no rights or privileges not enjoyed by others lest a working class be artificially "created" by policies inappropriately modeled on the experience of Western Europe.[51] Finally a flat assertion of managerial prerogatives was advanced: workers had no right to collective representation, nor was it permissible for them to participate in setting the basic conditions of employment.

> The factory owner hires workers, but not unions of workers, and therefore is not obligated to recognize the representation of workers. There are no questions which are necessary for the factory owner to discuss with elders, since it is not possible to permit questions about the length of work time and wages to be subjected to such discussion.[52]

In sum, employers grouped in the Petersburg Industrial Society found themselves in conflict with the Ministry of Finance, which had advocated not only the institution of elders but the decriminalization of economic strikes; and also at odds with the Ministry of Internal Affairs, which had supported legislation on elders as well as an expanded program of social welfare designed specifically to benefit the urban working class. Since its founding in 1897, the Society had been actively engaged in a critique of labor legislation and equally aggressive in its defense of proprietary rights, arguing strenuously against any governmental policy which might promote the development of class organizations of workers within or outside the factory gates, and remaining steadfastly resistant to discussions with any collectivity of workers regarding the conditions of employment. Such positions suggest not so much the "backwardness" of the Society's views on the worker question, but rather an understanding of employer interest which hinged on the presumption of management's exclusive right to control the labor it purchased.

Russian Engineers and American Utopias

The social and economic ferment at the turn of the century also proved central to the development of the Russian engineering profession. This period witnessed the first really significant increase in the number of engineering students, yet also the continued inability or unwillingness of Russian employers to hire them due to the economic downturn. These factors combined to encourage engineers to define more explicitly their professional persona and to organize in pursuit of their interests.

With the significant growth of industry over the course of the 1890s, as well as its obvious dependence on foreign expertise, Witte pushed forward the plans of his predecessor Vyshnegradskii to expand engineering education in the Empire. Witte also saw to the establishment of a number of commercial schools and fostered the creation of independent economics faculties, which had heretofore been linked to juridical faculties and largely divorced from practical concerns.[53] The new educational institutions began to produce a new generation of specialists: between 1896 and 1902 the number of higher technical schools doubled, as did enrollment at existing institutes. Specifically, this entailed an increase in the number of engineering students from about 4,000 in 1895 to 13,000 in 1904, while the number of graduates per year rose from approximately 400 to 1,000 over the same period.[54] Just as important, the substance of engineering education began to change since the new institutes were developed along the polytechnic model, which stressed a broad-based technical education and applied research. The new curriculum contrasted sharply with the older emphasis on theory and narrow specialization in one field of technology; attention now turned to the development of technical and entrepreneurial skills appropriate to the practical needs of industry. By the first decade of the new century the older, elite institutions were also undertaking curricular reforms of a similar nature.

Not only was a new generation of engineers exposed to a significantly different curriculum; these young men went to school at a time of considerable ferment in the educational institutions of the Empire, as students struggled over issues of academic freedom and against the repressive power of the state and in the process developed a substantial critique of the autocracy.[55] Many technical students were politicized by these experiences: some joined the Social Democratic Party, while others would express radically democratic views in the period of the first revolution.[56]

The expression of progressive, even radical views was doubtless also shaped by the fact that many newly trained specialists entered the job market in the midst of a serious economic crisis and consequently faced the unhappy prospect of unemployment.[57] Having been schooled in the importance of technology to Russian industry and having developed a sense of accomplishment in the technical skills they had mastered and could now offer their country, the economic crisis threatened to make these engineers victims of the very economic backwardness they had been trained to overcome. It must have been with considerable frustration that these young professionals looked for work, especially given the fact that many had endured considerable financial difficulty in order to graduate.[58] Many turned to professional associations for help, in the process, argues Harley Balzer, providing an important stimulus to the further organization of the profession, but also, it seems likely, infusing a particular energy and perhaps even anger into the development of these associations.[59]

These various experiences combined to shape the values of a new generation of engineers and to foster the emergence of a particular professional ethos strongly infused with a technocratic vision of the future Russia. While this vision had earlier roots, the increased number of graduates from the new polytechnicums seemed to create a "critical mass" within the profession that was ultimately able to advance this vision quite forcefully.[60]

Elements of this new professional ethos can be seen in the efforts of a group of engineers in the winter of 1903–1904 to enrich the activities of the St. Petersburg Society of Technologists.[61] Stating that they "recogniz[ed] the social tasks of educated technicians [*intelligentnago tekhnika*] and desir[ed] to expand and enliven the activities of the Society of Technologists," they proposed a three-part program concerned with the "moral and intellectual strengthening of ourselves as a corporation," "the social activity (of engineers and technicians) in the sphere of industrial life," and "(our) activity outside the sphere of technology." Specific areas of study within these broader programmatic concerns were outlined, as were proposals to expand the journal of the Society to address general questions of industry. The group's program was circulated to both Petersburg and provincial engineering associations; at the same time members of the group actively participated in an expanded range of lectures given at the Society in first months of 1904.

These initiatives apparently combined to attract a significant number of engineers to Society activities. This interest, in turn, encouraged the initial group to put forward a variety of proposals preparatory to the annual meeting of the Society of Technologists on May 23, 1904. They advanced a particular group of candidates for election to the board of directors of the Society; advocated the introduction of secret balloting for certain offices; and suggested that a new section on social and economic problems be added to the Journal of the Society and that a special editor for this section be hired. (Significantly, they proposed V. E. Varzar, a man with a long-established interest in labor questions and decidedly progressive views, to head the new section.) Moreover, these discussions in the early part of the year laid the basis for the organization of the Union of Engineers and Technicians, which emerged from the banquets of October and December 1904 and formed in the immediate aftermath of Bloody Sunday.

The proposals articulated by this small group of engineers (ultimately to number about forty) illustrate not only an active interest in the professional study of scientific and technical issues and a desire to popularize important developments for a broader public, but also an interest in the practical affairs of industry, as well as a concern to address what they called "the social and moral tasks of technicians."[62] Indeed, one good illustration of the role these engineers sought to play in the struggle with Russia's many political and economic problems was provided by the lead editorial in the new "Political-Economic Section" of the journal *Vestnik Obshchestva Tekhnologov*, which they managed to launch less than a year later.

Sounding the themes of intense international economic competition and the importance of science-based technology to industry, the editorial stressed the need of "backward" Russia for the trained engineer. Only those nations which adapted to the most modern of the scientific and technological advances would survive the ruthless economic struggle, and crucial to survival were the services of the technologist. But this central figure in the economic life of the nation was not only an economic actor; he had important social responsibilities and needed to concern himself with a broad range of national problems. Clearly one of the most vexing of these issues was the "worker question" and the difficult position of the engineer between the "hammer and anvil" of labor-management conflict. The Russian technologist, though, could not "lock himself up in the narrow sphere of specialized questions," but had to cultivate a broader mental outlook. He "must not drag along on the coattails of private entrepreneurial interests, but, conscious of his social tasks, loudly raise *his own* voice" for his own socioeconomic convictions. And, stressing that there was probably no other social group as interested as engineers in seeing that "the spontaneous internecine war of labor and capital" adopt a more tranquil character, the editorial hoped that Russia might "take on the cultural forms characteristic of the West."[63]

Worries about Russia's place in a world defined in Darwinian terms, concern about the "worker question" as well as the ambiguous role of technical personnel in the resolution of labor-management conflict underlay, in important respects, the striking interest of many Russian engineers in the views of Frederick W. Taylor and the emergent scientific management movement.[64]

The managerial reform movement came of age in *fin de siècle* America, a period characterized by various social reform movements (Progressivism), dramatic advances in industry (the "second" industrial revolution), pronounced labor conflict, and a significant increase in the number of trained engineers available to industry. The dominant value which Progressivism brought to this setting was a faith in the possibility and desirability of constructing a "rational" social order. Concerned with increasing the "efficiency" of social institutions, Progressives sought to harness the achievements of science, technology, and the professions for the benefit of society at large. Imbued with a deep faith in positivist philosophy, Progressives believed that society could be restructured with the aid of "objective" scientific truths. Progressive America, in short, nourished the technocratic vision of many of its leading engineers and entrepreneurs.

The father of the scientific management movement, Frederick Winslow Taylor (1856–1915), was a graduate engineer who began his work life as a common laborer at the Midvale Steel Company in Pennsylvania and soon progressed through the ranks to become Midvale's chief engineer. Here in the midst of skilled metalworkers, Taylor developed his initial concern with the problems of labor-management relations and his obsession with the rational organization of industrial operations.[65]

Believing that the source of labor-management tension was an ongoing conflict over productivity and wages, Taylor asserted that what management most wanted were low labor costs and what workers most wanted were high wages. Once labor and management realized the mutual benefits to be reaped through a cooperative effort to increase productivity, conflict would be overcome. By substantially increasing the availability of goods and the ability of workers to purchase them, and by insuring the profits legitimately due employers, labor and management would be freed from the crippling struggles of the past. Taylor's conception of social conflict and its resolution thus rested on fundamentally productivist assumptions. His "system" was built on the belief that workers were not really interested in exercising control over the nature and conditions of their work; nor were they concerned with questions about power and authority in the workplace. Rather, their "real" interest lay in producing more and better.

The "mental revolution" required to bring about Taylor's vision of "hearty brotherly cooperation" in pursuit of increased productivity entailed a fundamental reorganization in the tasks of management.[66] Instead of merely overseeing the self-directing work of independent craftsmen, management had to tell the worker exactly how to do his job. Thus began minute studies of the labor process, the detailed planning of the workday, and the preparation of specific tasks and the tools to perform them. Ultimately, the systematization of the technical skills of the work force would be congealed in advanced technologies, reducing still further industry's dependence on the "human" factor in the process of production.

Management also had the new responsibility of motivating workers to perform their predefined tasks and insuring their compliance with the new methods. Labor's collective solidarity thus had to be broken. The early proponents of scientific management dealt with these challenges by developing elaborate wage incentive schemes. Utilizing Taylor's differential piece rates, Gantt's "task and bonus system," or a variety of others, management pressed workers to compete with each other, while goading the individual worker to focus on his own material gain.[67]

"Scientific" managers thus sought to secure control over labor productivity by a systematic appropriation of workers' skills, by a strict division of conception from execution in the production process, and by undermining collective solidarities. The new creed entailed a fundamental simplification of work processes, a progressive de-skilling of the worker, and a substantial alteration in the patterns and relationships that had heretofore defined the shop culture.[68]

America in the early Progressive era and Russia in the waning years of the tsarist autocracy could not have afforded a more striking set of contrasts. A confident industrial America looked forward to decades of world prominence, while a troubled Russia seemed locked in a Promethean struggle to define its future socioeconomic and political fate. The perception of the worker as consumer and complex psychological being seemed grotesque in a setting marked by crushing poverty and a fabric of violence and degradation, while the bright and expansive vision of Western science and technology and the productive capacity of industrial America seemed to mock the reality of daily life in Russia. Yet despite the vastly differing contexts, many Russians and Americans were posing the same questions: How was labor conflict to be resolved? How could industry decrease its reliance on the highly paid skilled worker and tap the abundant sources of unskilled (peasant or immigrant) labor? How could productivity be increased so as to maximize the utilization of scarce or expensive resources? How could management find more effective ways to monitor the production process and bring down the high costs of operation?

For engineering professionals in Russia, the promises of scientific management suggested a means by which Russia could more rapidly overcome its backwardness and end its problematic dependence on Western expertise. As important, with technical personnel acting as impartial arbiters of Russia's destiny, the debilitating conflicts between labor and management could be transcended. The technologist as midwife to the new society was an immensely appealing idea, particularly given the increased numbers and reduced opportunities for native engineers at the outset of the century. For the less professionally committed,[69] the doctrines of scientific management suggested a methodology of profit maximization and labor control.

Disarray and Discontent on the Eve of Revolution

In the period following the Obukhov defense, the strike activity of Petersburg metalworkers fell off sharply. Until the outbreak of an extraordinary
wave of strikes in early January 1905, the collective protests of metalworkers
remained modest. This could scarcely have been otherwise, given the depth
of the economic crisis besetting the metalworking industry. Petersburg workers thus observed from afar as the autocracy shot down workers in Rostov-
on-Don, Tikhoretsk, Zlatoust, and elsewhere during late 1902 and early 1903,
and as major strikes rocked Southern Russia in the summer of 1903.

If the economic downturn was the key factor in curtailing the strike actions
of metalworkers, another reason may be found in the organizational disarray
of the various socialist groups working in the factories. Major arrests followed
in the wake of the spring-summer strikes of 1901 and continued unabated
under the repressive regime of V. K. Plehve, who was appointed minister of
internal affairs following the assassination of D. S. Sipiagin on April 2, 1902.
There can be little doubt, however, that the intense conflicts within Social
Democracy wreaked equal havoc on the affairs of local organizations, at once
breaking the ties of citywide groups with individual districts and factories
and alienating workers by their fractious debates.[70]

Indeed with some exceptions, Social Democrats remained remarkably de-
tached from working-class life throughout the pre-1905 period, some diverted
by the student movement, others by arrest or exile, and still others preoccupied by the identification of the "orthodox" and the "opportunist" in all
manifestations of political activity. Thus P. N. Lepeshinskii could write at the
outset of the century that "the proletariat accepted active participation in the
political demonstrations of the students, in the majority of cases without the
knowledge of their leaders and sometimes even against the will of local Social
Democratic organizations."[71] Nor had the situation improved by the end of
1904: "Factory life found no echo at all in the circles; the smoldering unrest
. . . that was finding expression in the powerfully developing Gapon movement, in which the yearning of the working masses for broad organization
and class unity was so clearly displayed, was ignored as Zubatovism."[72]

This distance from the life of the working class alienated many activists,
sending some to work with Gapon and others to propagandize on their own.
Thus V. V. Sviatlovskii described the Karelin group which would prove so
important in pushing Gapon's Assembly in a more political direction as
"'eagles' . . . that is, people dissatisfied with the party but more or less
[politically] conscious, having been in a party and left it, and always an
important and influential group among the Petersburg proletariat."[73] Others
noted that those workers who were attracted to SD circles were "mostly
extremely young, only just getting out of their apprenticeship, and did not
enjoy any influence in their factory sphere."[74] Petr Garvi, commenting on SD
work elsewhere in the Empire, concurred: "In the Party organizations were

gathered mostly callow youths, hotheaded and resolute but weakly linked to the working masses and uninfluential in the factories. The old Social Democrats among the workers—the real vanguard of advanced workers formed in the period of propagandism and of so-called Economism—these old workers for the most part stood aside."[75] Social Democracy in these years was in great disarray, unable to cultivate viable organizational links with Petersburg labor, while the youthful militants the SDs had touched remained too "wet behind the ears" to influence more experienced workers. But as the young militants acquired skill, a decent wage, and literacy they began to gain an audience.

The upheaval born of Witte's industrialization left smoldering discontent and a developing oppositional milieu in the capital. If the worker protests of 1901 were largely the product of the economic conjuncture, nonetheless they bore an unmistakably political coloration. The "quiet" politicization that had occurred over the course of the 1890s and the increasingly charged atmosphere at the turn of the century combined to encourage some metalworkers to respond politically to the mounting ferment in society. At the same time, the many changes in polity and society underlay the student demonstrations and public protests of "awakening society." And this activism of the social elites provided workers with a model which was not supplied by the splintered socialist left, enmeshed as it was in doctrinal disputes of little relevance to most workers and focused instead on the construction of an underground network of conspiratorial committees that excluded the vast majority of workers. "Society's" form of protest, which was at once visible and dignified, satisfied labor's longing to make public and hence legitimate its deeply held concerns.[76] Such forms were perhaps all the more attractive to "advanced" workers who were prepared to seek a broader social alliance against the autocracy and who had historically shunned contact with the average "gray type."

IV

LABOR-MANAGEMENT CONFLICT
IN THE REVOLUTION OF 1905

On the night of January 26–27, 1904, the Japanese attacked the Russian fleet at Port Arthur, beginning a war that was very largely the product of the provocative policies pursued by the Russian government over the past decade. Many of Nicholas's ministers, among them Witte, had grown increasingly wary of an aggressive policy in the Far East, recognizing that Russia could ill afford to squander its resources in this way. Nevertheless, a government divided at the highest levels and led by the reactionary Minister of Internal Affairs von Plehve embarked on the war amidst a flurry of racist rhetoric.[1]

The war developed within the context of mounting ferment in educated society (*obshchestvo*). By the end of January, liberal zemstvo men and urban professionals had joined to create the Union of Liberation with the goal of forcing change on the reluctant autocracy. Steadfastly opposed to any concessions to society, Plehve continued to block the efforts of even moderate elements to expand the parameters of permissible debate. But events soon conspired against the minister. The shocking defeat of the Russian army along the Yalu in April was only the first in a series of ever more embarrassing military failures—and with each defeat the criticism of the government grew more insistent. By the spring of 1904, a wave of terrorist attacks had descended on high officials, culminating in the assassination of Plehve himself on July 15.

Almost six weeks following Plehve's death, Nicholas appointed a man of considerably more moderate views to the Ministry of Internal Affairs. Sviatopolk-Mirskii's public articulation of the government's confidence in society at once signaled the beginning of a "political spring."[2] The iron regime of Plehve was to be relaxed by the return of some opposition leaders to the capital, by a somewhat greater freedom of assembly, and by a loosening of press censorship. Liberationists immediately perceived in these concessions the weakening of governmental authority. Through the fall of 1904, they not only voiced increasingly explicit demands for reform, but sought to mobilize oppositional sentiment on the basis of a series of banquets marking the fortieth anniversary of the judicial reforms and through the formation of political-professional unions.[3]

The increasingly open expression of anti-government views in the press fueled tensions already building within the ranks of Petersburg metalworkers since the beginning of the year. Growing if not yet overt conflict within the industry was in part attributable to the pressures released by the outbreak of the Russo-Japanese War: metalworking plants, particularly those owned by the state or working primarily on state contracts, were flooded with urgent orders for weaponry and rolling stock. With the new orders, employers were relieved somewhat of the economic crisis besetting their industry; workers, however, were forced to fulfill the urgent orders by means of long hours of overtime on piece rates cut repeatedly by supervisors. In May and again in August, to cite just one example, the St. Petersburg city governor (*gradonachal'nik*) warned General Vlas'ev of the Obukhov Plant that dissatisfaction was mounting: in the shell shop, overtime was required four to five nights a week, but when workers managed to increase their earnings as a result of intensive labor, their rates were lowered "without warning and in an arbitrary [manner]."[4]

Labor Conflict at the Outset of the Revolution

Acute pressures building among the laboring population of the capital contributed to the development of the Assembly of Russian Factory Workers, founded by a young priest, Georgii Gapon, in August 1903. It was not until the second half of 1904 that the Assembly's membership grew dramatically and took on an increasingly political coloration.[5] By year's end, thousands had flocked to the district branches seeking a place to associate with their comrades and a way to articulate their concerns. Many, perhaps a majority, of Gapon's recruits came from the metalworking plants of the capital: some, undoubtedly, were religious and monarchist; others, however, held more radical views and reflected developments in the capital's work force over the previous decade.[6] Thus diverse segments of the capital's work force came together in what Gerald Surh has aptly described as Russia's first mass organization of labor.

At the center of Gapon's movement were the workers of the Putilov plant. In late May, the Assembly had opened its first and soon to be its largest branch in the Narvskii district, not far from the factory; this local rapidly became the focal point of Gapon's energy and interest.[7] Precisely because of the rapid growth of the Assembly and its authority among his work force of some 12,000, S. I. Smirnov, director of the Putilov works, began to shed his initial enthusiasm for Gapon and to perceive in the Assembly the dangerous seeds of trade unionism. The dismissal of several of its members by the rude and despotic foreman Tetiavkin, himself deeply hostile to the Assembly, confronted Gapon with a challenge to the basic legitimacy of his project and provoked the conflict which by January 3, 1905, led to a full-scale strike at the Putilov works.

The Putilov strike immediately gained the sympathy of tens of thousands of other workers. Labor unrest spread throughout the capital with stunning rapidity, resulting in a near general strike by January 7.[8] Quite clearly, Gapon's locals had become a key staging area for the mobilization of labor: not only was Gapon's famous petition read, discussed, and affirmed at these branch meetings, but the demands Gapon had helped work out for the Putilovtsy were shared. But something more took place at these locals over the course of the first week of January; workers, to borrow a phrase from the Chinese peasantry, began to "speak bitterness."

> A kind of mystical, religious ecstasy reigned throughout the meeting; thousands of people stood shoulder to shoulder for hours in the dreadful heat and closeness, eagerly listening to the artless, extraordinarily powerful, simple, and passionate speeches of their exhausted fellow worker orators. In content, all the speeches were poor, the same phrases were repeated again and again: "we cannot bear it any longer," "our patience has already come to an end," "our suffering has gone beyond all measure," "better death than this life," "impossible to flay three skins from a man," and so on. But all of this was said with such striking, touching sincerity, so very much from the depths of the exhausted human soul, that the same phrase, spoken for the hundredth time brought tears to the eyes [and] compelled you to feel it deeply. . . .[9]

The experience of finally coming together, speaking openly, and giving witness to the suffering of their lives now informed the consciousness of thousands of workers. Powerfully motivated, Assembly members and supporters throughout the city prepared to share their concerns with the Tsar. On the cold gray wintery morning of January 9, thousands of Petersburg workers formed up in columns preparing to go to the Winter Palace. From various parts of the city, workers and their families walked against a biting wind, carrying icons, portraits of the Imperial family, and a petition of grievances.[10] By midafternoon, hundreds lay dead or wounded, victims of a senseless slaughter.[11] A panicky government deeply fearful of its own subjects had fired the opening shots in what now became the Revolution of 1905.[12]

The meaning of Bloody Sunday for thousands of Petersburg workers could be captured in a single phrase: We have no Tsar. For, in a murderous scene repeated throughout the city, the assault of troops on unarmed petitioners broke in a matter of minutes the legitimacy of a political order that had commanded people's loyalty for centuries. This profound disillusionment was doubtless made all the more compelling because it had occurred within an already highly charged setting: in the week leading up to January 9, Petersburg workers had mobilized to mount a near general strike and had labored to develop a detailed set of demands. In the months prior to Bloody Sunday, morever, they had witnessed the increasingly open displays of contempt for constituted authority by members of educated society.

Bloody Sunday and the January strike movement more generally confronted the forces of order with a complex set of issues that would not be easily resolved. The political demands contained in Gapon's petition went considerably beyond those raised by metalworkers in 1901 and hence presented an even greater challenge to the state and its representatives within the factories. Broadly democratic in nature, metalworker demands conformed with the strivings of the Liberation movement and as such marked the emergence of a multi-class opposition to the autocracy. The petition forthrightly condemned bureaucratic arbitrariness and called for full civil liberties and a constituent assembly. Moreover, taken in conjunction with the economic grievances included in the petition but stated in far greater detail in the demands presented to employers during the January strikes, workers aimed to end autocracy both within and outside the factory gates. The new institutional structures workers envisioned were premised on their own active participation in defining the political and economic conditions which directly affected their lives.

The January events also confronted the old regime with an unprecedented level of strike activism. As Leopold Haimson has demonstrated, the strike wave beginning in Petersburg in January and continuing throughout the year was broadly based, involving numerous grades of labor in diverse branches of industry from a wide range of geographic settings. And while there is no question that metalworkers often initiated strike actions and provided leadership in a variety of ways, their rate of participation in strikes generally conformed to their relative numbers in the working class population as a whole. But it was also the case that significant variations characterized the strike activism of Petersburg metalworkers. Particularly notable was the role played by the giant, mixed-production factories that were state owned or working primarily on state contracts and which were situated along the periphery of the city.[13] Thus the workers of the Putilov, Nevskii,[14] Baltic, Izhorsk, Aleksandrovsk, and Obukhov plants were at the center of metalworker protest.[15] The highest concentration of metalworkers at such mixed-production giants was to be found in the Nevskii district: during 1905, it was the most strike-prone district of the capital, containing as it did the workers of the Nevskii, Obukhov, and Aleksandrovsk plants, as well as several major textile firms. The extraordinary strike activism of the Putilov plant made Narvskii district a close second.[16] Thus while the autocracy confronted a broadly based strike movement which directly threatened the established order, St. Petersburg's heavy industrialists, and the managers of state-owned factories in particular, faced an especially aroused work force militantly insistent on substantive change.

The demands presented by metalworkers to their employers in January 1905 illustrate a host of other factors fueling protest throughout the capital. In lists of twenty-one or twenty-five or even thirty-five points, workers spoke out against the oppression which defined their daily lives; and in a stunning recitation of the abuse and injustice which they now laid out in such compelling specificity, they demanded that the autocratic practices reigning in their shops be put to an end.[17]

The major issues raised by metalworkers included demands for an eight-hour day; the establishment of permanent commissions composed of elected representatives of workers serving jointly with management to resolve grievances and oversee dismissals; changes in the rate-setting process whereby rates would be determined by the foreman with the voluntary agreement of worker representatives from the shop and then be considered binding; the abolition of overtime and/or its payment at a higher rate; a minimum wage for unskilled labor; a guarantee of no reprisals for striking; and polite address. Workers also demanded, variously, the abolition of the search, the elimination of certain fines, specific wage or rate increases, the improvement of medical care, safety and sanitary conditions, and the establishment and/or restructuring of coops, savings banks, and schools.

Workers also raised a number of demands which focused on issues of dignity and mutual respect. And here, doubtless, the articulation of grievance after grievance had a mobilizing effect, for by looking at the particular, the nature of the social oppression that workers faced every day came into sharper relief. Especially revealing were the many criticisms of factory medical staff: these people were variously enjoined to "be more attentive to workers, especially the injured," to treat workers "humanely" and "courteously"[18] and to look carefully after the ill.[19] Among the extraordinarily detailed grievances of the Aleksandrovsk workers was a shop-by-shop indictment of lower level supervisory personnel. Aleksandrovtsy demanded that eighteen persons be dismissed and six reprimanded, charging in the clear majority of cases that these people had used "insolent" [derzkoe], "beastly" [skotskoe], or "inhumane" [nechelovecheskoe] address with workers. Other charges included bribe-taking, inattention to workers, drunkenness, negligence, and plain "meanness."[20] And the overarching distrust of workers for nachal'stvo (the authorities, or, more loosely, the bosses) was neatly captured in the demand that management "must not resort to [its] usual tricks, to promises that later will not be kept, or to the assistance of the police."[21]

While focused on the factory, these various issues could not be viewed as simply or narrowly "economic." Demands seeking equal representation with management and binding wage agreements rested on such civic rights as the freedoms of speech, assembly, association, and strike. Workers could make little headway in the factory without fundamental reform in the polity. So too, the contemptuous relations conveyed by the use of "ty" with a worker could not be redressed solely within the confines of the factory. Managers might order polite address, but the social prejudices of doctors, engineers, and foremen could not be changed by command.

Labor's assault on established managerial prerogatives also impinged on "larger" issues: it was not only that workers wanted shorter hours and better wages—they now asserted their interest in the process by which wages were set, grievances adjudicated, and staff hired and fired. And these demands raised very real issues of power in the workplace. Thus, while metalworkers challenged the unilateral authority of employers and the structure of labor-management relations based upon it, they also and equally challenged the legitimacy of the established social and political order. At issue, then, was both the historic rightlessness of Russian labor and the specific conditions pertaining in the factories.[22]

For many metalworkers, conditions in the factories had deteriorated since the outbreak of the war. When, for example, Baltic workers met with Major-General Ratnik in January, the intensity of the work process was very much on their minds. They wanted an end to overtime and they insisted on an eight-hour day. Like their comrades throughout the industry, they sought a review of all rates based on a voluntary agreement between workers and the foreman, and they sought respectful treatment. Coupling complaints about exhaustion and fatigue with a range of accusations about the offensive actions of foremen, and demanding that they be required to work on only one machine tool at a time—an end to the "stretchout" as it was sometimes called—workers struck out at the faster pace of work that was accomplished by the coercive drive methods of foremen.[23] Tightly woven together, therefore, were demands focusing on the length and intensity of the workday, the rate-setting process, and the authority of foremen. To respond to even the purely "local" concerns of the work force, Ratnik and others would have to reexamine essential components of the work process.

At least for the managers of state-owned plants at the beginning of the year the incentive was there to do so. Russia was at war and required weaponry and rolling stock. The state's managers could not afford repeated work stoppages, nor could they tolerate assaults on their authority. Some, moreover, had already demonstrated a concern to improve the wages and hours of their workers. Men like Ratnik of the Baltic works and F. Kh. Gross of the Izhorsk works therefore approached the problems raised during the January strikes with a degree of flexibility.

Immediately following the outbreak of the strike, Ratnik and Gross forwarded the workers' demands to the Naval Ministry, and in their accompanying commentary suggested that some of the grievances were fully justified and a number could readily be met. Both, for example, felt a reduction in hours was possible; Ratnik agreed that a wage increase to one ruble for unskilled labor could be granted, while Gross favored changes in the existing piece-rate system. Although the forwarding of demands to higher authority necessarily meant a delayed response on issues of primary importance to workers, both directors hastened to order their subordinates to use polite forms of address, while Ratnik dismissed several particularly offensive foremen and lower level supervisors.[24] Ratnik and several other state managers also announced that pay for three days of the strike would be issued.[25]

The explosive character of labor protest, as well as the apparently conciliatory actions of some state officials, alarmed private employers and encouraged them to mobilize in defense of their interests. Meeting several times during the first week of January and then in almost continuous session following Bloody Sunday, employers grouped in the Petersburg Industrial

Society began to craft a policy in response to labor. One of their most immediate concerns was to coordinate actions with the state-owned plants and forestall what the Society viewed as the "dangerous precedent" of paying workers for time spent out on strike; another was to parry the request made by Minister of Finance V. N. Kokovtsov on January 6 to grant partial concessions on the "secondary demands" raised by workers. By January 18, the Society had drawn up a four-point program which was then circulated to all state and private factories in the capital. While it contained a response to labor's demands, it also can be read as the first faint outline of a political critique of the government.[26] The program stated:

1. The general points raised by workers, namely the eight-hour day, worker participation in wage determination and in the regulation of the internal order of the factory, and the elimination of fines for absenteeism and striking, were "not subject to discussion." The Society noted that it had informed the Ministry of Finance of the need to address these problems as quickly as possible in legislative form with the participation of factory owners and workers.

2. In regard to particular issues, it was not appropriate to enter into binding agreements prior to a general resumption of work.

3. Workers had been drawn to the present movement by factors external to the factory and not of an economic character. Therefore, given the absence of mutual alienation between labor and management, employers wished to meet workers with the following resolutions:

   a. in the given case, not to impose fines for absenteeism;
   b. not to employ measures to determine the instigators and ringleaders of the strike, or impose special punitive measures against them;
   c. to provide assistance to the families of the victims of the January 9 disorders based on the contribution of individual factories at a rate of 20 k./worker and distributed by the Petersburg Industrial Society;
   d. to make no distinctions in these grants between those who struck voluntarily and those who were forced to strike.

4. The present strike was considered a popular disturbance which violates the law in regard to hiring; not wishing to set a false precedent, employers will not pay workers for the time of the strike, but in an effort to help the extremely needy, will issue special assistance grants.[27]

On the issues of greatest importance to labor, Petersburg employers were intransigent; to the degree they displayed any sympathy with workers whatsoever it was reflected in their willingness to lift certain penalties for the recent strike in light of the bloodshed of January 9 and to petition the government to reexamine national labor legislation. The first response of both state and private managers, then, was to direct all major demands "upward" to the Ministries of Navy and Finance; to reject all but the most modest pleas for change; and to insist on a return to work. On issues of greatest moment to the minister of finance, the position of St. Petersburg employers was also disturbing. Again calling them to a conference on January 24, Kokovtsov reiterated his request for partial concessions. Considerably more exercised at this juncture by the suggestion that worker unrest was motivated by conditions in the factories, the Society responded on January 31 with a letter to Kokovtsov based on the ideas articulated in the January 18 program but including a far more pointed critique of the government.

Indignantly, employers now argued that economic grievances did not lie at the heart of labor protest; rather, protest was rooted in the general conditions of Russian life. Recent events were the manifestation of a "popular disturbance," "provoked and sustained by the surrounding atmosphere." Although employers had tried to conduct negotiations with representatives of labor, these discussions had been hampered by the absence of a "proper [*pravil'naia*] organization" of workers and the impossibility, in the existing situation, for workers "to gather and to discuss their needs in a lawful manner." Arguing further that the condition of the working class in all countries depended on the extent of industrial development and the general level of culture, the Society asserted that "the iron law of supply and demand and the inevitable conditions of competition do not permit us to place industrial workers in artificial hothouse conditions. . . . Russian industry lacks the capacity . . . to bear inappropriate demands." Noting, moreover, the general crisis and depression which befell industry at the turn of the century and which was in essence the product of the overall backwardness of the nation, employers protested their inability to "work at a loss" or to be guided by "motives of charity." Industry "is in a difficult situation and it gives to the worker what it can." Pointing to the ferment enveloping all segments of society, St. Petersburg employers claimed that the workers' movement was apparently the most serious source of unrest only because it expressed its grievances in a sharper, more violent manner. But, importuned the industrialists, woe to the government which was quick to react to this sort of protest, but slow to heed the "moderate and correct" solicitations of others. "The leaders of the workers' movement will achieve from below such results, that for the higher layers of society would be unattainable, and this will be the dangerous, logical consequence of the fact that crude demonstrations are listened to more attentively than proper statements." Criticizing as well the intervention of the police and administrative organs into the affairs of the enterprise, St. Petersburg employers suggested that it would be better if workers "knew that they could rely only on the law and that they must remain within the limits of the law." The memorandum concluded disingenuously that the resolution of labor unrest required "fundamental reforms of a state character."[28] Absent was a willingness to accord any legitimacy to worker pleas for change within the factory.

Petersburg employers were soon joined in their protest by industrialists from across the Empire, expressed in a torrent of memoranda sent to the government in the latter part of January. These memoranda would form the basis of the positions argued by industrial groups in the soon-to-be-convened Kokovtsov Commission on reforms in labor legislation. They also formed the essential basis of employers' political positions in the first period of the revolution. It is notable that the statement of the Petersburg Society was the least conciliatory toward labor and the most ambiguous in its concern for expanding the civil rights enjoyed by labor. And more generally, while St. Petersburg employers called for "fundamental reforms" and bemoaned the absence of legality and the problems created by the lack of certain civil rights, on the whole the memorandum was hardly a ringing appeal for liberal reform. As recent studies of the Russian bourgeoisie have suggested, significant differences separated representatives of industry from across the nation. Insofar as employers grouped in the Petersburg Industrial Society were concerned, its politics bore little relationship to the "bourgeois liberalism" espoused by some employer associations, and still less to that of most professional groups allied with the Liberation Movement.[29]

The actions of the Petersburg Industrial Society during January did not exhaust the efforts of employers to deal with the crisis in the factories. Reflective of the particular intensity of conflict within heavy industry, two important series of meetings occurred in the latter part of the month. On January 15, the Liubimov Commission was reconvened and over the course of the next several weeks studied the demands raised by workers in the Naval Ministry's factories and port facilities.[30] Then on January 26, 28, and 29, representatives from the St. Petersburg metals and machine-construction industry gathered; present as well were officials from factories under the aegis of the War Ministry's Artillery Department and the Ministries of Navy and Ways of Communication.

Taking up the long list of demands submitted by workers in the state's naval factories and ports, the Liubimov Commission found that a number of issues, including the eight-hour day, wage increases for women and unskilled labor, the introduction of three-shift work without a reduction in wages, and the opening of a special conference in which strikers might discuss their needs should be discussed in conjunction with the Ministry of Finance. On several other issues—e.g., the abolition of the search and rules governing the time, place, and frequency of distributing shop and piece-rate wages—the commission suggested reforms. It also recommended that heads of the ports and factories "instill in those who require it" [vnushit' komu sleduet] the need for polite forms of address with workers.

The commission refused to make concessions on a number of demands: it would not rehire those workers dismissed without the right of reentry into the plant, nor would it accept back those who had been fired for striking three years earlier; it would not alter rules specifying obligatory participation in savings funds; and there would be no pay for time spent on strike. In regard to work on more than one machine tool at a time, the commission indicated that it did not wish to prejudge this matter, but suggested that for the present such practices be avoided where possible.

On several other issues, the Liubimov Commission not only refused the demand but seemed to deny the existence of a problem. To workers, the length and intensity of the workday was of prime concern; much tension resided in long, exhausting, and poorly compensated hours of overtime. Yet the Liubimov Commission stated that the existing payment of overtime at time and a half was sufficient and refused to abolish overtime or place specific limits on the amount of extra work during a given year. The commission also declined to guarantee the inviolability of worker deputies, asserting that the dismissal of a worker at a given job might have nothing to do with his tenure as an elected representative. Workers speaking from bitter experience knew that their representatives had been arrested, exiled, and deprived of their jobs. Ministry officials appeared flatly to deny this, taking refuge in the right of management to hire and fire labor as the requirements of production dictated. High officials also maintained that no deductions were made at Naval Ministry facilities for spoilage not due to the fault of workers, hence wages were not lowered for this reason as workers charged. From the workers' point of view, such deductions were only one of many deceptions practiced routinely by their despotic supervisors.[31] Here again—as with the demand that management not resort to its usual tricks, false promises, or reliance on the police—an enormous gap separated the perceptions of the contending sides.

By all appearances, workers at state-owned plants had achieved very little in the weeks following Bloody Sunday. On major issues, the Liubimov Commission felt the need to coordinate its decisions with those which might be forthcoming from the Finance Ministry; when the commission concluded its initial deliberations in mid-February, therefore, no public announcements were deemed appropriate. On other issues, the commission seemed to deny the reality of the workplace as experienced by workers.

Managerial policies throughout the heavy industry of the capital emerged as fundamentally similar in the discussions taking place at the end of January among representatives of the metals and machine-construction sector.[32] After three days of deliberation, the conference resolutions included the following decisions and points of information:

1. Regarding the length of the workday:

   a. final establishment of a workday in the metals industry will be postponed until the general regulation of worktime is decided through legislative action.

    b. any decision must be made in conjunction with the question
       of the number of holidays.

    c. it is not permissible to establish a workday of less than 57
       hours a week. [This normally meant 10 hours daily and 7
       hours on Saturday.—HH]

2. Payment for unskilled labor in the industry varied between 60
   kopecks and one ruble per day; it was agreed to establish a norm
   of not less than 80 kopecks.

3. No changes would be adopted regarding pay increases for apprentices.

4. The demand to abolish overtime was recognized as "not subject
   to discussion." It was determined that at most factories overtime
   pay exceeded regular pay and that the majority had established
   a rate of time and a half for overtime.

5. Employers felt it useful to create sick funds with the participation
   of workers and employers in both dues payment and administration; and that the Ministry of Finance should be encouraged
   to include these matters in a general system of state insurance.

6. The search had been abolished in most cases; nevertheless, employers should reserve the right to utilize the search as the need
   arises.

7. Agreeing with the opinion that the present strike was a popular
   disturbance and noting that the law on hiring did not require
   employers to pay for time on strike, the meeting established that
   almost all factories issued one-time grants averaging three days
   of shop pay.

8. In regard to improvements in sanitary conditions it was found
   that this issue was of constant concern to employers and that the
   industry, in general, maintained conditions superior to those pertaining in other branches.

9. It was agreed that fines should not be eliminated; rather, the
   meeting established uniform norms of relatively modest size.[33]

Whether they were affiliated with the Petersburg Industrial Society, directors of major private metal and machine-construction factories, or officials
charged with the supervision of state-owned ports, metalworking plants, and
shipbuilding facilities, employers in the capital thus stood firmly opposed to
an expansion of the rights of labor within the factory and resistant to the need
for substantial changes regarding wages and hours. Comparatively minor
adjustments might be made; national legislation might be proposed; but the
established structure of labor-management relations was to stay wholly in-

tact. Their numerous conferences revealed both an impressive ability to mobilize and an appreciation for the seriousness of the moment. Nonetheless,
they offered labor little but firm rebuff.

The Shidlovskii Commission, Labor
Mobilization, and Employer Politics

The positions staked out by organizations representative of Petersburg's
heavy industrialists in January soon proved problematic. Some individual
employers granted concessions, but usually well within the guidelines established by the various employer conferences.[34] More to the point, however,
order had not been restored to the capital's metalworking factories. Not only
did work stoppages continue during the latter part of January and well into
February, but scattered attempts were now made by workers to introduce an
eight- or nine-hour day by simply walking off the job at the appointed hour.[35]
Employer intransigence was challenged from other quarters as well. The
newly organized Union of Engineers began to takè up the cause of labor
reform, arguing positions in striking contrast to those of the Petersburg
Industrial Society, while the government put forth a series of initiatives. By
the end of the month, the Kokovtsov Commission had been authorized to
develop national labor legislation touching on issues such as the length of
the workday, the lifting of punitive measures for peaceful striking, permissible forms of worker and employer organization, and insurance for illness and
accidents.[36] Moreover, a second commission under the chairmanship of Sen-
ator N. V. Shidlovskii was announced at the end of January to examine
specifically the grievances of Petersburg labor, the novel feature of which was
the election of worker representatives to participate in its deliberations.

In the immediate aftermath of Bloody Sunday, the election of worker
representatives to the Shidlovskii Commission was arguably the most important stimulus to the further mobilization of Petersburg labor.[37] Even before
guidelines could be issued, workers in some factories seized the chance to
elect representatives, while elsewhere they hurried to develop detailed instructions to present to Shidlovskii, demanding the full personal inviolability
of all those involved in the commission's work, freedom of speech, press, and
assembly, and the reopening of the Gapon Assembly's eleven locals that had
been closed by government order during the January Days.[38] Other workers
reiterated demands raised in early January, thus indicating how little had
been achieved since the beginning of the strike protest.[39]

In the event, Shidlovskii would not accept the preliminary conditions
presented by Petersburg workers; indeed, by February 20, the government
felt compelled to abandon its initiative. But for Petersburg labor a significant
process of political education had gone forward. Deputies had been elected
in individual factories and then joined together on a city-wide basis. After
the collapse of the commission, these electors remained at many plants to

form the core of ongoing factory committees or councils of elders. New structures were thus emerging that enabled workers to mobilize more effectively in support of their demands. Ironically, just as with Gapon's Assembly, it was the government's own initiative that provided a stimulus and organizational prototype for the further mobilization of labor.[40]

The organizational impact of the Shidlovskii campaign was particularly significant for metalworkers. There was, first, the simple fact that metalworking factories elected the largest number of deputies.[41] Second, because of the size of many metalworking factories, workers conducted discussions and elected representatives on a shop-by-shop basis, and then, at a second round, chose representatives from the whole factory. Thus the process of mobilization ran deeper and left a more lasting organizational legacy. Third, this mobilization occurred in a context in which a leadership cadre was already at hand: those "advanced, conscious" workers developing over the course of the past decade now came into increasingly regular and open contact with an aroused rank and file. Shop and factory level elections and the organizations which they spawned now expanded the scope of the labor movement.

Social Democrats of both factions gained as well. At the outset of the campaign they searched for a strategy which might reflect both their own skeptical attitude toward the intentions of the government and the enthusiasm of many workers for the project. They ultimately advocated worker participation at the first stage of the elections but boycott at the second if the government refused to guarantee basic civil rights. Their approach proved successful; and for the first time, Social Democrats found a way to link up with the mass movement as well as a means by which to capitalize on the organizational potential apparent in the government's initiative. The gap that had distanced so many Social Democrats from the labor movement and which had been so clearly reflected in their inability to recognize the growing power of the Gapon movement now began to close.

In the aftermath of the Shidlovskii campaign strikes in the metalworking industry fell off. In part, this may be attributed to the exhaustion, and the loss of wages, that attended such repeated work stoppages during January and February. The lower levels of strike activism, however, should not obscure the fact that labor-management conflict remained acute. Both at the level of the individual factory, and at the level of an emerging consciousness of class, workers continued their search for ways to alter the conditions of their civic and work lives, while employers sought strategies to defend their economic and political interests.

At the level of the individual factory, one reflection of the ongoing struggle was the imposition of lockouts: in these early months of the revolution such closures occurred at the Franco-Russian, St. Petersburg Freight Car, Putilov, Nevskii, Baltic, Obukhov, Orudiinyi, and St. Petersburg Pipe (Trubochnyi) factories.[42] Another measure of the continuing, indeed deepening, level of strife in the factories may be found in the changing actions of workers toward lower-level supervisors: if in early January workers presented demands for the dismissal of a foreman or the reprimand of a crew leader, by March workers were carting the offenders out in wheelbarrows.[43] The empowerment experienced by metalworkers in the first months of 1905 was being translated into a corresponding decline in the authority of supervisory personnel on the shop floor. Moreover, metalworkers continued to press for an eight- or nine-hour day and were able to make real gains at the state plants. On February 17, the nine-hour day was introduced by the Ministry of Ways of Communication for its railroad shops and depots; the Artillery Department followed suit on April 12, as did the Naval Ministry in mid-May. Despite the firm resistance of private employers, however, the issue of the eight-hour day continued to fuel labor-management conflict.

For Factory Inspector Chizhov, what was most noteworthy about labor unrest in those first few months of 1905 was not so much worker efforts to secure immediate improvements in their lives as the push to achieve the right of organization. Workers were convinced, asserted Chizhov, that only with the help of ongoing organizations could the concessions gained by their protest be defended.[44] Employers seemed to agree with Chizhov's assessment, for it was precisely on the issue of labor's right to organize that the Petersburg Industrial Society focused so much of its attention and concern. Indeed, it was in regard to this right that the Society seemed to reveal its views about reform in the polity more generally.

In a memorandum written by Chairman Glezmer on February 11, the attitudes of the Society toward worker organization were laid out in no uncertain terms. Glezmer asserted categorically that industrial workers must not be isolated from the general mass of workers, and that institutions created for their welfare must not be distinct from other, already established organizations serving society as a whole. While worker participation in the administration of these institutions was fully desirable, such participation must never be confused with worker participation in the affairs of industrial enterprises, which was "absolutely impermissible at any level and in any regard." And while Glezmer argued that the right to assemble and to present collective statements was fully desirable in principle, it was scarcely appropriate at the present time, given "the low level of personal development of workers" and the lack of correspondence between such rights and the level of civil freedoms secured by other layers of society. The chairman also asserted that whatever the form worker organization adopted at the outset, it would always and inevitably lead to a unification of labor on a national and international level. Yet notwithstanding the specter of the mighty international association of working men that he conjured up, Glezmer went on to stress that workers' low level of literacy, "lack of maturity, and ignorance" [*neosvedomlennost'*]were key factors limiting a speedy improvement in the conditions of labor.[45]

If Glezmer's memorandum reflected the Society's long-standing concern with the development of any autonomous organizations of labor, then the Society's six-point "Convention," adopted on March 15 and ultimately signed by 126 of the largest factories of the capital including 50 from the metalworking sector, was equally clear about the rights of labor to participate in setting conditions within the factory and suggestive as well of the further mobilization of employers in the early months of the revolution. Employers resolved, among other things, not to permit the participation of workers in the determination of wages and in questions of internal factory order, as such participation was deemed unconditionally impermissible. Any attempt by workers to enter into these questions was to be decisively rejected. Employers further agreed that the right of dismissal belonged to the factory administration and that any intervention by workers or their representatives could not be permitted. They also maintained that the establishment of a guaranteed wage for those working on piece rates, as well as the establishment of a minimum wage for day workers was impermissible. Wages were recognized as necessarily subordinated to the laws of supply and demand; any digression from this principle would set a harmful precedent for interference by workers.[46]

These intransigent positions indicated that the Society had no interest in accepting the right of labor to organize or any intention of permitting labor to participate in setting basic factory conditions.[47] And yet these views seemed to conflict with the Society's May 12 "Note" to Kokovtsov which asserted that the question of labor organization was "the basic, cardinal question," since all other questions hinged on whether "free labor unions in the European sense" would be permitted or not.[48] Such views appeared at even greater variance with the platform of the Progressive Economic Party— the political party formed under the auspices of the Society in the late summer of 1905—which advocated for labor the "freedom of union, assembly, and strike as a peaceful means of regulating labor-management relations, and, in particular, of regulating all conditions of labor."[49]

These conflicting emphases, however, were in part modulated by what employers were willing to view as "appropriate" areas for labor's participation. The role Petersburg employers apparently envisioned for organized labor had little to do with restructuring industrial relations within the factory: worker involvement in setting wages, hours, and internal factory order was repeatedly declared "absolutely impermissible." Rather, employers seemed prepared to accept labor's participation in the discussion of a range of problems broadly related to industrial life. These problems—e.g., insurance for accidents, illness, old age or disability; regulation of female and child labor, and the maximum length of the workday; reforms governing the labor contract, the factory inspectorate, industrial courts—could be usefully regulated by legislation emanating from a national representative institution or from other bodies which brought members of the industrial community together. Employers were prepared to argue for worker participation, equally and along with other interested groups, in deciding these issues; they were not prepared to negotiate directly and equally with organized labor on the specifics of the labor contract.

At the same time, the various positions put forward by the Society seemed to reflect a growing, if still confused, linkage between its conceptualization of labor-management relations and its views on reform in the polity more generally. One must recall, for example, that Petersburg industrialists joined in the oppositional ferment of January in large measure because of their perception of the ruinous consequences of the "illegal" and arbitrary actions of the government. At issue for them was a long history of confused and often contradictory policies emanating from the Ministries of Internal Affairs and Finance—policies made possible by the absence of firm legal norms establishing the competency and delimiting the authority of governmental institutions. Also at issue were a range of questions relating to the economic development of the country broadly conceived. Restrictive, hopelessly bureaucratic, and sometimes criminally corrupt practices constrained the development of those "healthy forces" so crucial to the welfare of industry and the population. Disastrous fiscal and agrarian policies had left the countryside impoverished and in turn hindered the growth of an internal market. Petersburg employers had argued first and foremost, then, for the subordination of the bureaucracy to the rule of law and for "appropriate" attention to the economic needs of the country.[50] Said somewhat differently, their opposition was directed against an *unreformed* autocracy, and what they hoped to accomplish by their protest was a coherent approach to national economic development.

In May, Petersburg employers returned to the theme of national economic development in their critique of several proposals soon to be discussed in the Kokovtsov Commission. The proposals, which had been made public in mid-March, regarded the shortening of the workday, provision by employers of medical aid for workers, and changes in the law governing strikes.[51] Petersburg employers were highly critical of this draft legislation, which they felt was ill conceived, hastily issued in response to worker unrest, and developed without respect to the needs of the nation as a whole. They also asserted that the complete lack of attention to the financial costs of the projects was rooted in the Ministry of Finance's concern to pacify workers rather than attend to the development of industry. In short, they roundly condemned Kokovtsov's proposals as economically unreal.[52] As in their January memorandum, so again in their May note they focused on the overarching backwardness of the country, the low level of literacy and labor productivity, and the shocks experienced by industry due to the recent economic crisis.

The Society's May 12 statement to Kokovtsov also contained a view of civil rights that might be described as qualified or contingent rather than conceived of as an inherent political "good." To be sure, employers called for reforms in the state structure and pointed to civil rights as "jewels" valued by all citizens. Yet their preeminent focus was on insuring that workers were given no rights that other members of society did not enjoy. The employers' quite cautious defense of civil liberties seemed primarily to hinge on the premise that *if* workers were to secure the right to organize—a right which presupposed other rights (e.g., the freedom of speech, assembly, strike, and personal inviolability)—*then* all others must secure this right.[53]

Taken as a whole, there was considerable ambiguity in the employers' arguments; they had yet to articulate a politically coherent position, much less a compelling vision of a reformed Russia. But there should be nothing especially surprising in this, given that these employers were very new to politics. Nonetheless, certain patterns emerged in the jumble of views they advanced which might be characterized as a protocorporatist conception of politics.[54] Their vision of reform at the national level did not entail a commitment to liberal parliamentary forms; they were concerned, rather, with the rule of law (*Rechtsstaat*) and with the regulation of the bureaucracy. And while they spoke in support of civil liberties, their call was scarcely unambiguous or fulsome. In important respects, moreover, they viewed Russia's economic backwardness as the preeminent national problem, and were profoundly concerned that the further development of the country be placed in "competent" hands.

Moreover, they were deeply wary of the free play of competitive social forces and had little interest in the creation of liberal institutional forms premised on the acceptance and legitimacy of autonomous and sometimes antagonistic social interests. They wanted to regulate labor-management relations and stated their willingness to include labor in this regulatory project; but, not surprisingly, they emphasized that labor's participation was not to entail any encroachment on proprietorial rights within the factories. Employers were apparently drawing a distinction between the political rights of labor exercised in the public arena and the exercise of these same rights within the factories, and basing the distinction on a spirited defense of the rights of property and the "imperatives" of national economic development. As well, they had apparently come to the conclusion at this juncture (i.e., before October 17, or more precisely, before the elections to the First State Duma) that the best safeguard for their rights lay in some national institution inclusive of all social groups and within which the voice of labor would be muted. Clearly, Petersburg industrialists recoiled from a conception of labor relations premised on a process of negotiation occurring between two equal and organized social groups and concerned with the definition of conditions within the factories.

It must be stressed, however, that the views articulated by the Society were not broadly representative of the positions taken by other commercial and industrial groups. Through the spring and summer, employers across the Empire remained divided over critical issues: politically, they differed over the competency of the forthcoming Duma, as well as the question of suffrage. At the same time, their inability to surmount issues of competitive economic advantage undercut developing class-based initiatives.[55] Perhaps the clearest expression of the many differences separating employers was the emergence—over the course of the late summer weeks following the announcement of plans for the Bulygin Duma—of five political parties representing the various wings of the commercial-industrial bourgeoisie. The limits of employers' unity on a national level were soon revealed, as well as the inability of the Petersburg men to assume a leadership role.

But precisely because of the political weakness that this proliferation of parties suggested, and because of the Society's fundamentally ambiguous commitment to the project of substantive political reform, employers in the capital would quickly reconcile themselves to the changed conditions following the October Manifesto and map out an alternative approach to the government and to labor protest. The transition from pre-October opposition to post-October accommodation would be a relatively easy one for those grouped in the Petersburg Industrial Society.

Defining the Role of Engineers

Petersburg engineers were among the first to seize the opportunity afforded by the fall banquet campaign[56] to organize a political-professional union, and stood at the very forefront of the Liberation Movement.[57] Led in their efforts at mobilization by the indefatigable L. I. Lutugin, a well-known geologist and professor at the St. Petersburg Mining Institute, and soon to be a moving force in the formation of the Union of Unions,[58] some 500 specialists met on December 5, 1904, at the Kontan' restaurant to sort out their views. Taking the current state of the economy as the focal point of their critique of the government, the assembled specialists argued forcefully, in a resolution that 492 would sign, that the necessary condition for the further development of Russian industry was the full flowering of civil liberties: without the complete inviolability of person, without free speech and press, meeting and association, industry would be crippled. Only with solid guarantees of these rights and only with the expansion of popular education, they asserted, could the productivity of labor be increased and economic growth facilitated. In what amounted to a first draft of their political platform, they concluded with a call for the convocation of a national legislative body elected by the people. The engineers then agreed in principle to form a union and to establish ties with existing engineering and technical societies: to this end they elected an eleven-man bureau with V. L. Kirpichev as chair and A. S. Lomshakov and Lutugin as vice-chairs.[59]

Events soon pushed the engineers further. Appalled by the massacre on January 9, Lutugin called another round of meetings on January 13 and 14, where some 250 specialists agreed to move forward quickly with the establishment of a union.[60] This group also composed the "Note of the 198" which rejected the government's claim that the tragedy of Bloody Sunday was a product of agitation on the part of revolutionaries, and argued instead that "disorder within the government" was to blame. Noting that "our industrial workers are completely deprived of legal means to defend their interests, and in particular, are deprived of the possibility to organize themselves for this goal in unions," the "Note" asserted that the striving of workers for civil rights was fully justified. In their advocacy of labor's right to organize and to strike, engineers thus took the lead in asserting "society's" interest in securing fundamental civil liberties for workers.[61]

Petersburg engineers sought to retain a leading position in the weeks that followed. They not only rendered immediate assistance to the victims of Bloody Sunday by setting up dining halls for the needy, but asked the city duma to undertake a comprehensive study of working class life in the capital so as to generate the necessary data for the development of policy in the future. They also pointedly recorded their attitudes toward the existing norms of industrial relations by passing a principled resolution censuring engineers who participated in the compilation of lists of "untrustworthy" workers. Moreover, meeting in conjunction with members of the Society of Technologists, leaders of the union agreed to establish a joint commission to study the labor question. Between February 4 and March 19, this commission played host to five mass meetings and became a focal point for the discussions surrounding the Shidlovskii campaign.[62] But these encounters would prove frustrating for the engineers: while they argued strenuously against participation in the government's commission and asserted instead that their own commission was the proper venue for the study of labor's grievances, Petersburg workers as well as their Social Democratic allies struck out in a different direction, seizing the opportunity afforded by Shidlovskii's project to organize in defense of their own interests.[63]

Nonetheless, within the first few months of 1905, the St. Petersburg Union of Engineers and Technicians had staked out a politically liberal position and offered itself to government and society as an expert on the "worker question." It had, moreover, demonstrated an impressive ability to mobilize engineers both within and beyond the limits of the capital: by mid-March, the union united 687 Petersburg engineers and by the latter part of April the figure had climbed to 850. The Petersburg group had also taken the initiative in calling the first All-Russian Delegate Congress of Engineers and Technicians of All Specialties which was held on April 22–24, first in Petersburg at the Polytechnic Institute and then in Terioki. The resolutions passed by this assembly of engineers were even more impressive for their radicalism. They argued forcefully for national self-determination and an end to discriminatory policies against Jews; for a constituent assembly elected by the famous "four-tails" formula (universal, equal, direct, and secret suffrage); and full civil liberties. Their platform regarding labor included a range of proposals for national insurance and protective legislation, as well as advocacy of the right to strike and to organize, conciliation boards, freedom to celebrate May Day, and a gradual reduction of hours to an eight-hour day.

The Congress also included a rudimentary code of ethics pertaining to labor-management relations. Stating that engineers were frequently asked to participate in "police-administrative repression,"the Congress recognized that "it was incompatible with the dignity of the engineer" to call for the assistance of armed force in conflicts between labor and capital; compile lists of so-called politically untrustworthy workers; dismiss workers according to lists compiled by the factory administration or police, or in general to fire workers or employees for political reasons; nor was it permissible to impose any sort of punishment for May Day. The engineers also called for an All-Russian Congress of Workers to elucidate their needs.[64]

Engineers turned their attention to problems on the shop floor as well. On March 18, for example, technical personnel at the Izhorsk works presented Director Gross with a detailed memorandum which discussed conditions at the factory in general and analyzed the twenty-five demands presented by Izhorsk workers in particular.[65] Their general comments were critical of upper management's attitudes toward the technical staff; most especially they expressed dissatisfaction with the current structure of labor-management relations as well as the level of technology and organization of work pertaining at the factory. Writing with a palpable sense of wounded professional pride, they asserted: "Up to now, we either remain passive spectators to the unrest in our shops, or we are called to meetings in the capacity of so-called informed persons, [as] the executors of the administration's plans, but not as technologists, consciously working in some branch of factory operations with the right of a decisive voice."[66] They stressed, moreover, that in their capacity as foremen and department heads they were the first to receive worker demands—and, one might add, the first to bear the brunt of worker hostility. Yet despite this pivotal position in labor-management relations, engineers complained that their opinions were rarely solicited or that their views were ignored by their superiors. In hopes of redressing these problems, they suggested that two commissions be established, each composed of foremen and technical personnel and under the chairmanship of the director or his appointed deputy. One would examine all decisions pertaining to labor-management relations; the other would examine technical questions (equipment, safety conditions, etc.).[67]

Convinced that their professional expertise was not properly appreciated by management, Izhorsk engineers were equally certain that their "exact and intimate acquaintance with the worker milieu" must be utilized in resolving the issues raised by the recent strikes.[68] They therefore provided a detailed analysis of worker demands; spoke in favor of political freedoms and an end to the persecution of workers and their deputies; argued generally that concessions must be granted but stressed that these must be made in a timely and planned manner; and suggested that a gradual increase in wages and a shortening of the workday would be "possible only with an increase in the productivity of labor, [which] in turn raises the question of greater technical independence for foremen and department managers than currently exists, unfortunately, at our factory."[69]

Then followed specific recommendations that echoed many of the same themes: to the demand that the current ceiling on piece-rate earnings be lifted, engineers not only agreed, but stated that limits on piece-rate earnings had a "corrupting" influence on workers and entailed a "lowering of the intensity and productivity of labor." In response to labor's insistence on an eight-hour day with the retention of current wage levels, engineers were sympathetic but cautioned that without a basic reconstruction of several shops and the corresponding changes in the level of technology and organization of work, such demands could not be met.[70]

If technical staff thus used worker demands as a means to express their own dissatisfaction with conditions in the factory, it was also clearly the case that the demands themselves forced managerial personnel at all levels to scrutinize more closely than in the past the work process and labor-management relations pertaining on the shop floor.[71] A good example is the demand for the eight-hour day, which focused attention quite explicitly on the problem of labor productivity and on the control workers exercised over the pace of work. Another is the issue of limits on piece-rate earnings. Deciding to lift the ceiling on these rates, Director Gross was sure that workers would now "strain every nerve so as to earn more," while management would learn "the real working capacity of workers, the productivity of their labor, and the time of performance, and consequently the exact cost of the work force."[72]

Such issues encouraged supervisory personnel to think in terms of piece-rate *systems* and the principles underlying wage determination, and therefore helped push engineers to the realization that the resolution of industrial conflict went beyond larger allocations to the wage fund and rested instead on a more fundamental reconceptualization of the work process. At the same time, changing perceptions of the work process also heightened the concern of many engineers with the obstacles to further development posed by managers like Gross and the autocratic system he served. Gross's unilateral exercise of authority and his repeated reliance on tsarist troops to maintain order only underlined the absence of a coherent system of labor-management relations and impeded efforts to improve the rationality and efficiency of the factory.[73] For Gross, however, developments over the course of the year seemed to confirm that the professional and political pretensions of engineers were dangerously linked: on October 16, some of his best technical and supervisory staff wrote to inform him that they intended to join the October general strike in support of the goals of the Liberation Movement. And while Gross did not shrink from dismissing key members of his managerial staff, he was unnerved by the experience: the notions of duty and loyalty that underpinned his conception of labor relations had been badly shaken.[74]

Through the first nine months of revolution, many Petersburg engineers were powerfully identified with the "all-nation" movement striving for substantive political reform. They were equally committed, both politically and professionally, to a broad-based economic development of the country. Thrust by their professional position into the very center of conflict between labor and capital, many initially advocated the development in Russia of that liberal institutional matrix for industrial relations that had been evolving in the West for some decades. They also sought changes in the work process which would permit real improvements in working conditions. At this juncture, few engineers perceived the claims of nation and of class to be irreconcilable, much less that workplace rationalization might generate more rather than less conflict.

The Bending of the Autocracy

On May 17, 1905, news of the naval disaster in the Tsushima Straits reached the capital. The Russian fleet that had steamed out of Kronstadt the past October and sailed half way around the world had been destroyed in a matter of hours and lay at the bottom of the sea. It was now made painfully clear to Nicholas that he must sue for peace; he was also forced to acknowledge that the regime's flagging prestige abroad was having punishing financial consequences at home. Unable to bear the burdens of war, the autocracy proved equally incapable of insuring domestic tranquility. The Tsushima disaster undermined still further the credibility of the government in the eyes of educated society and amplified its already urgent pleas for reform. At the same time, social conflict—which frightened both the autocracy and "society"—appeared to deepen and was variously illustrated by the expanding dimensions of agrarian unrest, the mutiny of the battleship Potemkin, the appalling levels of violence in Odessa, the massive strikes of the Ivanovo-Voznesensk textile workers, the demonstrations in the capital in commemoration of Bloody Sunday and against the call-up of reservists, and the long and bitter lockout of Putilov workers. Perhaps just as important for future developments, the end of the war meant the termination of government orders for military goods and rolling stock: as a result, the economic problems that had troubled heavy industry since the first years of the century soon returned.[75]

The spring and summer months were thus a time of continued tension throughout the Empire, and these tensions were not substantially relieved by the announcement of plans for the Bulygin Duma on August 6. Again educated society was in an uproar when it was learned that the much-awaited national assembly was to enjoy only consultative powers and to rest on an extremely limited franchise weighted heavily in favor of propertied and agrarian interests. Many now protested the disenfranchisement of large segments of urban, professional Russia and the total exclusion of industrial workers. Nor did the government's August 27 decree restoring university autonomy bring calm to the country. With the beginning of the academic year in mid-September, students resolved to open their lecture halls to the public; particularly in the capitals, the higher educational institutes became the center of the anti-tsarist movement and a unique meeting ground for workers, *intelligenty,* and the opposition-minded public. The mass political meetings that now occurred at Petersburg's higher educational institutions every evening provided a crucial opportunity for further mobilization against the autocracy; and this daily exercise in free speech and assembly proved critical to the launching of the October general strike in the capital.[76]

A less visible but nonetheless important mobilization was taking place in the metalworking factories of the capital, particularly those situated in the Nevskii district. In the wake of the Shidlovskii campaign, Nevtsy had made a variety of attempts to organize, relying in their efforts on the resources and the loyalties that had been accumulating within the context of the factory and the district for a considerable period of time. Leading this mobilization were workers of the three major mixed production plants of the district—the Nevskii Shipbuilding and Engineering Works,[77] the Obukhov Steel Works, and the Aleksandrovsk Engineering Works—factories that had played a central role in the strikes of 1901.

To understand metalworker protest at this juncture—as well as its place in the subsequent evolution of labor relations in the St. Petersburg metalworking industry—we must recall the particular situation of workers in the Nevskii district, and those elements that were common to other metalworking plants: large factory size; a diversified products line; factories that were owned by the state or worked primarily on state orders; factories located at the periphery of the city and large enough both to dominate the surrounding area and to create a "special world" which was perceived to be unique from other plants; and factories which employed a significant number of skilled, literate, and urbanized workers. Putilovtsy or Baltiitsy thus fit what might be called the "Nevskii-type" worker. All three of the factory "giants" which dominated the Nevskii district shared this set of characteristics and each was closely tied to the state: Obukhov was under the direction of the Naval Ministry and Aleksandrovsk was administered by the Ministry of Ways of Communication. Since the turn of the century and the scandalous Mamontov bankruptcy, the State Bank had been the principal stockholder of the Nevskii works.[78]

As we have seen, the Nevskii district was shaped by its own particular geography and history: located about 12 versts from the city center and surrounded by villages that stretched out into the Russian countryside, it developed somewhat in isolation from the other centers of working class and urban life in the capital. But the district had long been a focal point of liberal philanthropic and social democratic work, and over the course of the preceding fifteen or twenty years, *intelligenty* of various ideological persuasions had developed ties with Nevskii workers and had been instrumental in fostering the development of a stratum of politically conscious workers. It was the metalworkers of this district who had played the critical role in the strikes of 1901 and whose protest had demonstrated the emergence of an important layer of workers broadly sympathetic to the democratic strivings of the "all nation" movement of liberation. And it was these workers who had been shaped in important ways by the vagaries of the economic cycle: by the great expansion of the 1890s and the insatiable demand it produced for skilled cadres, but also and equally by the sharp decrease in earnings and the contraction in opportunities for advancement that attended the crisis at the turn of the century, and by the marked increase in the intensity of labor that accompanied the outbreak of the Russo-Japanese War.

By 1905, the experiences of the past two decades had produced a stratum of politically conscious metalworkers from the Nevskii district—as well as workers from Putilov, Baltic, and elsewhere with a similar history and set of characteristics—who were able to seize the many opportunities afforded by the revolutionary unrest to mobilize on behalf of their interests. Quite often, however, this activism rested on loyalties that had been crafted within the context of a particular factory, or, in the case of the Nevtsy, in a district where three giant metalworking firms were linked together by the peculiarities of geography.[79] In the aftermath of the Shidlovskii campaign, for example, Nevskii Shipbuilding workers were able to retain their elected representatives as the core of an ongoing factory council. This authoritative factory-based organization was not only able to mount strike actions over the course of the year, but to launch efforts—unsuccessful in the short term—in pursuit of the formation of a metalworkers' union in the spring of 1905.[80] The first attempts at union organizing among metalworkers thus occurred in the Nevskii district.[81]

Nevtsy also deployed a new weapon in the summer of 1905—the rent strike. In May, landlords in this district and elsewhere sought to raise their rates. Workers decided to fight back: first at the initiative of the Obukhov council of elders, and then in conjunction with the councils at the Nevskii Shipbuilding and Aleksandrovsk factories, workers resolved to pay 20% less in rents and called on their compatriots in neighboring plants to follow suit. Nevskii district workers then came together to form an Apartment Boycott Commission, which not only pursued a decrease in rents, but sought ways to protect comrades and neighbors evicted from their homes.[82] Here again, the factory-based organizations of metalworkers nourished collective action in support of important community-wide issues.

Nevskii district metalworkers thus brought to the great strike conflicts of October and November both an ability to organize and a proclivity to rely on factory and district based resources. They also brought a set of fundamentally democratic values, including a commitment to overcome the historic rightlessness of Russian labor as well as an insistence on substantive improvements in living and working conditions, values, and commitments which hinged on the sense of dignity and self-worth that had been built over the previous fifteen years and which rested on the acquisition of a valued skill, on the attainment of literacy and a more fully "cultured" life, and on the successful adaptation to the city. These values, moreover, permitted them to ally, however loosely and tentatively, with broader and not exclusively proletarian segments of society who also shared comparable civic aspirations. Nevskii workers would play a leading role in the strike movement of the fall; they would act alongside other workers and would become part of a larger effort which linked together diverse segments of Russian society in a loosely unified movement directed against the autocracy. But their activism did not hinge on an exclusively proletarian identity, nor did they pursue a specifically class-based politics.

The great October general strike in St. Petersburg had its origins in the "days of meetings" which brought workers and the opposition-minded public together within the walls of the universities in an increasingly electric atmosphere. The strike also had its immediate roots in the response of the capital's printers to the request of their Moscow compatriots to support their work stoppage. In an impressive demonstration of strike discipline and solidarity Petersburg printers called a three-day strike for October 3–6.[83]

In the midst of this stoppage, Nevskii workers began to strike on October 4, and quickly mobilized most other factories and mills of the district to join them. Numerous bloody clashes with the police ensued along the Shlissel'burg road; barricades were thrown up around the Aleksandrovsk and Nevskii factories in a scene reminiscent of the "Obukhov defense" four years earlier.[84] Obukhovtsy then joined on the 5th and resolved to stay out until the 10th,[85] while most of the other workers of the district decided to return to their factories on the 6th. It was in the midst of the strike on October 4–5 that the "Workers' Strike Committee beyond the Nevskii Gates" was formed, and it was this organization that issued a set of demands which characteristically wove together the "economic" and "political" concerns of the Nevtsy. Workers demanded a nine-hour day with a 20% increase in wages; a ruble a day minimum wage for the unskilled; freedom to gather and conduct meetings; noninterference by police in strikes and no arrests for striking; and finally a 50% cut in rents.[86] Obukhovtsy worked out their own set of demands which focused almost entirely on political issues: they sought freedom of speech and press, strike and union; inviolability of person and dwelling; the right to pre-electoral campaigning for the State Duma and election by universal, direct, equal, and secret suffrage; and immediate freedom and amnesty for all those arrested for their political convictions. Two final issues were of particular interest to metalworkers: demands that all state and private orders for heavy metal manufacturing be placed within Russia and that an eight-hour day be instituted.[87]

In assessing these strikes, the Ministry of Justice asserted on October 5 that "the present movement, which pursues exclusively political goals, is a direct consequence of the agitation taking place at the meetings in the higher educational institutions, and the strikes on Shlissel'burg road, in all probability, are the beginning of a general strike in Petersburg industrial enterprises...."[88] Ministry officials doubtless worried that Nevskii district workers would play a crucial role in the developing protests, although these strikes ended before Petersburg railroaders took the critical step: on October 12 they joined with their comrades in Moscow in a work stoppage that brought rail traffic to a halt. On the same day, workers from Nevskii, Aleksandrovsk, the Atlas plant, and all the major textile mills of the Nevskii district once again walked off the job, and as such became the first significant detachment of factory workers to join the railroaders in the October general strike. On the

13th, Obukhovtsy joined as well, as did all major factories on the Vyborg side. With the addition of metalworkers from such major factories as Putilov, Franco-Russian, Baltic, and St. Petersburg Freight Car on the 14th, the strike became general. Soon central Petersburg was crippled, as artisans, shopkeepers, service workers, and then professionals joined in the mounting protest.[89]

On the evening of the 13th, representatives from the striking factories of the Nevskii district as well as metalworkers from the Vyborg side met at the Technological Institute. Following the example of the Shidlovskii campaign, the thirty-five to forty assembled workers called on their compatriots throughout the capital to elect deputies on the basis of one representative per 500 workers and encouraged them as well to join the general strike. And so, in an effort that was initially directed at the formation of a city-wide strike committee, but which rapidly reached beyond the management of the strike, a collectivity composed mostly of metalworkers and their Social Democratic supporters proceeded to create an institution that would soon call itself the Petersburg Soviet of Worker Deputies.[90] Just as at the outset, so too through the life of the Soviet, metalworkers contributed the majority of deputies and played the leading role.[91]

Over the course of the next several days, the Soviet expanded its activities, variously meeting with representatives from the Union of Unions, ordering shops to open certain hours of the day, sending deputies to the city duma to request funds and meeting space, reiterating its call to the workers of the capital to elect their representatives, and in general adopting measures in support of the spread of the strike. Meanwhile, the regime mobilized to stop it. At the behest of Nicholas, General D. F. Trepov, the military governor of Petersburg, moved to restore order. On October 14 he issued his famous command to the troops: "Should the people resist, do not use blank cartridges and do not spare your ammunition."[92] He also ordered the halls of the higher educational institutes barred to the public. But the strike went on and the meetings continued; so did the repressive actions of the government. What increasingly appeared to be a stalemate by Monday, October 17, however, was broken by the autocracy late in the day: the regime bowed to the pressure of the strike and issued a manifesto pledging full civil liberties, an extension of the franchise, and legislative competence to the State Duma.[93]

Reactions to the October Manifesto differed markedly. Some cried victory and were clearly relieved that the struggle was now over; others were more cautious and saw in the Tsar's promises only the beginning of a long and difficult process of political reformation; still others cried fraud and vowed to continue the struggle for a constituent assembly elected by the famous four tails. As thousands took to the streets in joyous celebration, others embarked on a bloody rampage of pogroms against the "Yids and students" whose revolutionary actions had brought such disgrace to the autocracy. Taken as a whole, what became increasingly obvious in the weeks and months to follow was the beginning of a process of political differentiation, as various segments of the population clarified their views in light of the Manifesto and the emergence of legal political parties, and in response to the continuing social and economic crisis.

For most metalworkers of the capital, the battle would continue and in many respects intensify. They neither trusted the political promises of the government nor had they achieved the material improvements they had sought since January. So while some workers and many professionals began to return to their jobs in the days following the issuance of the Manifesto, most metalworkers stood firmly behind the Soviet's directive to remain on strike until October 21 as a sign of dissatisfaction with the government's concessions. As important, immediately following the events of October 17 and until the bloody bombardment of the Presnia district in Moscow on December 16, Petersburg's metalworkers joined in the "days of freedom" and very much helped to shape them. This was a time when workers and others sought to exercise their newly won civil rights by meeting freely, speaking openly, organizing all manner of associations, and reading an uncensored press. And it was a time when workers sought to implement these rights directly within the factories. Insofar as they felt it necessary to discuss their political or economic needs, they talked with their comrades or gathered by the thousands in the cafeterias and courtyards of their factories.[94] And insofar as they feared the mobilization of the right in the form of Black Hundred gangs, they appropriated factory materials to forge weapons and they organized in "fighting detachments" for self-defense.[95] Also central to their notion of democratic reform within and outside the factory gates was a reduction in the length of the workday so that they might have the time to pursue their civic freedoms. So, shortly following the return to work on October 21, and again at the initiative of Nevskii district metalworkers, the struggle for the eight-hour day was renewed.[96]

Employers experienced this six-week period as an unprecedented assault on managerial authority. In what surely appeared to them as an all-enveloping chaos they witnessed repeated work stoppages, ceaseless meetings and violations of shop discipline, the crafting of weapons, massive walkouts after eight hours to force introduction of a shorter day, and a seemingly unhindered stream of revolutionary rhetoric from the Soviet. Top managers now regularly heard remarkable reports from the shop floor: foremen complained that workers came to the factory simply to talk politics, read newspapers, discuss the "evils of the day," and in every possible way show their contempt for the shop administration. And the alarming incidence of physical assault on lower level supervisory personnel reflected only too painfully the degree to which the prestige and authority of shop personnel had fallen.[97] As disturbing was the behavior of technical staff. Some engineers had continued to support labor protest in the post-Manifesto period by staying off the job;[98] others had long since voiced their principled support of a substantial reduction in the workday;[99] while still others were sharply critical of the manufacturers' unyielding response to the eight-hour-day movement.[100] At the same time, the Union of Engineers sought in a variety of ways to demonstrate its support for the Soviet and its participation in the ongoing struggle for a Constituent Assembly.[101]

The political and economic implications of this crisis of labor discipline were profoundly disturbing to Petersburg employers in general and metal-working industrialists in particular. The continuing unrest in the factories after the October Manifesto discredited the arguments of those who had sought to minimize the economic strivings of workers and to propose instead that the mainspring of labor unrest was dissatisfaction with the existing political order. It now became clear that political reform was inadequate; workers were prepared to contest conditions in the factories and to go on struggling to secure substantive gains. Moreover, workers' self-implementation of "civil rights" in the factories during the "days of freedom" only served to confirm the beliefs of deeply conservative men like Glezmer that labor lacked the culture, maturity, and restraint required in a polity governed by representative institutions and the rule of law.

But the post-October protest of workers was even deemed inappropriate and unacceptable by "liberal" industrialists. Consider events at the Semenov factory. On October 31, workers here voted to introduce the eight-hour day. I. A. Semenov was present at the meeting and endeavored to convince the assembled workers that now was not the time to raise economic demands. Rather, he argued, it was necessary to struggle for political freedom and then later, when these freedoms were won, it would be possible to fight for economic improvements. Semenev failed to convince his audience. On November 7, he informed his workers that if they would not work under the old conditions, i.e., abandon the struggle for the eight-hour day, he would fire them. When they persisted, Semenov declared the factory closed and all workers dismissed. Moreover, Semenov threatened that not one dismissed worker would find employment in the machine-construction industry of the capital. Significantly, the Semenov factory was unique among Petersburg machine-construction plants in that it held patents on the machinery it produced and therefore faced no competition. As important, Semenov himself had stated to workers on October 31 that his factory could run successfully on an eight-hour day, even if other factories did not follow suit.[102] Clearly, the self-styled liberal Semenov had had enough labor activism. At issue was his understanding of the "appropriate" parameters of protest, and so when workers continued to fight for an eight-hour day rather than press for "political freedom," he was fully prepared to defend his prerogatives by means of blacklists and a lockout.

Employer strategy over the first nine months of the revolution had entailed an intransigent rejection of workers' "economic" demands, as well as an adversarial attitude toward the government. They believed that workers would accept change in the polity in place of substantive reform in the factory. This strategy necessarily collapsed when workers fought on in the post-October period. By the end of this month, therefore, the operative assumptions of Petersburg employers had been badly shaken, leaving their subsequent approach to labor and polity none too clear.

At the same time, the real cost of these "economic" demands came into sharper focus, since a cluster of important issues surrounded the shortening of the workday. First, worker efforts to "legislate" on their own the length of the workday clearly represented a conflict over control and power in the workplace, and as such, were directly challenging to managerial authority. Second, the length of the workday had been an historically divisive issue among manufacturers: time and again they had clashed over legislation regulating it. Most recently, their competing economic interests had contributed to the collapse of the Kokovtsov Commission. Equally indicative of the problem, Petersburg employers were troubled about the precedent set by the state factories as first the Ministry of Ways of Communication, then the Artillery Department, and finally the Naval Ministry acceded to the nine-hour day. Concessions to workers on this issue, therefore, would be granted at the price of employer unity. Third, the eight-hour day directly raised the problem of labor productivity and as such entailed major questions of labor discipline, the organization of work processes, and the level of mechanization pertaining in the shops, questions made all the more vexing given the current state of the economy. In sum, precisely those economic and political issues of greatest moment to employers were challenged by the actions of metalworkers: for the fact was that metalworkers both spearheaded the eight-hour-day movement and constituted the backbone of the Soviet, which in the "days of freedom" was showing all the signs of a revolutionary government in embryo. Employers, and most especially metalworking industrialists, took up the challenge by joining with the government in a massive lockout and by embarking on efforts to better organize their ranks.[103] The workers and employers of the heavy industrial sector thus stood at the epicenter of the conflict in Petersburg.

The struggle for the eight-hour day had scarcely begun, however, when the attention of Petersburg workers was diverted by two major political events: the mutiny of Kronstadt sailors on October 26–27 and the imposition of martial law in Poland on October 28. In an impressive mobilization of forces, the Soviet called for a political strike, and between November 2 and 7 more than a hundred thousand Petersburg workers stayed out in response to the call.[104] Once more, workers demonstrated their readiness to struggle over politics *and* economics, as well as their deeply rooted skepticism of the reforms granted on October 17. Yet the strike also revealed that limits had been reached: by and large, the November political strike failed to gain the support of the liberal intelligentsia, nor did it secure the backing of workers across the Empire. Indeed, labor protest in the post-October period tended to be confined to the capital cities, making Petersburg workers increasingly isolated and vulnerable.

At the conclusion of the political strike, many workers resolved to continue the eight-hour-day struggle despite clear signs of employer resistance. Meeting on November 1, a conference of representatives from seventy-two metalworking factories resolved that shortening the workday was impossible and that if workers continued to force the issue, factories would be closed. Placards carrying this message were duly hung on the following day. But what was particularly disturbing about the threatened lockout was the participation of the state firms: private industrialists and the state were closing ranks. At one session of the Council of Ministers during the November political strike it was agreed not to accede to demands of railroad workers for an eight-hour day; and apparently following a discussion between E. L. Nobel and Witte, the prime minister indicated his support for the closure of major state plants. On November 7, the government took the lead by locking out workers at the Aleksandrovsk, Orudiinyi, Baltic, Obukhov, and other factories; and when representatives of the Soviet met with Naval Minister Birilev on November 8 in an effort to get him to reopen the factories, Birilev stated simply that they would only reopen if work resumed under the following conditions: "No eight-hour day, and no meetings." On the 9th, Nevskii Shipbuilding was closed; by November 16, more than 100,000 workers, the majority metalworkers, had been thrown out of the factories in a devastating show of force by state and private employers.[105] As private employers well realized, without the agreement of the major state plants no lockout in the capital could be effective; with it, they might tame labor radicalism.[106]

The concerted actions of state and private industry thus broke the eight-hour-day strike movement. And although the Soviet endeavored to regain the offensive with a dramatic November 14 proclamation, indicting the regime as provocateur and attacking the retrograde alliance between the government and the bourgeoisie, it had sustained a major defeat.[107] Petersburg workers, especially metalworkers, now had to contend with mass unemployment as manufacturers utilized the unrest as a pretext to filter out "untrustworthy" workers, repressive actions which were facilitated by the cutbacks in state purchasing that attended the end of the Russo-Japanese war. As well, the presence of police and troops in the factories and the ban on meetings on factory premises undercut the ability of workers to organize in their own self-defense. Metalworkers had chosen an exceptionally difficult time to continue a struggle over issues of first magnitude to employers.

Equally important, the alliance between state and private plants reflected a larger reconciliation: with the government no longer isolated, it could begin to reassert control over a restive and rebellious population. Thus by the end of November, the regime felt strong enough to arrest the leader of the St. Petersburg Soviet, Khrustalev-Nosar', and a week later moved against the Executive Committee and the worker deputies. While the workers of St. Petersburg endeavored to mobilize in yet another general political strike, they now no longer possessed the strength and backing to do so. In the capital, the strike was met by another major lockout of metalworkers; in Moscow, it was met by a barrage of artillery shells.

V

RETHINKING LABOR RELATIONS "FROM ABOVE": STATE MANAGERS AND THE ENTREPRENEURIAL ELITE IN 1906

The arrest of the Petersburg Soviet and the shelling of Moscow's Presnia district demonstrated the renewed confidence of the government, but scarcely resolved the conflict between regime and people. While the forces of reform had been compelled to retreat, decisive battles still lay ahead. The relationship between the future Duma and the autocracy had yet to be clarified; peasant Russia had not been satisfied in its land hunger; the grievances of labor had not been addressed. Serious economic difficulties compounded the political issues at hand, simultaneously fueling the conflicts between labor and management and informing the attitudes of Russia's industrialists toward the problems of national development. As the new year opened, state and society remained locked in struggle over the nature and limits of social and political change.

In the breathing space provided by the repressive actions of the state, Witte's government worked to modify the concessions granted in the October Manifesto and to restore the fiscal integrity of the Empire. In the months before the opening of the Duma on April 27, a complex electoral system was devised; an upper house was added as a conservative counterweight to the lower chamber, while a host of powers were declared beyond the reach of the legislature and under the unilateral control of the autocrat. These and other regulations were promulgated on April 23 as Russia's new Fundamental Laws; as such, many essential prerogatives were stripped from the legislature prior to its first session. Nonetheless, the multi-staged elections to the Duma—and the expectation among some segments of the population that the new legislature would enjoy authority and legitimacy—contributed to a resurgence of political activism in the spring of 1906.

Witte had also been energetic in seeking to stabilize the regime's finances. By early April, the terms of a major loan were finalized with the French, which "saved" the autocracy from bankruptcy as well as any debilitating fiscal dependence on the Duma, and allowed the government to proceed with a vigorous suppression of revolutionary unrest. But Witte secured the loan by sacrificing substantial diplomatic maneuverability; in further undermining Russia's relationship with Germany, the regime was henceforth increasingly tied to the Anglo-French Entente. Witte's efforts to shield the regime from revolution at home thus had far-reaching foreign policy implications. And even in the short term, his accomplishments failed to improve his standing with the Tsar or insure that the Duma would bend to the will of the autocracy.[1]

The period between the calling of the First State Duma on April 27, 1906, and the dispersal of the Second on June 3, 1907, would constitute a critical period in the evolving relationship between labor and management in Petersburg heavy industry. For metalworkers, the struggles of late 1905 led directly to mass unemployment, and to an important mobilization around the issue of joblessness and the responsibility of the city to its working class citizens. Metalworkers also sustained a withering assault by the autocracy on their newly formed union, as well as stiff resistance by employers to their strike actions. Deep demoralization but also profound alienation began to characterize the labor movement, and, in part as a product of the repression that fell so heavily on labor in the second half of 1906, a working class more sensitive to its common concerns began to take shape. Gone now was talk of the "all-nation struggle." Voting for the parties of the radical left in elections to the Second Duma, Petersburg workers made clear that they had no interest in an alliance with the "bourgeoisie"; still less did they seek an accommodation with the autocracy.

The crisis of labor discipline that had emerged with such clarity in the "days of freedom" had a stunning effect on employers, who were now impelled to scrutinize closely the assumptions that had guided their understanding of labor-management conflict. While the government published new labor legislation which seemed to alter the institutional context structuring industrial relations, directors of the state-owned plants began to think seriously about rationalizing plant operations. Private employers surveyed their extant organizational resources and, finding them wanting, searched for more effective means to press their interests. Perceptions of problems in the factory, as well as management of the national economy, had begun to alter significantly.

Sorting Things Out at the State Plants

On December 9–10, 1905, officials charged with the operation of state-owned plants demonstrated that they had reached a turning point. By order of the Naval Ministry, the Baltic, Obukhov, Izhorsk, and New Admiralty plants were closed down and would remain so for more than a month. The directors of the state plants had made clear to their superiors that ongoing worker unrest made "normal work" impossible, while the upcoming holiday

season promised still further interruptions.[2] Thus the repeated work stoppages, the seemingly endless gathering of workers in the shops and the yards
and the cafeterias, the litany of complaints, the assaults on supervisory personnel, the intense struggle surrounding the eight-hour day had taken their
toll on management. It was time to take stock and assess the problems that
had led to such an explosion of discontent.

Yet the deeply unsettling actions of workers were not the only problem
besetting the state's managers. Well before the decision to shut down, they
had struggled with a complex web of issues which obviously included acute
labor-management conflict but also hinged on the increasingly tenuous economic situation of the metalworking industry. Already by late summer of
1905, orders received by these plants had fallen precipitously in conjunction
with the end of the Russo-Japanese War; the Izhorsk, Obukhov, and Baltic
factories projected cuts in work force size and a possible shortfall in the wage
fund.[3] And such difficulties doubtless played a role in bringing about several
high-level changes in the fall of 1905: at Baltic, P. F. Veshkurtsev replaced K.
K. Ratnik, while the head of Obukhov since 1893, General G. A. Vlas'ev, was
replaced by M. Z. Shemanov.[4]

Labor unrest, economic constraint, and new blood at the top combined to
bring about a wide-ranging reexamination of plant operations. Managers
simply had to bring down costs and restore labor discipline; through the fall
of 1905 and into the new year they commissioned studies and convened staff
conferences, questioned foremen and compiled statistical data, and ultimately
began to implement a vision of factory management substantially different
from the one that had guided their counterparts in the pre-1905 period.

Management studies quickly identified problems in several areas: wage
policy was inconsistent and failed to motivate workers; the role and authority
of foremen was ambiguous at best, confused and arbitrary at worse; uniform
regulations governing labor-management relations were largely absent; overall, the lines of authority were tangled. Moreover, problems in these areas
contributed just as clearly to high costs and low productivity as did the
technical obsolescence of equipment and the deterioration of physical plant.
By 1906, therefore, some staff had begun to see things in a new light: it was
now asserted that the problems they confronted were intertwined and that
the factory had to be understood as an integrated whole whose parts were
poorly coordinated at the present time. It was not simply that labor was
restive; rather, the shops were fundamentally disorganized, they relied on
outmoded equipment and production processes as well as woefully inadequate accounting procedures, and they utilized wage policies that failed to
instill discipline and diligence.[5]

At Obukhov, management sought to develop an approach which addressed, first, the absence of uniform personnel policies and rules of internal
order, and second, the inadequacies of wage policy. It was now recognized
that the "unreformed" factory had no comprehensive set of regulations to
guide the actions of supervisory personnel, only the scattered, unsystem-

atized rules in the workers' rate books. Since these rulings failed to encompass many of the problems that arose on the shop floor, disputes were perforce settled on an ad hoc basis. Over time, this had led to the development of a contradictory body of informal rulings, which in turn was productive of an "inexhaustible source" of disagreements.[6] Confusion was compounded for those workers or employees coming to Obukhov from private industry, for unlike private factories which were governed by the *Ustav o promyshlennosti*, the state factories were exempt from these regulations and labored under different statutes.

Reformers thus advocated the creation of "definite legal norms" and "complete uniformity" in the regulations governing the separate shops. With such rules, supervisory personnel would receive the guidance heretofore lacking. Workers, therefore, would no longer be able to manipulate the differing and informal rules to their own advantage; and with a coherent set of guidelines, managers would be less likely to concede to such pressures. The end result, it was hoped, would be a substantial lessening of the personalization of conflict on the shop floor.[7]

Top managers at Baltic, Obukhov, and Izhorsk were as one in delineating wage policy as a key arena of conflict. Already, in light of the demands of his workers in January 1905 to lift the ceiling on piece-rate earnings, Director Gross of the Izhorsk works had scrutinized existing wage policies and concluded that they "corrupted" workers and encouraged "goldbricking."[8] Now, new directors Veshkurtsov and Shemanov took the matter further and initiated more wide-ranging studies of wage policy and its bearing on labor-management relations.

They found a mass of difficulties. Prior to 1906, the pay that a metalworker received once every two weeks was based on the combination of a base pay and a simple piece-rate wage. The fixed base pay or "shop pay" [*tsekhovaia plata*] was usually calculated by the day, not by the hour. Base pay was supplemented by piece-rate earnings, which constituted an important element in the metalworkers' pay packet. At most plants, however, rates were set in each shop at the discretion of foremen or other shop personnel. At Obukhov, special premiums were used in some shops, while in others managers added to the base pay of their workers in five kopeck increments. No common guidelines structured these practices; as a result, a mass of different wage scales existed throughout the factory—and the industry—as did wide variations in the pay a worker received from month to month.[9]

Managerial personnel at Obukhov concluded that the old system failed to motivate workers to increase their productivity and provided no mechanism to distinguish quality in a worker's performance. Each element in the workers' pay packet had to be rethought. Thus reformers asserted that day rates "systemically encouraged the unconscientious and undisciplined worker" by compensating him at the same rate as the hardworking laborer.[10] They also came to believe that simple piece rates were inadequate, arguing that without incentive measures "it would be difficult to count on receiving from the skilled worker [*masterovoi*] more than two-thirds of his labor power, [since] he expends the remaining one-third only for supplemental pay in one form or another."[11] Any new system would have to evaluate the skills and experience of workers separately and motivate each worker individually, but would also have to eliminate those managerial practices that had contributed to these problems in the past. Reformers made clear their view that rate cutting and inconsistencies in rate setting fostered a solidarity that reduced the intensity of labor to that of the slowest worker. They also found that technical difficulties and poorly organized shops led to a mass of disagreements, since delays in issuing tools and materials reduced piece-rate earnings. And all these problems contributed to a pattern of excess staffing: while each shop had many more workers than necessary, nonetheless everyone adopted the pose of looking busy. As one observer concluded, given "the extraordinary solidarity of the workers, the managers of the shops had been forced to make all sorts of concessions so as not to risk their own safety."[12]

Looking to the latest in Western managerial practice for answers, reformers decided to adopt the Rowan plan, which permitted workers to earn a premium computed from the percentage of time saved in the performance of a given task, and then added to it a special method of classification unique to the Obukhov factory. Workers were to be divided into five categories (*razriady*), with a sixth covering simple manual labor. The categories were defined by the level of exactness, responsibility, and intellectual ability required of the worker. The intended result was that both workers and work would be qualitatively evaluated, with the number of workers so divided by skill as to correspond to the varying requirements of the work. When the plant resumed production in February, technical personnel were supposed to place workers in these categories; reformers also proposed an ongoing system whereby representatives from several engineering shops would test incoming workers and assign them to the proper category. The new wage structure was built on a fixed base pay calculated on an hourly, not a daily, basis. Simple piece rates were now replaced by the Rowan scheme. At the time these reforms were proposed, management envisioned the creation of a special rates bureau, which would determine rates when shop drawings were compiled and thus inject an additional control over the work process. However, this bureau was not fully or immediately developed and existed only as a consultative body during 1906.[13]

The reforming administration that took over at Obukhov thus began to sketch entirely new tasks for its shop personnel. Passive oversight of work processes was no longer deemed sufficient and was slated to give way to more active supervision. Operations were to be reinvigorated from top to bottom; a new "creative period" in the life of the factory was to open and promised to be of special import for the technical personnel. Indeed at Obukhov, management seemed rather proud of its innovative mentality, not to say consumed by the novelty of its "scientific" methods: technicians armed with statistical tables defining the "theoretical speed of work" bustled throughout the factory, while others focused on the problems of technical obsolescence and the relationship between production processes, wage structures, and the organization of work itself. Pleased with the initial results of their efforts, the authors of an April 1906 report characterized the new wage system as "fully just and impartial," one that all "conscientious persons" must come to "value." They claimed that the new policies had already led to increases in productivity and reductions in cost, and indicated that concern with speeding the work process would provide an important ongoing stimulus "to a whole series of reorganizations in the methods of work and in the technology of the factory." In sum, the Obukhov reformers set the goal of completely rooting out old habits of work.[14]

Yet later policy reviews made clear that the reformers of 1906 had overreached themselves: both the classification of workers and work had remained in the shops, as had a large portion of rate setting. The rates bureau, recognized as integral to the performance of both these functions (classification and rate-setting), had not been developed. The reforms had not, therefore, eliminated the personal discretion of shop level supervisors. Moreover, the Rowan system was constructed in such a way that premiums rose quickly to a certain point and then fell off sharply. Workers had identified this point and controlled their productivity accordingly. Quite in contrast to the intentions of the reforms, therefore, workers had found a way around the system and continued to control carefully the pace of work. As early as April 1906 a report noted that workers tended "to wreck [sorvat'] this new system which they called 'American.'"[15]

Obukhov reformers were certainly not alone in their interest in Western managerial systems. At Baltic, engineers also took a closer look at wage policy and found numerous advantages to the "progressive" wage incentive schemes being developed in the West. At staff meetings in December and January, for example, reports were presented and opinions exchanged on the Halsey and Rowan premium plans, as well as "Taylor's system."[16] While talk of "coefficients," sliding scales, and incentives to technical rationalization understandably appealed to the professional interests of many engineers, perhaps just as interesting was the stress reform advocates laid on the social benefits to be derived from the new systems. These new approaches, it was argued, would reduce labor-management conflict by providing better wages for the worker and increased productivity for the factory. As one Baltic engineer asserted, "[The Halsey system] calls forth an increase in productivity, a lowering of costs, an increase in worker earnings, and good relations between the administration and workers," although careful planning and gradual implementation of the wage reform were required to allay the "suspicion" and "conservatism" of workers. To avoid complications, statistical data had to be gathered to provide the basis for a "coefficient" suited to the conditions at Baltic, and a special calculation bureau established.[17] Director Veshkurtsov was apparently persuaded by these arguments. An hourly computation of wages replaced day-based rates when the plant reopened in

February, while the utilization of "American" methods, as incentive schemes were typically dubbed, came in the spring of 1907, presumably after the "proper" coefficient had been determined.[18] Still later, in 1911, a comprehensive plan for a rates bureau was developed.[19]

Discussions surrounding "innovative" wage systems encouraged managers to reframe their thinking about problems in factory economy. Many were now persuaded that day-rate wages had been an inexact measure of the work performed and had allowed workers to arrive late or take time off without punishment. Not only disciplinary issues were at stake, however. When plants closed early on Saturdays and on the numerous pre-holidays, workers had received a full day's compensation: management could now economize by simply paying labor an hourly rate for the time worked.[20] Similarly, an incentive wage addressed the problems of "goldbricking" and worker solidarity: premium plans would compel workers to be more attentive to the intensity of their labor; and by stressing individual achievement, workers would become increasingly interested in raising their own rates and correspondingly less concerned with exercising any collective control over the prevailing wage structure. Finally, predefined wage rates displaced the haggling that typically characterized worker-foremen relationships"; scientifically" determined rates would depersonalize the rate-setting process and remove it from the shop floor. Managers thus apparently believed that a "proper," objectively defined wage policy could substantially alleviate the intense social conflict that had exploded in 1905.

But not all supervisory personnel agreed with the new thinking and not all were ready to accept "progressive" wage schemes as an appropriate response to the problems of the recent past. At issue were alternative visions of labor management; and underlying these alternatives was a set of competing values and attitudes laid bare by the wholesale assault on Russia's autocratic institutions over the past year. Discussions at the state plants revealed a substantial difference between upper and lower management as regards the source of the difficulties, as well as fundamental differences within the senior staff itself.[21]

The many defensive statements made by foremen to their superiors reflected, in part, the fears and insecurities released by labor's extraordinary assault on their authority. There were also the social pretensions of foremen and shop supervisors and claims to special knowledge of their craft. When given the chance to lay out their grievances, then, it was not surprising that they wanted upper management to give them greater authority on the shop floor by clearly displaying confidence in their actions, and also by investing in them full control over labor management in their shops (e.g., foremen would be in charge of decisions concerning grants, dismissal slips, the setting of wages, fines for lateness, absenteeism and negligence, hiring, firing, and so on). Moreover, they sought access to more information on material and labor costs which would allow them to contribute to a reduction in expenditures, but also provide the information they needed to determine the proper wage rates. In their view, they had not been allowed to demonstrate their economic knowledge. Labor-management relations and factory operations would improve, they asserted, if the foreman became the "full boss" [*polnyi khoziain*] in his shop and enjoyed the complete confidence and full respect of the director and senior staff.[22]

Senior management saw things differently. For some, the issue was the foreman's lack of initiative, his inability to organize work properly, and a questionable level of technical competence. In the director's eyes he "lacked a serious attitude toward business" and needed to work harder. For others, the lack of system and order had led to the recent "chaos." For still others, the "abnormalities" were simply a result of the times. But senior staff agreed that supervision of the shop floor had to be enhanced, and to this end foremen had to be relieved of paperwork.[23] Recommendations proceeded along three lines: first, to reduce the foreman's paperwork, accounting should be transferred to the shop level. In late January 1906, clerical staff was in fact shifted from the central offices to the individual shops and departments.[24] Second, uniform rules of internal order had to be developed, lines of authority clarified from top to bottom, and the rights and responsibilities of each employee delineated. Finally, the duties of the lowest level of supervisory personnel—assistant foremen and crew leaders (*ukazateli*)—had to be codified. These people, it was now specified, must be literate, able to read blueprints, and have a basic command of arithmetic; they had to know their trade and be able to lead work. Their position in the shop administration had to be clearly defined so as to permit uniform career development (*chinoproizvodstvo*).[25]

Thus while senior staff wanted tighter controls exercised over material expenditures, labor costs, and the work process in general, and worried about the fallen prestige of foremen, they looked to a transfer of clerical staff to the shops and experiments with "scientific" wage systems for the answer. They also hoped that greater uniformity in personnel policies and rules of internal order would overcome the "chaos." But the effect of this approach was to lessen rather than enhance the authority of the foreman. His discretionary powers were to be reined in by the elaboration of more formalized rules and duties. Moreover, innovations such as rates bureaus or "progressive" wages threatened to deprive foremen of a key aspect of their power over labor, namely the setting of piece rates, and thereby diminish their authority on the shop floor as well as their importance in the managerial structure.[26] Additional clerical personnel located within the shop would be looking over the foreman's shoulders as well, judging the way he utilized materials or managed a job.

It is perhaps not surprising, then, that reforms at Obukhov, Baltic, and elsewhere were slow to be effected. Some staff found "American" methods offensive and threatening, one supervisor describing them as "exploitative" and hence inappropriate for a state factory, another dubbing them "keen-witted" and "sly," but unjust to the worker.[27] Others opposed the new wage systems, arguing that workers' inability to understand the complex mathematics that went into the computation of wages would give rise to conflicts; one suspects that many foremen were voicing their own anxieties in this regard as much as those of their workers.[28]

But there was more to these debates that the simple self-interest of foremen or the inertia of some middle managers. Reform-minded staff and engineers sought nothing less than an entirely new regime at the state plants, a total displacement of old patterns, habits, and attitudes. Thus one was fully convinced that "[t]he old had to be forgotten, [so that] the new order could not even give occasion to allude to the old."[29] Another stated bluntly that the "regime [at the Baltic factory] had been developed by bureaucrats [*chinovniki*] and not by technical personnel [*rabotniki*]."[30] At issue for these men was the dismantling of an existing system that was informal and personal, indeed almost criminally susceptible to bribery and favoritism. It was a system, moreover, that was fundamentally indifferent to the "imperatives" of technical modernization, rationality, and profitability. And so as they critiqued the old methods of management, they not only implicitly condemned many supervisory personnel for their backward and arbitrary ways, but also tried to impose entirely new standards, values, and goals by which to measure their performance.

Those "bureaucrats," however, may have had other performance criteria in mind. One thinks, for example, of Major-General Ratnik in 1901 as he grappled with questions surrounding the profitability of factory operations and hoped that gains in productivity would go toward improving the life and labor of his work force. Central to his concerns was the changing nature of his work force and a desire to respond in ways that might secure the "stability" and "morality" of those workers entrusted to him. One also senses the unease of Director Gross in 1905 upon receipt of recommendations from his engineering staff. Gross expected loyalty and discipline from his staff; their professional pretensions smacked of insubordination, while their participation in the October general strike seemed not only a violation of duty, but a reckless betrayal of legitimate authority. And those members of the Baltic staff who worried about "American" methods thought about what was "right" for workers in a state-owned plant, not in terms of profit and loss.[31]

So too, did one anonymous vice-admiral,[32] who insisted that the state's factories be administered in such a way as to reflect the ideals of "justice, right, [and] truth," ideals which were personified by the government and which had to be fulfilled by it. In his view,"[c]oncern for the material interests of the state factories [could] not have more or less weight than concern for the workers." Noting that arbitrariness at state factories embittered workers who then communicated their "just dissatisfaction with governmental institutions to thousands of peaceful, average men on the street," the vice-admiral concluded that the actions of factory directors thus became "generalized with the government itself and its highest personages."[33]

Such concerns and values were a far cry from the emerging technocratic vision of some engineering professionals. This new breed of men clearly felt constrained by the old regime; they wanted to create an environment which would better utilize and respect their expertise; and they wanted to move swiftly on with the tasks of "modernization."[34] Notions of duty and honor were simply inappropriate to the tasks of "modern" management; doing what was "right" for workers was not the issue. All would benefit from the gains in productivity brought about by a more "rational" organization of work; social conflict would dissolve with the progress of science and technology.

These conflicts had scarcely been resolved when the state factories re-opened in early February 1906. While "American" wages were introduced at Baltic and Obukhov, other elements of the reform proposals were enacted piecemeal in these and other Naval Ministry plants and port facilities.[35] One suspects that the resistance of those more conservative state officials to the technocratic vision of their colleagues was important in slowing the further transformation of labor-management relations at the state plants. But it was also the case that the fiscal crisis besetting the government constrained the ability of the state plants to invest in the newer, technologically more sophisticated machinery and processes that were a constituent element in the reform program.[36] Nonetheless, managers at the state plants had opened an important discussion that would soon attract the attention of a growing number of private employers; and these men would not be nostalgic about the depersonalization of labor relations nor would they want for the resources to make capital investments in new technology. Thus the alternative model of management pioneered at the state plants would ultimately come to have a great deal of relevance for employers in private industry. As for metalworkers in the capital, the "amerikanka" and "ekonomiia" was something new and demonstrated that important changes were on management's agenda.[37]

Defending the Interests of Heavy Industry

Private citizens rather than tsarist officials, the heavy industrialists of the capital responded to the dilemmas of late 1905 in a different manner than their counterparts at the state factories. Private employers not only confronted an unprecedented challenge to their authority within the factory but were forced to come to terms with an exceptionally unstable political situation in which newly created institutions promised a quite different distribution of power among social interests. At stake, it seemed, was both a shift in the relative influence of social elites and a devolution of at least some power to "the people." The initial response of Petersburg industrialists to the problems of political insecurity and labor discipline, therefore, was not so much an examination of past failures in managerial strategy as an aggressive attempt to organize their ranks more effectively. Mobilization proceeded along two lines. With the issuance of the October Manifesto they moved swiftly to bring the Progressive Economic Party into public view, hoping to secure at least some representation of industrial interests in the new State Duma. At the same time and in the midst of the eight-hour-day strikes in early November, they took decisive steps to form an employers' union. In the end, the Petersburg Society of Mill and Factory Owners would provide these men a more comfortable and durable type of association for the pursuit of their economic and political interests than that afforded by the modern political party.

Following the publication of plans for the Bulygin Duma in August 1905, several political parties representative of Russia's fledgling bourgeoisie began to take shape. Among them was the Progressive Economic Party, organized under the auspices of the Petersburg Industrial Society. E. L. Nobel, a leading metalworking industrialist, M. N. Tripolitov, an entrepreneur with interests in sugar beets and paper, as well as Ia. P. Beliaev, a man with huge holdings in the timber industry, took the lead in pressing their compatriots to join with them in a separate party representative of commercial, financial, and industrial interests. Members of the broader business community, however, particularly those who resided in the capital as spokesmen for industrial interests outside of it, voiced their concern with the narrowness of such a party and its consequent inability to win at the polls. Resistant to joining with other efforts to forge a party of the moderate center, the Petersburg Industrial Society pressed on alone. On October 21 it published the program of the Progressive Economic Party and ten days later, following another divisive meeting, it appointed what amounted to an ad hoc committee of the Society to pursue further the organization of the party.[38]

The program of the Progressive Economic Party advocated civil rights for the entire population and the rule of law; and while it looked forward to the development of a fully competent legislature with control over the budget, it rejected the need for a constituent assembly. Although the platform remained vague in its support of universal suffrage, it is nonetheless significant that the Petersburg Industrial Society had protested the exclusion of workers under the limited franchise proposed in conjunction with plans for the Bulygin Duma.[39] The party was particularly focused on issues of economic development and variously advocated protective tariffs, infrastructural development, the elimination of state enterprise in competition with the private sector, and the need for general and technical education aimed at raising the productivity of labor. While embracing the new Duma and the granting of civil liberties, the party cautioned against "reveling in freedom" and called instead for "tireless, constructive workmanlike activity in the name of progress and the powerful development of the country." Reflective of its economic nationalism was the party's insistence on empire: prefacing its political program was the slogan "Russia—One and Indivisible," a slogan certain to alienate non-Russian businessmen of the Empire.[40]

Among the most notable programmatic recommendations of the party as regards "the worker question" was a call for "freedom of union, assembly, and strike as a peaceful means of regulating labor-management relations and in particular, of regulating all conditions of labor"; the creation of conciliatory bodies to mediate contested issues to be "organized at the initiative of and with the general agreement of the interested sides"; and the elimination of intervention by the factory inspectorate in the regulation of the conditions of labor.[41] The goal of these planks appeared to be the self-regulation of labor-management relations by the industrial community. A second set of proposals, however, seemed to conflict with the first, since the platform insisted that industrial labor be seen as part of the entire working population of the country, not as a distinct class with unique needs and interests. Thus insurance, factory legislation, and social welfare programs should be extended to all forms of labor. Again, underlying the "social" program as a whole was the firm belief that national economic development would culturally and materially benefit the entire population.

As reflected in the program of the Progressive Economic Party, therefore, the political vision of the capital's entrepreneurial elite entailed a qualitative improvement in the nation's productivity; a pronounced economic nationalism; a concern for the establishment of civil liberties, the rule of law, and a fully competent State Duma; and a vague conception of new institutional structures for the resolution of industrial conflict which were based on the organized interests of labor and capital, the development of mediation bodies and the elimination of state intervention in these relations. Though never phrased as such, the party's basic message seemed to be: political restructuring is desirable and urgently needed for the purpose of national economic development. However, a certain tentativeness characterized the party's program which in turn highlighted both the political inexperience of its organizers—perhaps even their tenuous commitment to the positions staked out—and the institutional instability of the time. Thus, the very first paragraph of their "appeal" stated that no political program could pretend to immediate realization; rather, a program was to describe the political physiognomy of a party and serve as a guide to its actions.[42] Moreover, given employer unease about the organization of labor, one suspects that their advocacy of the right to strike and form trade unions was a concession to the political realities of the moment, i.e., the need for a minority to win the support of a wider constituency in an electoral campaign.

The vision presented in the public statements of the party assumed a different cast in the more private remarks of its leaders. At a gathering of industrialists on October 31, M. N. Tripolitov focused on the needs of industry and the threatening dimensions of the labor movement. Recognizing that times had now changed, he argued that to believe "that those patriarchal relations which existed between workers and industrialists can return is as naive as [the belief that] you can establish the relations which used to exist between landlords and peasants."[43] Pressing his point, he asserted that the "workers' question" had acquired "the force of a hurricane" and that the first "blows" of the workers' movement would fall on "us," as representatives of the political system. It was necessary, therefore, for industrialists to join together and develop the necessary "discipline, measures, and methods of struggle." Conjuring up images of class war, Tripolitov suggested that workers were so organized and disciplined that their leaders could simply "push the button," and the whole country would go on strike.[44] In comparison, industrialists were weak and disunited.

Tripolitov's anxiety about labor activism and his perception of the urgent need "to organize" doubtless reflected the concerns of Petersburg's heavy industrial elite, but put off other members of the business community who were less threatened by labor and more interested in building bridges to other segments of society to secure at least a few seats in the Duma, or who chose not to take any position whatsoever at this moment of high political instability. The Progressive Economic Party thus remained narrowly based, unwilling to transcend the preoccupations of the entrepreneurial elite, and unable to mobilize even a significant portion of the capital's business community. In the first round of elections it suffered total failure: on March 20, 1906, all 160 electors in Petersburg's urban curia went to the Kadet Party.

With the opening of the First State Duma on April 27, commercial-industrial groups were forced to confront the fact that they had sustained a crushing defeat at the hands of agrarian interests and rebuff by the party of the professional middle class. The Progressive Economic Party quickly dissolved into Octobrism.[45] With the lower house closed to them, Petersburg industrialists could only hope to secure a representation of their interests in the upper chamber—the reformed State Council—where the business community had a handful of influential spokesmen, including S. P. Glezmer.[46] But this chamber too was heavily weighted in favor of agrarian Russia, and industrialists remained skeptical of the ability and willingness of such a legislature to respond to the needs of their class.

By the spring of 1906, therefore, the effort of Petersburg's entrepreneurial elite to situate itself within the new and fragile "constitutional" order had failed. Indeed, never again would these men seriously engage in parliamentary politics. No doubt equally disappointed by the election returns, segments of the Muscovite industrial bourgeoisie would continue to pursue the organization of a political party—the Progressive Party—and an effective position in the Duma. But St. Petersburg industrialists would never align with the efforts of the Progressists, nor would they seek to organize their own political party in the Third and Fourth Dumas. Instead, they would circumvent the legislature and endeavor to influence segments of the bureaucracy through "representative" associations of big business, the most notable of which was the Association of Trade and Industry and its sometimes competitor, the Petersburg Society of Mill and Factory Owners.[47] Importantly, then, the Petersburg men chose not to pursue their interests by lobbying the elected legislature of the country, but rather focused their political energies on the autocratic state.[48]

The emergence of this alternative conception of political action at the outset of Imperial Russia's "constitutional" era suggests not only the weakness of the commitment of the capital's entrepreneurial elite to parliamentary politics, but also the inability or unwillingness of Russia's principal parties of the centrist right and left—the Octobrists and the Kadets—to pursue an effective alliance with leaders of the St. Petersburg industrial and financial community. And this failure of the parties to draw the capital's entrepreneurial elite into the parliamentary project could only reinforce the tendency of many employers to depict the Duma, and much of the rest of society, as unresponsive to their needs.

Just as importantly, the rise of these "representative" associations reflects the dilemmas of the period, for how were these powerful men to secure their influence in a polity historically insensitive, in their view, to the needs of national economic development, the concerns of the commercial-industrial bourgeoisie, and the interests of urban as against rural Russia? Recognizing perhaps too quickly their inability to shape the new institutional structures emerging out of the October crisis, St. Petersburg heavy industrialists tried to fashion some alternative way to press for their positions. Through the ostensibly "apolitical" form of "representative" associations, they began to carve out a different conception of political action based on the organized representation of important social interests, which were, however, still numerically weak in the Russian empire. Neither classically liberal nor traditionally monarchist, their politics suggested a transitional form that reached back to the patterns of petitioning, an estatist social order, and the "impartial" exercise of autocratic power in the interest of all *sosloviia*, and forward to a corporatist polity composed of organized social interests whose conflicts were mediated through the abundance of a flourishing national economy and the authoritativeness of an "above class" state power. The "retreat" to representative associations was therefore a predictable response to the defeat they had suffered in the elections and also consistent with their preeminent concerns: to press for national economic development in a polity historically resistant to their views and currently experiencing significant political instability and rapid social change.[49]

As leading members of the Petersburg Industrial Society struggled unsuccessfully to organize a political party, other activists within the Society tried to mobilize in response to the eight-hour-day strikes. Since the outset of this struggle in the last days of October, metalworking industrialists had been meeting in almost continuous session, endeavoring to craft a strategy to put a stop to labor's protests. The first fruit of their discussions was a resolution to reject any reductions in the length of the workday; the next was to secure the agreement of the major state plants to close down operations if workers persisted with the conflict.[50] Employers also revived the idea of "convention" by reconfirming and supplementing the March 15 agreement with the addition of a seventh point: industrialists now agreed not to enter into any dealings or agreements with "outside" [*postoronnyi*] organizations (e.g., the Soviet of Workers' Deputies or the trade unions).[51]

In the midst of this struggle key leaders of the metalworking industry began to assert that the Petersburg Industrial Society no longer provided the proper organizational framework for the capital's employers: the experience of the eight-hour-day conflict revealed the "urgent" need to organize by branch of industry. To this end, representatives from heavy industry met on November 7 and resolved to develop draft statutes for such an employers' association, to be known as the Professional Society of Metal Industrialists of the St. Petersburg Region (*Professional'noe obshchestvo metallozavodchikov S. Peterburgskogo raiona*). A committee quickly set to work under the chairmanship of B. A. Efron of the St. Petersburg Freight Car Company.[52] Between November 9 and December 10 it held eight sessions, reviewed projects developed earlier in the year by F. K. San-Galli and A. E. Vintergal'ter, studied the experience of German employer unions, and finally produced statutes defining the goals, areas of interest, structure, and membership of the proposed association.[53]

Only at the end of January, however, was the general membership of the Petersburg Industrial Society convened to discuss the work of the Efron Committee. Perhaps the Christmas holidays or foot dragging on the part of other members of the industrial community reduced the urgency to act. In any case, the general membership meeting did not accept the proposals of the Efron Committee, apparently fearing fragmentation along occupational lines.[54] But by March 24, a circular from Glezmer suggested that a set of compromise statutes had been worked out: a "common district organization" [*obshchaia raionnaia organizatsiia*] would be retained, but departments based on industrial branch would be added. At the same time, Glezmer urged that as a "proper resolution of the worker question" and as a counterweight to attempts by workers to "introduce violently conditions unacceptable for industry," the idea of "convention" had to be strengthened, while special strike funds had to be established.[55]

But it was not until June 10 that the issue was again pressed forward. In a circular which underlined "the extremely anxious mood of the times," E. L. Nobel and representatives of the metalworking group urged the Council of the Petersburg Society to secure a final decision on the draft statutes. Meetings were held on June 13 and 16 which finally adopted the statutes, which were in turn submitted to the *grado'nachalnik* on June 27 for confirmation.[56] It was well into the fall, however, and for reasons not wholly dependent on the industrialists, that the founding meeting of the Petersburg Society of Mill and Factory Owners took place.

The experience of organizing the Progressive Economic Party and the Petersburg Society of Mill and Factory Owners had revealed the limits of unity within the capital's industrial community. Efron's metalworking group had been at the forefront of both efforts to mobilize, but it had substantial difficulty in persuading other employers of the wisdom of their political positions, the appropriateness of their approach to labor protest, and the urgency of the need to organize. Statistics on membership suggest the differential impact of the crisis of 1905–1906 on various industrial branches. (See Table 5.1.)

However mixed the response of their colleagues to the project of employer

TABLE 5.1
Membership in the Petersburg Society of
Mill and Factory Owners

Branch	# of Firms		# of Workers	
	1897	1906	1897	1906
Engineering	22	66	9,840	52,510
Textiles	35	37	27,760	29,150
Other	41	64	16,935	27,680
Total	98	167	54,535	109,340

Source: TsGIA, f. 150, op. 1, d. 51, 1. 170.

mobilization, activists within the Society and its metalworking group seemed able to gain support for the imposition of a variety of punitive measures against the strikers. In November and December 1905 employers agreed to pay no wages for time lost due to strikes; to forewarn workers that if they went out on strike they would be dismissed; and to hire no workers from striking factories. The Society was also able to gather information from individual plants on the progress of strikes and circulate a bulletin to members with this information, as well as develop guidelines in the form of a booklet suggesting a variety of responses to labor unrest (e.g., fines, dismissal, factory closure, etc.).[57] But here too the limits of unity would soon be reached. Once the strike movement abated, employers began to vacillate in their commitment to these methods.[58]

A very real confusion was also apparent in employer argumentation regarding the nature of labor protest in the wake of the October Manifesto. Unlike the assertion earlier in the year that unrest was the manifestation of a popular disturbance provoked by "disorder" in the state system, it was now maintained that strike protest was the product of an insignificant group of instigators who lacked any real relationship with workers and who were able, by means of violence and intimidation, to compel the "passive" and "inert" mass to riot and strike. Given the obvious failure of the promised political reforms to quell labor protest, and still inclined to deny the economic dimensions of the continuing unrest, employers advanced the rather lame proposition that the problem lay with a small group of outsiders.[59] Such assertions underscored the obvious alarm of employers at the increasingly insurrectionary course of the labor movement in the post-October period, but also suggested the absence of any really compelling explanations for the continuing unrest.

Challenges to the positions heretofore argued by employers came from other quarters as well. Important among these in the second period of the revolution was the publication of new government regulations permitting certain forms of strikes (December 2, 1905)[60] and legalizing trade unions (the "temporary regulations" of March 4, 1906). Although these reforms had long been defended in certain government circles, their enactment forced employers to come to terms with a largely new institutional structure for the regulation of labor-management relations. Precisely because the members of the Society had publicly advocated both the right of association and strike and the end of administrative intervention in the "private" affairs of labor and management, they now struggled to find some justification for abandoning their own previously articulated positions.

Indicative was the argument laid out by A. E. Vintergal'ter at an August 1906 meeting of the Society. While recognizing the right of association for workers, he asserted that "unfortunately, to negotiate with worker trade unions is not possible for the simple reason that they do not exist at the present time. What exists now under the guise of trade unions are exclusively political organizations of labor, which bring terror and anarchy into life."[61] A few months earlier, the Society decided simply to ignore the suggestion of the Metalworkers' Union to participate in the establishment of a conciliation board, despite a plank in the Progressive Economic Party and a paragraph in the statutes drafted by the Efron Committee in support of such bodies.[62]

The Society also advanced the view that labor currently enjoyed "unfair advantages" by pointing to the paternalistic policies of an earlier period and the laws remaining on the books which constrained employer action in times of strike. They insisted, for example, that regulations governing the contract of hire had to be reworked in light of the legalization of strikes, for it was scarcely "fair" to require them to notify workers two weeks in advance of the termination of the contract; retention of this provision implied that employers would pay for strike time.[63] Employers also insisted that the protection of person and property had to be adequately insured in times of strike. But as would become clear from later lawsuits, what constituted "violence" and "incitement" and what "endangered" the person or property of the factory could be subject to quite divergent interpretations.[64]

In the post-October period, then, neither employers nor the government proved able to develop a consistent labor policy. Despite the creation of a new Ministry of Industry and Trade, the transfer of the factory inspectorate to its jurisdiction, and the articulation of a more "liberal" conception of labor-management regulation, the historic conflict that had divided the Ministries of Finance and Internal Affairs continued.[65] And necessarily so, since the question of what constituted legitimate protest in the reformed state structure had not been resolved; the boundaries between "justifiable" economic struggle and unacceptable "political" protest continued to resist definition. Indeed, through the second period of the revolution, neither the state nor the employers set these boundaries in a coherent manner, nor was a compelling ideological justification in support of a certain position articulated. In the wake of the fall crisis, Petersburg employers—very often in

VI

THE CHANGING NATURE OF METALWORKER ACTIVISM IN 1906–1907

Mobilizing the Jobless:
The Petersburg Council of the Unemployed

The dominant reality for Petersburg metalworkers in the winter of 1905–1906 was unemployment and the repression of all forms of labor activism. But with the publication on March 4, 1906, of the Temporary Regulations on Unions and Societies, and in conjunction with the elections to the First State Duma,[1] some modest forms of associational life for workers again became possible. Among the most interesting organizational initiatives to emerge in the second period of the revolution was the Petersburg Council of the Unemployed.

Already in the fall of 1905, the Soviet of Workers Deputies established a commission on unemployment to help those locked out in the November struggles. This work was soon halted, however, by police repression. Although some public organizations set up soup kitchens and comrades who continued to work tried to help through voluntary deductions from their pay, the needs of the unemployed continued to mount over the winter months. During March 1906, many of the workers who now routinely spent the day at soup kitchens scattered throughout the city began to mobilize, encouraged by a few sympathetic party organizers.[2] Doubtless relying on earlier experience, they elected deputies on the formula of two per soup kitchen, and on March 22, some thirty such deputies convened the first session of the Petersburg Council of the Unemployed.

Over the course of the next several weeks, a number of crucial decisions were taken. The leaders of the Council recognized the need to broaden the base of their movement and sought to establish ties to the factories and to those who still worked. Thirty more deputies were elected to the central body, while district councils were organized to link the jobless with the employed. Equally important was sorting out a strategy which properly defined the arena of struggle. Because workers had just suffered defeat on the national level and the issues surrounding unemployment transcended the specific factory, the Council resolved to focus on the municipal level. The specific needs of the unemployed also led in this direction, for as demands were articulated it became clear that fundamental community issues were at stake: the unemployed urgently needed assistance for food, rent, city pawnshop payments, and fees at city hospitals. Most of all, the unemployed needed work. The Council therefore sought a program of public works and mobilized to confront the city duma.[3]

On April 12, 1906, thirty representatives of the Petersburg Council of the Unemployed converged on the city duma. Initially, the town councilors proved responsive, at least in part because the capital's press had been carrying frightening reports about "the 40,000 unemployed and the 100,000 starving" and raising questions about the well-being of the urban population lest hunger and social distress go unattended.[4] The duma quickly established a commission to develop plans for public works. Agreeing to allocate 500,000 rubles to the unemployed—175,000 rubles for immediate relief, the remainder for public works—and even conceding to the demand that an equal number of worker representatives be seated on the commission—the *dumtsy* appeared remarkably conciliatory.[5]

The apparent ease with which the city fathers responded to the representatives of the unemployed was doubtless conditioned by the profound and deepening social fear that engulfed "society" in the wake of the fall crisis and which grew more intense during the unsettling months surrounding the first State Duma. As the unemployed fully realized, social fear lubricated the discussions in the city duma. "Society," to quote one of their leaflets, "was frightened by the possibility of an explosion of popular rage."[6] But it was not only apprehension about food riots, epidemic disease, or the prospect of a wave of urban crime; it was also an overarching anxiety over the uncertainties that still attended the political situation. Institutional flux, political instability, and what was perceived to be social chaos shaped the thinking of urban and rural elites in the spring and summer of 1906.

Reflective of this pervasive unease were the thoughts A. A. Polovtsev, an appointed member to the reformed State Council, recorded in his diary on July 5:

> The newspapers are full of news of plunder, armed robbery, and murder; the State Duma lays claim to the role of a national convention. . . . It sends its agents in all directions to organize an armed uprising. . . . The government has failed to display energetic measures; the army has become so corrupted that even the Preobrazhenskii regiment, which stands closest to the sovereign, has gone over to the side of the revolutionaries; it is difficult to walk along the streets because of the pursuit and attack of the unemployed and the so-called hooligans; threatening clouds are gathering from all sides.[7]

Social antagonisms were expressed just as sharply in the discourse of the unemployed movement. Most dramatic was the articulation of a loose but portentous linkage between diverse segments of the urban well-to-do (census society) and the capital's industrial bourgeoisie. Wrote Sergei Petrov (Vladimir Voitinskii) about the confrontational meeting with the *dumtsy* on April 12:

> Knowing neither labor nor need, unfamiliar with the difficulty of back-breaking work or with the torments of unemployment, living on someone else's labor, these gentlemen aren't used to the language that workers speak.
>
> Workers remember that none of these gentlemen lifted a finger to mitigate the calamity of unemployment while the unemployed silently endured their situation. Or didn't the "city fathers" know that 40,000 workers in Petersburg sat with their families without a piece of bread and were starving? They could not but know this, since they themselves and those close to them sacked these workers from the very factories and mills they themselves own, evicted these families from the very houses they themselves own, threw them onto the street, deprived them of food and shelter.[8]

In their identification of the city fathers with the industrial bourgeoisie, the unemployed explicitly broadened the definition of the forces arrayed against the workers' movement. Conflicts that had heretofore been confined to the industrial community (albeit with the frequent intervention of the autocratic regime) were now expanded into a more complex and differentiated but in the end deeply polarized urban community. Over the course of 1906, class and community were thus linked in new ways; and as new conflicts were joined, all involved were unavoidably forced to view power, privilege, class, and estate from a different perspective. In its reconceptualization of the "enemy" the Petersburg unemployed movement foreshadowed one of the most fundamental realities of 1917—a conflict in which "they" (census society, but also and equally bourgeois society) were pitted against "us" (the urban *nizy*, but also and equally the working class).

Identifying "them" also contributed to a clearer definition of "us." In the struggles with the city duma over aid to the unemployed a set of values were articulated that reflected the tension between workers and other segments of urban society. Thus, as representatives of the unemployed were quick to point out, "the flower of duma liberalism"[9] proved able to allocate funds swiftly for immediate needs,[10] but considerably less able to develop and implement programs of public works. These "handouts" were merely charity, an easy extension of the helping hand ethos of zemstvo liberalism and fully consistent with long-established relations of social dominance and subordination. But as the unemployed never tired of stressing: "We demand not charity, but our rights and we will not be satisfied with some sort of sop."[11] In their eyes, a program of public works was the central demand in their petition to the city duma on April 12; assistance with food and rent was simply an advance until work began. This pointed insistence on jobs-not-charity reflected a sense of the dignity and self-worth of an autonomous individual: a job was the only appropriate way for a worker to provide for himself and his family. Editorialized *Prizyv*, the principal voice of the Council of the Unemployed, "[w]orkers don't want to support [their] existence by charity or handouts. To get out of the current situation we demand work for ourselves."[12] Moreover, workers were entitled to employment from the city duma, not only by virtue of their membership in the urban community but because their current plight was the result of political reprisals. As one leaflet put it:

> In view of the fact that many of us are deprived of work because we tried to gain freedom for the entire people, we demand from the city duma of Petersburg immediate work, we demand that those millions in public monies which are in the possession of the duma be expended on the organization of public works.[13]

Here one senses that the thinking of these unemployed activists was informed by a basic perception of what was fair and just. In their view, it was plainly "right" to use public monies to support the needs of the population and plainly "wrong" for employers to use starvation and homelessness to silence legitimate protest. Moreover, it now appeared that the "city fathers" were complicit in the suffering of workers. Such perceptions expanded the dimensions of the conflict; already by late May, the alienation of the unemployed was finding rhetorical reflection in the statements of the Council.

> . . . at each step coming up against the sluggishness and disregard for the interests of the working class which distinguishes the Petersburg duma, the unemployed of the city of Petersburg have become convinced that they won't get much from the present census bourgeois duma of landlords and capitalists [*tsenzovaia burzhuaznaia duma domokhoziaev i kapitalistov*]. The interests of workers can only be served by a duma elected on the basis of universal, equal, direct and secret suffrage by the entire urban population.[14]

These and other representations of the antagonist illustrate the ability of the Council's leaders to politicize the issue of unemployment. Just as striking was the way in which the Council sought to build a more unified movement based on the values emerging directly out of the experience of joblessness. The specificity of the unemployment of late 1905 through the spring of 1906 gave the movement these possibilities. For the political sophistication of the Council of the Unemployed derived from the fact that the majority of its constituents were young, skilled metalworkers, precisely those militant elements thrown out of the plants at the time of the November lockouts and suffering from the "*fil'trovka*" ever since.

While there are no reliable statistics for 1906, those gathered between April and June 1906 by the duma's Commission on Unemployment and recognized as understating the problem nonetheless illustrate the general nature of the phenomenon.[15] Of the 12,933 registered unemployed, 7,016 (54.3%) were skilled metalworkers; 3,149 (24.3%) were skilled workers in other trades; and 2,768 (21.4%) were unskilled laborers, primarily from the large state-owned metalworking factories. Generalizing on the basis of the only available data (i.e., figures from the Gorodskoi, Moskovskii, and Vyborg districts), the clear majority of unemployed were literate, under the age of thirty, and, normally, well paid. (In Gorodskoi, 16% earned 30 rubles a month or less and 64% earned 40 rubles or more; in Vyborg, 30% earned 30 rubles a month or less and 20% earned 50 rubles or more.) Registration forms also make clear the reasons for dismissals: of the 560 registered unemployed of Gorodskoi district, 27% had been fired because of cuts in production, 40% for strikes, and 23% for "politics." In Vyborg, 29% lost their jobs because of cuts in production; 34% for strikes, and 23% for "political convictions" or "conflicts" with the administration.[16]

Unemployment was plainly not the product of economic dislocation alone; it was part and parcel of the ongoing political conflict in the post–October Manifesto period.[17] And precisely because many workers believed that their suffering was the result of the deliberate decisions of state and private employers to punish politically active workers, they seemed able to hold at bay, at least temporarily, the demoralization that normally attended prolonged idleness. Moreover, because these assaults appeared focused on discrete and identifiable groups of the urban population, a sense of class was reinforced by this experience of joblessness.

The Council of the Unemployed clearly fostered a sense of class by hammering away on the theme of proletarian solidarity and the commonality of interests that linked the employed and the jobless. Unemployed comrades had fought and suffered for the cause of freedom, they argued, and hence merited full support, all the more so since employers were now manipulating the situation to undermine conditions in the factories. Only on the basis of a common front could decent wages, hours, and conditions be maintained; only with a clear sense of the need for proletarian solidarity could the jobless be held back from the temptations of strikebreaking. The Council thus resolved to exclude strikebreakers from the ranks of the unemployed, as well as to register strikers and their families on the rolls, thereby making them eligible for free meals and other benefits. Moreover, the Council's propagandists stressed that unemployment was not the fault of the individual worker, but the product of capitalism. It was therefore the duty of every worker to support his fellow proletarians by giving aid freely, and to understand that the jobless were comrades in arms, not dissolute elements down on their luck. This vision of class solidarity was then actively promoted through the creation of funds in support of the unemployed. Already in late 1905, but increasingly in 1906, workers throughout the capital practiced a voluntary 1% deduction from wages.[18] In this way, bridges between differing segments of the working class were built.

In a similar vein, organizers for the unemployed addressed that scourge of working-class life, alcoholism: those comrades who criticized the unemployed for taking to drink were encouraged to look first at themselves and at those who continued to work and to come to terms with the harm that alcohol did to the working class as a whole. It was, clearly, the responsibility of all conscious workers to put aside alcohol, and more generally to conduct themselves in a dignified, self-respecting manner.[19]

The specificity of the unemployment of this period was important in another way. Young, skilled, literate, well-paid workers were tied to the city and the factory more closely than the unskilled or the day laborer; and as many observers now noted, those thrown out in late 1905 and early 1906 were the least able to fall back on the resources of the village.[20] These workers were the most dependent on factory wages and had the greatest stake in the urban community. They were now fundamentally dispossessed and had to turn to their comrades for help. Precisely because the throngs of unemployed illustrated that workers were in the city to stay, a clearer linkage between work and community became possible, as did stronger bonds to neighborhood and class.

As the months dragged on, however, the despair and bitterness of the unemployed understandably grew, as did the corrosive effects of joblessness on solidarity. Angry and frustrated, the Council mounted another demonstration on the city duma in mid-June to protest delays in the opening of public works projects.[21] While these protestations secured the allocation of further monies for the immediate needs of the unemployed and some public works projects did begin over the summer, nonetheless need continued to far outstrip the available aid.[22] With the dispersal of the State Duma on July 9 and the assault of the autocracy on labor organizations, however, the city fathers began to back away from their commitments to the jobless. By the fall they voted, by closed ballot, to terminate aid.[23] A few months later, moreover, leading industrialists pressured the duma to put a stop to the public works projects altogether. In mid-January, S. P. Glezmer addressed the city fathers concerning his dissatisfaction with this sort of program. Similarly, his colleague, A. Belonozhkin, director of the Putilov Factory, worked energetically to insure that upcoming orders for bridge reconstruction went to private contractors and not into the hands of the unemployed.[24] In all this workers perceived the power of the victorious antagonist: no longer as alarmed by the uncertainties that had surrounded the period of the First Duma or as threatened by a strong and coherent labor movement, the city duma and those it represented could take back the concessions that had been granted.[25]

But other factors also contributed to the collapse of the unemployed movement. By the second half of 1906, the very nature of unemployment began to change: politically motivated reprisals were gradually eclipsed by layoffs due to cuts in production and to an intensification of work. These changes had as much to do with an absence of orders and the generally difficult economic situation as they did with a set of decisions on the part of private industry to embark on a process of industrial rationalization.[26] As a result, the former homogeneity of the unemployed movement was eroded. If earlier the movement had been cemented by the knowledge that joblessness was a consequence of political protest, then later the causes of worker idleness became more diverse, less "heroic," and in important ways, more obscure. "Redundant" workers were fired; adult men were replaced by women and adolescents; new machinery did away with the "lazy" and the "less able." With the changing nature of these dismissals—and with the implementation of incentive wage schemes that focused workers on the pursuit of individual gain—the boss's assertion that "whoever isn't a fool and isn't lazy can always find a job" began to seem persuasive to the less politically committed. The proletarian solidarity that the Petersburg Council of the Unemployed had tried to forge was undermined.[27]

Thus, however impressive the mobilization of the jobless during the first part of the year, the movement could not withstand the corrosive effects of long term idleness brought on by the withdrawal of support for the unemployed by the city duma and by the changing nature of work in Petersburg heavy industry. With the waning coherence of the movement and the crippling demoralization of extended joblessness came despair and individual acts of violence.[28] In place of the organized struggles of the spring, the outrage of the unemployed began to blend in easily with the wave of "partisan" activities developing during the fall—the notorious expropriations, but also an epidemic of assaults on factory owners and foremen, police and high city officials.[29] In some cases, moreover, this despair found reflection in an insidious resentment toward those who continued to work, an angry assertion that "the satisfied don't understand the hungry"; or even in a peculiar expression of "factory patriotism" which was directed against those "outsiders" who got work at "our" factory or in "our" district.[30] But with the passage of time, this outrage was increasingly directed inward to find dehumanizing expression in alcoholism and suicide.[31]

The experience of unemployment thus contained destructive elements of envy and insularity, as well as a more positive ethic of collective self-help and proletarian solidarity, attitudes and behaviors which now entered the collective traditions of the Petersburg working class. Moreover, the experience of unemployment and the mobilization around it proved central to the further evolution of social conflict in the city of St. Petersburg. For census society, social fear sharpened its perception of the costs of political opposition and hastened its accommodation with the autocracy. And for labor, the treatment of the unemployed at the hands of the city fathers was interpreted as "proof," if it were needed, of the linkage between their employers and census society more broadly. At the same time, the issues surrounding unemployment—food, rent, access to city hospitals—as well as public works projects for the welfare of the city as a whole (e.g., stockyards, bridge repair, electric trams)—raised important questions about who "ran" the city and in whose interests and hence opened up new areas of involvement for working-class activism.

Organizing the Metalworkers' Union:
The Competing Claims of Craft and Class

Among the many initiatives undertaken by Russian workers in the fall of 1905 was the organization of hundreds of trade unions. Metalworkers had mounted their own efforts in this regard during October and November, indeed even earlier, but a variety of factors combined to prevent their success.[32] At the time, it appeared that metalworkers had focused their energies on the political conflicts at hand: playing the pivotal role in the organization and leadership of the Petersburg Soviet of Workers Deputies and spearheading the eight-hour-day movement had simply left them no time to devote to union organizing. As it turned out, however, few tasks proved more problematic for Petersburg metalworkers than unionization, for it was not only the "diversion" of politics, or the particular intransigence of employers in heavy industry, or the ravages of unemployment, or the assaults of the police that hindered their efforts, although these factors all played a part.[33] Organizing a citywide industrial union challenged deeply held craft, factory, and district loyalties and called into question the very meaning of "consciousness" for metalworkers. The early period of the Petersburg Metalworkers' Union thus revealed deeply sensitive issues and provided insight into those particularities that structured the dynamics of working-class formation at a critical moment of transition in Russia's history.

Over the course of the difficult winter months of 1905–1906, it fell to the Central Bureau of Trade Unions to assume the leading role in efforts to organize the metalworkers. The Central Bureau, which had been formed in the late summer–early fall of 1905 primarily but not exclusively by Menshevik praktiki,[34] focused on the organizational aspects of union construction (e.g., bookkeeping, member registration, the writing of model union statutes, etc.); as one of its key leaders, Viktor Grinevich, noted, the Central Bureau could do little else given that repression deprived organizers of the opportunity for any broad-based agitation among the rank and file.[35] But focusing on what was called the "internal organization" of a union proved consistently problematic for Mensheviks, for as we shall observe below, such an approach regularly drew activists away from the mass and from the project of grassroots organizing in the factories.

With the publication of the "Temporary Regulations on Unions and Societies" in early March, however, more open activity became possible. Several district initiative groups arose and with the help of party activists and the Central Bureau they were brought together. But while union activists clearly hoped that the bonds between the districts might be strengthened, it soon became obvious that metalworkers were deeply divided over whether a centralized, citywide industrial organization should be created or if one based in the separate districts and united on federative principles was more appropriate to their needs.[36] Also troublesome was the question of union dues. While supporting "in principle" fees based on a percentage of earnings, worker activists nonetheless moved to establish a fixed rate of 25 kopecks. At the same time a proposal to set dues by grade (e.g., less for apprentices and the unskilled) was rejected.[37] There was, too, the persistence of numerous craft-based unions within the ranks of metalworkers, as well as the competing claims of other trades within the major metalworking plants.[38]

TABLE 6.1
Movement of Membership by District
June 1 to July 15, 1906

District	To June 1	To June 15	To July 1	To July 15
Gorodskoi	102	308	536	991
Moskovskii	—	235	235	480
Narvskii	106	136	430	650
Vasileostrov	89	120	500	523
Peterburg	128	150	650	900
Vyborg	100	700	1,430	2,500
Nevskii	300	476	2,480	3,500
Totals	885	2,125	6,261	9,544

Source: Bulkin, *Na zare*, p. 151.

These issues, which highlighted the differing skills, wage levels and alle-giances of metalworkers and which threatened to undercut class-based soli-darities, had scarely been resolved when the *gradonachal'nik* released a curiously contradictory ruling: district gatherings to discuss and formulate the basic structure of the union could not be held prior to the full legalization of the union. Thus constrained, a group of metalworkers submitted to the authorities on April 11 the model statutes worked out by the Central Bureau. On April 30 at Dom Panina, with some 2,000 in attendance, the founding congress of the Petersburg Metalworkers' Union got underway.[39]

The debate between "centralists" and "federalists" occupied much of the meeting. Those who spoke for a district-based union, each with its own governing board and treasury, stressed that such an organization would be closer to the rank and file and enjoy greater mass confidence. While this position was in a minority and while a centralized structure was agreed on in principle, union development in the next months was nonetheless charac-terized by substantial district autonomy. Thus, the temporary governing board that the congress elected was chosen on the basis of three representa-tives from each district and not elected by the membership voting as a whole. As importantly, the districts secured effective control over union funds: 25% of the incoming revenues went to the districts, 25% to the center, and the remaining 50%, which constituted the strike fund, was also administered by the districts.[40]

Despite persistent organizational problems, the union began to grow. By mid-July, as Tables 6.1 and 6.2 indicate, the union boasted some 9,500 mem-bers, which nonetheless represented only about 12% of the work force in the

TABLE 6.2
Movement of Membership at the Largest Factories
June 1 to July 15, 1906

Factory	# of Workers	# of Members	% Organized
Nevskii	5,300	1,380	26.0
Obukhov	4,900	1,268	25.9
Aleksandrovsk	1,890	569	31.1
Putilov	11,700	515	4.4
SPb Metals	2,100	416	19.8
Baltic	5,050	275	5.4
Franco-Russian	3,500	209	6.0
Nobel	840	206	24.5
SPb Pipe (Trubochnyi)	6,200	170	2.8
SPb Freight Car	2,300	160	7.0
Totals	43,680	5,168	11.8

Source: Bulkin, *Na zare*, p. 152.

industry. In comparison with other important segments of the capital's labor movement, this was not an impressive figure; Petersburg printers, for example, had been able to organize 55% of their comrades.[41] Moreover, most members came from a handful of mixed-production giants, while more than a third (36.7%) came from Nevskii district. Indeed, one-third (33.7%) of the membership was concentrated in the "big three" factories of this district.[42] A union resting on such a narrow base was obviously problematic; but perhaps most troubling of all was the curious fact that district patriotism and craft particularism had its strongest reflection in the Nevskii district, that bastion of metalworker protest and the long-time focal point of Social Democratic work. It was here, for example, that the leading local unionists argued that the district-based delegate council should become the leading organ of the union, with the central governing board serving simply as its executive arm.[43] And it was this district that put up the strongest resistance to a unified fund managed by central institutions: only after the complete collapse of militant labor protest in the spring of 1908 did the Nevtsy finally agree to subordinate themselves to the center on this issue.[44]

Other problems bedeviled the union in these early months in addition to the narrowness of its membership base and the strong localist allegiances of its largest section. At times, union activists found themselves struggling against the Council of the Unemployed. Trying to build its stature among the rank and file, the union recognized the need to render assistance to the jobless, but also worried about the harmful effects of collections carried out in individual factories, which deprived the union itself of funds and strengthened "factory patriotism."[45] The Council, however, argued that help to the unemployed should not be rendered by each union individually, but must be organized in general, so as not to undermine class solidarity. The Council therefore asked the Metalworkers' Union to delegate its own representative and to participate in joint work. But from the union's point of view, organizing aid to the unemployed had to be done in such a way as to join the membership as a whole more tightly together and to demonstrate that the union was responsive to the material needs of its membership. These divergent views led to an "unpleasant clash" between the Council and the union. But perhaps more importantly, precisely because the need was so great in metalworking, the union lacked the resources to provide assistance to all; it therefore retreated to a position of granting benefits only to its members, and hence promoted rather than mitigated differences among metalworkers.[46]

Still more difficult were the battles with employers. During the summer of 1906 strikes broke out in a number of mid-sized machine-construction factories. These were important conflicts, not least because they entailed an effort on the part of the Petersburg Society of Mill and Factory Owners (henceforth PSMFO) to break the union. But these strikes typically began without the authorization, and in some cases, without the knowledge, of the union. In at least one case, jurisdictional squabbles between competing unions led to disastrous consequences. And in all cases where the union was involved, not only did the PSMFO refuse to recognize the union's right to represent workers, but the strikes ended in defeat or in extremely modest concessions.[47] In its first engagement in the strike struggle, therefore, the union did not fair well: it failed to establish its legitimacy in the eyes of the rank and file and was unable to secure the recognition of employers.

These strikes, as well as the continuing organizational battles between the center and the districts, remained unresolved when political events once again overtook the union: on July 9, Russia's first elective legislature was dispersed. Over the next several weeks scores of trade unions were closed, press censorship was vigorously carried out, martial law was imposed in the cities, and summary justice was meted out in the rebellious provinces by hastily created field court martials. Thus began the era of Petr Stolypin, who while retaining the post of Minister of Internal Affairs, assumed the chairmanship of the Council of Ministers.

On July 28, 1906, the Petersburg Metalworkers' Union was closed. While it continued to maintain a semilegal existence, increasing police repression furthered disintegrative tendencies apparent from the outset. Since repression fell most heavily on the union's governing board and central institutions, some of the locals were still able to continue their activity. The consequence of this interference was to break the union up into a few independent branches, to make still more complex the relations between the center and the districts, and to compound the difficulties of articulating policies for the union as a whole. Police and government intervention, in short, tended to reinforce the already pronounced pattern of factory and district "patriotism."

Looking back on this exceptionally difficult period, union activists recalled the litany of problems which they faced: organizational disarray, unemployment and economic crisis, police harassment, bitter factional dissension within their own ranks, and employer intransigence. Informing these accounts of the early period, moreover, was both a self-perception of weakness and an underlying anxiety over the issue of particularistic loyalties.[48] Thus the union's own history, written in 1909, stressed that

> as always, the dead seize the living. Factory and district patriotism weakened, but did not disappear. The absence of habits of joint work within the framework of a broad democratic organization—habits which only experience provides—engendered even among advanced workers a distrust in the union leadership, a fear that the union would degenerate into a bureaucratic apparatus which would crush any initiative from below. Comrades searched for salvation from this imagined danger in the preservation of the greatest possible independence, the broadest autonomy for the districts. It was necessary to struggle with these conservative strivings, but at the same time one had to take them into consideration. *The struggle for centralization*, a struggle both heretofore and still incomplete, characterizes the first period of union life.[49]

Indeed, so uncomfortable with this phenomenon were the union's historians that they chose to describe late 1906 and early 1907 as a period of "district anarchism," a time when the authority of the central board was largely ignored and viewed as "superfluous," a period in which strike leadership remained in the districts as did control of union funds. Over the course of these distressing months, the "obligatory resolutions" of the board were variously interpreted and implemented, while legal assistance, grants in aid, even bookkeeping was centered in the districts and varied widely from one branch to the next.[50]

Important in all this was the realization that a principal cause of union weakness was craft particularism and district patriotism. But coming to terms with this *tsekhovshchina* proved deeply perplexing, since these "conservative strivings" were displayed by "advanced workers." Said somewhat differently, union organizers were faced with the dilemma that the most militant, the most "conscious" metalworkers of the 1905 period—those who worked in the state-owned, mixed-production giants of the Nevskii district, as well as workers of similar type elsewhere—proved to be the most attached to allegiances built on craft and district lines, loyalties which union activists believed were antithetical to the project of industrial unionism and demonstrative of a distressingly "primitive" level of working-class consciousness.

The paradox resided in the specificity of the transitional moment of 1905–1907, for as a consequence of the struggles of the fall of 1905, as well as the resurgence of oppositional activity and its suppression in the period of the First Duma, the process of class formation was pushed in new directions. At this juncture the ambiguous social identity of the "Nevskii-type" worker came into sharper focus, while at the same time it became clear that the struggles of the recent past had drawn into the labor movement different segments of the work force in heavy industry. Politicized by their experiences, these cadres not only made an industrial trade unionism objectively possible, but contributed to a process of class reformation which ultimately posited a broader and more inclusive definition of class than that which was permitted by the greater particularism of the "conscious" metalworker of an earlier period. Integral to this process of class reformation was the sharper perception of the class antagonist which emerged in the wake of the November lockout and which became more refined during the second phase of the 1905 revolution.

If we look again at the "special worlds" of the Nevskii, Obukhov, Putilov, and Baltic factories, we will see they were just that—special, by definition unique, and hence not attuned to broader commonalities.[51] Because of their large size and geographic setting, these factory giants so dominated the surrounding area that they appeared to define "the world" in a way evocative of the peasant "mir." The "Nevskii-type" metalworker was a denizen of this "special world," and his identity was shaped by it. Even more fundamentally, his sense of self was built on a proud acquisition of skill, a good wage, literacy, and a more fully cultured life, qualities which contributed to his sense of dignity and self-worth and allowed him to join in a multi-class liberation movement, but which also distinguished him from other less accomplished and less cultured workers. These distinctive characteristics gave rise to an exclusivist attitude which was captured in a conversation recorded by Petr Garvi with Pavel Kolokolnikov in March 1906 as they rode a tram from the central city out to Nevskii district.

> —Yes,—said Pavel Nikolaevich thoughtfully,—Moscow workers are duller [*poseree*] than Petersburg workers. Nevertheless, workers of state factories are their own sort of worker aristocracy. They even take offense, or more precisely, they first and foremost take offense when they are called workers [*rabochie*]: "we are skilled workers [*masterovye*] and not common laborers [*rabochie*]." For them, unskilled workers [*chernorabochie*] are called workers [*rabochie*].[52]

Thus as Kolokolnikov perceived, and notwithstanding all the activism of skilled metalworkers at the state plants since the turn of the century, they were not yet secure enough in their proletarian identity to let go of older distinctions based on craft. Garvi captured this ambivalence in another way, describing the Obukhov worker Vasia Sokolov.

> He was not religious, but in the corner "for his wife" hung icons, and the gastronomic parts of church holidays were observed unswervingly: bliny with sweet butter, *kulychi* for Easter, and, of course, a good drunk [*vypivka*]. He lived comfortably, like the majority of skilled workers of the state Obukhov plant. He made 150–200 rubles a month, but when urgent work was given out with

premiums (on the "American" system) he could "pull off" up to 250 rubles. For holidays he had a good fur coat with a beaver collar and even a black frock suit [*siurtuchnaia para*] for trips to the city for public meetings or the theater. If for a textile worker somewhere in Tver province the sign of an association with culture [*priobshcheniia k kul'ture*] was brand new galoshes in the summer heat, then for the worker aristocracy of Petersburg it was to be dressed, characteristically, as the intelligentsia would dress, not for a visit to the district, that is in a Russian blouse and cloth cap, but for oneself—in public places, at evening parties, at the theater. Vasia Sokolov did not see in this a sign of "being bourgeois": he was always ready to go to prison for the workers' cause; he wanted to live not a wealthy life but a cultured life, as did the *intelligenty* with whom he was acquainted. The visits of the party intelligentsia with leading workers called forth in them an imitation of cultured habits of life, beginning with dress. Domestic life—like that at Sokolov's—remained nonetheless semi-peasant.[53]

Vasia Sokolov, married with children and living on the top floor of a wooden house in the village of Aleksandrovsk, conceived himself a fighter for the workers' cause, but combined within this representation aspirations to the intelligentsia as well as lingering attachments to a peasant past. To the degree that industrial trade unionism, indeed Social Democracy more broadly, sought to submerge these ambivalent social conceptions and to advance instead the vision of a common proletarian identity, then the organized labor movement was bound to challenge crucial elements of self-definition that had been built up over the previous decades among "conscious" metalworkers like Sokolov and hence undercut rather than strengthen the unionization effort. For both the self-esteem and the leadership role which was the product of a mastery of skill, literacy, and the adaptation to urban life and which stood at the center of the social identity of this sort of worker had historically depended on the absence of a mass labor movement, and on the still largely "protocapitalist" industrial development of the pre-1905 period. The events of the recent past had begun to change all this: vast new segments of the working class had been drawn into the struggle over the course of 1905–1907 and had been politicized by their experiences; economic crisis, unemployment and the changing nature of work in heavy industry had begun to alter work force composition; new working-class organizations had begun to forge different bases of solidarity than those that had pertained in the period of *kruzhkovshchina*; and, far more clearly than in the past, all sorts of metalworkers had experienced an intense and sustained clash with their employers.

These recent experiences began to generate new conceptions of working-class life and behavior. In this transitional moment, the relative valences between skilled, craft metalworkers and metalworkers of various types had not been sorted out; nor had activists come to an understanding of the ways in which the terms of struggle had begun to change on the shop floor in the aftermath of the "days of freedom"; nor had anyone seriously confronted the latent generational conflict emerging at this juncture.[54] In this context, some workers—exhausted and demoralized by the struggles of 1905—proved unable or unwilling to sustain an active commitment to the project of trade unionism; other workers, radicalized by the bruising experiences of 1906–1907, never embraced such a project. What emerges, however, is that the weakness of the union in its first phase of development might best be explained by the shifting and sometimes competing identities of metalworkers in a time of profound flux.[55]

Strike Conflict in the Summer of 1906

The oppositional mood that was apparent in the mobilization surrounding the Council of the Unemployed and the Metalworkers' Union in March and April 1906 increased over the course of the spring. In the highly charged atmosphere that accompanied the opening of the State Duma, the disaffection of labor found reflection in major May Day demonstrations, as well as in a resurgence of overt conflict on the shop floor. Strikes were called by segments of the labor force heretofore relatively uninvolved—bakery and candy workers, shoemakers, dock workers, tobacco workers—and by June, metalworkers, too, were mounting work stoppages at selected factories.[56]

Tension in the shops was manifested in other ways. Over the course of the spring a variety of "wheelbarrow incidents" occurred or were threatened, as hated foremen and other lower-level supervisory personnel were carted out of the shops in a ritual designed to humiliate the offenders.[57] Shop floor conflict was also expressed in a purge of the Black Hundreds. In a rite filled with righteous condemnation but also healing redemption, members of Black Hundred organizations were stripped of their insignia and weapons, forced to beg forgiveness for their disgraceful actions, and punished for their uncomradely behavior, sometimes in the form of a fine levied in support of the unemployed. Instructed in such a way as to what was proper proletarian conduct, these former transgressors were then readmitted to the fellowship of the working class.[58] Symbolically, by virtue of rituals designed to disgrace and disempower, and in fact, by the removal of hated personnel, threatening weapons, and offensive insignia, workers laid claim to the shop as their own turf.[59]

In important respects, the strikes that broke out in five mid-sized machine-construction factories in the June-August period reflected a similar struggle over "turf," that is, struggles to exert worker control over aspects of the work process and life on the shop floor that management had sought to alter or contest.[60] While none of these strikes raised overtly political demands—absent was a call for a constituent assembly or basic civil rights[61]—each was deeply infused with issues of power and authority and approached "politics" in a new way: politics at the point of production.

Strikes at the Erikson Telephone Factory and the Atlas Engineering Works began with clashes over issues of hiring and firing. In both cases, workers attempted to cart out offensive personnel; management forthwith fired the culprits, but workers immediately responded by imposing a boycott on the jobs of their dismissed comrades. Unable to replace the needed workers and thereby get out the work, the Erikson management imposed a partial layoff, while Atlas announced a complete shutdown.[62]

At Erikson, the partial layoffs were met by several decisive actions. The first was to refuse all piecework and while working on shop pay (*po tsekhu*) to deliberately slow output. Second, a partial strike was called in the assembly, warehouse, and packing shops, the point being to block the shipment of finished goods. Those workers slated for dismissal also began a work slowdown, utilizing the mandatory two-week notification period to inflict losses on the factory. Workers simply walked around, talked, played cards, and generally "wasted time." Eriksontsy also called upon the Woodworkers' Union and Metalworkers' Union for help.[63]

With the formation of a strike committee, a further set of demands was developed. These included a nine-hour workday with an hour and a half for lunch, a demand to replace hourly with daily shop pay and to pay wages on Saturday as a full day, to issue wages during working time, to hang a table of rates on piecework in the shops, to pay for strike time, and a pledge that no one would be punished for the strike.[64]

At Atlas, the announcement of a shutdown was also met by a "go-slow" action during the two-week notification period. Here, too, workers turned to the union. Frustrated by these actions, the administration closed the factory a few days prior to the expiration of the notification period. Workers now imposed a boycott on all jobs and work; a picket line was set up, blocking employee access and repeatedly preventing the shipment of goods. Again with the strike in full progress, workers articulated further demands: a reduction of the workday from ten and one-half to nine hours, daily in place of hourly shop pay, several specific wage demands, including one for a general increase of 30% in rates and base pay, recognition of a grievance committee, abolition of fines and overtime, and polite forms of address.[65]

Conflicts at the Kreiton Shipyards, Langenzipen and Company, and the Lemmerikh Engineering Factory similarly turned on issues of hiring and firing, pay cuts and attempts by workers to intervene in the determination of wage policies, and managerial efforts to intensify the work process. At Kreiton, workers contested the actions of a particular foreman and the way in which he set the conditions for wage payment as a particular job neared completion.[66] At Langenzipen, workers experienced a steady decline in rates and wages and an increase in fines; when they sought to participate in wage determination, their representative was summarily dismissed by management.[67] At Lemmerikh, workers' demands suggested resistance to a speedup: they stipulated that work should only be on one machine tool at a time, that the number of unskilled workers should be increased on certain jobs, and that the traditional Saturday half-holiday be paid as a full day. They also sought specific wage and rate increases, as well as worker agreement with foremen in determining rates.[68]

Taken as a whole, these conflicts were essentially defensive in nature: to protest "unfair" treatment or cuts in wages, or to reverse changes in the forms and methods of remuneration that worked to labor's disadvantage. In seeking to block the shift to hourly in place of daily shop pay and to retain full payment for the Saturday half-holiday when work ended at 2 or 3 in the afternoon (and by implication, the many pre-holidays that occurred over the course of the year), workers tried not only to maintain former levels of earning, but to forestall important changes in wage policy intended by management to recoup some of the economic losses of 1905 and to instill in workers a greater sense of time discipline. But workers also tried to shape the social environment of the shop through interventions that removed personnel who had in some way wronged them and by demands for polite forms of address. At issue for workers was an insistence on dignified and humane treatment; for management, worker involvement in issues of hiring and firing, much less the carting out of supervisory personnel, again encroached on the effective rights of private property and threatened or in fact entailed acts of violence against persons and property which were clearly illegal.

Control issues were also reflected in worker attempts to influence the pace of work by demanding the restoration of daily pay; by contesting a reduction in "extra" hands or the increase in workload which attended work on more than one machine tool at a time; by protesting overtime; or by worker efforts to engage management generally over the issue of time by demanding a reduction in hours. For management, the problem turned on gaining or regaining control over labor productivity, and at least in part, employers sought to do so by manipulating forms of remuneration. Like their counterparts at the state factories, they hoped to achieve a more disciplined and productive work force through such "capitalist" incentives to hard work as monetary inducement.[69] But in so doing, management was encroaching on what labor viewed as an acceptable—humane—pace of work.

Workers, furthermore, sought to press new institutional forms on management for the regulation of industrial relations: representation by the trade unions; the right to strike; grievance committees; and worker participation in wage determination. At issue was labor's newly won right to strike and form trade unions and the ways in which management now felt compelled to reframe and modify these rights. Important here was the effort of employers to expand the legal definition of *force majeure* to include the right to close the factory immediately, without obligation to pay workers for the two-week notification period when the *possibility* of violence against person and/or property existed. This was a very broad definition indeed of an "act of God" and reflected how hesitant employers were to accept the "liberal" approach to labor relations articulated in some government circles between late 1905 and early 1906. Moreover, employers insured that their arguments were voiced at the Senate level (and hence received a more conservative hearing) by filing legal suits for large compensatory damages. The blatancy of this action was not lost on labor.[70]

Central as well to an understanding of these struggles was the fact that labor and management confronted each other for the first time as organized social forces, in the form of the PSMFO and the Petersburg Metalworkers' Union. And doubtless in part because of the still unstable political environment in the spring and summer of 1906, each organization confused perception and reality in its respective evaluations of the strength, cohesion, and resources of the other side. Just as labor focused on the proliferation of employer organizations, their mobilization at the time of the November lockouts, and such ostensibly united and powerful national coalitions of businessmen as the Association of Industry and Trade, employers shuddered at the multiplication of worker organizations, the emergence of a Central Bureau of Trade Unions, and the unionization of some 9,500 "militant" metalworkers in the space of just three months.

In fact these summer conflicts revealed significant internal weaknesses and a quite notable lack of unity.[71] Nonetheless, both sides displayed a readiness to represent the antagonist as conscious of its class interests, coherently organized in pursuit of its goals and politically aggrandizing. Thus the PSMFO's facile identification of the "so-called trade unions" with militant organizations "pursuing revolutionary goals" and its consistent refusal to accept the unions as legitimate bargaining agents for "their" workers became central points in employer argumentation and practice.[72] Hence, too, the tendency of both labor and management to cast the conflict in absolute terms—in terms of the "principles" at stake—which encouraged each to fight with intransigence and to reject compromise out of hand. In the end, organizational forms that carried the potential to pursue conflict resolution by means of negotiated compromise settlements were constructed instead to advance confrontational positions.

The summer strikes therefore tended to generate new methods of struggle—work slowdowns, boycotts on jobs and work orders, pickets, and work stoppages in selected shops.[73] These tactics depended on high degrees of labor solidarity and on a willingness to manipulate consciously their knowledge of and control over the process of production. Employers saw in such tactics a deliberation and intentionality heretofore absent in labor protest; and they now asserted that such tactically sophisticated methods had little in common with the spontaneous, elemental nature of labor protest they judged characteristic of the previous year.[74]

The new and threatening tactics of labor, in turn, helped push employers and the PSMFO into an aggressive campaign to break the strikes and the union by means of blacklists and lockouts, strikebreakers and police, attempts to manipulate the judicial process, as well as tendentious appeals to Stolypin. At issue from industry's point of view was a defense of private property,[75] the corrosive effects of the revolutionary actions of "working-class leaders" on the mass, and the financial viability of their enterprises, indeed the well-being of industry as a whole.[76] By invoking images of anarchy, the collapse of industry, and the perilous consequences of an enormous army of unemployed workers far larger than the impoverished mass that currently existed, employers pleaded with the government to recognize the challenge it confronted.

What begins to emerge at this juncture is yet another aspect of the trauma experienced by Petersburg employers over the spring and summer of 1906. However fundamental the issues of worker control and the institutional matrix for labor-management relations, these concerns were ultimately transcended by the ways in which the summer conflicts threatened management's notions of what constituted appropriate and legitimate behaviors for workers. Here, in short, was another expression of that profound social fear gripping "society" as a whole in 1906, but played out in the specific context of labor relations within the metalworking industry at a difficult transitional moment when both workers and managers were endeavoring to understand the changing terms of struggle. Thus it became increasingly imperative for employers to articulate how behavior on the shop floor was inimical to social order, to somehow specify the difference between "legitimate" economic grievances, revolutionary manifestations, and what had occurred over the past two years.

They began by arguing that something had indeed changed. Dating the "new phase" in the workers movement from mid-April and specifically locating its expression at four machine-construction factories (Erikson, Lemmerikh, Atlas, Kreiton), employers noted that the current conflicts usually began with incidents involving violence against supervisory personnel and asserted that the strikes—and especially the new tactics—represented an attempt by worker leaders to regain influence over the working-class movement that had been lost since the failure of the eight-hour-day strikes in the fall. In no way revealing that specific policy changes enacted by management had contributed significantly to the outbreak of the strikes or that employer behavior had altered in any way, the PSMFO charged that working-class leaders "intentionally" launched strikes at carefully chosen factories selected on the basis of size and geographic location, and raised "deliberately" excessive demands that the respective managements could not fulfill.[77] At issue, it seems, was the very fact of organization, intentionality, "consciousness," if you will. Workers seemed "to know" what they were doing; and, in employers' eyes, the purpose was to shatter industry and thereby bring down the entire social edifice.

> With iron consistency the leaders of the workers' movement are pushing toward this [the collapse of industry and the creation of a revolutionary army of impoverished unemployed], and the whole question consists in whether or not the factories and plants can hold out until the renewal [*obnovlenie*] of state life and the cessation of anarchy.[78]

In this apocalyptic vision, "rational" assessments of the costs of labor's demands were less the issue than social control, particularly given the

charged atmosphere of 1906 when accepted norms of authority and legitimacy seemed to be crumbling. For, as the PSMFO noted with considerable
alarm, what *was* to happen if workers could commit acts of terror with
seeming impunity when the capital was under a state of emergency
(*chrezvychainaia okhrana*)?[79] In this context, therefore, the assault on supervisory personnel and the insistence on polite forms of address took on added
point. Demands for respectful treatment illustrated quite literally labor's
"coming of age"—its rejection of relations of subordination and the in-
fantilization that the continued use of *ty* (thou) implied. And in ways that
must have seemed wholly unnerving to management, workers lashed out at
formerly authoritative figures. Thus with a palpable sense of affront, a top
executive at Langenzipen wrote to the PSMFO in July: ". . . from our side,
they [the workers] were informed that 'demands,' as well as participation of
representatives from them, would not be recognized by us; moreover, we
fixed for dismissal one of the workers conducting himself especially im-
pertinently [*derzko*]."[80]

Just as surely as management would countenance no "demands" and no
worker participation in wage determination, it would abide no impudence
on the part of a worker. Incensed and threatened by the "insolence and bad
conduct" of workers, managers thus equated (and confused) labor's assault
on their own particular notions of authority and legitimacy with any and all
organized and/or collective expressions of labor's grievances.[81] Similarly, the
PSMFO repeatedly equated worker tactics with acts of "terror," and then
argued that the government had to provide effective protection for the factories as well as legal status for their employer organization. Only in this way
might industry "hold out" until "state life" was restored and anarchy
quelled.[82]

But employer "organization" remained an elusive goal in the summer of
1906. Unnerved by the test of strength in which they were now engaged,
employers displayed a hesitancy and self-doubt that undercut the project of
class organization. Consider the rather panicked plea for help written by the
director of the Atlas factory, A. F. German, to E. L. Nobel, a prime mover of
the PSMFO, on July 24.[83] Frustrated by the substantial losses suffered by the
factory and the failure of either the PSMFO or the authorities to render
sufficient assistance, German revealed his reluctance to implement a policy
of blacklisting lest the factory incur still further losses. Arguing that Atlas
was fully aware of the principled significance of the conflict, and had fought
it with determination because the outcome could well influence the future
standing of both sides, the administration nonetheless asserted that the task
it had assumed was too difficult. Workers had mounted a strong, fully
organized resistance; the police had failed to protect the factory; the firm
was under enormous pressure from its customers; the administration's allies
had not provided serious support. Given all this, German felt it impossible
to continue with its policy of repression and specifically the circulation of
blacklists. Moreover, the Atlas administration felt there was little recourse

but to enter into negotiations with the Metalworkers' Union. Fully cognizant of the implications of this step, the letter concluded that the factory would like to receive the approval of the PSMFO before taking such action, and added that, if required, it would honor its obligation to supply a list of its workers to the Society.[84]

The Lemmerikh administration betrayed similar anxiety. On August 23—after the resumption of work at the factory—management asked the PSMFO not to require a list of its workers in conformity with the recent resolution on blacklisting. The Society responded by saying that the issue did not concern Lemmerikh alone, but was a principled issue affecting the industry as a whole: it was important to show workers that industrialists would resist the workers' boycott by an organized boycott of its own. Several days later the Lemmerikh management complied, but asked that the list not be circulated until further discussion of the issue.[85]

The sense of weakness on the part of individual plant administrations, and the perceived need to cajole its members into united action on the part of the PSMFO, reflected the insecurities of the times, but also the limits of "class consciousness" in the summer of 1906. In these cases, the PSMFO was "out in front" of its membership, pushing it to stand firm on "principles" important to industry as a whole. Some wavered, and as they did their ambivalence revealed the "need" for an employer organization, but also the underlying uncertainty as to how to pursue the interests of industry at this juncture.

Metalworkers and their union were no less uncertain. For as much as one may appreciate the fears a union uniting thousands of metalworkers conjured up in the minds of employers or the way in which Petersburg "society" was haunted by lingering images of unemployed "mobs," limits on working-class strength and cohesion in the summer of 1906 were also readily apparent. Barely two months old and in a context of high unemployment, the Metalworkers' Union was drawn into five important strike conflicts which it lacked the financial resources and requisite experience to fight. In the midst of these conflicts, moreover, the union was closed down and what leadership and support it offered was provided through the district branches. But even more crippling than such "objective" factors as police harassment and financial constraint were the internal limits imposed by a membership still incompletely committed to the project of trade unionism.

Thus at Erikson and Atlas, workers turned to the union only after the strike was in full progress. Uninvolved at the outset, the union was largely confronted with a *fait accompli* and had to assume a responsible role too late in the developing conflict. Moreover, a failure to coordinate actions with the Woodworkers' Union in the Erikson strike contributed to the devastating defeat there. Very much in response to these unsettling realities, the union passed an important resolution in September—a sort of post mortem on the summer experiences—stating that it would offer material aid to strikes only when it was informed of the causes, judged the issues worthy of struggle, and itself took on strike leadership; the union henceforth would not support strikes called without its knowledge and approval.[86] But there was more than inexperience bedeviling the union.

Suggestive of the deeper problems of union organization in the summer of 1906 was the specific experience of Atlas workers. Atlas was located in the Nevskii district, where the union branch was dominated by workers from the Obukhov, Nevskii, and Aleksandrovsk factories. The organizational bureau for the district was composed entirely of workers from these factories; likewise, the membership of the district was overwhelmingly drawn from the "big three." Then, too, noted Garvi, the union tended to appeal to the "upper strata" of metalworkers in Nevskii district, while the "broad mass of metalworkers were not as yet psychologically prepared to enter the union."[87] And yet at a meeting called by Atlas workers on June 21 to discuss the union, the majority agreed to join: a few days later some 200 Atlas workers had registered.[88] The numerical dominance of the "big three" in the union, and a somewhat condescending attitude on the part of some *praktiki* to the "broad mass," may well explain the judgment subsequently reported by Bulkin that "the [Nevskii] branch took up leadership [of the Atlas strike] too sluggishly, limit[ed] itself only to financial support, and even that in insignificant dimensions."[89] Focused on the needs and concerns of one segment of the work force and perhaps diverted by the "larger" political issues surrounding the Duma, the local union leadership in Nevskii district and elsewhere may well have been insufficiently sensitive to the interests of workers like those struggling at the Atlas factory in the summer of 1906.[90]

In the end, metalworkers and their union again took away from the summer strikes the experience of defeat. In hard fought conflicts stretching upwards of two months, workers suffered complete failure or secured extremely modest concessions.[91] And in these defeats was the shape of things to come: unlike the settlements of 1905, in which concessions were made by management and compromise decisions were reached, the summer strikes of 1906 were almost without exception victories for employers and thereby foreshadowed the strike outcomes of the 1912–14 period. Similarly, to the degree that the summer strikes turned on issues of worker control they marked the first effort to resist changes in the organization of work adopted by management in the wake of the "days of freedom." In 1906, as well as subsequently, the engagement of these issues primarily by workers at mid-sized machine-construction factories signaled the waning leadership of the "Nevskii type" metalworker and the opening of a new phase of struggle, which brought to the fore a different sort of metalworker fighting a different sort of battle. By the same token, these strikes impelled employers to evolve strategies which might secure their effective control over production processes all too vulnerable to the machinations of labor and enhance their mastery over industrial relations all too exposed to the vagaries of autocratic power.

Social Democracy and the Dilemmas of
"Bourgeois" Revolution in Russia

The disarray besetting labor at the outset of 1906 was compounded by the divisive struggles within the Social Democratic movement. The defeats of December quickly dissolved into mutual accusations of failed strategies and adventurist leadership, but also revealed anew the fundamentally different conceptions of Menshevism and Bolshevism regarding the possibilities of the current revolution as well as the relationship of party to mass. During the heady days of 1905, many rank and file Social Democrats had pressed for the reunification of the party and plans had been laid for the Fourth (Unity) Congress of the Russian Social Democratic Labor Party to be held in Stockholm in early April 1906. But before it could convene, discord replaced the apparent harmony of the fall. At issue was the question of participation in the elections to the First Duma. More generally, however, were the very real differences that divided leading Mensheviks and Bolsheviks in their conception of the "bourgeois" revolution: how would it occur in the Russian context, what alliances should be made with the bourgeoisie, and what role would be played by the Duma?

Lenin had long been a harsh critic of Russian liberalism, asserting early on that the bourgeoisie would be unable to play the requisite role in overthrowing autocracy and establishing a democratic regime. But since the fall of 1904, his critique became sharper still. By June-July 1905, he had arrived at a fundamentally new conception of the bourgeois revolution in Russia, one in which the hegemony of the proletariat would be maintained and in which the tasks of the democratic revolution would be completed by an alliance between the working class and peasantry. Drawing a sharp distinction between the "big bourgeoisie" and the petty bourgeois peasantry, and judging the former to be totally unreliable and retrograde, he railed against any alliances with this section of the Russian bourgeoisie, and pressed instead for a "revolutionary democratic dictatorship of the proletariat and peasantry."[92]

With the October Manifesto and the struggles of the fall of 1905, Lenin's critique only deepened: the liberals had accepted the Tsar's counterfeit legislature and the response of the working class must be to reject the Duma and the elections to it, lest any "constitutional illusions" be nourished. Moreover, Lenin embraced the radicalism of the late fall and applauded the heroism of the December militants, seeing in these experiences a critical phase in the ongoing evolution of a specifically working-class consciousness. Perhaps most important for Petersburg metalworkers, Lenin's attention to the conflict between labor and capital reflected concretely the punishing lesson workers had just received at the hands of the "big bourgeoisie" during the November lockout. Many Bolsheviks thus embraced and legitimated the lived experience of the fall by seeking to clarify and deepen one of the constituent elements of the conflict on which it rested.

The leading voices of Menshevism, however, decried the adventurism of the "days of freedom" and called for realism and restraint. Now that a liberal party had emerged, it was appropriate for the working class to relinquish the leading role and to align with the liberals in pressing the common struggle against the autocracy. However restrictive the franchise and however vacillating the bourgeoisie, most Mensheviks argued, it was the task of the working class to exploit the Duma for agitational purposes and to foment conflict between the autocracy and the Duma, thereby continuing to deepen the revolution and to pave the way for the complete overthrow of the tsarist regime. But given the harsh lessons of November, a strategy premised on class accommodation seemed seriously out of joint with the acute labor-management conflict pertaining in St. Petersburg metalworking factories.

The differing theoretical assessments made by Bolsheviks and Mensheviks shaped their tactics and strategy in the second phase of the 1905 revolution. At a December 1905 conference of Bolsheviks in Tammerfors, it was decided to pursue an active boycott of the elections; and at an exceptionally acrimonous meeting in mid-February, the Petersburg Committee (dominated by Bolsheviks) confirmed this position. Mensheviks initially failed to agree on a general policy, and their first response was to leave the decision to local organizations; soon, however, most Mensheviks moved to a position in support of participation in the elections. Thus at the Fourth (Unity) Congress held in April 1906 and dominated by Mensheviks, it was decided to participate in the few remaining elections (namely those being held in the Caucasus) and that the SD deputies should then organize a fraction in the Duma. (Recognizing the agitational significance of the elections, Lenin now accepted this position.) For the leading lights of Menshevism, the boycott had been a foolhardy tactic born of the extremism of the late fall.[93]

How, then, should the boycott be evaluated? If the criterion for "success" was the degree to which workers refused participation in the elections, then the extreme parties scored an impressive victory, especially in the capital. In the workers' curia of St. Petersburg guberniia, 39% of the plants refused to participate; in the city, 49% of the enterprises rejected participation; while 70% of Petersburg's suburban plants refused. Moreover, where elections did take place, the full complement of workers typically chose not to turn out.[94] St. Petersburg workers thus seemed to embrace the critique presented by the radical parties: labor could gain little from a Duma whose electoral franchise was so skewed, nor could workers suppose that their interests would be defended by the liberal bourgeoisie. But the boycott tactic surely failed insofar as those worker deputies who were elected tended to be moderate or even conservative, since the more radically minded candidates had withdrawn from the process. Assessed in these terms, most radicals recognized their political error and hence were prepared to change course in the future.[95]

Ultimately, however, the significance of the elections in the workers' curia to both the First and Second Dumas (indeed, in the elections to all four Dumas) may well have had less to do with immediate politics than with the process of class formation, since the workers' sense of themselves as *workers* rather than as citizens of St. Petersburg or of the nation as a whole was magnified. According to the complex electoral law of December 11, 1905, the right of a worker to participate in the elections was premised not on his personal qualification or registration, but rather on the fact of his attachment to a particular factory or plant, specifically one at which he had worked for at least six months and one with a work force of at least fifty males. On the day of the election, workers were to gather in their factories and select their delegate(s). These delegates would then come together in a city assembly to select fifteen electors; these electors, in turn, went on to join with the electors from the urban curia (160 in number) to elect deputies for the Duma.[96]

While the place of employment might well have served in the eyes of tsarist officials as "the analogue of the village community,"[97] for workers, the factory—transformed as it now was by these officials into the venue for the first stage of a national electoral process—became in yet another way a site of class formation. Meeting on the familiar "turf" of the factory with "outsiders" formally excluded during the elections, workers would find little in this setting to encourage them to distinguish between "national" and class concerns. And since, in practice, employers routinely interfered to influence electoral outcomes, perceptions of the class-based nature of the national political process could only be enhanced.[98] Politics and a particular social identity were thus neatly linked in a multi-tiered electoral system which began in the shop and which at each subsequent stage (except the last) emphasized the distinctiveness of the worker as well as minimized the opportunity for discussion and association across class or *sosloviia* lines. Meeting in segregated groups provided little chance for one group to imbibe the discourse of another. Thus the worker remained a worker, not a citizen with other sources of identity beyond or in distinction to his identity at the workplace.[99]

In a certain sense, therefore, the curial electoral system may have effectively destroyed the "constitutional illusions" of both the St. Petersburg entrepreneurial elite and the metalworkers of the capital. The views of leading industrialists were totally submerged in the urban curia to the positions articulated by the Kadets and still more so in the Duma itself to agrarian interests. Workers, consigned to vote in a way that heightened their isolation and distinctiveness from the rest of urban society, indeed the nation as a whole, were nonetheless so numerically overwhelmed in both the urban curia and the Duma as to make participation in the legislative process appear wholly meaningless on anything other than a purely agitational level. In important ways, then, and most particularly when the parties of the left abandoned their boycott, the language of class became the only audible discourse in the workers' curia.

Whatever the assessment of the legitimacy or utility of the Duma, once convened, Russia's first legislative institution became the focal point of the political life of the nation and most particularly of the capital. From its very first session, relations between the Duma and government were marked by a confrontational style which placed the combatants on a collision course in very short order. Fresh from their electoral victory and aching for a fight, the Kadets led the Duma to respond to the Tsar's welcoming address by presenting a legislative program which challenged the recently promulgated Fundamental Laws and offered sweeping changes in Russia's agrarian relations. Offended by the temerity of the Duma, the government led by Prime Minister Goremykin responded with a dismissive rebuff, rejecting out of hand the Duma's legislative program. Goremykin's reply on May 13 provoked a firestorm of protest: the Duma swiftly voiced "no confidence" in the government and demanded a ministry responsible to itself. Thus within the first two weeks of its existence, relations between the government and the legislature had essentially broken down, leaving participants and observers alike in a tense political atmosphere anxiously awaiting the denouement.[100]

Petersburg workers responded with considerable interest to the debates and conflicts taking shape within the Duma; and at first the Mensheviks took the lead in trying to develop and deepen this interest by fostering ties between Duma deputies and workers. Thus Martov worked to form a Social Democratic fraction and then to craft its positions within the Duma, while other Mensheviks labored over the course of May to organize regular conferences between Petersburg workers and the SD fraction. Bolsheviks were somewhat slower to partake in this effort, reticent as they were about nourishing any "constitutional illusions" among the people; by mid-May, however, they recognized that the Mensheviks had seized an important opportunity for agitation, but perhaps more to the point, Bolsheviks now asserted with increasing urgency and clarity that the content of Menshevik agitation was antithetical to the proletarian cause. At this juncture, therefore, the bitter fractional strife developing over Social Democracy's attitude toward the Duma and the liberals deepened and was propelled still further by the conflict surrounding Goremykin's May 13 statement, the Duma's vote of "no confidence," and its demand for a responsible ministry.

The Mensheviks came out in support of the Duma majority and hence the demand for a Kadet ministry which it implied; the Bolsheviks stood firmly against. Nowhere was the fractional combat over this issue more intense than in Petersburg, with the Petersburg Committee dominated by Bolsheviks and led by Lenin, who battled openly with the Menshevik-controlled Central Committee and routinely defied its directives. At issue was the attitude of Social Democracy toward the nature and potentialities of parliamentary institutions, the posture of the SD fraction within the Duma, and the relationship of the SD fraction to the liberals. Said differently, the conflict Lenin saw developing within Russian Social Democracy turned on the emergence of a reformist politics. Critically important, therefore, was the articulation of a position regarding the Duma which sought not to work with the liberals or within the framework of the Duma in alleged pursuit of revolutionary goals, but rather to recognize that the Duma was "useless as a representative body," that it could not and would not articulate and defend popular demands, and that it only blocked the convocation of a constituent assembly. Just as importantly, Lenin argued, it must be recognized that the Kadets sought not the overthrow of the autocracy and the deepening of the revolution, but rather an accommodation with the old regime and a means by which to tame the revolution. Social Democracy, in short, could work within the Duma only in order to explode the illusions of those who believed revolutions could be fought and won by parliaments; revolutions were fought and won on the streets, by militant action and armed uprisings, not by virtue of parliamentary change or peaceful, evolutionary development.[101]

These fundamentally different theoretical perspectives shaped the tactical positions of Menshevism and Bolshevism once the autocracy moved against the Duma. On the morrow of July 9, Mensheviks called on workers to defend the legislature through strikes and demonstrations and thus advanced slogans "for the Duma." Bolsheviks, in contrast, urged workers not to squander their strength in partial protests or premature actions, but to conserve forces until the time of full-scale armed uprising. Moreover, they explicitly protested any formula built on a position "for the Duma." The immediate consequence of such divergent approaches was to preclude coordinated and decisive action in response to the Duma crisis. It was only following the uprisings in Kronstadt, Sveaborg, and Revel that Social Democrats called for a general strike to begin on July 21 in the capital; but given the two weeks of wrangling between Mensheviks and Bolsheviks over the goals and purposes of mass action at this juncture, as well as the inadequate preparation provided by the Menshevik Central Committee, the general strike failed to capture the support of many of Petersburg's most militant workers and certainly came too late to augment the actions of the mutinous sailors. By July 26, the strike had to be called off, with many Petersburg workers angered by the fiasco and the inept leadership provided by the Menshevik Central Committee.[102]

Meanwhile, Duma deputies, primarily Kadets, had responded to the dispersal order by earnestly issuing the so-called Vyborg Manifesto which called on the population to refuse to pay taxes or report for military duty until a new legislature was convened. The Manifesto was received with stunning silence. Thus, notwithstanding the considerable apprehension in the highest circles of government as to the consequences of proroguing the Duma, the moderate and radical opposition failed completely to deflect the assault of the autocracy. The drama surrounding the First Duma crisis and the social fear that pertained throughout the spring and early summer now began to subside.

The failure of Petersburg workers to rise in defense of the Duma was received with profound shock, even despair, in the leading councils of Menshevism. Seeing in this rebuff a demonstration of the distance which separated the party from the mass, the crisis of the First Duma was thus equally perceived as a crisis of Social Democracy. For the essential lesson of the July general strike seemed to be the chasm separating the Menshevik vision of revolution from the attitudes and capacities of Russian labor, or more precisely the terrible distance that continued to pertain between the underground, conspiratorial, and deeply contentious party and the broad, if still mostly "unconscious," mass of workers. At issue for the Mensheviks, however, was not so much that their vision of revolution had been shaken, but rather the reasons why the party had failed to break out of its conspiratorial, heavily intelligentsia-dominated structure and to develop instead a broadly based mass movement capable of purposive action. It was imperative, therefore, to address the issues of party reform. Out of the despair of the summer thus came renewed interest in Axelrod's notion of a workers' congress, as did the origins of what would soon be termed "liquidationism."[103] Focusing on party-mass relations, however, the summer crisis seemed considerably less jarring insofar as the Menshevik understanding of bourgeois revolution in Russia was concerned. Their experiences provoked no major reassessment of the notion of a "two-staged" process of revolutionary development, nor did they lead to any substantive change in Menshevik attitudes toward the Duma or the Kadets.[104]

Just as importantly, furthermore, developments since the late fall of 1905 seemed to define the limits of the possible for Mensheviks in wholly different ways than for Bolsheviks. Not only did *praktiki* like Garvi despair of the "political backwardness" of the mass,[105] but leading theoreticians of Menshevism like Martov worried about the seething hatreds bubbling up from below—the frightening reality of the pogroms and the unpardonable "excesses" of the *partizanshchina*.[106] This fear of unleashed hatreds was akin in some important respects to the social fear gripping eduated society and it was at least in part due to such emotionally charged perceptions that people like Martov became all the more wedded to a belief in the need for a substantial period of bourgeois democracy and capitalist development: Russia was not "objectively" prepared to go further.

For many Mensheviks, the fight in the summer of 1906 "should" have revolved around the Duma and the government, and workers "should" have aligned with the Duma majority in pursuit of "national" objectives. Instead, despaired Mensheviks, workers proved unable to respond to this task because they were politically backward or indifferent to events of national significance or frightened by the thought of new reprisals.[107]

And yet the subjective experience of labor in the second phase of the revolution pushed relentlessly against the "classic" boundaries of the bourgeois revolution.[108] Since the November lockout and the onset of mass unemployment, through the lessons of the boycott campaign and the clashes with the city duma over public works, with the defeats of the summer strikes and the closure of their union, metalworkers had been living through struggles which revealed concretely the class nature of the conflicts in which they were engaged. As a result of the specificity of the historical moment, a more fully class-conscious movement was beginning to emerge, even though the tasks of the bourgeois revolution remained woefully incomplete. In failing to appreciate fully this subjective experience of class struggle, Menshevik practice in the second period of the revolution began to diverge sharply from working-class reality. And so while Martov and others worked to "cool off" the overheated atmosphere and continued to insist on tactical alliances with the Kadets in the elections to the Second Duma, proletarian wrath seethed, finding outlet in "fighting detachments," "exes," and the maximalism of the Bolsheviks or SRs. And the more this outrage bubbled up, the more Mensheviks felt it imperative to tame it and sought to do so by building an open, mass, legal labor movement based on a disciplined and coherent notion of what in their view was relevant and "objectively" possible at a given historical juncture.

The elections in the workers' curia to the Second State Duma soon revealed, however, how discredited a politics of moderation was in the eyes of Petersburg labor by the winter of 1906–1907. Most important was the complete triumph of the radical left over the Kadets and the other "bourgeois" parties of the center and right. Liberalism had no appeal to the working class, editorialized *Rabochii po metallu*; "[w]orkers want not freedom for capitalist exploitation, but freedom for their struggle against it."[109] Just as revealing of working-class attitudes was the apparent strength demonstrated by the SRs, as well as the weakness of Menshevism, but the relative strength of Bolshevism when representatives of the respective factions stood in direct competition with SR candidates. These seemingly puzzling electoral outcomes had been most in evidence at the major mixed-production metalworking plants— the very bastions of the "conscious" metalworkers during the first phase of the 1905–1907 revolution.

The leading theorists of Menshevism and Bolshevism were quick to put forth interpretations of the weakness displayed by Social Democracy in the workers' curia of St. Petersburg. The Bolsheviks attributed SR success to the Menshevik position in support of an electoral alliance with the Kadets in the second round of the electoral process. Workers, argued Lenin, were pushed by Menshevik tactics into the arms of the SRs, who represented a more radical alternative.[110] Mensheviks searched for the socioeconomic determinants of working-class behavior. Unemployment and political reprisals had derailed the organized struggle, argued Martov, leaving "the middle type" (*seredniak*) to search for an escape from his unbearable life through sympathy with terror or dreams about a return to the land.[111]

Yet this fundamentally reductionist claim could not be confirmed or denied on the basis of hard evidence. While it was undoubtedly true that many skilled, urbanized, "conscious" metalworkers from the state plants had been fired, it was not demonstrably the case that those who remained had affective ties to the land or that such ties determined voting behavior.[112] The Menshevik position, in asserting that votes for the SRs reflected the rank and file's residual ties to the land and *consequently* their "backward" views, took little account of the politicizing experiences of 1905–1906 for large segments of the work force in heavy industry, the longer-term trends of urbanization and the rise of a hereditary proletariat in metalworking, or the ways in which the very meanings of "consciousness" may have begun to shift over the course of the first revolution. Nor is it possible, given the paucity of evidence as well as the particular structure of the electoral process, to determine either the numerical weight or the party allegiances of those skilled, urbanized, "conscious" metalworkers who continued to hold jobs in the major state plants or the ways in which the lingering parochialism of many such workers—the craft particularism and district patriotism of the "Nevskii-type"—might have influenced electoral outcomes.[113]

Yet it seems equally dangerous to posit that the relative strength of the most extreme parties (Bolsheviks and SRs) constituted the triumph of a "revolutionary" consciousness among significant segments of the Petersburg work force. The Bolshevik-SR vote most probably reflected the early stages of a profound process of radicalization, which was bound up with a sense of outrage and revulsion against the barely reconstituted authority of the post–October Manifesto state and the continuing prerogatives asserted by *obshchestvo* as against *narod*. The electoral outcomes may well represent the first clear signs of a rejection of the moderation of Menshevism, but they do not signify a wholehearted commitment to either the Bolshevik vision of socialist revolution or the SR vision of land and freedom. Working class attitudes and behaviors, as well as even nominal party affiliations, remained quite fluid.

With the elections in the worker curia over, the radical parties moved on to articulate positions regarding alliances in the next round of the electoral process. Here again, Bolsheviks and Mensheviks divided sharply, with Bolsheviks advocating an alliance with the SRs and Trudoviks, while the Mensheviks continued to insist on the danger of a rightist victory and hence the need for a bloc with the Kadets. Intense fractional fighting and much electoral campaigning defined the life of the radical left in the capital through January and well into February. In the end, two Bolshevik deputies were elected to the Second Duma, G. A. Aleksinskii from St. Petersburg city and Ivan Petrov from St. Petersburg guberniia.

However involved many workers became in these elections, nonetheless another reality increasingly intruded on life in the working-class districts. Not only did the massive layoffs continue and conditions in the factories worsen;[114] the cost of food began to rise precipitously, and as it did some workers began to sack the bakeries. By late February, activists were trying to organize around this issue and advocated pressure on the city duma to regulate prices on basic necessities as well as the development of municipal food cooperatives.[115] As with the mobilization surrounding unemployment, so now with the problem of bread prices, workers began to grapple with issues of fundamental concern to the community.

And yet events on the national level would again intervene to shape developments within the local community. For the Second Duma turned out to be more "leftist" in composition than the first, and within a few short months deadlock was reached with the government of Petr Stolypin. On June 3, 1907, the prime minister acted, suspending the Duma and promulgating a new electoral statute in specific contravention to the Fundamental Laws. With the launching of the Third of June system Russia's first revolution came to an end. As Stolypin turned to the reimposition of "law and order," a period of great political repression, as well as continued economic distress, took hold in the working-class districts of the capital.

The Formation and Reformation of Working-Class Identities in the 1905–1907 Period

The experience of intense political and economic conflict over the course of more than two years, the taste of freedom in the fall of 1905 and the despair of unemployment, arrest, and exile thereafter, and the repeated practice of collective action in pursuit of working-class demands were part of the legacy of 1905–1907 that came to inform the collective consciousness of Petersburg metalworkers. It was an experience that brought vast new segments of the work force in heavy industry into conflict both with the autocratic state and with a newly, if still incompletely mobilized, segment of the capital's industrial elite. And it was an experience that changed the terms of struggle on the shop floor just as surely as it reformed essential aspects of working-class identity. In consequence, both labor and management emerged from the first revolution with substantially different perceptions of "the other."

The particular events of this period made possible, in important respects, the rise of a more coherent, less fragmented conception of working-class identity within the heavy industry of the capital. Not only did loyalties to craft or district begin to fade by the end of the first revolution, but lingering attachments to a peasant past or ambiguous aspirations to join the intelligentsia attenuated as well. For it was no longer possible for many metalworkers "to go back" to the village, nor was it conceivable to follow the intelligentsia into that desperate spiritual and intellectual retreat that attended the imposition of Stolypin's Third of June regime. Moreover, in the aftermath of the "days of freedom," many "Nevskii-type" workers suffered such a withering assault as to remove them from participation in the labor movement of the capital: hundreds were arrested and exiled; thousands were thrown out of work. And in due time, the processes of industrial rationalization that were launched in 1906 would reduce still further the relative numbers of skilled cadres as new methods of work relied increasingly on semiskilled and unskilled laborers. Thus while the effective influence of the "conscious" metalworker of the pre–October Manifesto period was substantially reduced by the objective changes occurring in the 1906–1907 period, the values and attitudes of this sort of worker remained an important part of the collective traditions and subjective perceptions of the Petersburg working class. Among the most significant of these legacies was the dignified bearing of a skilled worker who conceived himself an autonomous individual with mastery over his life and work, and who insisted that he be accorded respectful treatment.

At the same time that the leading role of "Nevskii-type" workers began to wane, a less fragmented conception of working-class identity began to take shape which hinged on the identity of the worker as a worker not only in the factory, but in the urban community and in the nation at large. Through the experience of mobilizing around such issues as rent control, public works, and food prices, metalworkers could begin to perceive themselves as part of an urban community whose critical point of definition resided in the fact of social class as reflected in the enormous distance separating the "city fathers" from life in the workers' *kvartaly*. Through the curial system of elections to the State Duma, moreover, workers could again see the centrality of class as against citizenship as the key determinant of political participation on the national level. Here again the specificity of the historical moment was important, for workers' first experience in a national electoral process took place within the factories and not on some more "neutral" ground, and it occurred in an atmosphere seething with social fear and proletarian wrath.

Moreover, as the changes launched first at the state factories during this period began to envelop the private sector there would be relatively fewer opportunities for metalworkers to remain independent factory artisans, or for peasant migrants to remain only temporarily in the city, or for worker *intelligenty* to stand high above a "dark," prepolitical mass and focus their attention on the camaraderie of the study circle (*kruzhok*) rather than the struggles of the shop floor. Gradually eclipsing this earlier reality were newly emergent norms of working-class life, based on the collective experiences of workers who were becoming more homogeneous in their urban and industrial *stazh*, increasingly similar in levels of skill, literacy, and pay, and more conscious of their identity as workers in the factory, the community, and the nation. Contributing to this newer identity was the concrete experience of class struggle, which took place with particular intensity in the metalworking plants of the capital in the late fall of 1905 and which was shaped by encounters with the city duma over issues of unemployment and public works. Contributing as well was the vigorous reassertion of managerial control over the course of 1906–1907—that arbitrariness (*proizvol*) workers had hoped to contain through the imposition of "factory constitutions" in 1905—which further cemented workers' perceptions of the defeat they had suffered at the hands of a class enemy. And however anguished the Mensheviks were as regards the relationship between party and mass, there could be no question that the radical parties of the left had gained access to and influence over the workers of the capital to a degree unprecedented in the pre-1905 period. Whether Menshevik, Bolshevik, or SR, workers far more regularly than in the past imbibed a radical critique which interpreted the experiences of the recent past in class terms and asserted the ultimate victory of "the people" over state and "society."

The legacy of 1905–1907 for metalworking industrialists would be equally substantial. Not only had they witnessed the collapse of labor discipline; they had suffered from a punishing economic downturn since the turn of the century whose end was not yet in sight. This "dual crisis" of the metalworking industry made necessary, indeed inevitable, substantive change in the commercial, technical, and supervisory structures of their plants. But the revolution had also made inevitable a painful confrontation with one of the overarching realities of tsarist Russia—its overwhelmingly agrarian structure and the political outcomes that flowed from this reality. The inconsequence of Petersburg's entrepreneurial elite within the chambers of the State Duma, but also within the worldview of Petr Stolypin, made politics by some other means a necessary component of employer thinking in the aftermath of the first revolution.

VII

FINANCIERS, EMPLOYERS, AND ENGINEERS: CONFRONTING THE IMPERATIVES OF ECONOMIC MODERNIZATION

The political settlement arising out of the June 3, 1907, coup d'état of Prime Minister Stolypin rested on the belief that rural Russia would act as midwife to the birth of a new political nation and a reformed state structure. From the opening of the Third Duma in the fall of 1907, however, Russia's landed nobility set as its overarching goal the preservation of its prerogatives in rural Russia and the maintenance of its primacy in the realm. Such a narrowly conceived politics in the postrevolutionary period amply demonstrated many nobles' singular insensitivity to the claims of urban-industrial Russia, the hollowness of their pretensions to leadership, and the continuing vitality of their particularistic values. And so by virtue of his unwarranted faith in the ability of this anachronistic estate to utilize wisely the power invested in the legislature and by the exclusion of the vast majority of the population from the constitutional project, Stolypin undercut his own effort to create a more fully authoritative state system. By late 1908 it was clear that his reform proposals for rural Russia would not pass successfully through the Duma; by the spring of 1909, the Naval Staffs crisis revealed how substantially his authority had been eroded and how far the fragmentation of the Octobrist Party had progressed; and by the spring of 1911, the Western Zemstvo crisis sealed the political fate of his system. Well before his death at the hands of an assassin in September 1911, Stolypin's carefully crafted system had unraveled, and with it effective governmental leadership of the nation.[1]

Stolypin's coup nonetheless ended Russia's first revolutionary crisis. For the elite, a period of relative calm finally descended; for much of the rest of the population, years of repression, reaction, and demoralization set in. Having secured a tenuous sort of breathing space, the government began to confront the host of domestic and foreign policy problems that had accumulated since the onset of Russia's most recent time of troubles. Paramount among these problems was the stabilization of the state's finances and the

154

reconstruction of its armed forces. The costs of revolutionary upheaval and unsuccessful war had been enormous, and Stolypin's minister of finance, V. N. Kokovtsov, now struggled with the fiscal consequences. He did so not only in the context of continuing economic stagnation but in a political setting which forced the government much more clearly than in the past to maneuver between the competing claims of agrarian and industrial Russia. At the same time, the sinking of the Baltic Fleet and the routing of the army in the Far East seemed to require not only a massive investment in rearmament but redoubled efforts to project Russia's power in the international arena.

No less substantial were the problems confronting Petersburg's entrepreneurial elite. At the level of public policy, they faced a difficult struggle to assert the claims of big business before a skeptical polity and society. However gifted a statesman, Stolypin had little understanding of the world of Russia's emergent haute bourgeoisie; still less had the agrarians who dominated the Duma and the State Council, and who increasingly held the ear of Nicholas. In such a political context and given the fiscal situation of the state, substantive conflict over the national economic agenda necessarily shaped the waning years of the Imperial period. From the point of view of the entrepreneurial elite, this conflict was all too often accompanied by reactionary and xenophobic protests about the allegedly corrupting influence of foreign capital and the unwonted power of the monopolies, or by the crude anti-Semitic claims of the anti-bourgeois right. And all too often the government seemed to pander to these ignorant protestations and shortsighted claims, apparently blind to the imperatives of national economic development.

At a different level, metalworking industrialists continued to suffer from a decade-long economic downturn which lingered on until mid-1909; as well, they were now forced to deal with the substantial losses incurred from the labor conflict of the 1905–1906 period. Workers had won wage increases and cuts in the length of the workday; more costly had been the collapse of managerial authority. Coming to terms with the "chaos" that had reigned in the factories thus became a first priority for individual factory owners, but also for the Petersburg Society of Mill and Factory Owners.

A few metalworking plants now embarked on ambitious programs of comprehensive rationalization; many others moved more haltingly, variously acquiring more advanced technologies, or reorganizing accounting methodologies, or experimenting with new wage and time management schemes. This process of restructuring was facilitated in large measure by major Petersburg commercial banks, which had themselves recently undergone consolidation and reorganization. The restructuring of the industry was also pushed forward as the economies captured by rationalizing strategies began to be reflected in the marketplace and hence began to pressure other plants that had been more hesitant in reforming their manufacturing and managerial practices. At the same time, the PSMFO pursued an aggressive anti-labor policy, at once refusing to countenance the Metalworkers' Union as a legitimate bargaining agent and seeking to define unilaterally conditions pertaining across the industry. And whether at the "advanced" factories or the "semi-feudal," employers sought to recoup losses and control by broadly practicing a policy of "takebacks." Taken as a whole, this managerial offensive brought significant change to the industry and opened up new sites of conflict—at the point of production, in the local politics of Petersburg, and at the national level.

Russian engineers were central to the process of industrial rationalization, yet they often brought entirely different motivations to the task than did employers and financiers. For while engineers and entrepreneurs were surely united in a conviction that the nation's future lay in further industrial development, nonetheless 1905 had revealed that serious conflicts in values and priorities often divided them. Each had conceived political reform and social progress in sometimes starkly different terms; each had taken different lessons from 1905. Some engineers now projected a thinly disguised contempt for those industrialists who pursued no larger vision of the future than the unhindered exercise of their proprietary prerogatives. In consequence, the historic division within Russia's middle class between the professional intelligentsia and the industrial bourgeoisie was perpetuated and reinforced.

It was precisely the desire of many engineers to articulate a "larger" vision of the future that propelled them to critique "the capitalists" as well as the state. In the post-1905 period, the voice of professional engineers could be heard with growing force and clarity, not least because Russia's educational institutes were producing more technical personnel than ever before. What these professionals were saying about the "imperatives" of national economic development was very much grounded in a positivist faith in the liberating power of technology and the ability of experts to resolve socioeconomic problems. With increasing confidence, Russia's technical intelligentsia began to advance a sweeping and sophisticated set of arguments which underlay their particular notion of progress, justified their claims to a special role in Russia's future, and exerted a powerful influence on the nation's pre- and postrevolutionary modernizing elites.

One of the more striking aspects of the discourse surrounding industrial rationalization and "the science of management" in early twentieth century Russia, then, was the way in which it reflected and embraced the fascination of many Europeans and Americans with the boundless potentialities of science, technology, and the professions. More striking was the power of these ideas. In part because of the confident assertion by engineering professionals that the new "science" of management was socially neutral, while advances in technology were "objectively" value free, an ideology of modernization that was technocratic, productivist, and premised on the authority of experts began to appeal to people of radically divergent political convictions and social standing. Not only would engineers of quite different political persuasions consciously distance themselves from the self-interested actions of the "bourgeoisie" or view with scorn the antediluvian attitudes of tsarist bureaucrats. Leftists of the stature of Lenin would come to embrace Taylorism and Fordism with the enthusiasm of converts; like so many other Social Democrats of the time, he came to view these approaches to factory organization as socially disembodied techniques and hence amenable to a "de-coupling" of the exploitative from the progressive. And beyond the apparent ability of this ideology to transcend substantial social and political differences was its power to transcend the great divide of 1917, uniting as it did Leninist Bolsheviks and some of Imperial Russia's leading engineering professionals through the 1920s.[2]

The Rise of the Petersburg Financial Oligarchy

One consequence of the economic crisis at the turn of the century was a pronounced process of concentration in both the heavy industry of the Empire and its commercial banking system. Over the course of the first decade of the twentieth century, a few major banks secured a commanding position over the remaining joint-stock commercial banks operating in the Empire; by the end of the decade these big banks had solidified into a small number of powerful banking monopolies. Most important were the Russian-Asiatic, the Petersburg International, the Russian Foreign Trade, and the Azov-Don banks, all headquartered in Petersburg. Together, they came to dominate Russia's private financial markets and to control much of the heavy industrial sector.[3]

The dominance of the big Petersburg banks rested in part on the changing pattern of foreign entrepreneurship and on the acute capital scarcity experienced by heavy industry over the first decade of the twentieth century. In the wake of the turn-of-the century economic crisis, foreigners withdrew from direct participation in Russian industry and shifted instead to a strategy of passive portfolio investment, particularly with the restoration of investor confidence toward the end of 1907 due to the passing of the revolutionary crisis and the stabilization of the ruble. Russian banks channeled these foreign monies into the credit-starved heavy industrial sector by reorganizing the financial structure and consolidating the debt of a given enterprise, in the process gaining control over the firm as majority stockholder.[4] Nowhere was the linkage between the big banks and industry more evident than in the machine-construction sector.[5] By the prewar years, principals of the major Petersburg banks either sat on the board of directors or held stock in most of the significant metalworking firms of the capital, as well as many others elsewhere in the Empire, thereby personally connecting these enterprises in an increasingly apparent pattern of interlocking directorates. Positioning themselves as intermediaries between foreign financial interests and Russian industry and directing the flow of investment capital into the development of Russia's heavy and extractive sectors, the Petersburg banks thus came to occupy a strategic position in the economic life of the Empire.[6]

A handful of Petersburg financiers stood at the center of this process of concentration. Key among them were A. I. Putilov, chairman of the board of directors of the Russian-Asiatic Bank between 1910 and 1917, A. I. Vyshnegradskii, director of the Petersburg International Bank from 1906 to 1917, and M. M. Fedorov, president of the Azov-Don Bank from 1907 to 1911. As Alfred Rieber has shown, these men had a great deal in common: all had graduated from St. Petersburg University, served for more than a decade under Witte in the Ministry of Finance, and left public service in the wake of the 1905 revolution to pursue careers in the private sector.[7] They were remarkably successful in their endeavors: on the eve of the world war, Putilov and Vyshnegradskii sat on the board of directors of dozens of major machine-construction, electrical engineering, metallurgical, mining, and railway concerns, in addition to being heavily involved in such powerful syndicates as Prodamet, Produgol, and Prodvagon and such influential business organizations as the Association of Industry and Trade.[8]

Through their careers and as a product of their efforts one glimpses the constituent elements of a multifaceted process of monopolization taking place in the late Imperial period. Putilov and Vyshnegradskii were, first, key players in the transformation of Russia's commercial banking institutions over the 1900–1914 period. Second, they sought to defend and to expand the role of the syndicates and cartels that had originally emerged in response to the turn-of-the century economic crisis, but which continued to exercise, in their view, an important regulatory function in the market. Finally, through their investment strategies they pursued the concentration of the heavy industrial sector, first through financial reorganization of individual enterprises under the aegis of their banking group, next through the linkage of these enterprises via interlocking directorates, and then into conglomerates which aspired to the horizontal and vertical integration of key sectors of the economy.

The problems perceived by these powerful men and the choices they made in response to them shaped the further development of Russia's heavy industry and the labor relations that pertained within it. Their investment choices clearly favored the development of select sectors—in general, heavy rather than light industry, in particular defense and machine-construction. Placing the needs of production over consumption, they chose to postpone more immediate and substantive gains in popular welfare. And while they were fully supportive of a vast rearmament program, they were disinclined to invest in less profitable but crucial undertakings such as infrastructural development—risky ventures they felt the state should assume. Their activity also reflected an effort to regulate the market and "organize" Russian industry, in the interests of big business rather than those of the small producer and agriculture, but also in the hopes of eliminating divisive domestic competition and enhancing Russia's ability to compete effectively with the powerful Western economies operating both within the Empire and internationally.

Independent men, focused on Russia's further economic development, they were not the tools of foreign banking or arms interests, but rather important participants in the evolving system of Western capitalism. They were concerned to improve the productivity of Russia's heavy industrial sector by pursuing significant economies of scale, by investing in new technologies and the mechanization of work processes, and by examining Western managerial strategies. At the same time, and reflective of the thinking of their patron Sergei Witte, Putilov and Vyshnegradskii were neither advocates of an unrestrained market nor opponents of extensive state participation in national economic development. Indeed, like Witte, they appeared supportive of an approach to Russian development that might be termed an "economic" Rechtsstaat, that is, the establishment of orderly and regulated economic structures by means of a "rational" division of market shares and spheres of production, and by "positive" and appropriate intervention of state organs into the national economy. Their pursuit of the "commanding heights" of finance and industry was surely also a means to secure influence in the economic development of a country whose political institutions and social structure denied them such a role.[9]

Access to the decision-making bodies of the government had always been important to an industry overwhelmingly reliant on state demand;[10] and this dependence on state orders not only tied the industry to shifts in the government's economic priorities, but fostered the sort of intimate contact between state officials and metalworking industrialists in which public service and private interest became intertwined and often confused. What amounted to a revolving door between the defense industry and the government's purchasing agents helped to bind the capital's entrepreneurial elite to the old regime, particularly so as the state allocated increasingly enormous sums for the rearmament program. This too was another avenue to attain influence in a government historically insensitive to the claims of private industry, but one that tended to impede the articulation of a mature and consistent class politics.

Access to the decision-making bodies of the state was important in another sense. The settlement arising out of the Third of June coup d'état gave considerable political weight to the attitudes and perspectives of the landed nobility; as well, the Stolypin administration envisioned major reforms in both communal land tenure and local administration. This increasing focus on the needs of rural Russia, the budgetary allocations which this focus implied and the political power the landed nobility came to hold in the Third and Fourth Dumas necessarily affected the interests of Russia's leading entrepreneurs. Throughout the 1907–1914 period, the competing interests of big business and the landed nobility found regular reflection in conflicts over the issue of Russia's apparent dependence on foreign capital and the appropriateness of monopolistic agreements governing key sectors of the economy.

Hostility toward the monopolies took several forms. When in the spring of 1908 rumors began to circulate concerning the formation of a metallurgical trust in South Russia, more than a hundred rightist Duma deputies petitioned

Stolypin to block its organization. Although he agreed to do so, ultimately disagreements between the potential participants prevented the formation of the monopoly.[11] Also indicative of the general distrust of big business was the stance of S. V. Rukhlov, the rightist Minister of Ways of Communication from 1909 to 1915 who pursued a vigorous anti-trust policy, in particular trying to break the power of Produgol, the coal syndicate. Considerably more embarrassing for the magnates of heavy industry was a series of Senate "revisions" conducted over the 1908–1911 period concerning the activities of major monopolies in the metalworking sector and the revelation of their extensive illegal dealings with high government officials.[12]

Anti-foreign sentiment was no less important to an industry so heavily reliant on foreign investment. In February 1908, for example, the Stolypin administration was condemned by the Congress of United Nobility for the state's mounting indebtedness to foreign financial interests, as well as its failure to address seriously the developmental needs of the countryside. In the end, noble interests secured a substantial shift in government allocations in support of the zemstva and gentry agriculture; meanwhile, the patriotic press continued the attack against foreign influence in the Empire's economy. In these and other forums, hostility toward the dimensions of foreign involvement in Russia was strong and remained so throughout the inter-revolutionary period.[13]

Substantive differences even divided big business from the ministries ostensibly most responsive to the need for industrial development. Kokovtsov, for example, was concerned first and foremost with fiscal stability, and pursued a tight budgetary policy throughout his tenure in office. He rejected the position advanced by the Association of Industry and Trade in support of so-called productive expenditures (e.g., state investment in railroad construction, port facilities, favorable tax policies for industry, and the like), and the argument that such expenditures, by expanding the tax base, would ultimately enlarge the state's coffers.[14] Big business thus found itself at odds with the Ministry of Finance over a key policy issue.[15] By 1914, frustration had reached the point that Iu. P. Guzhon, a leading Muscovite metalworking industrialist, could remark at the Eighth Congress of the Association of Industry and Trade: "We cannot but recognize that the minister of trade and equally the minister of finance are completely separated from us in outlook; they do not live our life; they do not understand our problems as we do; they look on industry and trade with different eyes."[16]

Despite the enormous economic resources the St. Petersburg entrepreneurial elite came to possess, they proved unable to secure decisive influence over public discourse on key economic issues, nor were they able to attain the commanding position in determining the state's economic agenda. While able to prevent the dissolution of the monopolies and maintain public relations at a level that did not impede the flow of foreign capital into the Empire, their power and position must be seen as constrained by agrarian and reactionary interests at court, in the Duma, and in the bureaucracy. Economic strength was thus not coupled with a commensurate level of social authority or political power. Summing up the position of the entrepreneurial elite on the eve of the war, one recent observer has concluded:

> On cultural matters they [the Petersburg and Baltic region industrialists] could not hope to challenge the dominant position of the imperial court and the nobility who set the tone for the artistic, literary, and academic life of the capital. They edited no newspapers, presided over no salons, sponsored no theaters, built no museums; in a word, they offered no alternative to the established social order. Thus, the great wealth and economic influence of the northwestern entrepreneurs had little resonance within the political system and even less effect upon the cultural values and beliefs of society.[17]

Their painful social isolation and political impotence in the national arena reinforced in the Petersburg entrepreneurial elite its own predilection to place economic issues before all else. In the context of the times, the only way in which they might hope to play a role at the national level was by embracing *apparently* "apolitical" representations of their interests and by forcefully defending the notion that *the* answer to Russia's problems resided in economic development.

Protecting Employer Interests

There were, however, many sites of political conflict in the waning years of the Imperial regime. In the Empire's capital city, the PSMFO fought to assert a decisive role in setting the agenda for labor relations and in organizing their colleagues in defense of proprietary prerogatives. In the absence of an active labor movement in the 1907–1912 period, the PSMFO appeared both internally united and exceptionally powerful in the local arena. From this position of strength, it worked tirelessly and often successfully to restrict the voice of labor within industry. By the 1912–1914 period, the PSMFO had emerged as the most militant anti-labor association of businessmen in the Empire, yet its very intransigence alienated many potential allies.

In the aftermath of the first revolution, the PSMFO, but most particularly its Engineering Section, sought to define unilaterally work conditions throughout the industry, attempting to systematize work rules, impose uniformity, and exercise control over the labor market. The Engineering Section even aspired to coordinate the wage policies of member firms. Choosing to ignore key demands voiced by labor in 1905, Petersburg employers did not elaborate a new institutional matrix for the regulation of labor-management conflict and continued to deny the need for any structure within the factory that would permit workers to air grievances in a regular and orderly manner. Moreover, they repeatedly rejected worker requests to recognize the Metalworkers' Union as a legitimate bargaining agent. Instead, the strategy pursued by the PSMFO endeavored to preempt conflict by the prior definition of conditions on an industry-wide basis.

Illustrative of this approach to labor relations was the work of the PSMFO's Pankov Commission, organized in 1907 and chaired by I. P. Pankov of the St. Petersburg Metals Factory. Its task was to compile a standard paybook and rules of internal order appropriate to the needs of the metalworking industry of the capital. The importance of establishing uniformity in these most basic contractual documents had been recognized earlier and had been discussed by metalworking industrialists in December 1904 and again in October 1905.[18] Private industrialists had also met with representatives of the state factories on this question in the latter part of January 1905, seeking to obtain a clearer picture of the conditions pertaining in all the capital's metalworking factories.[19] But it was not until the work of the Pankov Commission that concrete steps were taken.

The first fruit of the commission's work was published in June 1908 and distributed to the major metalworking plants of the capital. Model contractual documents governing labor and management were issued in four parts, purposefully delineated so as to avoid approval of the entire package by the factory inspectorate. Thus a seven-point "Rules on Hiring" was to be hung on the factory gate and not entered into the standard paybook, stipulating among other things that the manager of the given shop was responsible for hiring; that the worker was required to have a medical examination performed by the factory doctor; and that a trial period lasting no more than seven days take place during which the worker was subject to all existing factory rules. An additional three-part section entitled "Conditions of Hire" was to be inserted in the paybook. These regulations covered the wage package, and delineated the relationship between shop pay and, if offered, piece pay and the conditions under which the latter might be given. Also separate and subject to confirmation by the inspectorate was a detailed set of "Rules of Internal Order," which contained over twenty points and discussed such matters as the issuance of wages, rules governing lateness, appropriate behavior in the factory, the length and distribution of work time, and so on. Finally, a twenty-four-point "Table of Fines" listed punishable violations of factory order, but refrained from specifying the size of the fine.[20]

The concern to establish uniformity also found reflection in another initiative of the Engineering Section. In March 1908 it encouraged its members to embark on an important set of changes in wage policy. Judging an hourly based computation of wages to afford a variety of advantages to industry, members were urged to abandon day-based wage systems.[21] And while most metalworking industrialists did indeed shift to an hourly based system, the PSMFO would be frustrated in its subsequent efforts to introduce uniform rates scales prior to the outbreak of the First World War.[22]

In effect, the model contractual documents worked out by the Pankov Commission, as well as the directive on hourly based wage systems, represented a prior agreement among a monopolistic group of employers to offer but one set of conditions to labor. "Regulating" labor relations in such a way, member firms of the PSMFO placed the definition of crucial elements of the contractual relationship beyond the reach of workers, indeed beyond the control of the state as represented in the factory inspectorate. In so doing, employers not only tried to narrow the areas open to negotiation; they endeavored as well to reduce the incentive for workers to change jobs (or to strike) in pursuit of better employment elsewhere.

The PSMFO also sought to exercise a much greater control over the labor market. One major project concerned the organization of a so-called Inquiry Office,[23] an idea discussed earlier but realized in 1909. The stated goal of this office was the gradual selection of a "trustworthy cadre of workers" and indirectly "the promotion of factory discipline, which [had been] shattered in recent years and without which a proper industrial life [was] impossible."[24] Employers had experimented with blacklisting in the summer strikes of 1906, but now institutionalized the practice, as well as the collateral effort to identify a cadre of strikebreakers. Association members were entitled to use the office as an employment bureau, but were required to report all workers they had fired, as well as those hired without the services of the office.[25]

The identification of a "trustworthy cadre of workers" was an ambitious— perhaps impossible—task, but it was facilitated by an industry-wide PSMFO effort in 1908 to catalog those workers potentially eligible for grants and pensions due to accidents. Concerned lest a worker deceive multiple employers into providing a disability grant, the PSMFO compiled a card file on some 45,000 accident victims covering the 1904–1907 period and subsequently updated it up to April 1909. Valuable in its own right, the work on registering accident cases also provided useful experience for the project of a general registration of workers.[26]

Efforts at what might be dubbed a negative regulation of the labor market—attempts to identify strikebreakers and company spies or to get rid of the aged and infirm—could only go so far in providing the type of workers the industry needed. Particularly as economic stagnation began to give way to economic expansion around 1910, employers became increasingly concerned about another aspect of the labor market, the problem of skilled labor shortages, especially given the competition of the large state-owned factories in the capital.

Responding to this concern, the PSMFO organized a commission under the chairmanship of M. S. Plotnikov of the Lessner Factory in the latter part of 1911,[27] which set out to address the insufficiency of trained workers at metalworking factories, and to examine at the same time the question of apprenticeship. As employers pondered the reasons for the inadequate supply of skilled workers, a number of explanations were advanced. For some, the problem resided in legislation restricting child labor: factories were simply deprived of their natural source of apprentices.[28] Others suggested that the major factories had historically relied on workers trained at small shops, where boys had learned a basic trade and then moved into the factories. Now, it was claimed, the shops preferred to hire adult workers fired from the factories, since the shops found it increasingly difficult to retain apprentices, who wanted to move into the big plants as soon as possible.[29] Others contended that shops continued to utilize apprentice labor, but that these workers left as soon as they could, often seeking to open their own small shop in far-off Siberia. This emerging trend was explained by the fact that wages in Petersburg failed to keep pace with the cost of living.[30] Others highlighted a different facet of the issue. Well-trained workers could still be found in the provinces, where they learned their trade from small artisanal enterprises; the big Petersburg factories, however, were developing workers who in the main were only able to work on a given machine tool and who remained wholly unfamiliar with other aspects of metalworking.[31] The problem, in other words, was the growing specialization of heavy industry and the way in which it was reshaping the labor market.

At the commission's first session in January 1912, Chairman Plotnikov noted that a decline in the number of trained workers had been apparent since 1905–1906, but had grown progressively worse. Without the requisite cadres, he argued, the metalworking industry would be doomed. Just as worrisome, skilled workers had become such a valued commodity, they could present virtually any demand to the employer.[32] Perhaps most troubling of all, however, was the explosive potential of skilled labor shortages to undermine employer unity. As the intense conflicts of the 1912–1914 period would reveal, employers wavered over the uniform imposition of fines, the identification of strike "instigators" and the compilation of blacklists for fear of losing valued skilled labor to their competitors.

While the commission would continue to study the problem, its initial response was to suggest that the PSMFO encourage the organization of vocational schools for twelve- to fifteen-year-olds and not wait for the government to act on the problem. Furthermore, Plotnikov cited the efforts of his factory—Lessner—to institute an apprenticeship program, and bemoaned the failure of others to follow suit.[33]

The aspiration of the PSMFO to articulate a uniform labor relations policy for industry as a whole was paralleled by an effort to stimulate a community of interest, indeed a united front, among employers. One aspect of this endeavor was the work of the PSMFO in collecting and disseminating a wide range of information on strike actions, labor legislation, court rulings, and the like. Characteristic in this regard was the work of the Inquiry Office in times of labor conflict. Building on the methods developed in 1905–1906, a data sheet on the cause and duration of labor conflicts was devised, to be filled out by factory administrators at regular intervals, daily if worker disturbances were frequent.[34] Similarly, the PSMFO issued a weekly bulletin registering strike activity. The bulletin aimed to verify and correct press reports, to inform employers of the demands of workers at various factories, and to provide information on the actions taken by managers in response.[35] The PSMFO thus facilitated the circulation of relevant information and in turn encouraged employers to view labor protest not only in its larger, city-wide context, but in a more systematic manner.

Another aspect of the PSMFO's work concerned the publication of various handbooks. One, compiled in 1907, was a "reference book" on the hiring and firing process.[36] A second edition, updated and expanded in 1911, provided employers with information on the legislation governing industrial relations, the compilation of a contract of hire, and dealings with the courts.[37] Not surprisingly, these handbooks encouraged employers to take full advantage of the law and its lacunae to defend their interests.[38]

The PSMFO was equally energetic in its approach to the courts and methodically pressed to expand the effective rights of employers by securing favorable judicial rulings. In 1907 it organized a Judiciary Committee and, noting its usefulness, assigned 6,000 rubles for its activities in the following year.[39] The PSMFO also kept employers abreast of recent legislation and court actions by apprising member firms of the practical applications of rulings on labor problems. And to the extent that a more coordinated approach to judicial and legislative institutions resulted in favorable decisions, the PSMFO enlarged the employers' sphere of action in labor-management relations. The society thus played an important role in educating industrialists, encouraging them to utilize the legal system in a sophisticated manner, and urging them to develop a more activist approach to the expansion of their rights.

Taken as a whole, the PSMFO's aggressive defense of employer interests reflected an effort to reestablish most elements of the "autocratic" factory regime. Restoring managerial authority in the aftermath of 1905 very largely meant securing the unilateral right to define all essential conditions of labor. Employers wanted neither to bargain over wages and hours, nor to allow worker participation in setting the rules of factory order. The PSMFO's strategy hinged on mobilizing member firms to agree on a prior regulation of conditions industry-wide. But what distinguished the post-1905 "autocratic" factory order from its prerevolutionary predecessor was the effort of some metalworking plants to "modernize" their strategies of control by employing new technological processes and "scientifically based" methods of time and work discipline without fundamentally reconceiving the archaic institutional structures governing labor relations. By the 1912–1914 period, the tensions spawned by the implementation of new work practices could no longer be contained within the outmoded structures.

The thinking that informed the PSMFO's approach to labor relations paralleled in some important respects the attitudes of the financial oligarchy to the problems of national economic development. The common thread uniting financiers and managers was a concern to "organize" the various arenas in which they operated. Finding competition and conflict unproductive, these men consistently asserted the value of regulation and control. Thus the financial oligarchs viewed syndicates, cartels, and trusts as important regulators of the market; they advocated as well the prior division of production spheres and market shares. Similarly, the PSMFO worked to implement standard rates books and rules of internal order, as well as bring about a more reliable and predictable labor market. And their effort to standardize conditions industry-wide resonated with the attempts of many individual metalworking firms to create orderly hierarchies of command and execution by means of various rationalizing schemes. Thus rejecting unrestrained competition and pluralistic forms, the Petersburg entrepreneurial elite looked instead to corporative structures, preemptive regulation, and monopolistic agreements.

Engineering Professionalism and
the Struggle to "Modernize" Russia

Engineers and entrepreneurs shared a common concern for Russia's economic backwardness and its vulnerability before a more economically powerful West. Yet as the 1905 revolution revealed, these proponents of economic growth differed substantially over a range of issues. For most Petersburg employers, the central task of the postrevolutionary period was to reimpose discipline in the factories and insure the economic viability of their operations. But for many engineers, coming to terms with Russia's recent time of troubles meant more than finding ways to restore order; these events had raised serious questions about their professional identity as well as their role in responding to the overarching developmental needs of the Empire.

As we have seen, many engineers had entered the 1905 period clear about the need for political reform and critical of the social conditions pertaining in the factories. Many had joined in the banquet campaigns, the Union of Unions, and the October general strike.[40] But coming out of this experience, many seemed convinced more than ever that Russia's economic backwardness lay at the heart of the problem and had to be overcome.

Most obviously, the abysmal conditions that had led to so much labor protest reflected an unacceptable level of labor productivity, a problem in turn connected with irrational patterns of factory organization and out-of-date technology. Social strife appeared embedded in the problem of economic backwardness; it rested equally on the self-interested positions articulated by labor and capital, neither of whom seemed able to transcend their particular class concerns and work in concert for the betterment of Russia. Finding themselves at the center of labor-management conflict, many engineers had come to believe that they had to define a "third" course above and beyond the claims of labor and capital and that only they, as disinterested experts, could act for the nation as a whole. Moreover, Russia's international standing was clearly compromised by economic backwardness; in an era of intense international competition only those with a modern industrial structure could hope to survive.

Confident in the power of science and technology to solve the problems of humanity and disillusioned by the process of political change, engineers began to sketch a vision of the future to be attained by economic development. Said one of Russia's leading engineers, V. L. Kirpichev, in 1913: "The golden age is in the future. We get to it by the path of technical improvement and invention. We are led to it, directed, shown the way by engineers."[41] Said differently, as political options closed off in the Stolypin era, a technocratic vision emerged as increasingly compelling. What politics seemed unable to resolve, a higher level of material culture could; a modern, industrially advanced Russia might free the people from poverty, ignorance and the social conflict embedded in it. Gradually, a vision of an industrially advanced Russia began to eclipse the vision of a politically free Russia.

By the same token, because political reform appeared unattainable, the realm of the political had to be redefined. For many engineering professionals, it seemed increasingly clear that economic development could not be conceived as a matter of political choice. There could be no question of the imperative need to modernize, nor could a largely illiterate citizenry be expected to determine the ways in which this task was to be accomplished. Decisions of a purely scientific and technological nature belonged in the arena of impartial professional expertise and were not matters usefully dealt with in the sphere of bureaucratic or parliamentary politics; nor should the resolution of these issues be unduly bound up with the interests of private industrialists. Moreover, the conflicts of the recent past had revealed hopelessly tangled labor-management relations. To overcome these destructive patterns of interaction, both sides had to be subordinated to the discipline of advanced technologies, rigorous commercial procedures, and clearly defined hierarchies of command and execution. Power and authority in the workplace could no longer depend on proprietorial right or the craft control exercised by workers.

One of the themes that emerged in the interrevolutionary period, therefore, was the assertion that neither the government nor the industrial bourgeoisie was suited to the task of leadership in the struggle to modernize. Correspondingly, the claim that the professional engineer was uniquely qualified for the role was advanced. So too, the notion of a national plan of economic development defined and implemented by experts was advocated, as was the argument that professionals had to lead the way in the rationalization of factory industry and in the restructuring of labor-management relations. For the rationalization of industry was not only a matter of concern to individual enterprises; at issue was increasing the efficiency of socially necessary labor, and, along with it, increasing the national wealth.

Following the first revolution and through the vehicle of multiplying professional associations and an expanding professional press a self-conscious effort to delineate the engineer's identity can be observed.[42] In part, this heightened concern with defining the professional was reflected in discussions concerning engineering ethics, adequate and appropriate compensation, and the requisite elements of a comprehensive engineering education.[43] More generally, components of an "ideal" type were sketched.

The engineer, many maintained, could not be locked up in a narrowly defined sphere of technical questions; his outlook had to include an appreciation for the social and economic problems at hand. Because, wrote I. Russak, "engineers are the carriers of material culture," because they are "the organizers and leaders of the productive forces of the country," the engineer could not simply be "a good specialist in a certain field of technology." He had to "possess a broader intellectual outlook."[44] Expanding their own horizons, engineers had to reach out to other areas of expert knowledge in pursuit of the economic good. Concluded one engineer in a discussion of the "science" of management: "only by means of the mutual collaboration of representatives of a whole series of pure and applied sciences, the representatives of psychology, physiology, medicine, sociology, political economy and so on, can a well-balanced and complex structure be built for the young science."[45] Wrote another regarding the operational, organizational, and administrative tasks of an engineer:

> [In these areas] the engineer's profession presents increased demands to him, both in the sense of his mental horizons and requisite knowledge, but also in the sense of thinking itself, and here in particular it is appropriate to note that the question resides not in the quantitative side of knowledge and thought, but in its qualitative [aspect]. This means that the tasks which we are now speaking about require knowledge and thought not only of a technical nature, but an economic, sociological, legal, political, ethical, and also (terrible to say) philosophical nature.[46]

Because the engineer had to be a leader of men, he had to enjoy moral authority and be perceived as an impartial actor working in the interests of the economic development of the nation as a whole. He could not play the role of policeman or informant, for such behavior clearly violated professional ethics. For Russak, "engineers must not only be carriers of material culture, but must provide an example of social solidarity and moral beauty." Unlike the physician or lawyer who typically work with separate individuals, engineers

> stand close to the mass, they lead it, they organize and direct its mind and energy in a definite direction. Here is a broad field of activity for the engineer, therefore he must be fully armed not only with scientific knowledge, but with moral authority. The success of the undertaking and the well-being of many depends on his tact, steadiness, and impartiality. The technologist, being the mediating instance between the worker and the employer, must be able to act in an exemplary manner, and for this his moral authority must be high.[47]

For Russak and others, the success of American and English engineers resided in their "firm will, social instinct, and moral authority." And it was just these qualities that Russian engineering associations had to cultivate; indeed these associations were to become the "laboratory" in which the virtues of "social discipline, broad initiative, and moral steadfastness" were to be developed, for it would be the task of their members to organize and lead those "nameless gray blacksmiths of national happiness and well-being."[48]

Nonetheless, few engineers were able to articulate the uniqueness of their vision in a cogent and generally accessible way; and precisely this failing, P. Engel'meier maintained, had kept engineers from assuming the role in government that was appropriate to their training and worldview.

> In fact, of ten engineers who read the present article, no doubt nine will shrug their shoulders just at the term "technical worldview" [*tekhnicheskoe mirovozzrenie*] since they've not heard of such a thing. The very best, experienced and no longer young engineer, realizing, say, a whole series of marvelous technical enterprises and in fact demonstrating the vitality of his worldview, usually doesn't know that a technical worldview exists and is not able for himself or for others to explain the particularities of his intellectual constitution and to justify by generally meaningful arguments his completely correct, but purely instinctive conviction that in the contemporary social structure the functions of the engineer lie at the very center of the state mechanism. . . . And that is why—in part—the imprint of something gray invariably lies on the engineer, [something which appears] more appropriate at the factory, than at the helm of the ship of state."[49]

The engineer, concluded Engel'meier, must not only "feel the superiority [*prevoskhodstvo*] of his profession over others"; he must learn to articulate an intellectually defensible position in support of its primacy. One way to do so was to elucidate the role which technology had played in the "general progress of culture."[50]

An exalted sense of mission sometimes coupled with extravagant claims to superior knowledge helped inform a worldview that allowed engineers to subordinate others to their particular vision of the future. Just as Russak viewed men as objects to be mobilized, others asserted that precisely because engineers "organized" and "directed" the mind and energies of men, engineering education had to take up the issues at hand. Wrote E. P. Ivanov:

> For the most part engineers have to operate on that great raw material which is man. The study of this raw material in our technical schools is utterly ignored. One can correctly know the worker only standing side by side, shoulder to shoulder.
>
> And until a person is, in the closest way, acquainted with workers, with their methods of thought, expressed in their manners, their view of things, [then] he who is in the role of a director is in a very unsatisfactory position.[51]

In this ultimately coercive and dehumanizing vision, the worker was reduced to one factor among many in the process of production, an objectified "raw material" to be worked on and molded by the engineer. And for some, it was precisely the transformative power of "scientifically based" managerial systems that proved so compelling. *Utro Rossii*, for example, praised the Taylor system as "an invaluable weapon in the struggle with the ideology of idleness," not because it would result in gain for the industrialists, but because it would effect "a major shift [*perelom*] in the psyche of the working class." Taylor's system was the "best pedagogical measure" for developing a healthy attitude toward work. "The discipline on which the system is based is understandable to each worker and it cannot be represented as an arbitrary violation of his peace. This discipline turns the worker for a few hours a day into part of a machine but immediately after this he sees material advantage in a full subordination to the mechanism and already he is unable to return to the former ideology which possessed him."[52] Unconcerned by the implications of such forays into the psyche of the worker, the editors of *Utro Rossii* had little difficulty in transforming an image of mechanized humanity into a happy vision of a brighter future.[53]

One leading engineer-industrialist, I. A. Semenov, asserted that Taylorism had the power to "free the worker from the centuries-old oppression of false tradition."[54] Another, R. V. Poliakov, suggested that precisely because many Russian workers were "less developed," they had fewer traditions, technical habits, and routines to overcome; hence it would be easier to educate them in the direction of Taylor's system.[55] Thus, however one viewed it, Taylor seemed to be the "right thing" for Russia—appropriate either to its small pool of skilled urbanized workers or to that vast reservoir of peasants coming into the factories.

Still other observers stressed that a key benefit of "properly organized and specialized factories" was the chance to pay workers a higher compensation and thereby "sober them up from socialist doctrine and break them to the factory." With higher pay for the worker, lower costs of production, and the elimination of foreign competition, the commonality of interests uniting workers and factory owners would finally become clear.[56] For those many Russians concerned about increasing the national wealth, *Promyshlennost' i Torgovlia* seemed to sum up the problem most succinctly: "In view of the insignificant productivity of our workers, the introduction of this system [Taylorism] has for Russia even greater significance than for Western Europe or the United States of North America."[57]

But as the doctrines of scientific management became increasingly popularized and vulgarized, many professionals also sought to rescue the "science" of management from the crude representations of self-interested industrialists or benighted dilettantes.[58] Some engineers were at pains, therefore, to distinguish the particular and the partisan from the universally valid and objective. To S. F. Geints', for example, Taylor's studies "openly pursued narrow entrepreneurial interests."[59] He argued, however, that individual systems

> may be so constructed that the good and correct in them is outweighed by the bad and the harmful. For the science [of management] itself there can be no such suspicions and misgivings; it is free from preconceived motives of private gain and detached from class interests. In this regard it becomes completely possible to establish those normal conditions according to which the appli-

cation of living labor would generate the highest possible productivity, and at the same time guarantee to workers and society a defense of their legal rights and interests.[60]

Another engineer asserted that the new science of management

gives to society a weapon for the planned organization of production, for the elimination of a destructive squandering of the forces of nature and humanity, and for the creation of harmony between the inclinations of a person and the maintenance of those activities necessary for society.

The power and efficacy of these weapons encounter obstacles from the side of the reigning socioeconomic conditions, which are not slow to distort and deform the basic ideas of the new science and to adapt it to the needs of capital, just as this was done with machines. But in the conditions of capitalism any process has two sides, and there can be no doubt, that parallel to the adaptation of scientific systems of organization to the temporary needs of capitalists, will develop and strengthen another side—the influence of broad public organs on all conditions of production and distribution."[61]

Claiming to serve the interests of science and society as a whole, many engineers actively sought to distinguish the "professional" opinions of disinterested experts from the self-seeking positions of the "capitalist." Indeed, one undercurrent in engineering discourse was a rather thinly disguised contempt for the Russian factory owner. Commenting, for example, on the recent fashion among employers to adopt hourly pay, one engineer grew sharply critical of their inability to see that the utility of such wages resided in a far more comprehensive reorganization of the factory as a whole. For engineer Sharpant'e, the issue was order and rationality in the goals of increasing the national wealth rather than a concern for private entrepreneurial gain; he had little use for the many employers who remained skeptical about the new discoveries in factory organization or who proved blindly wedded to the old way of doing things. Nor did he believe that rate determination could be left in the hands of old-line foremen, "who were guided in the setting of prices by their own, sometimes very doubtful experience [*opyt*]."[62]

Other engineers came to embrace the various wage systems emerging out of the new "science" of management not because of profit maximization, but because so many believed that the old wage policies created an enormous amount of wholly unnecessary conflict; many saw in the new wage systems a means to social harmony. As one engineer put it, "life itself" required the two "hostile camps" of labor and capital to act together, for without each other neither could exist. They therefore had to find a "point of contact" which would make "peaceful coexistence" possible. Such a point of contact, argued Krzhizhanovskii, resided in the formula which was best expressed by Taylor: "the highest wage along with the minimum cost of production." And while he noted that no wage system was ideal, nonetheless such systems could "bring us closer" to the regulation of serious disagreements between capital and the working class.

> With the selection and introduction of a new, more rational and just system of compensation, when the worker adapts to the new regime, the long-standing, constant, and deep dissatisfaction begins to cede its place to a certain feeling of satisfaction, which is the result of the increased, completely determined and constant wage, a consequence, in turn, of correctly organized labor, which proceeds calmly, without tension, and which also exerts a certain influence on the moral side of the worker mass, which recognizes that their labor is paid fairly and that there is no need for them to consciously limit their productivity and pretend to be working intensely, thereby deceiving both themselves and the employer.[63]

Similar arguments justified the advocacy by so many engineering professionals of a "systems" approach to factory organization. Technical journals carried countless articles on the proper organization of instrument shops, on the structure and functions of planning departments, on the organization of forging shops, on plant layout, on accounting procedures and costing. In essence, each forwarded the notion that by virtue of an orderly, regulated, impersonal hierarchy of command and execution productivity might be enhanced and labor-management conflict eliminated.[64] "Systems," it appeared, had the power to transform shops into productive, indeed fundamentally congenial, units of enterprise.[65]

Central to the project of defusing conflict in the factory was a depersonalization of labor-management relations which was to be accomplished by managerial systems premised on a strict division of labor. Such an approach specified that each employee hold precisely defined tasks and responsibilities; that written communication replace oral instruction; that senior personnel be appropriately distanced from the labor force; and that rate-setting be removed from the foreman and the shop floor. In this orderly world of command and execution, nothing would be left to the discretion of the individual; labor and management would no longer be burdened with arbitrary processes or haphazard regulations. As one leading proponent of scientifically based systems argued, a strict delineation of administrative functions "facilitates the work of each person and to a considerable degree eliminates the dependence of production on the personality."[66]

Just as the engineer sought to remove technical, and increasingly administrative and supervisory, decision-making from the industrialist, so too he sought to strip the worker of any claims to craft knowledge. For A. V. Pankin, the "preparation, heat treatment, and grinding of cutting tools must be taken from the hands of workers and placed in the experienced hands of the appropriate specialists."[67] Lifting the burden imposed on workers by wrongheaded notions of skill, argued scientific reformers, would contribute to the building of a "friendly partnership" between labor and management.[68] Concluded Poliakov and Khmelev, "practice indicates that specialists standing outside the given plant" are best suited to the tasks of comprehensive reorganization.[69]

And so it appeared to the engineers that neither the industrialist nor the worker possessed the skills to organize the factory properly. That task belonged to the disinterested engineering professional whose work was informed by the perspectives of a wide variety of other experts. Possessed of a belief that order, system, and higher productivity could surmount social conflict, labor and sometimes management became the object of transformation and the focal point for the almost missionary zeal of Russia's technologists. Coupled with their claims to superior knowledge and an abiding faith in the power of science and technology, they felt compelled to assert the primacy of their role in assaulting Russia's backwardness. The way to a brighter future seemed to lie in radical gains in the nation's productivity and in the transcendence of narrow class interests; Russia would "get there" with engineers at the helm.

Engineers also felt called to lead owing to the absence of long-range planning on the part of others. As engineer Aronov observed the proceedings of the Sixth Congress of Representatives of Industry and Trade in May 1912 and thought about these deliberations in the context of the approaching end of the Third Duma, he found them almost completely devoid of any substantive understanding of the tasks of the present and the future. Hobbled by the narrow perspectives of their estate and unable to rise above their particularistic concerns, these representatives of "united industry" failed to appreciate the needs of state. "In essence," mocked Aronov, "the Congress of United Industry stood at the very same level as the Congress of United Nobility." And while they loudly and routinely complained about the "oppression" of industry, continued Aronov, in point of fact they exercised a very real influence in the day to day drafting of legislation, the work of diverse governmental commissions, and so on. Tired of the constant harping about their problems, Aronov was equally critical of their lack of a program for the development of the productive forces of Russia. Despite all their talk, "no one had yet seen such a plan."[70]

Just a few years later one of Russia's leading engineers and educators, V. I. Grinevitskii, surveyed the tasks involved in mobilizing Russian industry for the war effort and ultimately reorienting it to peacetime production. The need to develop a national economic plan stood at the forefront of his thinking; so did the conviction that neither the efforts of the government nor those of private industrialists would be adequate to the task. Grinevitskii insisted that the government "lacked sufficient closeness to life, technical knowledge, breadth of views and initiative," while industrialists lacked "objectivity" and a sufficiently broad vision. Professor Grinevitskii judged that only Russia's technical organizations, in conjunction with its "scholarly-economic organizations," possessed the requisite objectivity, expertise, and practical experience to do the job, a job made urgent by the "primitiveness" and "passivity" that had characterized the prewar economy.[71]

For those who viewed the government as obscurantist, private industrialists as parochial, and workers as backwardness incarnate, the ideas advanced by many engineering professionals must have been compelling. Beyond the engineers' own pretensions to superior knowledge and the obvious need to insure that their services were utilized was the apparent relevance of their thinking to the problems revealed by 1905. Labor-management conflict had an enormously destructive potential; industry had suffered catastrophic losses from a decade-long period of crisis, depression, and lingering stagnation; Russia's productivity scarcely corresponded to its resources and capacities. The reflections of engineering professionals on Russia's recent crisis suggested that conflict was a product of poorly organized shops, arbitrary wages, and ill-trained supervisory personnel. Harmony could be achieved when shop floor relations were depersonalized; when wages, hours, and conditions were "objectively" determined; and when up-to-date technologies were properly implemented and maintained. Higher rates of productivity would eventually lead to an improved standard of living, the requisite basis for a more modern, more civilized nation. Precisely because these arguments were persuasive they began to influence the choices being made in Russian industry.

Engineering ideology was a powerful set of propositions emerging out of the experiences of Russia's professional middle class in the early twentieth century.[72] Russian engineers arrived at their technocratic positions by virtue of a concern for their country's backwardness vis-à-vis the West; through a belief in the ability of science and technology to provide answers; by a set of apparently progressive convictions which sought to overcome social conflict and bureaucratic inertia; and by their own professional need to be needed. Similarly, engineers' reflections on what went wrong in 1905 made Western theories of factory organization appear increasingly "right": labor protest had gotten out of hand because of poor management and irrational patterns of work. Scientific management contained strategies to recover the economic losses of the recent past, increase productivity, and discipline both labor and management.

The attitudes of professional engineers were significant, moreover, because they began to reshape the social environment of the factory. Following the 1905 revolution, increasing numbers of technicians began to populate the shop floor. Many came with brash claims to superior knowledge; many were determined to impose "scientifically" conceived systems on the labor force; many saw workers (and very often managers) as objects to be transformed for the greater benefit of the nation. And as engineers tried to "deal" with primitive work methods, their new approaches to industrial organization began to influence the way workers were "handled."[73] While we will observe below that much metalworker protest developed in response to the engineers' fixation on reorganization, efficiency, and regulation, more portentous for Russia's future was the power of engineering ideology to obscure other ways of seeing just as ever-larger segments of educated society became consumed by the project of "modernization."

VIII

RATIONALIZING THE METALWORKING INDUSTRY

The Modernization of Physical Plant and the Reorganization of Business Procedures

Whatever the struggles at the level of public policy, whatever the tensions that pertained between employers and engineers, the big banks as well as individual firms nonetheless had to develop appropriate investment strategies at a time when the government was shifting its economic priorities and in a context of lingering economic stagnation. The production profiles of many metalworking plants necessarily began to shift, for, given the changed demand, these plants could either shut down, retool, or grow into new markets.

To a degree, the industry began to expand in the area of agricultural machinery; and especially during the pre–World War I period, the electrical engineering industry developed rapidly, responding to the needs of expanding urban economies for power, light, trams, telephones, and transformers.[1] Big shifts came in the transportation sector, affecting manufacturers of rails, ties, and bridge structures, as well as the producers of rolling stock. After a sharp decline around the turn of the century, the rate of construction of new track began to stabilize. (Table 8.1.) The production of locomotive engines fell

TABLE 8.1
Construction of Railway Track, 1890–1914

Period	# Kilometers
1890–1894	4,600
1895–1899	12,800
1900–1904	6,200
1905–1909	5,200
1910–1914	6,400

Source: Gatrell, "Industrial Expansion in Tsarist Russia," p. 103.

TABLE 8.2
Producton of Rolling Stock, 1906–1913

Year	# Locomotives	# Wagons (Passenger and Freight)
1906	1,305	22,665
1907	736	15,579
1908	653	10,267
1909	499	6,611
1910	580	9,045
1911	367	9,448
1912	308	12,153
1913	632	20,819

Source: Sovet s"ezdov, *Statisticheskii ezhegodnik na 1914 god*, p. 260.

dramatically after 1906 and did not substantially recover before the war, while output of freight and passenger cars fell seriously between 1906 and 1911, but largely recovered by 1913.[2] (Table 8.2.)

Manufacturers of rolling stock shifted to other types of machine construction, diversifying into the production of steam boilers, turbines, pumps, cranes, presses, and the like. Many giants of the industry like Putilov, Nevskii, and St. Petersburg Metals looked to armament orders to fill the void; on the eve of the war Putilov and others had moved decisively into naval defense contracting and ship construction. (Table 8.3.) State plants like Obukhov and Baltic began retooling on the basis of enormous contracts let for the reconstruction of the fleet, and in response to the development of the dreadnought

TABLE 8.3
Composition of Output at the Putilov Works, 1900–1912

Year	Defense %	Railway Equipment %	Metallurgical Products %	Value of Gross Output (mil. rubles)
1900	14.6	53.3	28.8	n.a.
1905	26.8	54.1	7.5	n.a.
1908	31.0	n.a.	n.a.	n.a.
1910	42.2	34.9	14.0	14.2
1912	45.8	29.6	14.3	22.7

Source: Gatrell, "Industrial Expansion in Tsarist Russia," p. 107.

TABLE 8.4
Concentration and Productivity of St. Petersburg
Metalworking Factories, 1894–1913

	# of Plants	# of Workers	# of Workers per Factory	Growth of Workers as % of 1893	Prod. (in mil. rubles)	Prod. (rubles per worker)	Growth of Prod. as % of 1893
1894/95	148	36,000	243	100	63.0	1,750	100
1900	163	64,513	396	179	97.2	1,507	154
1908	183	53,945	295	150	107.0	1,984	170
1913	230	87,518	380	243	209.0	2,388	332

Source: Kruze, "Promyshlennoe razvitie Peterburga," p. 16.

and the many technological changes required to produce this new class of warship. And while a major share of the government's huge allocations for the fleet was earmarked for the state-owned plants, nonetheless much of the auxiliary nautical equipment, as well as much of the naval ordnance, was produced in private firms developing rapidly on the basis of state contracts. Especially in the 1912–1914 period, the Petersburg metalworking industry expanded with the manufacture of gunsights and cartridges, shells and troop transports, heavy armor plate and gun turrets—in short, the industry grew on the production of a vast array of equipment consumed by a modernizing army and navy financed lavishly by a government concerned with its place in the world.[3]

An important shift in production profiles, a concentration of the industry, as well as the increasing control exercised by the big banks over the heavy industry of the capital took place over the course of the first decade of the twentieth century, but intensified with the economic upswing on the eve of the world war. Retooling, the reorganization of production processes, and expanding applications of power had the consequence of increasing productivity and bringing about shifts in the deployment of labor resources. Thus the electrical energy utilized in the metalworking industry of the capital grew from 24,021 to 42,723 horsepower (or by 78%) between 1894 and 1908, with perhaps 20% of this increase taking place in the 1900–1908 period. By 1913, usage had nearly doubled again, rising to 83,897 horsepower.[4] A substantial investment in physical plant and equipment is further indicated in Table 8.4: despite the exceptionally difficult economic circumstances between 1900 and 1908, output increased by almost 10 million rubles even as work force size fell by some 17%.[5] And while some of these gains in productivity were the result of speed-ups induced by the introduction of new wage systems and tighter controls over time, increased output was also the result of technical modernization.

TABLE 8.5
Growth of Fixed Capital in St. Petersburg Heavy Industry, 1911–1913

Factory	1911 (millions of rubles)	1914 (millions of rubles)
SPb Metals	3.80	9.00
Nevskii	8.51	10.00
Putilov	12.00	25.00
Russian Society for the Production of Shells and Military Supplies (formerly Parviainen)	—	10.00
Lessner	1.65	4.00
SPb Freight Car	2.50	7.75
Koppel'	1.65	2.39
Pneumatic Machine	1.00	1.50
Phoenix	6.00	5.00
Northern Tube Rolling and Engineering	.60	.60
Northern Engineering and Boiler (formerly Til'mans)	2.00	2.00
Zigel'	3.00	3.00
Russian Engine Construction and Engineering	5.22	7.85
Russian Shipbuilding (f. 1911)	—	10.00

Source: Sovet s"ezdov, *Statisticheskii ezhegodnik na 1914 g.*, p. 261; Rozenfel'd and Klimenko, *Istoriia Mashinostroeniia SSSR*, p. 92.

Still more investment occurred in the immediate prewar years, as illustrated by the growth of fixed capital in selected Petersburg factories. (Table 8.5.) Aggregate data for the industry as a whole indicate that some 51% of the basic capital in metalworking went into new equipment.[6] Other surveys of the Empire's machine-construction and metalworking industry covering the 1908–1915 period confirm the technical progress being made in this sector, particularly the acquisition of new machinery. Typically, plants gained economies from the increased usage of fuel and motive power, as well as from utilization of fast-cutting, self-hardening steel.[7]

The modernization of physical plant may be observed in some detail at several factories in the capital. Between 1907 and 1909 the Aleksandrovsk engineering factory laid new narrow gauge track, completed the construction and equipping of several new shops, erected electrical hoisting cranes, adapted to pneumatic drive, purchased the "latest" machine tools, and reorganized its warehousing facilities.[8] Similar changes could be glimpsed elsewhere. At the Baltic factory automatic hammers were installed, while Vulkan acquired new machine tools.[9] St. Petersburg Metals also invested in machine tools, built new shops, and updated operations. The largest machine-construction factory in the capital by the prewar period, St. Petersburg Metals enlarged the size of its work force from about 1,700 to 3,000 between 1900 and 1913, while increasing output from 3.7 million to 8 or 10 million rubles; fixed capital grew from 3.8 to 9.0 million rubles between 1911 and 1914. Particularly over the 1909–1913 period, the factory shifted substantially into the production of military goods.[10]

Elsewhere, the board of directors of the St. Petersburg Freight Car Company decided in 1907 to invest in new equipment so as to reduce expenditures on the work force; between 1911 and 1914, its fixed capital grew from 2.5 to 7.75 million rubles.[11] Following the acquisition of the old Parviainen company and its reorganization as a joint-stock corporation under the aegis of the Russian-Asiatic bank, one million rubles were allocated for the steel foundry and another several thousand rubles to supplement equipment. By 1914, just a few years after its incorporation, the fixed capital of the firm had been increased to 10 million rubles.[12] Also in the prewar period, the G. A. Lessner Companies expanded with the construction of a second factory, while such leaders in the electro-technical field as Siemens-Halske and Shukkert—once independent firms that had virtually merged by the early 1900s—developed an additional plant in 1913, the newly built Siemens-Shukkert plant for the production of dynamos.[13]

Reflecting the increased demands on the state factories in light of the rearmament program, the Izhorsk Works invested heavily in its armor-producing departments, adding a new open hearth shop as well as large-scale presses. New furnaces, machine tools, and cranes were installed, while the engineering assembly shop was retooled for the manufacture of internal combustion engines. Other shops within the engineering division were not fundamentally rationalized, however, and some products—chain, for example—continued to be hand fabricated.[14] At the Obukhov Steel Works, electricity was gradually brought to the shops: machine tools were given electric motors, while electric cranes replaced the old mechanical ones. Consumption of electricity increased from 2,100 thousand kilowatt-hours in 1907 to 3,700 thousand kilowatt-hours in 1912, a 76% increase. Acetylene welding and metal cutting were introduced; riveting, previously done by hand, was dramatically modernized.[15]

Engineering studies of technical obsolescence in the metallurgical and locomotive departments of the Nevskii factory undertaken in 1909 revealed an urgent need for reorganization. Of 338 machine tools in the engineering shop of the locomotive department, less than half were deemed suitable for use; a mere handful (just 43) were judged to meet the "demands of modern technology." More than half were found to need either major repair or complete elimination. The forging capabilities of the factory were also deemed primitive, with difficulties here reflected in wasteful expenditures on iron, copper, and steel. Comprehensive renovation of the metallurgical department was undertaken in the prewar years, when agreements between the Nevskii and Putilov factories transferred orders for some rolled goods to the latter plant; the requirements of both factories for large and specialized casts and forgings were to be satisfied by the construction of a new steel mill. Reforms in the locomotive department were undertaken immediately, however, with at least one Nevskii engineer traveling to England to study production processes in metalworking plants there. An extensive new shop was equipped and all engineering work was transferred to it "on the basis of a strict division of labor." Specialized milling and grinding machines were installed, in addition to other technical changes which "in the opinion of the administration [would]fundamentally alter the relationship between wages and the productivity of labor."[16]

Following an intense struggle with the Petersburg International Bank for control over the Putilov Works, the Russian-Asiatic Bank secured the dominant position early in 1912; within the year, the Nevskii works had been acquired, and by the eve of the war Aleksei Putilov and his bank had pulled together eight leading machine-construction firms in a defense-related conglomerate possessing enormous resources. Capitalized at 25 million rubles, the Putilov works undertook major reconstruction: the metallurgical department was reorganized; new equipment and machine tools for the artillery department were purchased; several shops within the engineering department were retooled; and the internal transport system was improved with the laying of new track and the expansion of rolling stock.[17]

Investment in physical plant and equipment had a number of consequences. Because, for example, the manufacture of armaments at some plants was different from what had been produced before, as well as more technologically sophisticated in many cases, the changes that began to take place in these factories affected not only the composition of the machine tool park, but the work process itself. Certain weapons systems—as well as many of the components produced by the electrical engineering industry—could be manufactured by mass production techniques; the assembly of parts by semi-skilled labor had thus begun to replace the fabrication of whole machines by skilled workers at some of the capital's factories.[18] More generally, across the various sectors of the industry, shifts in the products line of a given firm would normally entail the closure of some shops and the reorganization of equipment and processes in others; applications of hydraulic power, electricity, or fuel-driven machinery replaced processes heretofore dependent on the physical strength or dexterity of the worker.

Overall, however, these changes took time and did not occur uniformly throughout the industry: new machinery and new processes came on line gradually; much of the old machine tool stock necessarily remained as reorganization proceeded; shifts in the deployment of labor resources took place on a shop-by-shop basis, perhaps even individually. As well, the pace of technological change was governed by the differential access of individual firms to adequate levels of capitalization and sources of foreign expertise. As a result, backwardness and modernity in industrial plant commingled, insuring, among other things, a continuing demand for skilled cadres both to install and maintain the new equipment and to man the older stock. Nonetheless, the major shocks of the early twentieth century—economic crisis, war and revolution, a shift in the government's economic priorities—produced substantial change in the equipment and production processes employed in Petersburg's heavy industry.

The many changes in physical plant and technology gradually led to shifts in the industry's labor employment practices and in work force composition, but the nature and extent of these shifts were obscured by other factors. In the immediate aftermath of 1905, punitive layoffs, combined with the reduced demand that accompanied the lingering economic stagnation, led to reductions in overall employment in the industry; but technical rationalization and the intensification of work also contributed to the declining demand for labor.

While there are no really reliable figures on unemployment and its causes, the 1909 survey of the Metalworkers' Union estimated that 20,000–25,000 metalworkers were jobless in 1907–1908, and the union's historian, Fedor Bulkin, suggested that 10–15% were unemployed in 1908–1909.[19] *Kuznets* reported a 36% curtailment in work force size at eight major metalworking plants of the capital over the course of 1907.[20] According to one survey of jobless metalworkers between January and November 1908, while dismissals for repressive reasons (strikes, conflicts, lockouts, political convictions) played a major role, accounting for 42.5% of discharges in 1907 but falling to 26.9% in 1908, dismissals due to cutbacks in production had already reached 49.3% in 1907 and continued to climb to 69.0% in 1908. The survey further noted that a significant cause of unemployment was the increasing intensification of work processes: wage incentive schemes and to a lesser extent new technologies had increased labor productivity and as a result employers had been able to economize on work force size.[21] Recall also the recognition on the part of the leaders of the unemployed movement that the causes of joblessness had shifted over the 1906–1907 period and that young, skilled, literate, and well-paid metalworkers had been particularly hard hit.[22]

Shifts in the industry's labor employment policy were reflected in other ways as well and it appears that both technological rationalization and the changing perspectives of management played a part in bringing them about. Thus the *fil'trovka* began to weed out many types of workers, not only the politically suspect, but those who were undesirable from the point of view of factory economy. For employers focused on reducing costs, the removal

of old and ill workers became a prime target, to be carried out before they
sought grants to cover illness or accidents, or demanded to go on pension.
New rules began to come out specifying upper age limits on hiring, in one
case not over thirty-five and in another not over forty.[23]

Young people were affected in a different way. With the simplification of
work processes came the degradation of meaningful apprenticeship programs. In the post-1905 factory, an "apprentice" might be held in one position
for a longer time than required, learning what was increasingly becoming a
much less complex skill or employed on identical processes as adult workers,
but at a lower rate of pay. In either case, the employer capitalized on the
cheaper labor of young people.[24] As well, the number of women employed
in the capital's metalworking plants began to grow: *Metallist*, citing factory
inspectorate data, noted that female employment in the industry had increased by 33% between 1901 and 1910, while the male component grew by
only 8%.[25]

This hiring of young people and women was often perceived as a generalized assault on skill. Already in August 1907, the metalworking press was
speaking of "major technological changes which [were] displacing workers,"
while a detailed discussion of the Aleksandrovsk engineering factory in 1909
stressed the depth of the processes of rationalization which were restructuring all aspects of life in the capital's industry:

> Extraordinarily profound changes in the relations of labor and capital have
> been introduced in recent years. Collecting themselves from the violent shocks
> of the revolutionary period, capital has endeavored with all efforts to recon-
> struct internal relations at the factories and plants in accordance with the latest
> word in capitalist exploitation.[26]

One union official, who surveyed 38 plants in 1909, found that many
dismissals were accompanied by a decrease in rates, and at the same time,
adult workers were replaced by adolescents, men by women, trained workers
by common laborers. While technical modernization was sporadic, various
improvements were observed in the forge shop at Putilov (new riveting
processes had dramatically increased the speed of this operation), new machine tools and cranes were installed at United Cable and Langenzipen, and
a range of improvements had occurred at the Aleksandrovsk works.[27]

For some workers, these changes resulted in dismissal, reassignment to a
different shop or to a less desirable job, or work on new processes which
paid less and required a greater intensity of effort. By and large, however,
demand for skilled workers remained quite high, especially in the prewar
period, as the rapid expansion of the industry required more workers, and
as the technological development of the industry demanded skilled cadres
able to install and maintain the new processes.[28] Indeed, from management's
point of view, the absence of adequate reserves of skilled labor posed a threat
to the industry and to the united front of employers.[29] Overall, though,
technological change and the reconceived employment practices of manage-

ment began to alter the social context pertaining in the shops where adult, skilled, male metalworkers labored.

The problems experienced by employers also made imperative greater attention to commercial and accounting procedures.[30] If, earlier, firms rarely maintained records to document expenditures on materials and labor, scarcely knew in any detail the costs of production, failed to monitor work flows closely, or refused to employ the requisite technical and administrative staff to generate this information, management was now persuaded of the utility of cost-benefit analysis and the economies to be realized by more sophisticated accounting methodologies. If, earlier, pay office clerks labored over torn and dirty workbooks and the barely legible notations of foremen, now worksheets, rating tables, instruction cards, and the like supplemented the workbook. These far more detailed printed forms gradually allowed for the gathering of crucial data on the organization of production processes and passed them on to management for analysis and subsequent action. Further systematization included the installation of timeclocks, with the punchcard constituting an additional record of account with the worker. Office procedures became more specialized and simple mechanical devices were applied to routine operations. Filing systems organized blueprints and drawings for the needs of the planning department; heretofore such documents had remained in the shops, under the physical control of foremen and workers.[31]

All this required an expanded administrative and technical staff.[32] And, as we have seen, these newly trained professionals, conscious of the value of their skills, formed their own associations, published their own journals, and organized conferences, persuaded, among other things, of the urgent need to assault Russia's primitive industrial practices.[33]

A pattern of increased reliance on such personnel was apparent in data cited in the 1909 survey conducted by the Metalworkers' Union.[34] Such a trend is also suggested by materials gathered by the Central Statistical Administration; while not limited to St. Petersburg these data show a continuing industry-wide expansion in the employment of technical and administrative personnel over the 1913–1918 period. (Table 8.6.) As this table illustrates, the technical and administrative staff in metalworking was significantly larger than in other branches of the economy. Moreover, the ratio of workers to technical personnel in the machine-construction sector was particularly high—more than double that which existed in Russian industry as a whole.

The metalworking industry in general and Petersburg machine-construction factories in particular were thus increasingly reliant on the services of trained professionals; their presence came to influence not only the production processes and business methodologies utilized in the industry, but the social composition of the workplace as well. More so than in other sectors of the economy, supervisory personnel became increasingly visible in the shops and offices of the capital's heavy industry. With this personnel came a more articulated hierarchy of command and execution, more formalized relations, and a still greater distance between workers and employers. And while

TABLE 8.6
Employment of Technical and Administrative Staff in Selected Industries, All-Russia, 1913–1918

Sector	# of Factories with Data on # of Employees	# of Workers in Them	Total # of Employees	In Which			# of Workers per Employees	# of Workers per Technical Staff
				Directors and Managers	Technical Staff	Other Employees		
IX. Metal processing								
1913	103	24,824	2,281	104	534	1,643	10.9	46.5
1914	103	24,966	2,486	106	567	1,813	10.0	44.0
1915	103	29,582	2,880	107	643	2,130	10.3	46.0
1916	103	34,859	3,449	106	689	2,654	10.1	50.6
1917	103	34,524	3,601	101	720	2,780	9.6	48.0
1918	103	20,126	2,746	102	522	2,122	7.3	38.6
X. Machine construction								
1913	113	117,410	11,758	241	3,596	7,921	10.0	32.7
1914	113	134,712	14,260	247	4,475	9,538	9.4	30.1
1915	113	175,333	17,637	268	5,118	12,251	9.9	34.3
1916	113	216,268	21,971	276	5,962	15,733	9.8	35.6
1917	113	232,845	25,996	281	6,069	19,646	9.0	38.4
1918	113	124,789	20,323	256	4,213	15,854	6.1	29.6
All sectors								
1913	2,029	856,165	58,382	2,380	11,343	43,756	14.7	75.5
1914	2,029	860,921	63,241	2,407	12,462	47,529	13.6	69.1
1915	2,029	909,796	68,136	2,483	13,230	51,896	13.3	68.8
1916	2,029	943,155	75,424	2,462	14,356	57,768	12.5	65.7
1917	2,029	979,915	85,039	2,527	15,334	66,279	11.5	63.9
1918	2,029	806,904	78,554	2,468	12,970	62,370	10.3	62.2

Source: "Fabrichno-zavodskaia promyshlennost' v period 1913–1918 gg.," *Tsentral'noe statisticheskoe upravlenie: Trudy,* vol. 26, vyp. 1 and 2, pp. 68–9, 74–5, 118–9.

technical and administrative staff were employed to implement reforms envisioned by management, they undoubtedly brought their own concerns and priorities to the task, at once influencing the thinking of their employers and shaping the experience of workers on the shop floor.

We can look closely at the practice of several leading metalworking plants of the capital to see in detail the changing perspectives of employers regarding technical rationalization and improved commercial and accounting methodologies.[35] At the Atlas factory, for example, a variety of problems led to the introduction of a new accounting system modeled on the practice of the Berlin firm of L. Lowe, as well as that of several American factories. Prior to the changes that were implemented in 1906, the work of the accounting department had focused on the commercial aspects of business operations, rather than problems in the factory's economy. Preliminary calculations consisted in crude estimates of the cost of the work; typically a clerk went around to the shops twice a day, and, according to information supplied by workers, the time expended on each order was figured. Verification was by the profit and loss of the entire factory, determined at the end of the fiscal year. The cost of an article was calculated "by the eye," while prices were often guided by the prices of competitors. A. F. German, Atlas's owner, recognized that such methods relied "exclusively on the memory, conscientiousness, and attention of clerks and workers." He was therefore concerned with the development of accounting procedures which would free management from its problematic dependence on individual persons in the lower-level administration.[36]

Under a new system introduced in 1906, incoming orders were analyzed by senior technical personnel in conjunction with shop managers, thus utilizing both the theoretical and practical expertise of the staff. Each order was divided into parts and further subdivided into operations. Various colored "cheques" or forms routed the order through phases of the production process; at the completion of the work the cheques were compiled and tabulated in the main accounting office for a final determination of the time, labor, and materials utilized. Management derived several benefits: it was no longer reliant on the discretion of lower-level personnel, analysis of individual aspects of the production process permitted further specialization, profit and loss was calculated on each order, and work flows were considerably speeded.

This contributed in turn to the development of new mass-production techniques at the Atlas factory, for which unskilled labor was specifically trained. Further economies were achieved by the close observation of workers through time study, on the basis of which detailed instructions were elaborated which minutely prescribed the various individual manipulations the worker was to perform. An array of new forms, worksheets, and the like recorded the worker's name and number, the work station, the beginning and end of a task, the shop pay per hour, actual work time and the percentage of time economized on the task, and the premium earned. The shift to new accounting methodologies and detailed written forms thus permitted management to conceptualize factory operations in a more sophisticated manner, which in turn helped to elucidate problems in the plant economy and identify specific areas in which the factory could successfully compete. As well, the reforms provided essential data to reorganize basic production processes, calculate wages, and monitor working time.

At Semenov, widely regarded as a model machine-construction factory, six departments worked under the general administration of the factory: a commercial department, a section for the preparation of work, another for the distribution of work, a third for the determination of time and workers' wages, in addition to a design office, and a council, consisting of department heads and the director of the factory. Such an organizational scheme had been developed, in part, to facilitate the training of requisite foremen and supervisory personnel, as Semenov had found that the strict delimitation of the functions of each department eliminated costly expenditures on more generally competent personnel trained in several areas. In Semenov's words: "Up to now, the typical foreman was a universal man who acquired those skills which permitted him to direct work by long years of experience. His knowledge had become an art and since his sphere of competence was great, then, generally speaking, the productivity and quality of his labor was not great."[37]

Central to operations at Semenov was the detailed specification of each aspect of work. Time study was employed to fix the exact time in which a task should be performed; piece-rate systems and a premium plan were elaborated in conformity with these tests; machine tools were studied to determine the speed and depth of a cut, the materials to be used, and the time utilized in the task. All these data were recorded on specially designed forms developed by technicians, statisticians, and clerks working to collect information on time and productivity and to transform it into detailed instruction cards, work sheets, and wage formulas given out to foremen and workers. Copies of these various forms circulated through the relevant departments for analysis, in the end making possible exact determination of the cost of individual items, as well as the overall profit and loss of the factory.

On the cutting edge of the new practices, Semenov provides one of the best illustrations of the integration of diverse aspects of the rationalization process: the utilization of advanced technologies, the subdivision and functional specialization of work and staff, the increase in written documentation to structure factory operations, the expansion of administrative staff with an attendant increase in overhead expenses, and the application of a variety of Taylorist methodologies (e.g., time study, progressive wage systems, and the provision of detailed specifications for the operation of individual machine tools).

The application of more advanced technologies to the production process and more sophisticated accounting procedures to plant operations thus began to alter established patterns of work in the industry. And while much remained unchanged in the capital's metalworking factories, a qualitatively new sort of thinking began to animate the offices of many firms. These new approaches were stimulated, in part, by the perspectives of the St. Petersburg financial oligarchy, whose vision of a more economically powerful Russia hinged on developing large-scale organizational forms able to increase the productive might of the nation and compete in the international arena. These productivist concerns, as well as the technocratic views of many engineering professionals, were in turn conditioned by the way in which these men perceived domestic realities and developments elsewhere. For them, the key problem lay in Russia's economic backwardness; the task was to overhaul an industrial structure mired in antiquated machinery, primitive work methods, a general absence of entrepreneurial initiative, and crippling legislative regulations. In their view, the world economy was incontestably shaped by advances in Western managerial science and by the organizational forms adopted by Western finance capitalism. Russia simply had to respond to these realities. All these pressures and perceptions influenced the choices made in Petersburg factories; all had an impact on labor-management relations in the post-1905 period.

Reforms on the Shop Floor: Wage
Policy and Controls over Time

Employers in Petersburg heavy industry experimented with other changes in work practice over the course of the inter-revolutionary period that were far less costly and time-consuming than the reorganization of production processes or business procedures. Particularly in the area of wage policy and the utilization of work time, management sought to achieve substantial savings as well as greater labor discipline.

As we have seen, employers had begun in 1906 to identify wage policy as a source of numerous problems.[38] Haggling over rates produced conflict on the shop floor; rates set by individual foremen tended to vary from shop to shop and resulted in significant inconsistencies across the factory, as well as industry-wide; wages earned by the day or on simple piece rates permitted workers too much latitude in determining the pace of their own productivity. "Goldbricking" was thought to be one consequence of such lax policies.

In the private sector, an important change in wage policy was signaled by an industry-wide shift from day-based to hourly based wages in 1908. On March 1, 1908, the Petersburg Society of Mill and Factory Owners sent a circular to its member firms regarding the wisdom of hourly computation of wages. It noted that several factories had already adopted this measure, that it had not only "direct practical significance," but was extremely important in the question of setting similar rates for similar branches of production.[39] A March 4 meeting of the Engineering Section unanimously resolved to adopt hourly wages and on March 13, it sent a circular outlining its views. Paraphrased, the document stated:

1. Hourly pay, which is a smaller accounting unit, presents a certain convenience in the establishment of a correct system of shop-hourly pay [*pravil'naia sistema tsekhovykh pochasovykh plat*];
2. It facilitates accounting with workers when they do not work a full day or when they work overtime;
3. It creates disadvantageous circumstances for the worker if he is late;
4. It instills in the worker the conviction that shortening the workday on Saturdays and pre-holidays will have an adverse effect on his earnings;
5. It makes it possible to establish uniform rates of compensation in similar plants for shop pay [*po tsekhu*];
6. It can facilitate the establishment in the future of uniform rates in similar plants for piece work [*na sdel'nyia raboty*] as well.[40]

The circular further directed its members to use a half-kopeck as the basic unit of account in order to insure sufficient "elasticity." All private metalworking plants of the capital were to adopt this measure simultaneously—although a particular date for the transition was not specified—while representatives of the state factories were to be informed since the PSMFO believed that "unity in this [policy] with [the state] plants is especially important."[41]

The PSMFO's directive implicitly recognized that work discipline and monetary incentives might be fruitfully linked in a new wage policy. Such a realization marked a significant departure from earlier employer thinking on these issues, which had not been particularly sensitive to the potential of monetary incentives in bringing about greater labor discipline and increased productivity, nor rigorous in conceptualizing wage policy from the point of view of time management. Now employers looked much more closely at expenditures on work time: with calculations by the hour and by the half-kopeck, inaccuracies built into larger units of account could gradually be eliminated, as could the discretion exercised by shop personnel when they rounded off an hour to facilitate computations. Real and immediate savings were the result: not only was the worker more easily docked for lateness or "laziness," but industrialists could free themselves entirely of the cost of paying a full day's wage (typically ten hours) when the plant closed early on Saturdays and the numerous pre-holidays (when a seven and one-half–hour day was the norm).[42]

The shift to hourly computation of wages also served as a starting point for the development of more sophisticated piece-rate schemes. The objective of these "progressive" plans was to break the collective control workers exercised over their productivity by using monetary incentives that stimulated their competitive drive. The underlying logic was to encourage harder work by the promise of higher earnings, rather than to compel intensive labor by means of long hours, low wages, and the coercive drive methods of foremen. Coupled with monetary deterrents to discourage lateness, absenteeism, or demands for a shorter day, monetary incentives were designed to increase labor productivity and undermine labor solidarity by focusing workers on the pursuit of individual gain. As well, foremen who once "managed" their workers by bribe-taking, favoritism, arbitrary rate-cutting, and the with-holding of wages could be reined in by more systematized wage policies implemented from above and governing the entire factory. Taken together, the changes in wage policy apparent in Petersburg metalworking plants indicated that management was beginning to replace its more primitive and overtly coercive forms of labor discipline with considerably more sophisti-cated capitalist methodologies that hinged on monetary stimuli. Getting workers to internalize these sorts of stimuli suggested the appealing notion of a self-regulating system of control.

In addition to the adoption of hourly based wages, some firms began to alter their piece-rate systems.[43] Change in this regard differed widely from factory to factory: some firms experimented with the complex plans devised by Taylor, Halsey, and Rowan, while others opted for less sophisticated schemes that often amounted to little more than a poorly disguised policy of rate-cutting. From the point of view of labor, something new and unsettling was occurring on the shop floor, apparently orchestrated by the PSMFO. The journal of the Metalworkers' Union put it thus:

> Since the time when the Naval Ministry took the initiative and in 1906 intro-duced the American system at Obukhov, St. Petersburg factory owners have not stopped avidly looking at this new invention. When their leaders were convinced that the system was well conceived and workers were prepared to endure all, Glezmer [S. P. Glezmer, chairman of the PSMFO] lifted the conductor's baton and said: Gentlemen, begin! And at all factories belonging to the Society of Mill and Factory Owners, preparations began for the intro-duction of the American system.[44]

Unease was also registered at union meetings[45] and in worker slang. Talk of "American wages" or the "Amerikanka" or the "ekonomiia"—the loose jargon used by metalworkers to describe all manner of piece-rate systems and changes in methods of recording wage rates—began to figure in worker correspondence from the factories found on the back pages of the labor press. Judging by these alarmed comments, at least a dozen firms had implemented some sort of "American-based" plan during the 1906–1914 period: Phoenix, Kreiton, San-Galli, Vulkan, Struck, Siemens-Halske, Obukhov, Baltic, Nevskii, Semenov, Atlas, Glebov, Pneumatic Machine, and the Sestroretsk Arms Fac-tory.[46] The total number was undoubtedly higher.[47]

Other factories restructured wage policy by changing the way work was rated, issued and recorded. By some accounts, the establishment of rates bureaus became the *idée fixe* of many industrialists; in St. Petersburg they existed at the Lessner, Nevskii, Nobel, New Admiralty, and Semenov plants, and perhaps at Obukhov and Baltic.[48] According to *Metallist*, rates bureaus existed at some plants "according to the German model," and determined wages by "scientific methods."[49] Workers at United Cable confirmed they were sweated "po-germanskii," but noted wryly that other aspects of factory life remained "po-russkii."[50]

Determining "objective" rates was but one of the tasks of the rate bureaus; they also occupied themselves with time-motion studies and the generation of a new array of printed forms given to the worker when he was issued a task. These were variously called order sheets (*nariadnye listy*),[51] (*kontrol'nye listy*), or a check or card system. Typically, the worker was required to note when he began and ended a task. In some cases, the time allotted for a task was specified, in others the procedure and materials the worker used was defined.[52] When the rate on a particular piece was not designated in the rates book or on a table hung in the shop, it was to be noted on the order sheet prior to the beginning of work.

The widespread utilization of new forms for the rate-setting process encouraged the state's Office on Factory Affairs to issue additional guidelines. A May 1909 ruling specified that all such forms be considered supplementary books of account with the worker, presumably subject to verification by workers or the factory inspectorate if conflict arose.[53] Another ruling followed in November 1909 in response to queries by the PSMFO: while the rates book was subject to a stamp tax, other rating forms were to remain exempt.[54] Both rulings suggested the need to tighten the various regulations governing the use of these newly important forms. Nonetheless, the labor press and the Metalworkers' Union remained concerned with the abuses that attended the introduction of these procedures and began to advise workers of their legal rights,[55] while workers continued to complain of irregularities and stressed that the multiplicity of new forms easily eluded the control of the factory inspectors.

Management's heightened concern with the relationship between labor discipline, wage policy, and time management not only resulted in the appearance of time-work specialists on the shop floor, as well as new forms to document actual work time and monitor work flows, but changes in the rules of internal order governing the structure of the workday, revamped fine schedules to insure enforcement of the new rules, automatic punch clocks and turnstyles, new "fine whistles," and work assignments on multiple tasks. Linked with the new wage systems and the expanded staff of supervisory personnel, managerial control over work time was significantly extended by these diverse methods.

The changing structure and pace of the workday can be glimpsed in several of the capital's plants. For many Petersburg workers, the workday began with the factory whistle signaling the start of work at 6:30. In the Narvskii district where the giant Putilov works was located, three whistles sounded—at 5:50, 6:20, and 6:40, with the last indicating that the worker was ten minutes late. A similar pattern structured the dinner break, and again a "fine" whistle blew to mark lateness. Like their counterparts at other metalworking factories, Putilovtsy carried a square metal number that was used to check in, a process which took a few minutes as the many workers of the plant lined up to hang their numbers on a wooden dock or drop them in a box. Long-established practice had allowed a worker to enter the front gates by 6:30, hang his number, pass across what was often a considerable extent of yard to the far-flung shops, and begin work at 7:00 without a penalty fine. Shop tradition also permitted a "free time" period, five to fifteen minutes before the start of work in the morning and after dinner.

In February 1912, these practices were changed by Putilov's newly appointed director, S. G. Labunskii. Concerned that work was not begun promptly and trying to effect a greater control over the admission of workers into the factory grounds, the new director introduced a second, oval number. Workers now deposited the square number upon entrance into the factory and the oval number when they reached the shop. The "fine" whistle was changed to 6:45 and 1:45, with penalties for lateness strictly enforced.

Workers protested that the workday had been lengthened and began to organize a strike to demand the abolition of the new system, as well as the introduction of a nine-hour day. In some shops a sit-down strike was called, while elsewhere workers destroyed an electrical bell, newly erected to sound the fine in the hot shops. But with minor alterations, the new rules stayed in force.[56]

At the Nevskii factory a somewhat different procedure was employed. As in the past, workers were required to pass through the entrance gate and deposit their number, but later a new automatic barrier was installed within the factory yard. It took some five minutes to reach this second checkpoint, and workers were required to pass through it prior to the fine whistle. If they failed to do so, they had to return to the front office and get a special fine pass, at the cost of twenty kopecks. They were now docked for each minute of lateness, when in the past delays of up to five minutes were ignored.[57]

In the fall of 1913 turnstyles were installed at the Obukhov factory, designed to control the lines of workers as they punched in at the newly erected time clocks. Workers complained that this procedure added an extra fifteen minutes to the day. In November, several hundred Obukhovtsy demonstratively refused to punch out; this was followed by a strike of considerable duration, but one that ended in failure.[58]

Before the outbreak of the war, automatic time clocks had been installed at many of the capital's metalworking factories, affording a strange contrast to the simple wooden docks which had heretofore been used. Relying on the back pages of the labor press, workers at United Cable, Glebov, Shukkert, St. Petersburg Pipe, St. Petersburg Metals, and Tiudor let their comrades know that such devices had begun to shape their lives.[59]

Punch clocks, additional "numbers," new fine whistles and bells, closing gates, turnstyles, and vigilant supervisors became management's most visible (or audible) weapon in the struggle over work time. All effected tighter controls over the traditional "free time" workers enjoyed at the beginning of the day or after the dinner break. Supervisors intensified observation of the bathroom and guarded against smoking, drinking tea, or wandering off to another shop. They insured that wash-up at the end of the day didn't begin too early and made certain workers stayed at their benches. And they levied fines.[60]

Indeed, the imposition of fines in the inter-revolutionary period seemed to pursue new goals. If earlier, fines were designed to punish workers financially, and at least prior to 1886 put money in the employer's pocket, they now seemed to bear a more clearly disciplinary character. Sketchy data describing patterns of fining for all Russia, gathered by M. S. Balabanov in the 1920s and more recently by Iu. I. Kir'ianov, suggest that the frequency of fining increased in the years following the first revolution, as did the imposition of fines for improper work.[61] More impressionistic material from the metalworkers' press confirms the increased use of fines and often mentions the fault finding and petty carping of foremen.[62] Such penalties thus suggested that an old practice was bent to new purposes: fines were imposed to enforce compliance with changing methods and standards of work.

The sharper focus on time and work discipline was reflected in many other ways as well. In the model rules of internal order developed by the Engineering Section of the PSMFO in June 1908, tardiness, even for one minute, was to be fined and the worker not allowed through the factory gates after fifteen minutes.[63] In 1912, the PSMFO resolved to issue paychecks after the end of work, arguing that workers wasted too much time.[64] Elsewhere, management tried to lengthen the workday by eliminating time and one-half for overtime.[65] At still other factories, speedups were effected by assigning workers to operate more than one machine tool at a time; that is, the worker was required to perform different operations on different benches simultaneously.[66]

Managers also utilized time studies. At some plants, the use of stopwatches seemed more a method of intimidation than an instrument of careful analysis. At the Glebov factory, the director had his "foremen go around with watches and check up on workers," while at St. Petersburg Metals, workers complained that their "fattened foreman comes up to the bench, takes out a watch and says to workers: set it with more traction, at a faster pace and take it with greater force [vziat' s truzhku]."[67] Elsewhere, however, chronometry was practiced in earnest.[68] Explained I. A. Semenov:

> We study machine work individually. In detail, the capacity and speed of the machine tool is studied. By means of arithmetic calculations, the necessary machine tools are selected and the time necessary for the processing of an article is computed. Then the most advantageous combination is formulated and the worker is told at what speed to feed the machine, at what thickness the shaving must be, and so on. . . .
> All norms are strictly verified and observation goes on constantly.[69]

Often the practitioners of time study were young technical students on training assignments in the factories; and their age, their social background, as well as their methods seemed to have combined to become particularly offensive to the work force. At Baltic such students, acting as assistant foremen, administered tests to incoming workers and observed their performance with stopwatches.[70] The Nevskii factory employed students in its rates bureau (scornfully dubbed the "funeral bureau" by workers), and it was these young technicians who studied the machine tools and the workers and who then calculated speeds and wage rates.[71] In 1913, a sixty-day strike at the New Aivaz factory broke out over the issue of time study, a conflict that began when the student Balik was carted out of the shop in a wheelbarrow.[72]

It was precisely this sense of constant, intrusive supervision that rankled workers and tugged at their sense of autonomy and which, as we will observe in greater detail below, they fought with such tenacity in strike actions breaking out over issues of time and conflicts with supervisory personnel in the prewar period.[73] In important respects, though, management had engaged the struggle over time in response to labor conflicts in 1905 which had centered, at least in part, on the attainment of an eight-hour day. Combined with assaults on the authority of their foremen and concessions given under duress on wage rates, employers were pushed to articulate new policies in the post-revolutionary period designed to restore labor discipline, reduce labor costs, and deal with problems of lingering economic stagnation. But whether they reorganized their operations or not, employers sought to establish order and discipline in the shops. Metalworkers, whether they were subjected to new methods or old, simultaneously resented the reimposition of autocratic practices and feared that managerial innovations would spread through the industry.

IX

THE UNEVEN STRUGGLE IN
THE YEARS BEFORE LENA

In the years between 1907 and 1912, a deceptive quiet descended on the Petersburg labor movement. Beset by unemployment, weakened by the effective collapse of their organizations, and troubled by the many changes taking place on the shop floor, Petersburg metalworkers proved largely unable to resist the assaults of the state or the managerial offensive. Indeed many metalworkers struggled simply to cope—with the increasing cost of living, the overcrowded housing, the dangerous conditions that pertained in the disease-ridden slums of the capital. Demoralized by the defeats they had suffered, many workers turned their anger inward to destructive bouts of drinking, self-punishingly long hours of overtime, or the final despair of suicide.[1] Social Democracy mirrored this disarray in a distressing series of "expropriations" and in the rise of Liquidationism—both currents a reflection of the contracted possibilities for change.

In these difficult times, the Metalworkers' Union barely limped along: membership dwindled and regular participation in the life of the union all but ceased. The governing board, composed principally of Menshevik *praktiki*, worried about the weak links between the leadership and the rank and file and wondered what to do. And while they worked hard on the journal, on developing legal and medical assistance for their members, on perfecting the internal organization of the union and participating in conferences on various social issues, these Menshevik *praktiki* did very little organizing at the grass-roots level. Believing that an open, legal labor movement would finally emerge, they waited patiently, poised and ready to lead "the movement" when it revived again.

Labor in the Years of Reaction

As we have seen, high levels of unemployment pertained in the metalworking industry through 1910. Most intense from the early months of 1907 well into 1908 (with some data suggesting rates as high at 38%), joblessness then began to moderate from the latter part of 1908.[2] By 1910, factory inspectorate reports began to note the recovery of the metalworking industry, beginning with the smaller factories working for the domestic market, which grew in conjunction with the good harvests of 1909 and 1910, and then in the major plants, which expanded at least in part due to the huge state outlays for the rearmament program. In 1911, the inspectorate reported an increase in the number of workers employed by St. Petersburg industry in iron processing by 14% over 1910, and in machine construction by 21%.[3]

The degree to which real wages simultaneously fell in this period is difficult to determine, but in very general terms it seems safe to say that nominal wages were more or less stable in 1906 and into 1907, fell in 1908–1909, and began to increase modestly in 1910.[4] According to the Union's 1909 survey, wages actually rose somewhat between 1906 and 1907, but then declined in 1908 due to the general shift of metalworking industrialists to an hourly based computation of wages in March of that year, as well as the elimination of full pay on Saturdays and pre-holidays. Union sources also note "a whole series of attempts to transfer to the 'American system'" which were everywhere coupled with a sharp lowering of rates.[5]

As regards piece-rate scales, union sources paint a widely varying picture. At some plants, frequent cuts in rates had not occurred; in others, a lowering of rates was accompanied by technical improvements, and workers had not suffered an overall loss. In still other factories, the decrease in rates took place in conjunction with a marked intensification of labor, and only a faster pace of work allowed workers to maintain their former wages. Finally, the expanded use of overtime, the restoration of fines, at some plants the replacement of men by women and adults by adolescents, also influenced the downward course of wages.[6]

Whatever the objective change in wage levels, general perception was unambiguous: worker correspondence to the labor press leaves the unmistakable impression that rates were routinely cut and the pay packet diminished in all manner of ways. These perceptions, though, were bound up with a sense that many things were changing for the worse, so that a general if amorphous anger fueled grievances over wages. At issue, then, was not only the size and form of remuneration, but a host of other changes that were altering life on the shop floor. But at the same time, and as a product of the experiences of 1905–1906, workers brought to the shop a more skeptical attitude toward authority and a much sharper perception of supervisory personnel as enemy and antagonist. With time, consequently, the key flash points of labor-management conflict would center on these managerial personnel and the reforms they were implementing in the area of time management.

Workers recorded their distress by conveying a sense of exhaustion with the killing pace of work, by suggesting that so much was changing that even managers had lost sight of what they wanted, and by protesting the petty faultfinding of their foremen. Wrote one: "We work like horses. It is impossible to leave your place for a second."[7] Another felt that workers couldn't "forget for a minute that the vigilant eye of the boss, who rul[ed] with an iron hand, [was] constantly upon them."[8] At Nevskii, "The smallest delay, a minute breather, [was] now seen as slacking off and frequently serv[ed] as an occasion for the foreman to send you for a dismissal slip."[9] At the repair shops of the Nikolaevsk railroad, the boss's penetration into the "minutiae of factory life [had] quite perceptibly affect[ed] workers."[10] At the Baltic works "orders pour out one after another and each snatches some sort of worker right."[11] Everywhere, it seemed, "the strengthened staff of foremen vigilantly follow each move of the worker: God save you to talk with a neighbor, take a smoke, leave the bench, sit in a group, or still worse, glance at a paper. Fine, Fine, Fine!!"[12] At St. Petersburg Metals, workers complained that their foreman forced too fast a pace. Knowing that nothing good could come from all this pressure, they nonetheless did everything according to orders, and "of course, working with force [broke] some part of an expensive, specialized foreign machine tool. . . ." And then there was "some state examiner" who had presented "impossible demands for work." So a situation developed in which "one isn't right, another is no good and all is carping and faultfinding. In a word, they go to such extremes that they themselves don't know what they want and what they demand."[13]

The many changes that attended management's greater concern with time discipline further contributed to the workers' sense of encroachment. Particularly offensive were the stopwatch and the automatic punch clock. Union sources observed that "All factories began to acquire automatic control clocks which noted with a red line the slightest lateness. Every week, the minutes and seconds were lumped together and presented to the worker in his paycheck as a bill."[14]

But just as disturbing was the withdrawal of "free time" before the beginning of work and after lunch; or the loss of flexibility in rules governing lateness and checking in; or the right to drink tea or take a smoke.[15] At issue were changes in the heretofore accepted norms of factory life which had never been codified in the work rules, but which management had tacitly accepted. In the different world of the post-1905 factory, formal regulation eliminated the small but valued "freedoms" built in by workers to modify the length and pace of the workday.

Also disorienting were changes in work force composition. Union reports observed that women had replaced men at the United Cable Factory and adolescents had taken over adults' jobs at the St. Petersburg Cartridge Case Factory (Patronnyi) plant.[16] In some places common laborers were put on machine tools, not to train them to become metalworkers (slesari), but "in view of economy."[17] Other plants expanded the use of adolescents, and when adult workers left or were fired, they were replaced by assistants (podruchnye) "who, working for a year, year and a half, [were] already seen as lathe-operators."[18] Similar patterns could be observed at Diuflon. Noting the much increased use of child labor over recent years, one worker bemoaned the fact that they were scarcely trained. "They look upon apprentices as a cheap work force and aren't concerned whether [they] learn something or not."[19] When new workers were being hired on at Rechkin, one old-timer warned: "You came from small shops where there was one whip—the boss. Here you will find several. You will be searched like some sort of thief or criminal."[20]

At St. Petersburg Pipe Factory automatic machine tools were installed which not only lowered rates but, workers assumed, would soon displace skilled cadres.[21] The use of common labor in place of skilled was noted as well in the tram repair parks and at Vulkan.[22] In yet another case, workers at Siemens-Halske complained that the administration, trying to reduce costs as much as possible, had placed inexperienced workers "who perhaps have never seen a machine tool before" on the benches and this had "naturally" led to the increase in accidents at the factory.[23] Wrote one Langenzipen worker: "They constantly fire and again hire, so that the work force is extremely fluid [*tekuchii*]."[24] Combined with all this were the many complaints about the growing staff of foremen and supervisors whose numbers seemed all the greater given that work force size was cut or remained static in the years of reaction.[25] Perceived changes in the age, gender, and skill characteristics of the work force combined with the increased presence of supervisory personnel altered the social landscape of the shop and contributed to a sense of life off balance.

Workers were also quick to note the changed behavior of foremen once the bosses regained the upper hand in the aftermath of 1905. One had been "like silk" during the revolution, but had now returned to his former ways; others had "trimmed their sails to the wind." And if earlier, one could talk humanly with a foreman and bargain on rates, now he would hit the boys in the shop, scream at them like cattle, and pass out different rates for the same work.[26] In fact, the position of foreman became increasingly problematic in the post-1905 period. At some factories, rationalized procedures which stripped them of much of the their former control over the shopfloor served to undermine their authority in the eyes of workers. Elsewhere, though, their gruff and autocratic methods became especially offensive to workers who had challenged just these sorts of practices during the "days of freedom."

Some rank and file workers had their duties shifted as well; these new obligations could call into question old loyalties. As management began to expand the administrative staff of the shops, workers were sometimes promoted to fill the new positions. In letters to the labor press, workers complained that a "formerly conscious worker" had "forgotten his past." Or, once Ivan became foreman, he turned into an "exploiter," even to the point of hitting apprentices and "crudely," "insolently" dealing with workers.[27] But while the problem seemed serious enough for the union to pass a resolution in October 1910 which reaffirmed that all foremen be excluded from the union, by and large the new positions were filled by trained engineering and technical personnel.[28]

Relations within the work gang also changed. At many factories these small work groups were led by a senior worker. During the revolution workers had been able to democratize the gangs, securing the right to elect the senior and participate in the division of work. The senior had then acted as a mediator between the work group and the shop administration and had represented his workers' interests. At the Nevskii factory the senior simply executed the gang's decisions, but later these relations were altered and the senior became "some sort of boss."[29] At the railroad repair shops in the Nevskii district, workers noted that the "physiognomy of the senior had changed." He became increasingly close to the administration and began to act like a boss. Workers here lost their right to elect the senior, who now fell under administrative protection.[30]

Taken together, a keen sense of constant, oppressive supervision was linked with a perception that further assaults were to be anticipated: management seemed to be experimenting, engaging in some sort of trickery, and the consequence of it all was harmful to labor's well-being.[31] Thus when the PSMFO directed its members to implement hourly in place of day-based wages in March 1908, union discussions developing in response to this offensive not only focused on the harmful effects of the hourly wage but judged it a first, transitional step to still more refined and exploitative methods.[32]

Confronted with supervisors computing rates and wages in different ways, stopwatch-toting foremen ordering a faster pace, and guards monitoring the automatic punch clocks, workers variously experienced the new methods as offensive, confusing, and intimidating. And there was more. Management had sought to defuse conflict by depersonalizing relations on the shop floor. In some factories, rate setting had been taken away from the foreman (and with it the informal haggling that had heretofore pertained) and placed in the hands of rates bureaus, time-work specialists, or engineers. Hiring practices had been codified and in some cases special hiring committees had been formed so as to eliminate the favoritism, bribe-taking, and vodka "treats" that had often accompanied the hiring process in the past. Written documentation replaced oral communication; regulation tightened up a loose workday. As management strove to create more orderly lines of command and execution, as "systems" began to replace people, work relations became increasingly structured, formalized, and impersonal.

From labor's point of view, this impersonality obscured accountability: it was no longer clear who was directly responsible for a rate cut or the hiring of adolescents to do the work of a *slesar'* or the firing of a long time worker. When workers struck out at supervisory personnel or at the pace of work they prescribed, they were striking out more clearly than in the past at "the system"—at the reconceived managerial structures in which individual foremen had little remaining responsibility (or authority) within the factory. Just as telling in terms of the human relations on the shop floor, what constituted order and regulation in the eyes of management to workers appeared as dissimulation and evasion. What for employers was a "rational" response to the crises that they faced, became for workers a bewildering set of changes that were meant to disarm them—by muddying the lines of responsibility through allegedly clear and orderly administrative systems, by making obscure the calculation of rates and wages, by pitting worker against worker in a race against time to earn at a higher rate, and by encroaching on the informal, heretofore accepted norms of the shop floor.

Furthermore, these disturbing and unpredictable changes in the factory were not simply perceived in economic terms; for many, the managerial offensive was punishment for the rebelliousness of the recent past as well as a vigorous attempt to restore the arbitrary and autocratic power heretofore held by managers over labor. Moreover, to the degree that foremen and "former" comrades "trimmed their sails" and collaborated in the imposition of the new regime, many workers doubtless felt a sense of betrayal; certainly employer efforts to take back concessions granted in 1905–1906 would be experienced as such. Wrote one embittered worker in late 1906: "Bosses energetically use the situation [the economic crisis and unemployment] and under the threat of dismissal, they lower rates, make deductions, and impose severe fines. At the factories, now, an arbitrariness reigns that would have been unthinkable a year ago."[33] Editorialized *Kuznets* in 1908:

> "Attack on all fronts"—such is now the slogan of the employers. The main goal of their efforts is the destruction of all the achievements of the "days of freedom," a decisive return to the good old times of "unlimited" exploitation, the abolition of the last vestiges of the "factory constitution," the destruction of all types of worker organization. . . .
>
> "We are now the bosses of the factory, not you"—openly stated the manager of the engine department to a deputation of Semiannikov workers.—"If you do not want to obey, we will close the factory."
>
> "Obey or be fired!"[34]

For Petersburg metalworkers, workplace rationalization was largely experienced as part of the defeat they had suffered in 1905–1906. In victory, employers felt free to act unilaterally; in defeat, workers were mostly powerless. The tenor of shop relations in the aftermath of 1905 therefore reflected deep resentment at the loss of gains seized in a moment of revolutionary possibility, but also anger in the face of managerial initiatives which workers were unable to resist. When union leaders were asked rhetorically what workers had gained from the movement of 1905–1906, they responded:

> The answer to this question lays bare before us one of the most acute contradictions of the capitalist structure: any step of the working class on the path of liberation is utilized by capital for the establishment of new forms of oppression and exploitation. Any shortening of the workday or increase in pay is accompanied by an increase in the intensity of labor, any increase in the productivity of labor increases the cadre of unemployed.[35]

Here, clearly, "economics" and "politics" were conflated; the line between labor's struggle for "liberation" and capitalist exploitation within the factory was blurred.

Similarly, anger among union activists about the worsening conditions on the shop floor mixed easily with despair over the difficulties of daily life:

Is it surprising that 1907–1908 gave an unheard of development of suicide among workers, of crime, prostitution, and drunkenness; that cholera rained down on the workers' *kvartaly* with such success, reaping an abundant harvest! Does not the responsibility for all these calamities fall on the entire contemporary social order and its representatives—the "commercial-industrial class"?[36]

Just as many in the unemployed movement of 1906 had linked "the bourgeoisie" with the city's elite more broadly, so activists a few years later associated "the commercial-industrial class" with "society," holding all responsible for the terrible plight of the urban lower classes (*nizy*). Meanwhile, workers may have experienced a heightened sense of social isolation by virtue of the withdrawal of the radical and liberal intelligentsia in the aftermath of 1905.[37] The difficult conditions of the 1907–1912 period, interpreted by trade union activists through a discourse of class, thus contributed to a generalized if still repressed rage against the "entire contemporary social order."[38]

Also developing in the relative social isolation of the workers' quarters was a sense of what constituted an appropriate code of proletarian conduct. For as the labor press documented all the negative and destructive aspects of working class life, the opposite or more positive behaviors emerged in contrast. As harsh as the condemnations of the many ways in which workers themselves participated in their own oppression often were,[39] nonetheless the routine airing of such complaints on the back pages of the labor press acted as a most basic form of consciousness-raising.[40]

Thus workers criticized the long hours of overtime that many continued to perform or even request. Working extra hours not only took jobs away from the unemployed; it very often entailed obsequious behavior before a supervisor just to "score" a few extra hours. In such a way, workers became dependent on the whims of a foreman, allowing him to pick and choose who would get the overtime, hence sowing discord among all involved. Workers, admonished activists, needed the time to rest, to read, and to participate in social and family life.[41]

There were also many attacks on the *pogonka*, the drive to earn higher wages at the expense of all else, on the grounds that the pursuit of a few extra rubles undermined the health of the worker, and also brought harm to others. In correspondence from the factory, workers detailed the many ways in which rates were broken and offered advice on how to stop it. At Siemens-Halske, foremen tried to give out rates *after* the task was completed. But, counseled one writer, this practice could be fought since workers had the legal right to refuse any task on which an order form was not issued in advance. Foremen at Siemens-Halske also gave out jobs to "the most downtrodden," who would then try to work as fast as possible "so as to ingratiate themselves" with the boss.[42]

At Glebov's machine construction factory, the older turners were fired and replaced by new ones, who were ordered to work until 9 pm; in other shops, a great deal of overtime was required as well. Major rate cuts had occurred and apprentices had been forced to do difficult and responsible work. And the sad result of all of this was drunkenness and even fights.[43] At Franco-Russian, a foreman put two workers on one machine tool: one was to work by piece rate, the other on shop pay, and in such a way the boss was able to drive down wages.[44] With the introduction of automatic machine tools at the St. Petersburg Pipe Factory, rates had fallen sharply, for "among the workers on the automatic machine tools there [was] not one member of the union, and they agree[d] to work under any condition."[45]

A Baltic worker commented that the apathy, the "deathly calm," that had come over workers had resulted in a desire either "to serve" the administration and display "trustworthiness" or an effort to earn an extra kopeck or two, without giving any consideration whatsoever to the harm this entailed. Other shops at Baltic raced to complete work, thereby "giving the administration sufficient reason to lower rates," while "the former avant garde of the factory"—the electro-technical shop—had become so servile as to participate in the icon lamp funds.[46] At San-Galli, a new foreman, "alluding to his American experience, forced us to work without interruption or rest." Argued the writer, "we must oppose the tricks of this foreman with our solidarity and not bring down each other's rates when we turn in a job."[47]

At United Cable, "[t]hanks to the American sweating system, on some jobs the workday has been stretched to 14 hours. Workers have been divided into privileged and so-called "hard labor" men [*katorzhnye*]. It is the duty of the "hard labor" men to prepare the article, even to adjust the machine tool, but the privileged worker only has to stand at the machine tool and he alone gets the money for three. Thanks to this, antagonism and rate breaking and the like exist." And so having studied "the question of payment by the job [*akkord*]," United Cable workers resolved to agitate against it "in view of its baneful effect on the health [of the worker] and its demoralizing influence on labor solidarity."[48]

Moreover, there were many complaints about the ways in which alcoholism undermined the workers' cause. Rather than pay union dues or help an unemployed comrade, too many workers wasted their wages on drink.[49] And there was also the problem of giving "treats" or "gifts" to managerial personnel, or agreeing to do personal work for a foreman and hence becoming his "lackey."[50]

In these various injunctions against overtime and rate-breaking, drinking, and pandering to foremen, workers outlined the constituent elements of a proletarian ethic, reiterating in a different voice many of the same values articulated earlier by the unemployed movement. In criticizing obsequious behaviors, workers were called to maintain a dignified bearing, and to behave as mature, autonomous individuals. In rejecting overtime and rate-breaking, workers called attention to issues of labor solidarity. In indicting alcoholism, workers called for self-respect. In bemoaning a passive acceptance of existing conditions, workers underscored the need for an activist, organized labor force. In protesting the crude and demeaning language of supervisors, workers sought a basic human decency. In criticizing "gifts" to administrators and contributions to the icon lamp funds, workers called on their comrades to give to genuinely proletarian causes.

All this easily slipped from view in the demoralizing years of reaction. Much more obvious was the absence of strike protest, the weakness of the union, the apparent disarray of life in the conspiratorial underground. Amidst the teeming, disease-ridden slums and the dog-eat-dog atmosphere on the shop floor it was doubtless difficult to discern much proletarian comradeship. But as Kir'ianov has argued, both the first revolution and the years of reaction were important periods in the self-definition of Russia's classes.[51] In isolation and in difficult material conditions, Petersburg workers controlled their anger and punished themselves with destructive bouts of drinking and exhausting hours of labor; but they also began to conceive their world in stark opposition to the rest of Petersburg society. Explaining the remarkable explosion of collective action in 1912, one unionist wrote eloquently about the impact of the past few years:

> Now we have seen with our own eyes that all the efforts of the government, the black hundreds, and the bourgeoisie to transform the worker into a mute beast have not only failed, but have suffered the most decisive fiasco. Precisely in this ill-fated period, the worker matured all the more *as a person*. And only by this growth of the human personality are we in a position to explain the enormous protest against the Lena shootings.[52]

Individually and collectively much had changed for metalworkers during the years of reaction. As managers and the state dismantled elements of a "constitutional" order; and as foremen in one factory lorded over workers, while supervisors elsewhere "scientifically" managed them, metalworkers who had "been around" felt betrayed. But at this juncture, political repression and economic stagnation made overt protest impossible and therefore disguised the radicalization that had occurred. As we shall see, what was construed by the governing board of the Metalworkers' Union as worker apathy turned out to be a militant rejection of reformist trade unionism.

Problems and Patterns of Union Development, 1907–1912

Over the 1907–1912 period, the Petersburg Metalworkers' Union struggled simply to survive. Membership consistently declined, while the governing board waged a battle, unsuccessful on balance, to enlist the active participation of those members who remained by getting them to pay dues, attend meetings regularly, assume the responsibilities of organizers or delegates, and maintain ties with the journal.

Statistics tell part of the story. Throughout the inter-revolutionary period, membership sharply fluctuated and never again reached the figure of 12–13% organized metalworkers claimed by the union in the early years of its existence. Indeed, the initial success in recruitment was extremely short-lived, for membership patterns indicate a precipitous decline beginning early in 1908. (Table 9.1.) The "softness" of the union can be gauged in other ways as well. Reports in the metalworkers' press document a broad pattern of irregular and inconsistent dues payment. Of the 4,602 who left the union in 1908, for example, 92.9% were excluded for failure to pay dues.[53] And when the union undertook a re-registration drive in 1909, almost 40% of those on the membership rolls turned out to be "dead souls" (i.e., those who had failed to pay dues).[54] Nor had things improved over the course of 1910: reviewing the past eleven months, a union meeting called attention to the fact that some two-fifths of the membership had failed to meet this most basic obligation.[55] Similar patterns pertained in rank and file participation in union meetings.[56] Membership, in short, was often more nominal than real.

The reasons for union weakness in this period could certainly be found in

TABLE 9.1
Percentage of Organized Metalworkers, 1906–1914

	# of Members	# of Metalworkers in St. Petersburg and Suburbs	% of Organized Metalworkers
July 1, 1906	6,254	79,000[a]	7.9
January 1, 1907	10,200	77,000	13.2
July 1, 1907	6,200	—	—
January 1, 1908	8,778	66,000	13.3
July 1, 1908	7,809	—	—
January 1, 1909	6,771	58,000	11.7
June 1, 1909[b]	6,011	—	—
January 1, 1910	3,675	59,000	6.2
July 1, 1910	4,037	—	—
January 1, 1911	3,895	69,000	5.6
July 1, 1911	3,753	—	—
January 1, 1912	3,353	79,000	4.2
July 1, 1912	2,510	—	—
July 1, 1913[c]	5,023	102,000	4.9
January 1, 1914	10,273	122,000	8.4

Notes: a) Total number of metalworkers is given in round numbers.
b) The number of members for the first half of 1909 is given for June 1909. In June 1909 the union began a re-registration which sharply reduced membership figures.
c) Between August 1912 and April 1913 the union was closed, and therefore no information was available on its membership.

Source: Bulkin, *Na zare*, p. 304.

the near-constant police harassment suffered by the union and its journal, the rapid turnover of leading personnel due to arrests, the extreme hostility of metalworking industrialists toward unionization, the difficult economic conditions obtaining in heavy industry until 1910, and the generally repressive political environment characteristic of the Third of June regime. Despite all the many objective factors which hampered union growth, however, activists routinely ascribed union problems to worker indifference, apathy, and lack of discipline.[57] At the same time, many workers grumbled about the inaction of board members and delegates, and their inability to penetrate deeply into the lives of workers on the shop floor.[58] In this circular dance of charge and counter-charge, the fragility of the union at the grass roots came painfully into focus.[59]

With a dwindling membership, an unstable board, and a mass of unorganized workers, the union could play no effective role in labor-management relations. And however understandable union "softness" was in a period of economic stagnation and political repression, its weakness became all the more glaring when conditions began to change around 1910. At this juncture—the transitional period between 1910 and 1912 when the economy improved and strike activism revived—a major debate about the reasons and remedies for union problems broke out on the pages of the metalworkers' press. Under the rubric of "What is to be done?," mostly Menshevik activists struggled to find ways to expand the organization and solidify the commitment of its members to the project of trade unionism.

How should the union go about this task? Some argued for an expansion of mutual aid activities; others called for militant strike actions. Some pointed to the need to organize factory-based union cells, others wanted to rethink the content of the journal, still others tried to sort out the consequences of increasing or decreasing the level of dues. Some bemoaned the absence of a genuine sense of class consciousness among all too many metalworkers; others believed that serious attention had to be given to the issue of developing appropriate strike tactics. But however one might respond to these questions, one truth ultimately stood out: the union had not yet found effective strategies to deal with the day-to-day problems facing the rank and file and hence enjoyed no real authority on the shop floor.[60]

In trying to sort out how to capture the allegiance of the mass, activists began to explore the ways in which heavy industry had changed since the glory days of worker activism in the first revolution. Argued one unionist, Iurii Chatskii, the outcome of the strike struggle prior to 1905–1906 hinged on a particular set of circumstances that no longer obtained. At that time, every peaceful economic strike was treated as a manifestation of political struggle and was punished as such. Moreover, strikes usually broke out spontaneously, catching not only the unorganized employers unawares, but many workers as well; in this context, employers made concessions which they could easily take back later. Such patterns culminated in the enormous semi-economic, semi-political strikes of 1905; and it was these strikes that so aroused the working mass, popularized the very idea of strike struggle, and inculcated into the worker mass a whole series of general economic demands.[61] But, continued Chatskii,

> In the new period of industrial upswing and economic struggle, workers enter under sharply changed circumstances. Disparate employers are now united into powerful professional organizations, the pyramid of which is crowned by the Congress of Representatives of United Industry.
>
> The introduction of a "representative order" provides to the entrepreneurial class, both directly and indirectly in regard to economic questions, decisive influence in the legislative chambers—the State Council and State Duma. The "Europeanization" of employers has been neatly adapted to the "Europeanization" of the methods of struggle with the workers movement: lockouts, blacklists, the organization of strike breakers, and so on.[62]

But the economic struggle was particularly difficult in the Petersburg metalworking industry, "which consists of gigantic plants belonging either to the state or to private owners united in a powerful organization—the Society of Mill and Factory Owners." Here, in order to compel employers to deal with the union as an equal, "the union would have to encompass not 3–4,000 but tens of thousands of metalworkers and possess a treasury not of 17–18,000 rubles but hundreds of thousands of rubles." The reality, now, was that the union did not enjoy strong and solid ties with many metalworking plants of the capital.[63] In this unequal struggle, commented another writer, only some 5% of the work force in heavy industry was organized, although these workers confronted employers who had mobilized some 55% of their colleagues.[64]

Yet another unionist noted that "over the course of the past several years the capitalists have not slumbered. . . ." Unfortunately,

> [w]e cannot boast of such successes. In many regards we are now in a worse position than we were in 1904 or 1905. True, then we didn't have a union, but we had something else. Think about it yourselves, what is more important: a union with 3,500 members out of 80,000 metalworkers, [when you take into consideration] the lack of sociability [*odichalost'*] among the working mass, the absence of a spirit of comradeship, the complete disconnectedness of workers and their obliviousness to common interests—or the absence of the union, but [with the presence of] a militant mood among workers, their desire to fight for their rights, a faith in their own strength and a pride in the workers' slogan: "all for one, one for all."[65]

Conscious of the current weakness of the union, the author warned the unorganized mass: "Remember, comrades, that with a small number of members, our union will never be able to give you what you want from it—it will not be able to lead your fight with employers, nor render you support in time of struggle, unemployment and on other such occasions. . . . Only a strong, cohesive organization uniting a significant percentage of Petersburg metalworkers can fulfill these tasks."[66]

There was, however, another dimension to the problem that at least some activists perceived in the immediate aftermath of 1905.

> While the main attack of the proletariat at the time of the revolution was beaten back; while the struggle for such basic demands as the eight-hour day was not successful; while the capitalists took back much of what was achieved by workers or introduced militantly—nonetheless factory oppression was significantly mitigated. That shameful slavery that workers lived under before the revolution cannot be restored. The old "patriarchal" rightlessness has already died and cannot be resurrected.
>
> The capitalists fully understand this and therefore at the present time try to act in a more deceptive, a more clever [way], not by the old-fashioned oppression and enslavement; [rather] they try, surreptitiously, to introduce new methods of exploitation and cunningly wrap new fetters around workers.[67]

In a context, then, in which the relative strength of labor and management had substantially shifted, metalworker strike actions also had to change. Unionists stressed that strikes must not continue to break out without the knowledge and agreement of the union;[68] nor could they continue to be spontaneous actions in which workers failed to take into consideration such factors as the overall state of the industry, the number of orders on hand at any given factory, or the condition of the labor market.[69] And perhaps, argued "A. V.," workers should no longer take on the "giants" of the industry, since conditions here were so very different than in the days of the first revolution. Earlier, at the state factories, the notion of tight commercial accounting was entirely absent and this permitted such plants to grant concessions. State and private factories like Obukhov, Baltic, and Putilov no longer made concessions to worker demands. So wealthy were the "big industrial magnates of capital" that they could permit themselves the "luxury of principles."[70]

"A. V." proposed another arena of struggle. At mid-sized private plants like Vulkan and Geisler, as well as smaller plants, the chances for successful strike struggle were greater. Because of their size and because they worked for the private market, they were more sensitive to financial loss, more vulnerable to competitive pressures, and hence more concerned with strict commercial accounting. These conditions made employers more flexible regarding worker demands. Moreover, argued "A. V.," market competition encouraged employers at these plants to introduce more modern methods of work and a greater division of labor; and this in turn had created a new type of "trained" worker, adapted solely for work at the given factory. The owners of such plants, continued "A. V.," valued such workers and this would have to reflect positively on the type of demands workers were able to make. Just this sort of environment was "the most advantageous for the trade union movement and the easiest to yield to organization."[71]

Still better was the situation of the small enterprises, since their owners were not organized, and standing alone, they found it difficult to resist. "A. V." concluded by noting that "the working mass itself instinctively senses this. At the time of the recent enlivening of the strike movement namely this stratum of workers, workers of small and mid-sized industry, displayed the greatest activism. This is what occurred in Petersburg. Workers in large-scale industry were silent. Isn't this the answer of the mass to the question, what is to be done?"[72]

These discussions revealed just how closely the problems of trade union organizing were tied to developments within the industry. Big business appeared considerably more organized than previously,[73] while some plants had embarked on a process of rationalization. For "A. V." such changes opened new possibilities: the union might secure positive strike outcomes at the small and mid-sized plants because these firms were vulnerable to the competitive pressures of the market, they were less organized than the magnates of heavy industry, and they had come to rely on a special type of worker who was uniquely valuable to the specific employer.

Others also recognized that the union was too weak to take on the giants of the industry, but were less sanguine about the changes taking place in the mid-sized firms. For the problem of articulating appropriate strategies in response to a managerial offensive aimed at mobilizing heavy industrialists and substantially altering conditions on the shop floor was intrinsically difficult. It was simple enough to recognize the intensification of labor brought about by new wage incentive schemes; but it was considerably more difficult to conceptualize how workers could modify new technologies or production processes that were altering work force composition and undermining labor solidarity.[74] And what was to stop the mid-sized firms from joining the PSMFO as soon as these plants faced serious working class protest?[75]

Other members of the union were also struggling with these issues. A steady stream of articles on the "American system" appeared in the union press over the 1907–1912 period,[76] while at least some members of the board insisted that a special commission be established to study the problem in depth.[77] There was, too, the experience of the Semenov factory, where in the latter part of 1911 workers were confronted with a multifaceted process of rationalization and called on the union for help.

The situation at Semenov, however, illustrated how powerless the union was in dealing with the problem of workplace rationalization or in gaining access to the management. Despite the fact that some 55% of the factory was organized,[78] the union proved unable to mount any effective opposition whatsoever. At least in part, the problem lay in the ambivalent attitudes of some activists toward the "American system."[79] "In principle," wrote S. P—skii, "we cannot argue against this system because it is a higher form and leads to the improvement of production, which not only doesn't conflict with our interests but even goes in our favor." And while conceding the many negative aspects of such a reorganization, nonetheless P—skii, like so many other Russians of the day, fell victim to the "imperatives of modernization."[80]

Importantly, however, P—skii went on to articulate a variety of measures which might mitigate the extremes of the new system at Semenov. Thus he proposed an eight-hour day so as to preserve the health of the worker in the context of an intensified pace of work; the organization of a rates commission from representatives of all the shops, the management, and the union; the ratification of rates by means of a multiyear contract; and the determination by workers in conjunction with the union board of daily norms of output.[81] P—skii clearly hoped that the board would engage these issues seriously, for he felt that such involvement would help mobilize workers around the union. In effect, this was P—skii's answer to the question, "What is to be done?" As he had argued elsewhere, what was needed was union organizing at the grass-roots level—most especially the organization of factory union cells engaged in all sorts of activities directly related to life on the shop floor.[82]

While S. P—skii urged the union "to take the initiative and provide assistance" to the Semenovtsy so as to "figure this thing out," union members at the plant level remained confused and lacked appropriate leadership. Wrote one activist, "union members don't do anything and don't elucidate how to meet this situation and how to struggle with it."[83] And despite the fact that a November 26 meeting of the board resolved that the only way "to paralyze this system of modern exploitation" was through organized pressure to achieve a shortening of work time and the establishment of a contract,[84] it appears that very little was actually done.[85] Reflective of the lack of leadership on the shop floor, one Semenov worker remarked in February 1912: "While almost none of us has come to an understanding of this system [ne razbiraetsia v etoi sisteme], nonetheless we feel that something advances upon us [nadvigaetsia], and that it will be necessary to respond."[86] All available evidence suggests that no strike action against the "American system" was mounted at Semenov.

Whether the problem resided in the rank and file membership or at the top, both leaders and led recognized that the union needed to "win some" in order to build its base; but precisely the difficulty of "winning" against employers empowered by virtue of greater organization and more refined production processes contributed to union weakness. To be sure, new strike tactics were elaborated, but they were not implemented in practice and hence failed to contribute to the mobilization of metalworkers in support of trade unionism.

Just as problematic for union leaders as effectively engaging the changing terms of labor-management conflict was the continuing issue of factory autonomy, a problem that had existed from the outset but which bedeviled praktiki throughout the 1907–1912 period. Editorialized Kuznets, factory autonomy in the matter of economic struggle was a "harmful vestige of the past. Changing conditions urgently demand[ed] the centralized and planned conduct of struggle, the organ of which can only be the trade union."[87] Factory-based activism, however, would not go away. That bastion of localism, the Nevskii district, nearly seceded from the union when its right to have a paid secretary was challenged in early 1909.[88] And well into the spring of 1910, the frustration of the board with those departments seeking greater "autonomy" only deepened. In their view, the locals had every possibility to display the broadest sort of independence and initiative and therefore board members could not see how or why the locals felt constrained.[89]

At issue, however, was not only the "problem" of autonomy, but appropriate forms of organization. For it was not demonstrably the case that industrial trade unionism was the most effective means to mobilize labor; Petersburg metalworkers had rallied around factory-based organizations like strike committees and councils of elders time and again, and had been central in pioneering such organizational forms as the soviet. Moreover, the very goals and purposes of working class activism may have been at issue: wary of activism expressed outside of the union, fearful that "wildcat" actions would go too far in challenging employers and the state in these difficult years, unionists may in fact have been been engaged in a struggle over the appropriateness of a reformist or revolutionary labor politics.

The years of reaction helped to disguise these underlying problems. Precisely because it was so difficult to organize on the grass-roots level, precisely because of the many ways in which economic stagnation, the managerial offensive, and police harassment hampered dedicated *praktiki*, they began to turn their energies in other directions. Thus they focused on the "internal" organization of the union: proper accounting of dues and membership; work on legal aid and medical assistance; participation in various social congresses, and work on the journal.[90] And precisely because the union and its journal were "sometimes open, sometimes closed—all by order of the *gradonachal'nik*," the board was forced to adapt to the limited possibilities and work where work was possible.[91]

But just these sorts of activities isolated the leadership from the mass and contributed to a psychology of "small deeds." In its effort to keep the union alive, the leadership was forced to moderate its activities and confine itself within the narrow parameters acceptable to the autocracy. Unable to assert their leadership in the strike struggle, some unionists took up other issues. Many *praktiki* focused on orchestrating a petition campaign in 1911, commemorating the anniversary of legislation granting the freedom of assembly. Others hoped to increase union membership by expanding mutual aid. But others, both within and outside the union, opposed efforts focused on the legislature and argued caustically that medical aid or unemployment benefits had to come out of employers' profits, not out of the worker's pocket.[92]

While it was understandable why a "small deeds" psychology took hold of many *praktiki*, and why simply surviving the onslaught and keeping the union afloat appeared the essential task, the consequence of all the "internal" organizational work was modest and shaky ties to the rank and file, all the more so given the mounting alienation workers felt toward employers and the state. And so despite all the hard work of the mostly Menshevik governing board over the years, the vision they held of a Europeanized trade unionism developing in Russia was failing to take root among the capital's most advanced segment of workers. The "crisis" of the party that had opened so dramatically for Mensheviks in the spring and summer of 1906 was now reflected in the "crisis" of the Metalworkers' Union on the eve of the Lena Goldfields massacre.

As in 1906, the fear of going too far held most Mensheviks to a position in support of the Duma, and to a belief that the "all nation struggle" against the autocracy might again be resurrected. The leadership of the union thus advised against "premature" strikes or urged workers to present their grievances to their Duma deputies. Increasingly, however, this strategy conflicted with the developing outrage of workers in the factories and in working class communities, and was effectively critiqued by Lenin and the Bolsheviks as antithetical to the revolutionary project. A militance born of the defeats of 1905–1906, the mobilization of employers, and the repressive actions of the state was undercutting the "Europeanized" forms Mensheviks longed to develop.

X

LABOR AND MANAGEMENT IN CONFLICT, 1912–1914

A new era of conflict opened in urban Russia with the massacre of striking workers in the far-off Lena Goldfields of Siberia on April 4, 1912. When word reached the capital that hundreds had been killed or wounded, Petersburg exploded with strikes and demonstrations. Amid this outpouring of anger, Minister of Internal Affairs Makarov flatly informed the public that labor protest would continue to be met with armed resistance: "So it has been, and so it will be in the future."

The Lena strikes proved a pivotal event, unleashing years of building resentment within proletarian Petersburg, while also helping to ignite oppositional sentiment within broader segments of society frustrated by the incompetence of the autocracy. For the effective unraveling of the Third of June system and the passing of Stolypin had ushered in a period of drift in the highest reaches of the government. Without strong leadership, the Council of Ministers split into warring factions. At the same time, no viable parliamentary majority emerged in the Duma: the right-center bloc of the Stolypin era was not recreated, nor was the moderate left able to forge a coalition. And as autocratic ministers grew increasingly weary of the seemingly endless interpolations hurled by the radical deputies, some entertained the idea of doing away with Russia's frail democratic institutions altogether.

Labor unrest and the "crisis of the elites" worried the capital's entrepreneurial elite, but the economic upswing and the enormous allocations for rearmament permitted a certain optimism. Indeed, the economically buoyant conditions after 1910 seemed to recall the halcyon days of the Witte era. Yet precisely because of the improved economic situation, workers were again able to engage in strike struggle, a struggle made all the more difficult for employers by the serious shortage of skilled labor. Furthermore, the very rapidity of growth placed extreme demands on the urban infrastructure which neither the city fathers nor the entrepreneurial elite proved able to surmount: housing stock remained grossly deficient and overcrowded; health and sanitation were woefully neglected; public transportation was inadequate, while the cost of living soared upward, depriving the city's poor of the most basic necessities.

These changing conditions opened up new problems and possibilities for

Petersburg metalworkers and their would-be Social Democratic leaders. The socialist intelligentsia was now able to launch a number of ambitious publishing ventures, providing Petersburg workers with a much expanded labor press. At the same time, Social Democratic deputies learned to use the Duma forum as an effective agitational weapon. Many new labor associations were also born in this period, some arising in conjunction with the new insurance laws passed by the Duma in 1912, while others resumed activities suppressed during the years of reaction. But despite a receptive environment for socialist influence in the labor movement, neither wing of Social Democracy effectively led or controlled the remarkable strike activism displayed by metalworkers in the prewar years. And while some activists worried that Petersburg metalworkers would become dangerously isolated, the intensity of labor-management conflict in this industry spilled over into a critique of the entire established order as metalworkers challenged the basic premises of authority in Russian polity and society.

The Rebirth of Metalworker Activism

When Petersburg metalworkers walked off the job between April 14 and 22 to protest the Lena shootings, they began seriously to reengage a strike struggle that had been suspended over the previous years of reaction.[1] The Lena strikes were, in effect, a generalized protest against the established order of things: "we consider not only individual representatives of the administration and of capital guilty in the shootings, but the entire contemporary Russian order and, especially, the Third State Duma."[2] Economic and political concerns were closely intertwined, for the Lena protests were soon followed by massive May Day demonstrations, and then by a rash of "economic" strikes which in fact raised substantial questions about order in the factory.[3] By the fall of 1912, thousands of metalworkers were again downing tools over a number of essentially political issues. Demanding freedom of coalition and press, metalworkers also and equally demanded shorter hours and better pay. Breaking out in particular shops or factories, protests also spilled onto the streets.

Employers soon responded. At the outset of the Lena crisis, they chose to regard the demonstrations with a degree of restraint and resolved to suspend existing agreements specifying the imposition of fines on striking workers.[4] Shortly thereafter, however, when employers caucused in anticipation of the May Day demonstrations, they emerged disunited. A few counseled continued restraint, arguing that the imposition of fines was inopportune and would only provoke further unrest. But the majority favored compliance with previous agreements and hence punishment for absentee workers. In the event, only a handful of firms levied fines for May Day. Over the course of the next several days, the PSMFO met repeatedly, as the angry minority that had imposed fines—and incurred strikes as a result—hurled demands that the noncomplying firms be prevented from hiring away the striking workers and compelled to provide some sort of restitution. At the same time, the Minister of Trade and Industry took the PSMFO to task for fanning the flames of labor conflict by levying fines for May Day and threatened in turn to impose penalties on firms which failed to fulfill government contracts on time.[5]

Underlying this disagreement within the PSMFO was a set of market pressures, and most particularly a concern lest striking workers find employment in competitors' firms. "Categorically" opposing the imposition of fines, I. P. Pankov from St. Petersburg Metals asserted that at the present time "there are no workers" and "factories squabble over them."[6] Skilled labor shortages were having the effect of undercutting employer unity. But also troubling to Petersburg employers was the government's threat to invoke penalty clauses for delays in fulfilling contracts. Given the buoyant economy and the massive rearmament orders, factories were generally flooded with work and easily incurred delays, all the more so with strike actions. Concern over this issue thus led to a concerted effort on the part of the PSMFO to lobby the relevant governmental agencies to permit waivers in case of strikes. This effort was in turn part of a larger strategy, initially articulated in the period of the first revolution but pursued with increasing vigor between 1912 and 1914, which sought a coordinated response to the labor movement on the part of both state and private firms. In the short term, however, the PSMFO failed to get the support it desired from the relevant ministries.

Activists within the PSMFO pressed on. Concerned by the collapse of employer unity, and doubtless by the continuing strikes, many insisted that the 1905 Convention be revised and that stiff penalty clauses for noncompliance be written in. On May 10, a commission was appointed to draft a new document; by June 20, the draft was presented for discussion in the Council of the PSMFO, which adopted it and declared it in force on June 28.[7]

The 1912 Convention represented a considerably more rigid defense of proprietorial prerogatives than the agreement of March 1905 and the supplemental provisions of 1908, as a comparison of the two documents illustrates. The 1905 Convention envisioned a decrease of the workday only if approved by the legislative process, while the 1912 version stipulated that the current workday be accepted as the norm and that no change without the prior agreement of the interested section of the PSMFO be permitted. The 1905 agreement asserted that workers could not be allowed to participate in the determination of wages, questions of internal factory order, and in hiring and firing. The 1912 Convention reaffirmed these principles, but also specifically rejected the permanent representation of workers in the form of deputies or elders, and further stipulated that the intervention of "outside" associations such as trade unions was impermissible. Absent in the 1905 Convention were provisions for blacklisting; the 1912 agreement regularized blacklisting and also required member firms to report all relevant data on labor protest to the Society. The 1912 Convention reaffirmed the 1905 position regarding no payment of wages for strike absences and opposing the establishment of a minimum wage, and then added supplemental provisions: the number of holidays were not to be increased without the agreement of the PSMFO; all demands which conflicted with the Convention or which were not related to the internal life of the factory were to be rejected categorically, and no concessions were to be made due to threats or violence. Unlike the 1905 Convention, financial guarantees and penalties were elaborated, and unlike the supplemental agreement of 1908, no provisions for the imposition of fines on striking workers were outlined. Because collective fining remained a divisive issue, it was not included in the 1912 Convention.[8]

While the 1912 Convention reflected a hardening of managerial positions toward an accommodation with labor, and most especially toward any permanent representative organizations of labor,[9] the fact that the majority of member firms failed to sign the agreement until March 1, 1913, revealed a considerable degree of hesitation and ambivalence.[10] Unfortunately, the evidence permits no clear distinctions by industrial sector and hence it is not possible to identify those plants in full support of a militant position and those less certain or opposed. Available figures suggest only that larger firms were more inclined to ratify than smaller plants.[11] But there can be little question that the Engineering Section played the critical role in pushing the harder line. Metalworking industrialists initially proposed a new convention; B. A. Efron of St. Petersburg Freight Car Company chaired the commission that wrote it.[12] Also indicative of the influence of the heavy industrialists in the councils of the PSMFO was the election of E. L. Nobel, long-time chairman of the Engineering Section, to replace S. P. Glezmer as president of the society as a whole on June 20, 1912.[13]

This tough stance was also undoubtedly influenced by a cluster of strikes breaking out in the immediate aftermath of May Day.[14] While two[15] particularly long and bitterly fought conflicts began in protest to the imposition of a May Day fine, and hence fueled the anger of these firms with their erstwhile colleagues in the PSMFO, workers soon voiced other grievances. Brief protests occurred elsewhere over the fining but were soon followed by strikes of longer duration over other issues. Indeed, in one of the most celebrated conflicts of this period—the ninety-one-day strike at Siemens-Halske in protest against the fine—the other grievances presented tend to cast this "principled" strike over May Day into a somewhat different light.

To be sure, the 1,200 Siemens-Halske workers vigorously protested the fine and demanded that May Day be recognized as a legal holiday. But this issue must be set into a larger context. Following a two-month-long strike in 1906, relations with foremen and engineers had deteriorated, while conditions had worsened. More recently, and especially at the newer of the two Siemens-Halske facilities in which younger, less skilled cadres predominated, workers grumbled about the "fully determined arbitrariness" of foremen who had lowered rates by 20–30% and complained about the "American" system of control clocks.[16] Grievances building over a considerable period of time now found expression in a detailed set of demands developed shortly after the outbreak of the strike on May 10.

In addition to demands concerning rates and wages, workers endeavored to exert control over aspects of work organization that had been altered: they variously protested the way "checks" [*talony*] were given out; they demanded that a table of rates be hung with the signature of the factory inspector; and insisted that control clocks be placed elsewhere. Moreover, they wanted certain pre-existing conditions to be restored: the end to piece-rate sheets and a return to the old method, as well as Saturdays and pre-holidays paid as a ten-hour day. Worker demands also spoke to a number of "dignity" issues. They insisted on polite address, wanted hot water available in clean containers, and at the conclusion of the strike, demanded that the rehiring process proceed without a medical examination. They also wanted management to recognize a council of elders.[17]

Particularistic as some of these demands might appear at first sight, in fact they reflected changes occurring more broadly in the metalworking industry of the capital since the first revolution. "Checks," piece-rate sheets, and control clocks were something relatively new at this factory but also elsewhere, while reduced pay on Saturdays and pre-holidays constituted a rollback from earlier practice.[18] So when the opportunity presented itself in May 1912, Siemens-Halske workers began to resist managerial initiatives which had apparently been adopted since 1906, contesting the new regime in the shops and seeking to regulate the now intensified pace of work. The ninety-one-day strike was thus fought over something more than the May Day fine. Moreover, some workers perceived that still other issues were involved which also transcended their particular factory. Monitoring a meeting held outside the city, an Okhrana agent quoted one worker describing the strike "as a struggle of the workers of the capital against the union of mill and factory owners."[19]

Siemens-Halske workers had indeed been forced to contend with the employers organization. Perhaps because of the intensity of conflict touched off within the PSMFO over fining on May Day, the Society became particularly concerned with this strike. It was presumably with the assistance of the PSMFO that the Siemens-Halske management was able to mobilize a cadre of strikebreakers; but perhaps more importantly, the PSMFO also intervened by sending a delegation to the Ministry of Internal Affairs to pressure the police to arrest and exile several hundred workers involved in the conflict.[20] Ultimately, the ninety-one-day stoppage ended with extremely modest concessions on the part of management. On both "principled" and other grounds, workers at Siemens-Halske had suffered a substantial defeat.

So would many other metalworkers in the spring and summer of 1912. Like their comrades at Siemens-Halske, many chose to contest changes imposed unilaterally by management in the years of reaction.[21] Thus many workers tried to control (or subvert) the way in which work was issued and compensated, by seeking to regulate the use of worksheets, order cards, and the like, or by insisting that rate tables be hung in each shop in a visible place, or by demanding a guaranteed minimum wage. At issue here was not only the workers' concern to increase the size of the wage, although that was certainly a common demand. Apparent as well was a strong underlying suspicion that the various innovations in issuing, rating, and recording wages operated to the disadvantage of workers. Also widespread were demands designed to overturn the changes in wage policy advocated by the PSMFO in March 1908.[22] Thus workers at Rozenkrantz, Franco-Russian, St. Petersburg Metals, Russian-American Metals, Struck, Izhorsk, and elsewhere demanded day-based wages in place of an hourly computation, and/or a full day's compensation for Saturdays and pre-holidays.

As we have seen, metalworkers had long sought a shortening of the workday and an end to compulsory overtime or overtime paid at straight-time wages; in the 1912 strikes, workers continued to press these issues. But now they advanced a new demand which reflected the strains caused by the greater intensity of labor: they wanted a month-long leave of absence. There were as well a grab-bag of complaints that highlighted abusive practices workers wished to eliminate: an insistence on polite address, the adequate provision of soap and rags, clean hot water in the shops, a regulation of the length of apprenticeship and its appropriate compensation, hiring without a medical examination, privacy in the lavatory, and respectful treatment by medical personnel. Generally across the industry, metalworkers also insisted on the recognition of elders or some other form of factory-based representation.

Jumbled together in these 1912 strike actions were offensive and defensive demands, control issues as well as bread and butter issues, challenges to constituted authority within the factory but also jabs at the political assumptions and social biases that legitimated such authority. In this period, workers contested the "takebacks" and acted on the realization that the managerial offensive had generated new methods of labor exploitation that differed qualitatively from the patterns of the past. Very often, however, worker resistance to these changes was wrapped up in demonstrative strikes apparently protesting entirely different issues or in political strikes demanding freedom of coalition and an uncensored labor press. Just as the managerial offensive and the political reaction had been experienced by metalworkers as part of a piece—and fundamentally as punishment for the revolt of 1905—so now metalworkers began to mount a combined assault on the economic and political order that oppressed them.

Neatly suggestive of the growing conflict between labor and management over control issues on the shop floor, as well as the intertwining of economics and politics in the context of a renewed strike struggle, was the experience of Nobel workers. Management here had begun to reorganize work processes in late 1911 or early 1912, as its patent rights for the diesel engine neared expiration. Writing in the midst of the Lena events, one worker explained that with the approach of the expiration of the patent the Nobel management began to focus attention on the shop floor.

> The old administration, capable only of extorting "rubles" from the workers' pockets by fines for smoking, washing up before the bell, etc., was replaced

by a new administration with a broader range [*razmakh*]; the rates bureau became the absolute master of worker wages, attempts were made to improve factory technology, [and] to make the worker an appendage to a fixed, narrow operation.[23]

In other words, management was shifting away from older and cruder methods of labor discipline to more sophisticated attempts at labor control. Meanwhile, E. L. Nobel was assuming an ever more pivotal role in the PSMFO.

As a worker correspondent observed the changes at the Nobel factory, he saw that much had been done to exploit the labor force, but far less to improve technology. Rates had been cut by 30–50% and night work had become routine.[24] On April 2, 1912, five workers were fired, allegedly for absence from work, in fact because they had protested the lowering of rates. The next day the entire factory struck, but due to poor organization the protest soon collapsed.[25] One can only suppose that when Nobel workers joined their comrades on the streets to protest Lena and celebrate May Day, the specific grievances of the shop as well as the common outcry against the autocracy were woven together in the angry activism of metalworkers generally.

The Differing Strategies of Social Democracy in the Labor Movement

The upsurge of labor protest in the spring and summer of 1912 intensified debates that had been seething within Social Democratic and trade union circles since the end of the first revolution. Standing at the very center of these debates, the Metalworkers' Union became the bellwether of Menshevik and Bolshevik fortunes in the prewar years. Led by Menshevik *praktiki* through the closure of the union in August 1912, an entirely Bolshevik governing board would be elected to take over the newly reconstituted Metalworkers' Union in 1913.

As we have seen, metalworkers entered the strike wave of 1912 poorly organized within the framework of the union. Just weeks before the Lena protests, moreover, Petersburg's city governor closed the union down. Despite the fact that activists succeeded in registering a new set of statutes quickly, recruitment into the new association proceeded slowly.[26] In fact, metalworker activism in the post-Lena period largely bypassed union leadership.[27] Closely tied to the specific grievances emanating from the shop floor and proceeding under the direction of elders or factory-based strike committees often formed after the work stoppage had begun, metalworker strike actions increasingly reached beyond the enterprise level to find expression in city-wide street demonstrations and protests. This method of struggle— factory-based, often demonstratively on the streets, and simultaneously political and economic in motivation—proved exceptionally difficult for union officials to direct.[28]

In the five months of its legal existence in 1912,[29] union activists, primarily

Mensheviks, articulated a set of concerns which were familiar in terms of the past history of the union, but especially troubling given the upsurge of labor activism. The renewed strike protest redirected the debate over the reasons for union weakness that had occupied the pages of the metalworker press since 1910 into a set of impassioned pleas to organize and solidify ranks within the framework of a union. Indeed, many now perceived a challenge to trade unionism itself in the recent strike protests. Increasingly frustrated, *praktiki* lashed out against the "spontaneity" of the spring and summer strikes and the absence of coherent organization. They hurled scornful protests at those "hotheads, intoxicated by their own mood and the excitement reigning in St. Petersburg," who judged trade unions to be a "harmful undertaking" which only interfered with the workers' struggle.[30] They also found problematic factory-based strike committees and councils of elders if they were not solidly tied to the union and asserted that only the union could offer the sort of discipline, solidarity, and "cultural uplift" that would insure long-term improvements for the working class.[31]

Union leaders were worried with developments by mid-year: metalworkers had routinely sought organizational form by demanding employer recognition of elders or by hastily constructing strike committees, while at the same time embarking on strike actions without the slightest effort to inform, much less seek the approval of the union.[32] Perhaps most disheartening, a mere handful of metalworkers had chosen to join the union in a period of otherwise heightened activism. And as time passed and the union was suppressed by the police, activists complained bitterly about the indifference of the mass and its "negligent attitude" toward the reconstitution of a legal union.[33]

Also troubling to union activists was the confused intermingling of economic and political demands. Many Menshevik leaders argued that it would be a "great mistake" to mix economic and political protest; they went on to stress the independent significance of the struggle with employers for improving the conditions of labor and insisted on the need to give this struggle an organized, planned, and systematic character.[34] By the fall, the Menshevik newspaper *Luch'* was damning the spontaneous upheaval as an expression of a dangerous "strike fever," a recklessness profoundly harmful to the interests of the labor movement.[35]

Lenin and other Bolsheviks advanced a decidedly different analysis of the recent strike struggles, forcefully propagating their views on the pages of *Nevskaia zvezda* and *Sotsial demokrat* in May and June.[36] Hailing the strikes precisely because they involved the interaction of political and economic demands, embracing and encouraging the expansion of such strike actions because they drew increasing numbers of workers into active opposition, Lenin and his colleagues advanced the notion that just these sorts of strikes would evolve into the revolutionary mass strike which would topple the existing order.

> [T]he proletariat . . . is drawing the masses into a revolutionary strike, which indissolubly links politics with economics, a strike which wins the support of

the most backward sections by the success of the struggle for an immediate improvement in the life of the workers, and at the same time rouses the people against the tsarist monarchy.[37]

Lenin further stressed that "[s]tubborn mass strikes are inseparably bound up in our country with *armed uprising*." And while explicitly rejecting any call for an uprising at the current time, he clearly sought to establish the connection between strikes and revolution in Russia.[38]

At the same time, Lenin lashed out against those who sought to reign in these strikes and to confine them to the attainment of "partial" demands. The Lena shootings, argued Lenin, were a "reflection of the *entire* regime of the June Third monarchy." It was not a matter of fighting for "one of the *rights* of the proletariat," but a matter of the "general lack of rights typical of Russian life."[39] Denouncing those who sought gains for labor by "orderly and harmless demonstrations," Lenin's polemic harked back to the 1911 petition campaign when union activists groveled before the Duma, supposing they might secure rights by appealing to its president.[40]

Attacking "the liquidationist" position, Lenin wrote caustically against all those who cautioned workers to refrain from "mixing" economic and political strikes or who saw in the current unrest the beginning of a period of primarily economic conflict. Lenin insisted that workers must (and already did) understand "the great necessity and the great fundamental importance of precisely such intertwining."[41] And while Lenin agreed on the need to develop the trade unions, he maintained that the union was neither the only nor the chief means of giving organizational form to the labor movement. Work must focus on the illegal party, which in turn would exploit all opportunities afforded by the legal labor movement.[42]

These differing conceptions of the nature of the strike movement rested on fundamentally different assessments of the current political conjuncture and the tasks of the working class. At issue for the Mensheviks was not only what they saw as a confused and impulsive sort of striking which had little leadership and few realistic objectives, but an evaluation of the political moment which seemed propitious for an alliance with the liberal bourgeoisie (the Kadets) against the forces supportive of the autocracy (the gentry and bureaucracy). And with the example of European trade unionism ever before them, they continued to insist that Russia's untutored masses required the experience of a mass-based, open, and democratic trade unionism as the essential prerequisite to conscious political action.[43]

Mensheviks argued, therefore, that the labor movement should refrain from excessively radical and unrealistic political slogans. Workers should, however, pursue the strike struggle to secure real economic improvements; and they could do so, at least in part, by winning the sympathetic support of "society." Cautioning against too much militance, Mensheviks worried that intemperate strike actions would alienate the liberal bourgeoisie and thereby undermine the campaign for freedom of coalition and speech, rights that were crucial to the development of a European trade unionism in Russia. Said somewhat differently, Mensheviks asserted that the economic and political strikes of workers were appropriately and necessarily divisible; that strong and stable trade union organizations had to be built and that these associations were the appropriate organizations to conduct a disciplined strike struggle in pursuit of the economic interests of the working class. Moreover, workers should ally with liberal groups in the upcoming Duma elections and do so on the basis of such "partial" demands as a fully sovereign, popular representative body, a revision in the agrarian laws of 1906, and an eight-hour day.[44]

Lenin's position on the current strikes flowed from an entirely different conception of the contemporary political moment. Arguing against any alliances with the liberal bourgeoisie and ever on the alert for "revisionist" thinking about the allegedly progressive potential of the Duma, he pressed for the adoption of an electoral platform based on the "unmutilated" slogans of an eight-hour day, a democratic republic, and a confiscation of gentry lands.[45] In similarly uncompromising terms he stressed that just as workers should not pin their hopes for democratic rights on the Duma, so neither should they seek to advance their economic interests by tempering in any way the aggressiveness of their strike struggle. "Whereas the liberals (and the liquidators) tell the workers: 'You are strong when you have the sympathy of "society,"' the Marxist tells the workers something different, namely: 'You have the sympathy of "society" when you are strong.'"[46] A militant stance of no alliance with the liberals, as regards economics or politics, was one of the cornerstones of Lenin's political thought.[47]

How, then, did all this polemical heat affect Petersburg metalworkers in the fall Duma elections? Judging by the turnout, most displayed a marked indifference toward the electoral process: many metalworkers either refused to participate in pre-electoral meetings or declined to vote altogether.[48] When the autocracy disqualified some twenty delegates from the workers' curiae, however, one-day protest strikes broke out across the city, in the end forcing the government to permit new elections.[49] Thus it would appear that Petersburg workers wanted the right to vote, even if most chose not to exercise it.

At least for Mensheviks, worker reaction to the fall elections was disquieting. Six of nine deputies elected from the labor curiae were Bolsheviks; moreover, workers refused to embrace a strategy based on alliance with other anti-autocratic forces. While Bolsheviks might embrace the process of class definition that they observed occurring since the first revolution, most Mensheviks worried about the isolation of the labor force and the growing bitterness of the conflict in urban Russia.[50]

Strike Activism and Its Consequences in 1913

Over the course of 1913, strike protest intensified. As in 1912, metalworker strikes tended to combine economic and political issues; but particularly distinctive now were the growing number of strikes fought over questions of order in the factory, "principled" issues, and out of sympathy and solidarity with other workers. Meanwhile, the Engineering Section of the PSMFO pursued increasingly vigorous anti-labor policies. Although successful in their efforts to defeat strikes once they had arisen, industrialists proved wholly unable to stop their outbreak or tame the expanding dimensions of conflict.

The "big" strikes of the summer and fall of 1913 illustrate patterns common throughout the industry. Among the most famous was the conflict at Lessner. On the morning of April 23, the body of Iakov Strongin was found hanging in one of the shops. A suicide note explained that he had been falsely accused by foreman Laul' of stealing several hundred brass screws; Laul' had threatened to fire him and to mark theft as the cause of dismissal in his workbook. Having no way to prove his innocence and hence feeling unable to save his honor, Strongin took his own life. Outraged by the incident, workers demanded the immediate dismissal of Laul'. Learning on the following day that their demand had been categorically refused, workers announced a strike that was soon met by management with a lockout. The conflict lasted 102 days at the "new" factory and 68 days at the "old," securing the sympathetic support of Petersburg workers and the spirited resistance of the PSMFO.

The single demand of the Lessnerovtsy was the dismissal of the offending foreman; and after the strike began, an insistence that no worker would suffer for the strike and that rehiring would proceed without a medical examination. As was typical of so many metalworker strikes of this period, the conflict at Lessner revolved around offending supervisory personnel;[51] and in seeking to remove a foreman who was unacceptable, workers came out forcefully in pursuit of a basic right to exercise some control over their work environment and to insist on humane treatment by all administrative personnel. In all likelihood because this need was so deeply felt, other Petersburg workers responded with financial contributions of some 18,000 rubles, the provision of food and shelter for the children of needy strikers, the imposition of a boycott on all work that the Lessner management shipped out to other firms, and a strike of solidarity by workers at the "old" plant that lasted upwards of two months.[52]

The tenacious struggle that this issue evoked at Lessner, as well as the type of support it received from metalworkers generally, reflected at least in part developments affecting conditions across the industry and the fact that a foreman or supervisor very often became the lightening rod for all the grievances metalworkers harbored about quite diverse changes on the shop floor. The Lessner factories, both located in the Vyborg district, had grown significantly over the recent past: a new factory had been added, the corporation's fixed capital had grown, a shift from day-based to hourly forms of compensation had been introduced, a rates bureau had been established, and generally at the new factory, younger, less skilled cadres had been hired on to operate the newer equipment and processes.[53] At the same time, Lessner executives M. S. Plotnikov and A. A. Bachmanov had assumed an increasingly major role in the PSMFO, the former heading the commission on skilled labor shortages, the latter on methods to prevent strikes.[54]

Lessner workers, like metalworkers elsewhere in this period, turned to the Metalworkers' Union for assistance only well after the conflict had begun. Prior to this time a factory strike committee, elected on a shop-by-shop basis, provided leadership. With the participation of the union, and at its suggestion, management was asked in July to take the conflict to a court of arbitration. The union firmly stated that labor would be willing to comply with its decision; management, however, declined the offer.[55] Remaining intransigent, the Lessner administration proved willing to fight until the full defeat of the strike. Through the combined efforts of strikebreakers brought in from Sweden, the arrest of most of the strike committee, and the enforcement of blacklisting through the offices of the PSMFO, the strike at New Lessner ended in complete failure on August 2.[56] Consistent with the agreements undertaken by member firms of the PSMFO, the Lessner administration held to the principle of no negotiations with "outside" groups.

Despite the defeat of the strike, what seems important to stress in this conflict was the level of solidarity workers displayed. Support for Lessnerovtsy came from metalworkers across the city and certainly transcended the particularistic interests of an individual factory. Furthermore, the fact that Lessner workers chose to overlook the union at the outset illustrated not so much a "primitive" labor radicalism or tsekhovshchina, as Menshevik commentators were likely to suggest, but rather a considered decision by workers at the point of production to engage in an unmediated confrontation with managerial authority. In effect a wildcat strike which bypassed the more "sober" judgments of the union, the Lessnerovtsy demonstrated a militance which overflowed the bounds of trade unionism.

Another "big" strike broke out in the summer of 1913 at New Aivaz. The Aivaz factory was founded in 1898 and reformed as a joint-stock company in 1912. Located to the north of the Vyborg district, and manufacturing electric light bulbs, sighting devices for infantry rifles, and a range of industrial machinery, in 1913 the factory employed some 1,350 workers on three shifts, approximately 400 of whom were female. Perhaps as many as 400 Aivazovtsy were union members, and the factory was reportedly one of the strongholds of Bolshevism in the capital. Apparently in the wake of the 1912 financial reorganization, technological and administrative changes were undertaken. By the spring of 1913, repeated conflicts had arisen over the lowering of rates and the use of time study. Already in mid-May, a technical student named Balik—a time-work specialist from St. Petersburg Polytechnic —had been hounded out of the factory to the whistles and shouts of the workers for his rigorous application of chronometry and his contemptuous attitude toward the work force. The strike and lockout that broke out in mid-July were ostensibly concerned with the "carting-out" of Balik in a wheelbarrow; in fact, the struggle centered on the many changes taking place in the work process and on a sharp decrease in rates.[57]

As described by A. Zorin,[58] dramatic changes had been occurring at New Aivaz and at other leading firms as well. As various tools and processes were modernized, the multi-competent metalworker was replaced by a specialized laborer whose working gestures were simple, monotonous, and unthinking; the standards which had heretofore governed the trade were destroyed; while apprenticeship was denigrated. Initially on automated machine tools, then on finishing processes, the skilled metalworker had been forced to concede his place first to an unskilled male, then to a female. Some highly skilled, highly paid jobs remained, of course, but these were mostly in the new occupational categories created by the changing requirements of the industry—the gauge maker, the instrument maker, and the adjuster, for example.[59]

In this context, conflict had developed over the lowering of rates, the use of time study, and the rapidity with which the reorganization had proceeded. Workers complained that some machines had been timed too fast and quickly broke down; that work had become too intense; that repair work mounted up and cut into piece-rate earnings. When Balik suddenly reappeared on July 9, passions flared and workers wheelbarrowed him out.[60] Management demanded the culprits be turned over; workers refused. A strike began on July 13, met a few days later by a management-imposed lockout.[61]

At the forefront of this conflict was the sort of worker who had historically constituted the backbone of the metal trades—the skilled male metalfitter (*slesar'*). But the trades had begun to change; the Aivaz fitters who led the strike were characterized both by their youth and anger, but also by lesser skills than those possessed by the fitters of an earlier day. At Aivaz, these young militants sought to intervene in a process that was displacing them and reducing their wages; and they sought to resist what they described as the refined slavery of Taylorism.

> New Aivaz is the first major factory where the American system of Taylor has been introduced, with its division of labor, machine-ism, and time study. Our conflict is a struggle against this approaching new refinement of slavery, against a callous, merciless oppression. To win our strike is to secure all Petersburg from the savage extremes of the American system, to take the first step in the subsequent difficult and crucial struggle. What will become of New Aivaz if the workers of Petersburg leave it without their help? It will not be a factory, but a "workhouse," with its horrible bondage; it will be a brutal laboratory of human exploitation, where the latest word in technical science will be bought at the price of hunger, humiliation, sweating, illness, and premature death.[62]

Fueling conflict at the Aivaz factory was deep resentment toward managerial systems which were perceived to deny the humanity of labor.

While the Aivazovtsy fought tenaciously, they suffered defeat in a conflict lasting two months. The postmortem on the strike written by its leaders suggests that the wheelbarrow incident greatly interfered with a serious process of organizing begun in opposition to the managerial reforms that had been enacted earlier in the spring. Recognizing that a strike would be long and difficult, not least because both the "downtrodden and humble" elements of the work force (women and repair workers) and the "privileged" segments (gauge makers and adjusters[63]) were either hostile or hesitant toward a strike action, workers had begun to think through their demands and had created a special organization based on shop representation. But when Balik was carted out and the administration demanded that the culprits be turned over, the strike took on a different appearance. Under the pretext of this incident, management was able to shift attention away from the issue of wage scales and to shut down the factory for six weeks, using the time to proceed with its reforms. Moreover, management also tried to bargain with wavering groups of workers, aiming to undermine solidarity and fight off the challenge posed by the young fitters.[64]

The Aivaz militants had been pulled into a premature struggle. Those workers who had been hostile to the strike characterized it as a "boyish prank" (i.e., the carting-out of Balik), thereby contributing to the "bad press" the strike initially received. At the same time, the union chose to view the conflict through the prism of the Balik *skandal*; it therefore appeared as a reckless and impulsive strike action, begun without the knowledge or approval of the union and provoked by an undisciplined assault on an offending administrator. Thus on July 28, the union passed a resolution of censure regarding the use of wheelbarrows, while at an August 3 meeting it refused requests for grants. Moreover, the August 10 issue of *Metallist* carried no reportage whatsoever on the strike. It was not until August 17 that the union reconsidered its previous judgment and called on Petersburg workers to support the strike.[65] At the August 25 general membership meeting, the struggle of the Aivazovtsy was applauded and a few days later grants were issued to striking union members. But it was too late: strike contributions totaled only 726 rubles on September 1, some six weeks into the strike, although they nearly doubled over the course of the next two weeks, reaching 1,378 rubles by September 14.[66]

With financial support lacking, the Aivaz strikers faced an uphill battle trying to keep wavering elements in line. But they still worked to develop their demands and a strategy to force management to bargain with the entire labor force. The demands they eventually presented sought a minimum base pay for a variety of specific categories of workers and particular rates on certain types of piece work. They also sought a future relationship with management whereby further changes would not proceed at the expense of worker wages and that polite forms of address would be observed. The Aivazovtsy did not take a position opposed to technological modernization; rather they sought to minimize its effects by elaborating a rates structure which would protect the position of the fitters and at the same time prevent the exploitation of cheap female and adolescent labor.[67]

As the reorganization neared completion in early September, management tried to open separate negotiations with the adjusters (*ustanovshchiki*). The latter wavered but agreed not to respond to management's offer. Another ten days passed before representatives of all the strikers entered into discussions with the administration. As management no longer wished to play the Balik "card," negotiations proceeded on a variety of wage issues, a demand for an eight and one-half–hour day, on the procedures to be followed for rehiring, on the institution of elders, and a number of other matters. Management resisted virtually all the demands, but was careful to offer minimum wage concessions to selected groups. Feeling unable to press on, the Aivazovtsy accepted a return to work under worsened conditions.[68]

But the resistance of management was not the only reason why the Aivazovtsy lost their strike. Important too was the fractional conflict within the union. Since April and the founding meeting of the newly reconstituted union, Bolsheviks and Mensheviks had been locked in a bitter struggle for control over the governing board.[69] And at least in part, it was their divergent assessments of the current strike movement and the different ways they proposed to run the union that accounted for the complete victory of the Bolsheviks in elections to the board in August. It may be that prior to the Bolshevik victory in August, the Aivaz militants were handicapped by a less than sympathetic response on the part of Menshevik unionists still in a leadership role. At the very least, it is clear that early assessments of the Aivaz strike as a rash and impulsive act lived on into August and continued to dog the Aivaz militants through most of the strike. Also clear was that the governing board had little real knowledge of conditions at Aivaz, a fact that might be explained by the continuing problems experienced by the union in linking up effectively with the rank and file, or because the Aivaz plant was known as a hotbed of Bolshevism. But once the conflict was framed as breaking out over the use of a wheelbarrow, rather than as a struggle concerning the reorganization of work processes and rating policies, the union felt justified in not mobilizing the rank and file in support of the strike. Therefore, union members and Petersburg workers more generally did not hear the "full story." As a result, Aivaz strikers found themselves waging a rearguard action, returning a second time to explain the strike to the union board and trying to correct the misunderstandings that had plagued them from the outset. Only toward the end of August did they receive the full support of the union and its membership.

What also emerges in this story is the very real militance of the Aivaz strike leadership, its attention to issues of organization before the Balik incident, and its subsequent demand to management for representation within the factory through the institution of elders. The union did not appear to be an important factor in the thinking of the Aivaz militants before the outbreak of the strike, despite the fact that several hundred Aivaz workers were members. Nor does it seem the case that the Aivaz leadership had failed to give serious attention to the difficult organizational issues involved in waging a strike with a stratified work force. Rather, Aivaz workers chose to bypass the union and organize on the factory level. This choice most likely reflected a rejection of the cautious leadership of the union by Mensheviks and represented yet another expression of the sort of direct action under-taken by factory-based groups to confront managerial authority whenever it encroached on worker autonomy. Moreover, the Aivaz case illustrates the sort of influence Bolsheviks were gaining at the factory level. At Aivaz, New Lessner, and other factories in the Vyborg district especially, a pro-Bolshevik subelite was in the making, and it was assuming a variety of important organizational functions.[70]

What is also important to emphasize is that the Aivaz management waged a skillful battle, effectively utilizing the down time to complete its reorgani-zations and successfully manipulating wavering elements of the work force. In the end, management not only eliminated its third shift while maintaining the rate cuts of the spring; within six months of the end of the strike, the factory employed a work force of 1,250, of whom 600 were women earning a base pay of ninety kopecks while their male counterparts earned one ruble fifty.[71] Management, in other words, had been empowered by the reforms it had undertaken: it could win strikes and enforce the sorts of changes it deemed useful. Because Petersburg employers were strengthened by the many changes they had introduced since the first revolution, Petersburg metalworkers suffered a remarkably high rate of strike failure. For the same reason, the union proved unable to organize effectively. Powerful employers could refuse to recognize the union as a legitimate bargaining agent and because workers could not see in the union an organization able to defend them, they could see little point in mobilizing solidly behind it. Structural change in the metalworking industry of the capital undercut union organiz-ing efforts just as much as it spelled defeat for a remarkable number of strikes. And the consistent refusal of employers to deal with the union, and its consequent weakness, encouraged workers to pursue their interests through factory-based organizations and by direct challenges to managerial authority on the shop floor.[72]

In hard-fought strikes of considerable duration, workers at Lessner, Aivaz, and other factories protested the indifference of management to the well-being of labor, the length and pace of the workday, as well as such symbols of control as punch clocks, stopwatches and the intensified surveillance of the labor process.[73] Indeed, strikes over order in the factory, against supervi-sory personnel, and over time-management issues became the key defini-tional characteristics of metalworker protest in 1913.[74] In a survey of metalworker strikes for just the month of June 1913, for example, *Metallist* reported that out of fifty-three conflicts, workers had expressed seventeen demands for polite address, seven for the removal of offensive foremen, six cases each of sympathy strikes and strikes in support of apprentices, five demands to remove boycotted work from a given factory, and four demands to rehire dismissed comrades. Explaining these sorts of grievances, the journal argued:

> After several years of reaction, when the factory administration began to wield unlimited power [*bezgranichno vlastovat'*] in the factories, the appearance of worker demands which touched on some change or another in internal order became very characteristic. These demands indicate that factory absolutism draws to an end. Whether the bosses of the Society of Mill and Factory Owners want this or not, workers intend to render their influence over the course of factory life. On this point workers will have to overcome the determined opposition of the owners.[75]

Metalworker strikes were also distinguished by their significant length and by the high rate of failure they sustained.[76] Typical, too, was the tendency for strike conflict to be centered in the Vyborg district and in mid-sized, privately owned machine construction factories; generally speaking, these were the more "modern" factories utilizing more advanced technologies and managerial techniques, and employing a more homogeneous body of semi-skilled laborers.[77] But as strikes at Obukhov and Putilov illustrate, the giant metalworking plants owned by the state or working primarily for the state continued to play an important, if less dramatic, role in labor protest through the prewar period.[78]

In understanding the labor protest of this period, it seems important to stress the general interaction of metalworkers and the communication that pertained between them, whether this occurred on the streets in political-demonstrative protests or through the back pages of the labor press. For one of the more notable features of metalworker protest in 1913 was the increasing number of times they took to the streets, walking out over "economic" issues or engaging in one-day political strikes, particularly those commemorating occasions uniquely important to labor such as the anniversary of Bloody Sunday, the Lena shootings, or most especially May Day.[79] On these occasions, metalworkers filled the streets through collective acts which were visible and increasingly regular, and which steadily reinforced the bonds of solidarity as workers marched along together side by side. Unfurling illegal banners or singing revolutionary songs or confronting police were all experiences shared by increasing numbers of workers, and just such experiences helped to create new and potent symbols for the labor movement, as well as to reinvigorate long-standing memories of the old. By the same token, the struggles of daily life in the community—dealing with an increasing cost of living, overcrowded housing, and the absence of basic city services—brought working men and women together in a common fight against landlords, shopkeepers, and all the other representatives of urban authority. Important, then, was the accumulation of experiences which reinforced a class-based perception of the realities which confronted them. And given the proximity of metal plants in Vyborg and their particular volatility in the prewar period, the visibility and the regularity of protest here could only emphasize all the more a class-based apprehension of their world.

What was also central to the emergence of a more coherent sense of class was the nature of the challenge posed by the managerial counteroffensive. At issue here was not so much any systematic implementation of Taylor-like reforms across the industry, but rather the wide array of changes that were variously and unevenly transforming the factories and altering the relations of dominance and subordination on the shop floor. Workers could now "see" the scope and trajectory of these changes by reading the back pages of the labor press, by talking with comrades at other plants, and simply through contacts within labor organizations or conversations on the streets. Thus what latter-day historians have interpreted as singular reforms carried out in a handful of individual factories were more likely perceived by workers as all too illustrative of trends overtaking the industry.[80] Because workers grasped the commonality of their interests in the shifting relations of power on the shop floor, they began to challenge with increasing determination the new and aggressive ways in which management sought to exercise its authority in the workplace. Employer aspirations for control thus clashed with worker expectations of humane treatment.

Thus the politics of the street, just like the politics of production, contributed to the formation of an identity as proletarians that found reflection in the many strikes of sympathy with other workers; in the size and regularity of contributions to strike funds; and in the boycott of jobs at striking factories or the refusal to accept work shipped out from such factories. And this sense of shared identity became the stronger as workers saw that "society" was not with them on the streets.

Certainly by the end of 1913, many worker activists were conceiving metalworker protest in terms of a systemic critique of state and society. Wrote the worker-Bolshevik Kiselev[81] regarding the evolution of social attitudes toward such methods of struggle as carting out:

> [In 1905–1906] it was considered an indelible disgrace to be carted out on a wheelbarrow, since this was an indication of the moral degradation of the administrator, which was not approved by so-called "society"; and he left the factory not looking anyone in the eye. We see nothing of the kind now. That same student Balik at the Aivaz factory, because of whom the strike broke out, was at the time of a meeting of workers in the factory yard calmly looking out the window along with the administration and sweetly smiling, exchanging pleasantries with his colleagues, who obviously approved and did not censure him. And New Lessner, where there was a 102 day strike demanding the removal, only the removal, of a foreman who drove a worker to suicide. No one censured him, that is bourgeois "society," and the workers alone of all Peter were in solidarity with the Lessnerovtsy.[82]

Kiselev thus pointed to the moral chasm now separating workers from "society," arguing that in the years since the first revolution a much keener sense of class distance had taken shape.[83] No less damning was Zorin's vision of the inevitable distress caused by the powerful forces pushing capitalism ever forward.

> [I]f not today, then tomorrow, [if] not in 1913, then in 1914. Machine tools are modernized, the division of labor proceeds all the more deeply and broadly, work is increasingly simplified; and consequently, the capitalists' appetite for cheap, untrained labor, among whom are women, grows with every passing day. . . . It is necessary to intensify the struggle against the entire system, it is necessary to organize ourselves more strongly for new militant efforts. Even the blind know that our bourgeois world is governed by just one law: the pursuit of profit, the pursuit of gain.[84]

Weaving together the protest of metalworkers against a managerial authority that was perceived as inhumane and a social structure that was legitimated by values labor did not share, activists linked in yet another way the economic and political concerns of labor.

The PSMFO and Its Battle with Labor Militance

Already by January 1913, leading figures of the Petersburg Society of Mill and Factory Owners such as A. A. Bachmanov began to view strikes as having taken on an "epidemic character," while B. A. Efron began to advance the argument that a lockout, perhaps one month in duration, was the best method to "establish order."[85] Over the course of 1913, the Engineering Section substantially intensified its efforts to coordinate managerial response to labor protest and to forge a greater unity among its member firms. And yet despite an aggressive effort to tame labor radicalism and protect their proprietorial prerogatives, employers proved patently unable to secure the control they sought.

The activities of the PSMFO, and most especially its Engineering Section, proceeded along four lines. First, the Society pressed the relevant state agencies to waive penalty clauses for delays in contract fulfillment. Not only were these fees financially punishing, but in the view of many employers, they undercut their ability to successfully fight strikes.[86] Yet some state agencies proved less than sympathetic to the pleas of private contractors. The Navy, for example, was disinclined to waive penalties for delays caused by *any* strike, suspecting that some employers intentionally provoked stoppages precisely because they could not fulfill orders on time.[87] The Ministry of Trade and Industry also backed away from blanket waivers, convinced that manufacturers should be required to establish that a strike had, in actuality, hindered the fulfillment of a given order.[88] But by means of direct and aggressive petitioning, as well as discussions with representatives of the state plants, employers hammered away at their critics, trying to get industry's point of view across. By year's end, while the Engineering Section had been unable to secure the airtight guarantees it sought or to gain as broad an exemption from such penalties as it desired, nonetheless the issue had largely been decided in their favor.[89]

Second, the efforts of Chairman Nobel to secure the participation of representatives from the state factories in the regular deliberations of the PSMFO finally succeeded in mid-August. It was the belief of the Society that the implementation of uniform conditions across the industry, as well as a commitment on the part of state plants to join in a collective lockout, would contribute substantially to the suppression of labor unrest. With the active participation of the state firms, this work could now go forward.[90]

The state factories agreed to join in the efforts of the PSMFO to collect data on strikes and participate in the circulation of blacklists, but initially declined to provide ironclad guarantees as regards the imposition of a collective lockout.[91] Nonetheless, this degree of support undoubtedly facilitated the work of the Bachmanov Commission, formed in June to develop measures to prevent and fight strikes and to study the implementation of a lockout. Meeting through the latter part of 1913, the commission continued to look for firm commitments from the state's plants, and to examine a variety of legal and financial issues pursuant to the imposition of a lockout. Also during the fall, P. A. Bartmer of the Nobel factory was authorized to travel to Germany to consult with employer unions there on the practical aspects of utilizing a lockout.[92]

State representatives also participated in the work of the Pankov Commission on measures to standardize conditions at metalworking plants, the fourth major prong of PSMFO activity. Formed four years earlier and now revived, the Pankov Commission labored energetically to develop a set of model rules of internal order to cover the entire industry. The commission held nine sessions and voiced satisfaction at achieving "a greater closeness." However, the conferees fell short of the more grandiose goal of regulating wage scales across the industry, although they agreed to explore the possibility of setting minimum and maximum levels.[93]

By the end of 1913, however, metalworking industrialists remained locked in an ongoing struggle which showed no signs of abating. Judging by an annual report on its activities, the Engineering Section had come to believe that workers were considerably more organized than in 1905, and that their protest was largely due to the agitation of the labor press, the influence of worker deputies in the Duma, and the activities of a "worker center." Focusing on conditions external to the factory, employers displayed little inclination to see in the ongoing development of the industry an important source of labor conflict. Rather, a greater degree of organization and outside leadership appeared the cause of the attempts by workers to intervene in questions of internal factory order, and was responsible as well for the presentation of demands worked out according to a general "model," a model, employers believed, that was often indiscriminately applied and had little to do with the specific conditions at a given factory.[94] Believing that the worker mass was "led by a solid organization, acting in accordance with a definite, strictly elaborated program," the PSMFO argued that the only way to struggle with such an organization was "to oppose to it an organization able to realize the most stringent measures."[95] In fact, however, by choosing to fight for the complete defeat of strike actions rather than compromise settlements and by accepting an extraordinary number of lost workdays and the financially punishing costs of prolonged shutdowns, employers seemed to go beyond a defense of their "economic" prerogatives and a desire to break the union, and to engage in a far broader struggle for social control.

For it seemed now that employers saw the challenge that they faced as fundamental not only to their own well being, but also to the integrity of the country's defensive capacity and to the appropriate development of its economy. At the same time as they aspired to an ever more comprehensive control over the heavy and extractive industry of the Empire through the vehicle of a few powerful banking monopolies, metalworking industrialists responded to labor protest with a rigid insistence on their unhindered proprietorial right to run the factories as they saw fit. Pressed by worker activism and becoming more defensive as the battle intensified, they became even less inclined to respect the modest civil rights accorded to labor by the autocracy since 1905, much less to engage constructively in a broader dialogue about the creation of a more liberal constitutional order.

Over the course of 1913, therefore, employers endeavored to defend a fundamentally autocratic conception of their authority. So when, for example, some member firms began the process of implementing the Duma's new insurance programs and authorized worker meetings on factory grounds for the purpose of discussing the sick bay funds, the PSMFO worried that a precedent had been set and felt it necessary to reaffirm its principled position regarding the impermissibility of worker gatherings on factory premises.[96] And later in the fall of 1913 an in-house document laid out how complete a control industrialists wished to secure over the basic employment contract. Arguing that the essence of a contract of hire consisted in the obligation of the worker to be at work on designated days and for specified hours and to provide the factory owner with labor power at these times, the proposal asserted that the worker stood in violation of the contract if he failed to fulfill these obligations and that the employer should therefore be entitled to receive, without appeal to the courts, financial compensation. To this end, new regulations would be written into the initial contract of hire, whereby the worker would leave a certain sum on deposit which would be forfeited if he violated his contractual obligations (i.e., if he did not appear at the factory at the time of a strike or if he refused to work during the two-week notification of dismissal period).[97]

Nor could industrialists tolerate anything less than complete authority to direct the labor of the workers they purchased. Thus, deeply concerned about the growing refusal of workers at non-striking factories to complete orders transferred from a striking plant, the PSMFO insisted that employers had to secure the untrammeled exercise of their proprietorial rights and must fire any worker who refused to comply with the directives of management to complete an assigned task. At issue was not only the compelling need of each employer to assert and maintain his economic rights (*khoziaiskoe pravo*), but an obligation to his fellow industrialists to act in solidarity.[98]

Contesting the worker's "right" to discuss issues germane to his employment at the factory (e.g., the establishment of sick bay funds) and endeavoring to control ever more tightly the basic employment contract through a system of surety bonds, industrialists at the same time continued in their rigid rejection of any worker participation whatsoever in the setting of rates and hours, much less in the determination of rules of internal order or in the substance and procedures surrounding decisions to hire and fire.[99] Moreover, they sought to standardize these conditions in both the state and private sector in an effort to secure unilateral control by means of comprehensive and preemptive regulation. They continued on as well in their intransigent rejection of trade unions as legitimate bargaining agents. Taking specific note of the efforts of the Metalworkers' Union to intervene in strike conflicts and to forward the idea of arbitration, the PSMFO asserted that all such attempts were "from the very beginning and in all cases" energetically repulsed by the members of the Engineering Section.[100] And they were empowered to do so very largely because of the enormous economic resources they had come to command over the course of the past decade.

The PSMFO thus entered the new year ever more firmly convinced that the existing organizations of labor had to be broken and proprietorial rights ever more firmly defended. Labor, however, increasingly frustrated in its attempts to shape the relations of authority on the shop floor, took its struggle onto the streets.

Strike Conflict in the First Months of 1914

Over the first six months of 1914, the strike protest of St. Petersburg metalworkers became more intense and more intransigent. Increasingly political in thrust, seemingly spontaneous and anarchic, metalworker activism pushed employers and radical *intelligenty* alike to search for the reasons that fueled such relentless protest.

Many Menshevik *praktiki*, bitter and disillusioned by the losses they had suffered in key positions in the labor movement, argued that workers, in the main, still lacked a developed sense of class. And they worried that trade unionism had made so very little real progress.

> In vain, we—"the liquidators"—assumed that the working mass was with us. We were a small active force. The mass was indifferent. The unions for the entire 1907–1911 period stood at the same level. An influx of members was almost unobserved. The same of clubs. The mass did not come to us for help. Still more clearly, this indifference of the mass to our fully conscious class struggle was felt when we called it to the struggle for freedom of coalition.

> We were able to gather only a few thousand signatures. Of course, the chief culprit in our defeat was the reaction. But it is impossible to lay all the blame on it. No doubt other factors operated here. And one of the most important was the lack of culture, the class underdevelopment of the mass. It was not in a position to comprehend the complex program of political action of "liquidationism."[101]

Other Mensheviks stressed the changing social composition of Petersburg's labor force. Pointing to the influx of "raw" peasant recruits into the factories of the capital, as well as to the immature radicalism of "hot-headed" youth, many Menshevik *praktiki* argued that the absence of a mature work force undercut effective organization every step of the way; and it was precisely this primitive class consciousness that fueled the reckless strike protest and found organizational expression in the factory-based strike committees. The old problem of factory autonomy (*tsekhovshchina*) had seemingly reemerged and the broader solidarities of a developed trade unionism had been overwhelmed. For the same reasons, Bolsheviks had been able to manipulate this "gray" mass, swollen as it now was with migrants from the countryside. And these factors, it appeared, explained the declining fortunes of the Mensheviks. Thus one angry activist observed that "[b]y adapting to the primitive level of mass consciousness and to the no less primitive understanding by worker youths of [their] class tasks, Bolshevism gains its easy 'victories' in trade unions and other worker organizations."[102]

While it was clearly the case that Petersburg had again experienced an influx of peasant-workers,[103] it was not demonstratively true that such workers readily joined the metalworkers union (and hence were responsible for the ouster of Mensheviks from the governing board in 1913) or formed the backbone of the strike movement. As the debate over "What is to be done?" to help the union in the 1910–1912 period suggests, the leadership perceived itself to be in trouble well before peasants again streamed into the capital in significant numbers.[104] Nor was it demonstratively the case that unskilled peasant labor predominated at the mid-sized machine-construction plants situated in the Vyborg district which stood at the center of militant strike conflict, much less that these new recruits to industry led the factory-based strike committees.

Rather, the structural processes beginning to affect the industry tended toward the development of a cadre of literate, urbanized, semi-skilled operators, precisely those sorts of workers who headed the strike committees at factories like Aivaz and New Lessner.[105] And just as the epicenter of the strike movement had shifted from the giant, mixed production plants situated in more outlying districts to the mid-sized machine construction plants in the industrial districts closer to the city center, so too had the proletarian heart of the city—the Vyborg district—emerged as the largest branch within the union, a striking shift from the relative strength of the Nevskii district in the first period of union development. (Table 10.1.)

But Menshevik commentators were closer to the mark when pointing to

TABLE 10.1

Distribution of Members by District

DISTRICT	NOV. 1906 #	%	JAN. 1908 #	%	JAN. 1909 #	%	JAN. 1910 #	%	JAN. 1911 #	%	JAN. 1912 #	%	JULY 1912 #	%	JULY 1913 #	%	OCT. 1913 #	%	JAN. 1914 #	%
Nevskii	4,000	36.6	2,583	28.1	1,488	22.0	626	17.0	587	15.1	435	13.0	328	13.1	394	8.8	578	8.5	665	6.5
Vyborg	2,500	22.9	1,201	13.1	643	9.5	508	13.8	671	17.2	650	19.4	622	24.8	1,427	31.9	2,020	29.7	2,833	27.5
Gorod. 1st	1,040	9.5	1,190	12.9	1,116	16.5	385	10.5	377	9.7	312	9.3	370	14.7	459	11.4	460	10.1	641	10.1
Gorod. 2nd															53		231		397	
Peter.	1,120	10.2	1,144	12.5	436	6.4	700	19.0	824	21.2	631	18.8	286	11.4	709	15.8	986	14.5	1,554	15.1
Narvskii	800	7.3	695	7.6	697	10.3	398	10.8	470	12.1	384	11.5	268	10.7	215	4.8	426	6.3	700	6.8
V.O.	720	6.6	1,452	15.8	1,418	20.9	796	21.6	680	17.5	501	14.9	267	10.6	365	8.2	911	13.4	1,754	17.1
Moskov.	750	6.9	579	6.3	658	9.7	153	4.2	159	4.1	247	7.4	318	12.7	576	12.9	722	11.3	1,031	10.0
Sestro.	—	—	240	2.6	187	2.8	75	2.0	73	1.9	111	3.3	28	1.1	89	2.0	160	2.3	230	2.2
Kolpin.	—	—	104	1.1	128	1.9	37	1.0	40	1.0	65	1.9	23	.9	120	2.7	180	2.6	308	3.0
Porokhov	—	—	—	—	—	—	—	—	15	0.4	17	0.5	—	—	70	1.6	87	1.3	170	1.6
Totals	10,930		9,188[a]		6,771		3,678		3,895		3,353		2,510		4,477		6,811		10,283	

Note: a) 150 unemployed members were excluded from this total.

Sources: Rabochii po metallu, no. 1 (August 30, 1906), p. 5 and no. 7 (December 15, 1906), p. 4; 1909 survey, p. 74; *Edinstvo*, no. 1 (February 10, 1909), p. 14; Bulkin, *Na zare*, pp. 217, 276; *Metallist*, no. 19 (November 1, 1912), p. 11, and no. 9 (33) (October 4, 1913), p. 13; *Put' pravdy*, no. 1 (January 22, 1914), p. 3.

a generational gap within the labor movement.The Menshevik writer Sher' noted that the typical chairman of a strike committee, pushed forward and shaped by the spontaneous struggle of the prewar years, was a completely different sort of person than the typical union leader during the years of reaction. "They represented various periods of the movement, various habits and various psychologies, and they met each other with a certain amount of alienation within a single union."[106] Perhaps more pointedly, Bulkin observed that "[t]he experienced pilots of the labor movement [had] been replaced by ones who [were] inexperienced, but [who were] close in spirit to the masses. . . . "[107] Indeed, it seems likely that the caution of the old trade union leadership contributed to the formation of factory-based strike committees, led by young militants who were willing to launch wildcat strikes with little regard to their tactical prudence but with great sensitivity to the urgency of the grievances emanating from the shop floor. At the same time, these young rebels chose to appeal directly for contributions in support of strike actions through the labor press and enjoyed considerable success, thereby bypassing in yet another way the conservatism of the old union leadership.[108] Thus in important respects, the "Europeanized" trade union movement that the Mensheviks had tried to construct was rejected from below by the practice of thousands of ordinary metalworkers in the prewar period.

Bolsheviks offered another explanation for the militance of Petersburg's metalworkers. Like most Mensheviks, they pointed to the isolation of the labor movement from other segments of Russian society. But whereas Mensheviks saw great danger in this isolation and sought to construct anew the "all nation struggle against the autocracy" that had emerged in 1905, Bolshevism embraced the isolation as indicative of a mature class consciousness ready to act against autocracy *and* capitalism.[109] Hammering away at the linkage between economics and politics (life on the shop floor and the oppressions of the autocracy), Bolsheviks urged the strike movement forward, arguing that workers now needed to push beyond political strikes by going over to revolutionary meetings and revolutionary street demonstrations.[110]

Whatever the assessments of Bolshevism or Menshevism, there can be no doubt that worker-intelligentsia interaction over the past decade had a significant impact on Petersburg's labor movement. Radical *intelligenty* had come to the factories proffering a particular sort of worldview. Since the 1905 Revolution, significant numbers of metalworkers had come in contact with a Social Democratic (and to a lesser degree Social Revolutionary) discourse. By the prewar period, the opportunities to propagate a loosely Marxist worldview had expanded, for however modest, labor had gained certain rights and organizations since 1905 that had not previously existed. These included the opening (or reopening) of trade unions, an expanded labor press, various organizations associated with the implementation of the insurance program, a growing network of clubs and cooperatives, as well as labor deputies speaking with immunity from the Duma rostrum. These diverse

TABLE 10.2
Number of Lost Work Days in Economic Strikes
for Each Participant, All-Russia

	1906	1909	1911	1912	1913	1914
Metalworkers	11.0	1.9	9.3	13.4	11.1	6.1
Textile Workers	9.5	3.4	7.7	8.4	8.2	17.7

Source: Balabanov, *Ot 1905 k 1917*, p. 239.

forums were almost without exception led by or filled with Social Democrats of one type or another. As well, they were explicitly built as *worker* clubs or *worker* unions or *worker* sick funds and were exclusively concerned with labor's interests and grievances. Far more often than not, the goals and purposes of these organizations were understood through the medium of a Marxist discourse. So while the particular loyalties of rank and file workers to one faction or another might remain fluid, an identity based on class was considerably more solid and pervasive.

By 1914, metalworkers were embracing a language of class and acting on it. As the result of an historically specific interaction between Marxist discourse and objective conditions, class analysis could take on compelling explanatory force. Perhaps the best illustration of this perception of class was provided by the massive demonstrations launched by metalworkers in support of the protest of largely female rubber workers in March 1914. Women at the Treugolnik plant had fallen ill, apparently the result of toxic fumes emanating from a new shoe polish. Many refused to return to work, but management trivialized their complaints as "mass psychosis" and threatened a lockout.[111] Metalworkers supported these women though massive one-day solidarity strikes lasting from March 17 to March 20. Here was an understanding of the commonality of class interests that transcended a particular factory or a particular trade (or even gender). At issue at Treugolnik, once again, was a concern for the basic well being of labor and an insistence that state and society be held responsible for conditions which were patently injurious to the worker.[112]

Also important in defining class was the shifting territory of struggle. By 1914, metalworkers' "economic" strikes had become shorter, and the proportion of political strikes had increased. (Tables 10.2 and 10.3.) There were growing numbers of metalworkers on the streets, engaged in one-day collective protests which very often entailed direct confrontations with the police. Challenges to constituted authority were not only occurring routinely within the factories, but increasingly on the streets—as workers refused to obey police orders to disperse or engaged police physically by throwing bottles or rocks.[113] And these workers were not, in the main, joined in their monumental struggle with authority by other members of urban society.[114]

TABLE 10.3

The Economic and Political Strikes of Metal and Textile Workers

	Metalworkers						Textile Workers					
	1906	1909	1911	1912	1913	1914	1906	1909	1911	1912	1913	1914
Economic strikes	21.2	58.1	74.0	16.2	22.8	11.7	46.1	94.2	98.0	32.9	56.6	41.8
Political strikes	78.8	41.7	26.0	83.8	77.2	88.3	53.9	5.8	2.0	67.1	43.4	58.2

Note: Data are given as the percentage of strike participants.

Source: Balabanov, *Ot 1905 k 1917*, p. 235.

TABLE 10.4

Outcomes of Economic Strikes, All Russia

Result	Metalworkers						Textile Workers					
	1906	1909	1911	1912	1913	1914	1906	1909	1911	1912	1913	1914
In favor of employers	39.3	83.0	71.0	56.7	63.1	75.4	34.9	50.8	45.3	63.4	63.6	57.7
Compromise	26.7	4.3	26.9	38.5	29.1	20.1	29.6	45.3	34.3	30.9	26.4	36.1
In favor of workers	34.0	12.7	2.1	4.8	7.8	4.5	35.5	3.9	20.4	5.7	10.0	6.2

Source: Balabanov, *Ot 1905 k 1917*, p. 238.

The month of March seemed to signal a turning point in metalworkers' confrontation with both employers and the state. March began with one-day protests by workers at several major factories (among them Langenzipen, Siemens-Halske, Zigel, and Aivaz) at the government's preparations for war. Between March 6 and March 12, thousands had come out to protest the repression of the labor press and the closure of the Metalworkers' Union. On the 13th and 14th, demonstrations again broke out, this time in support of a Social Democratic interpolation in the State Duma concerning the Lena massacre. In response to the spreading disorder, the St. Petersburg *gradonachal'nik* announced his intention to use armed force if street demonstrations and violent assaults on the police continued. With the protests over the Treugolnik poisoning, the PSMFO indicated its frustration by imposing a mass lockout, begun on March 19–20 and lasting until the 24th.[115]

Thus the government now countenanced the use of arms on the streets of Petersburg, while employers boldly deployed the weapon of a collective lockout to tame the *political* protests of their workers and announced their intention to use it again should labor unrest persist.[116] Yet metalworkers fought on, seemingly undeterred by the loss of wages or the threats of police, arguably more emboldened by their own repeated demonstration of collective solidarity.

There were, however, limits to employer unity on the eve of the war. An acrimonious debate was going on between several member firms concerning a shortening of the workday, and the PSMFO struggled through the spring to carve out a united position on the further imposition of collective lockouts.[117] But challenged yet again by an explosive mass strike in July, eight factories on the Vyborg side now came together to impose a collective lockout, ultimately to be joined by scores more enterprises.[118] These eight metalworking factories epitomized the many distinctive patterns defining the industry over the recent past; certainly it was fitting that the metalworkers of Vyborg, who by the immediate prewar period stood at the epicenter of strike protest, should be the prime subject of a collective lockout. Taken together, these plants represented key suppliers to the military and had been very much involved in the massive prewar expansion of the defense sector; several had played critical leadership roles in the PSMFO; most had implemented innovative managerial systems and/or modernized production processes over the recent past; most were linked to powerful banking interests; and most had sustained repeated closures over the past several years.

The July strike—which saw well over 100,000 workers on the street and united some 75 firms in a lockout—crested before news of the German declaration of war reached Petersburg. In Russia, as throughout Europe, the outbreak of hostilities brought industrial conflict to an abrupt and artificial halt. By early summer, both labor and management stood on opposite sides of the barricade. Both were more organized than in the past and both more determined to continue the fight. Despite defeat after defeat for labor (Table 10.4.) and punishing financial losses for management, neither displayed a willingness to negotiate or compromise.[119] At the enterprise level, the strike weapon had lost effectiveness. Employers had been empowered by the many changes they had undertaken since the first revolution and their intransigent stance illustrated their determination to hold onto their unilateral authority within the factory and their social prerogatives more generally. Workers, however, increasingly moved the struggle onto the street, searching for new tactical approaches to contest the powers which oppressed them. They were able to do so in part because of their growing unity as a class, and in part because the deepening conflict between educated elites and the autocracy revealed the vulnerability of constituted authority.

EPILOGUE

In seeking to explain the radicalization of Petersburg metalworkers in the late Imperial period, I have emphasized the importance of labor-management conflict, of which the struggle surrounding workplace rationalization was one aspect. What I have tried to demonstrate is not so much the implementation of a particular process of rationalization, but rather the centrality of politics at the point of production. I have also sought to show that while a consciousness of class emerged among Petersburg metalworkers, this was a contingent phenomenon shaped especially by the interactions of workers and the radical intelligentsia, by the changing structure of the metalworking industry, and by the experiences of metalworkers in the year or so after the issuance of the October Manifesto. In the specific context of high unemployment, police repression, and significant political instability, the taking back of gains seized during a moment of revolutionary possibility and the experience of a managerial counteroffensive influenced the way metalworkers thought about their world and made the sort of analysis offered by Social Democrats compelling.

A consciousness of class grew in the difficult years between 1907 and 1912; it shaped a grass-roots rejection of the cautious trade unionism advocated by most Mensheviks, and it influenced the way in which metalworkers perceived urban society more broadly. The radicalism that percolated through working-class communities on the eve of the war derived not so much from the protests of dislocated peasants flooding into the capital in search of wages, nor was it the result of the hardships that accompanied the breakdown (or incomplete development) of the urban-industrial infrastructure.[1] Rather, it rested on a perception that "society" did not suffer from overcrowded housing or epidemic disease or the absence of public services or the increasing cost of living, but instead remained indifferent to labor's struggle for security and respect. And those workers who protested these inequalities most vehemently had been around the factories for years: their identity had been forged by intense strike struggle; their sense of self had come to rest on their literacy, a living wage, and identification with the city.

To the degree that Bolsheviks proved sensitive to metalworker anger,

240

metalworkers voted Bolsheviks into leadership positions. But this relationship need not be construed as evidence in support of Bolshevik hegemony in the labor movement by the prewar period. The concrete organizational ties constructed between Bolsheviks and rank and file workers doubtless remained weak, while many workers were unquestionably repulsed by the fractional combat. Important, rather, was the way in which Bolshevik positions "made sense" to increasing numbers of metalworkers; and in the 1912–1914 period, this message could be carried through a variety of mediums and venues (e.g., the Duma forum, the Bolshevik press, the insurance campaign). Said differently, a particular "way of seeing," far more than party affiliation or membership, informed metalworker militance on the eve of war and revolution.

Also important to this study has been the exploration of ideologies of "modernization," particularly the technocratic and productivist vision embraced by leading engineers and entrepreneurs. By the prewar years, a fascination with "Amerikanizm" and the "imperatives" of modernization had engaged broader segments of educated society, finding reflection in debates over scientific management in "thick" journals, as well as in the discussions taking place among the socialist intelligentsia on the pages of the labor press.[2] Perhaps most important in this discussion, from the point of view of industrial conflict and the envisioning of a post-capitalist order, was the way in which so many leftist thinkers came to interpret the "science" of management as a set of concepts and techniques that could be lifted out of their social context (capitalist relations of production), freed of their exploitative aspects once capitalist profit maximization had been eliminated, and utilized for the benefit of humanity; techniques, in other words, that would no longer be alienating once utilized in the service of socialism. For some, like the future Menshevik-Internationalist chronicler of the Revolution, Nikolai Sukhanov, Taylorist methods could free the proletariat from exhausting labor; for Lenin, the techniques of scientific management could lead to radical gains in productivity, and under proletarian auspices, a society of material abundance and social equity.[3]

Lenin and other socialists were not only influenced by the productivist aspects of the "science of management" and the imperatives of overcoming backwardness; their judgments were also colored by the economic determinism of Second International Marxism, its general disregard for the serious study of the labor process and hence its neglect of the early Marx's focus on the problem of alienation. And like so many of their European counterparts, Russian socialists on the eve of World War I failed to come to terms with one of the root causes of labor's alienation in the conditions of early twentieth century capitalism: they failed to appreciate the disempowering of labor that was a product of the structural changes occurring in the metalworking industry, as well as the indignity and sense of injustice experienced by workers as the relations of power and authority in the workplace were transformed.[4]

So while Lenin and many Bolsheviks proved deeply responsive to the intransigent militance of Petersburg metalworkers, they misconstrued some of its
most fundamental sources.

Finally, this study has sought to articulate the attitudes and values of one
important segment of Imperial Russia's industrial bourgeoisie, the St. Petersburg entrepreneurial elite. Magnates of heavy industry and leaders of the
financial community, these men pursued a vision of economic development
and labor management which ill fitted Russia's fledgling representative institutions, much less the democratic project more generally. Quickly abandoning the pursuit of their interests within the Duma and choosing instead
to cast their lot with the bureaucracy, those organized within the PSMFO
embarked on an ultimately futile effort to maintain their proprietorial prerogatives within the factories and their authoritarian perspectives on polity
and society more generally. In what I have characterized as a "proto-corpo-
ratism," I see the politics of these employers in broadly similar terms as those
chosen by other industrial magnates in the aftermath of World War I when
parliamentary institutions failed and corporatist politics seemed the answer
in Italy, Germany, and elsewhere.

NOTES

The Selected Bibliography gives full bibliographical information for all sources cited in abbreviated form in the Notes.

Introduction

1. Engelstein, *Moscow 1905;* Surh, *1905 in St. Petersburg.*
2. See especially his "Russian Bebels" and "On the Eve."
3. McKean, *St. Petersburg Between the Revolutions.*
4. Bonnell, *Roots of Rebellion;* Swain, *Russian Social Democracy and the Legal Labour Movement.*
5. The literature on these themes is vast. Most important to my thinking on issues of class formation and class consciousness has been the work of David Montgomery, E. P. Thompson, and Ira Katznelson. On the "second" industrial revolution see especially Landes, *The Unbound Prometheus,* and Noble, *America by Design.* On the particular role of metalworkers see Haimson and Tilly, eds., *Strikes, Wars, and Revolutions.*

1. Petersburg's Metalworking Industry in the Post-Emancipation Era

1. For discussion of post-Emancipation economic development in general and St. Petersburg's industrial growth in particular see Portal, "The Industrialization of Russia"; Gatrell, *The Tsarist Economy;* Bater, *St. Petersburg, Industrialization and Change;* Zelnik, *Labor and Society; OIL,* vol. 2, chs. 2–4; Bulkin, *Na zare;* Stolpianskii, *Zhizn' i byt;* and the 1909 survey. For a fine sketch of the city and its workers ca. 1900, see Surh, *1905 in St. Petersburg,* ch. 1.
2. Kireev, "Promyshlennost'," pp. 101–4; *Ist. Put. zavoda,* pp. 18–36; Okun', *Putilovets,* pp. 3–19.
3. Kireev, "Promyshlennost'," pp. 104–5; Bulkin, *Na zare,* pp. 25–26; Blek,"Iz praktiki," p. 119.
4. Paialin, *Zavod i. Lenina,* pp. 33–40, 78.
5. Bulkin, "Ekonomicheskoe polozhenie," table following p. 92; Kireev, "Promyshlennost'," p. 97.
6. Labor statistics for these years are inadequate, but according to data based on statistical handbooks (which tend to underestimate work force size), employment in heavy industry grew from 19,977 in 1867 to 28,288 in 1879, then dipped to 21,409 in 1884 and slowly increased to 24,841 by 1890. Estimates of the value of production illustrate a similar fluctuation: from 20,040,000 rubles in 1867 to 48,225,000 in 1879 to 33,255,000 in 1884 to 39,909,000 in 1890. Kireev, "Promyshlennost'," p. 97. By way of contrast, employment figures based on the city census of 1881, that is, before the sharp economic downturn of the 1880s, indicate that 31,371 workers labored in metalworking and machine construction, which represented approximately 14% of the capital's work force. Bernshtein-Kogan, *Chislennost', sostav i polozhenie peterburgskikh rabochikh,* p. 74.
7. Little biographical information survives on the entrepreneurs and managers who developed the capital's heavy industry. At best, the outlines of a collective profile may be sketched, but very large gaps remain. Unfortunately, this is especially true for the top managers of the state factories, some of whom played crucial roles in the development of the industry in the early twentieth century. See generally Rieber,

Merchants and Entrepreneurs; King, "The Emergence of the St. Petersburg Industrialist Community"; and Gindin, "Russkaia burzhuaziia v period kapitalizma."

8. *Ist. Put. zavoda,* pp. 39–40, 50–51.

9. Rieber, *Merchants and Entrepreneurs,* p. 366.

10. See the discussion in Gindin, "Russkaia burzhuaziia v period kapitalizma."

11. As quoted in Zelnik, *Labor and Society,* p. 303.

12. King, "The Emergence of the St. Petersburg Industrialist Community," ch. 6 and pp. 315–29. See Table 5.1 below.

13. Most Soviet labor historians have rigidly correlated revolutionary consciousness with degree of proletarianization; they have thus sought to document the emergence over the course of the late Imperial period of a permanent, hereditary working class in the cities with no meaningful ties to the land and to ascribe to this working class a particular worldview. Few Western historians have found this approach satisfying, but perhaps no one has so undermined it as Reginald Zelnik, who has provided richly nuanced portraits of Russian workers and their sense of self. See his "Russian Bebels," *A Radical Worker,* and "On the Eve." See also Johnson, *Peasant and Proletarian.* Perhaps the most sophisticated discussion of the historiography and statistics on the formation of an hereditary proletariat by a Soviet historian is Ivanov, "Preemstvennost' fabrichno-zavodskogo truda."

14. I have been helped in thinking about these issues by William Rosenberg, by E. P. Thompson's classic study, *The Making of the English Working Class,* and by the insightful essay of Ira Katznelson, "Working Class Formation."

15. Kutsentov, "Naselenie," pp. 173–74, 178.

16. Korol'chuk, "Ob osobennostiakh ekspluatatsii," pp. 153–55; 1909 survey, pp. 92–93.

17. Korol'chuk, "Ob osobennostiakh ekspluatatsii," pp. 152–53, on the greater development of *kustar'* in the Central Industrial Region. See also, for example, the early biography of Matvei Fisher, born in a village in Iaroslavl' in 1871, as sketched by Zelnik in "Russian Bebels," pp. 417–19.

18. See discussion in Ivanov, "Preemstvennost' fabrichno-zavodskogo truda."

19. Despite the fundamental change in the social and economic status of peasant migrants to the city, autocratic policy dictated that they remain ascribed to the peasant *soslovie.*

20. *Ist. Put. zavoda,* p. 45.

21. Zelnik, *Labor and Society,* pp. 234–36.

22. Semanov, *Peterburgskie rabochie nakanune pervoi russkoi revoliutsii,* p. 49.

23. Kutsentov, "Naselenie," pp. 178–79.

24. Blek, "Usloviia truda rabochikh," p. 80.

25. Rashin, *Formirovanie,* p. 565. Theodore von Laue notes that in the metal trades of the Empire, year-round employment increased from 89% to 97% between 1893 and 1899. See his "Russian Peasants in the Factory," p. 62; see also Korol'chuk, "Ob osobennostiakh ekspluatatsii," p. 159.

26. These comments draw on the insightful discussion by Zelnik of the formation of the working class and the peasant-worker "transition." See his "Russian Workers and the Revolutionary Movement," pp. 216–22.

27. Rashin, *Formirovanie,* p. 591.

28. Semanov, *Peterburgskie rabochie nakanune pervoi russkoi revoliutsii,* p. 55.

29. Rashin, *Formirovanie,* p. 579.

30. For a sampling of this often disparate data, see Kutsentov, "Naselenie," p. 192; Bulkin, *Arkhiv istoriia truda,* kn. 9, pp. 90–95; and Semanov, *Peterburgskie rabochie nakanune pervoi russkoi revoliutsii,* passim, ch. 3.

31. According to the city census of 1900, only 1.3% of the work force in metalworking was female, while just 5.3% of its work force was under 16 years of age. Semanov, *Peterburgskie rabochie nakanune pervoi russkoi revoliutsii,* pp. 44, 46.

32. Volk, "Prosveshchenie i shkola," pp. 676, 677.

33. There is no adequate English translation for the terms *zavodskie* and *fabrichnye*. The former usually refers to workers at large, mechanized factories, preeminently metalworking plants, who were generally more skilled than workers elsewhere; the latter typically refers to the less skilled workers at smaller, less technically sophisticated plants, very often textile mills, although many of these mills had become both large and modern by the late nineteenth century.

34. As translated by McKinsey, "From City Workers to Peasantry," p. 638.

35. Ibid.; Kropotkin, *Memoirs of a Revolutionist*, pp. 325–26.

36. Plekhanov, *Russkii rabochii*, p. 12. Emphasis in original.

37. Ibid., p. 11, 15–16.

38. Ibid., p. 15–16.

39. Ibid., pp. 24–25.

40. Levin, "Obshchestvennoe dvizhenie v Peterburge," p. 324.

41. Ibid.

42. Plekhanov, *Russkii rabochii*, p. 24.

43. Kanatchikov's memoir is virtually devoid of contacts with women his own age.

44. Timofeev, *Chem zhivet zavodskii rabochii*, p. 5.

45. See, for example, Kanatchikov's comments on some of his fellow pattern makers, *A Radical Worker*, pp. 14–23.

46. *Ist. Put. zavoda*, p. 49.

47. Buzinov, *Za Nevskoi zastavoi*, pp. 20–21.

48. "Thus a special type of worker was created in the hot shops—a strong man, often a Hercules; [a man] without skills [who nonetheless] was desirous of earning as much as a turner. To accomplish this, he had to expend strength without limit, he had to bear the heat, forget about time, and he almost always had to suffer a hernia." *Ist. Put. zavoda*, p. 49.

49. See the experiences of Kanatchikov when he first arrived in Moscow. *A Radical Worker*, pp. 7–13. Even following 1905, workers of the hot shops were recruited through the *zemliachestvo*. See Okun', *Putilovets*, p. xxiv.

50. Vladimir Fomin, a worker at the Baltic factory and a member of the Brusnev circle in the late 1880s and early 1890s, recalled: "Each 'senior' drew from his own village, first, his own relatives, second, his favorites, friends and so on. This subdivision, at the outset, made the introduction of propaganda more difficult because much effort was expended on 'rooting out' the hostile attitudes of the 'riazantsy' to the 'skoptsy' or to the novgorodtsy, who were openly called 'chechens.'" Cited in Korol'chuk, "Ob osobennostiakh ekspluatatsii," p. 157. *Skoptsy* was a play on words, meaning both castrati and people from Pskov, *pskovtsy*.

51. Timofeev, in noting what a great luxury meat was for the workers, calls attention to the "*nekul'turnye*" habits of a typical hot shop worker: "I clearly recall a certain stoker who could never forget the time he was sent away on a job where he was given as much meat as he could eat. 'I would eat it on its own,' he said, 'without any bread. I'd pick the fattiest piece and let the grease run down my beard.'" *Chem zhivet zavodskii rabochii*, p. 15. Such manners must have scandalized "advanced" workers, while at the same time calling forth bittersweet memories for men such as Kanatchikov who had left the village for the city.

52. A Putilov worker discussing 1905 remarked: "One must say that the furnace workers stayed behind because they had to stay behind due to the nature of their work, and not because they were inveterate monarchists—production required it. One cannot just leave a Marten furnace and go out, since this threatened the entire plant with a work stoppage. The old men [of the shop] never went on a one-day strike." Pozern, ed., *Putilovtsy v 1905 godu*, p. 27.

53. Buzinov, *Za Nevskoi zastavoi*, p. 20.

54. See, for example, Shotman's description of the Obukhov factory at the turn of the century in "Zapiski starogo bol'shevika," p. 146.

55. Timofeev writes: "While talking with one such [skilled] worker recently, I heard the most unexpected opinion about workers who kept their ties with the village. 'These "villagers" have hurt us a lot in the last strike,' he told me decisively. 'In what way?' I asked. 'Well, they all shouted, "Strike! Strike!" so we went on strike until the factory closed down.' 'Then what happened?' 'Then they all packed up and went back to the village, leaving us high and dry. The landlord threatened to throw us out of our rooms, and we had no money and no food.' 'Well, what do you make of this?' 'They're just holding back the worker's cause. They don't feel they have to organize the way we do, and why should they? Once they see that things are getting bad, they head for the village right away, saying, "The rest of you boys, you can just make do the best you can." That's why the bosses don't give us unions—because not everyone demands them.'" *Chem zhivet zavodskii rabochii*, pp. 17–18.

2. The Industrialization of the 1890s

1. Crisp, *Studies in the Russian Economy*, p. 26; Tugan-Baranovskii, *The Russian Factory in the Nineteenth Century*, p. 274.

2. *IRL*, vol. 1, pp. 179–80; Semanov, *Peterburgskie rabochie nakanune pervoi russkoi revoliutsii*, p. 10.

3. Kutsentov, "Naselenie," p. 184. For a much more detailed and careful discussion of St. Petersburg's labor demographics see Surh, *1905 in St. Petersburg*, pp. 6–50.

4. Kruze, "Promyshlennoe razvitie," p. 17.

5. Rozenfel'd and Klimenko, *Istoriia mashinostroeniia SSSR*, p. 60.

6. Ibid., p. 111.

7. For one statement of this problem see ibid., p. 134.

8. Crisp, *Studies in the Russian Economy*, p. 31.

9. 1909 survey, p. 19.

10. Rozenfel'd and Klimenko, *Istoriia mashinostroeniia SSSR*, pp. 52–53; Balabanov, "Promyshlennost' Rossii v nachale XX veka," pp. 62–63.

11. Balabanov, "Promyshlennost' Rossii v nachale XX veka," p. 61.

12. *Ist. Put. zavoda*, ch. 2, passim; Zhukovskii, "Ekonomicheskoe razvitie Putilovskogo zavoda," pp. 144–45.

13. *Ist. Put. zavoda*, pp. 44–45.

14. Ibid.

15. Ibid., pp. 35–45; Stolpianskii, *Zhizn' i byt*, pp. 158–61; Zhukovskii, "Ekonomicheskoe razvitie Putilovskogo zavoda," pp. 140–49.

16. Paialin, *Zavod i. Lenina*, pp. 56–64, 74–78; Gindin, "Antikrizisnoe finansirovanie," pp. 127–31.

17. Zelnik, *Labor and Society*, pp. 336–40; *Ist. Put. zavoda*, pp. 47–48; Paialin, *Zavod i. Lenina*, p. 94; Blek, "Usloviia truda rabochikh," pp. 116–17; Okun', *Putilovets*, p. xxiv.

18. See the comments of Svirskii, who observed that he, like everyone else, accepted the searches indifferently; but "now" (after his participation in circle study had begun), he felt a "deep sense of shame." *Zapiski rabochego*, pp. 48–50. See also Kanatchikov on the medical examination, *A Radical Worker*, pp. 51–52.

19. The artel' was a collectivity of peasants and later workers, organized to work or live together.

20. *Ist. Put. zavoda*, p. 24.

21. Data from a survey of private industry in European Russia and the Caucasus conducted by the Factory Inspectorate in late 1903 suggested how serious the shortage of trained personnel was. In the machine-construction sector, of 1,144 upper-level managerial personnel only 286 or 25% had completed a higher technical school; 76

had a secondary and 90 had an elementary technical education. Of the remaining 692, 19 had received a higher, 133 a secondary, and 222 an elementary general education. As regards the 812 foremen surveyed in this sector, 228 or 27% had a technical education, of whom 46 had a higher, 31 a secondary, and 151 an elementary technical degree. See "Tekhnika ili rutina rukovodit nashei promyshlennost'iu," pp. 200–2.

22. Bogdanov, "Deviatisoty gody," p. 14; see also the comments of Timofeev, *Chem zhivet zavodskii rabochii*, pp. 90–100.

23. See, for example, Paialin, *Zavod i. Lenina*, pp. 57–58; Timofeev, *Chem zhivet zavodskii rabochii*, p. 96; *Ist. Put. zavoda*, pp. 47–48; and Svirskii, *Zapiski rabochego*, pp. 48–50.

24. Paialin, *Zavod i. Lenina*, pp. 57, 73.

25. Semanov, *Peterburgskie rabochie nakanune pervoi russkoi revoliutsii*, p. 120. The Shlissel'burg road was a main thoroughfare running along the southeastern part of the city and into the suburbs.

26. Paialin, *Zavod i. Lenina*, p. 56.

27. Kniazev, "Nikolai Petrovich," *Vospominaniia o Vladimire Il'iche Lenine*, p. 118.

28. Svirskii, *Zapiski rabochego*, p. 61.

29. Ibid., pp. 14–15.

30. Timofeev, *Chem zhivet zavodskii rabochii*, p. 98.

31. For a detailed discussion of the development of engineering education in tsarist Russia see Balzer, "Educating Engineers"; see p. 367 for the number of graduates.

32. Teplov, *Zapiski Putilovtsa*, pp. 11–12.

33. Administrative staff at Obukhov was almost exclusively drawn from the military, especially the Navy. Lower positions were often filled with retired soldiers and NCOs. Rozanov, *Obukhovtsy*, p. 25. See also Paialin, *Zavod i. Lenina*, p. 87. Illustrative, too, was the comment voiced some years later in a professional journal on the "census, caste, and guild [*tsekhovyia*] differences which remain in us, [and are] an inheritance from serfdom and a bureaucratic regime." See *Trud tekhnika*, nos. 1–2 (January 27, 1908), pp. 33–34.

34. Buiko, *Put' rabochego*, pp. 17–19.

35. *IRL*, p. 179; see map.

36. The Narvskii district grew by 37.1% over the decade. *IRL*, p. 179. Workers tended to refer to the entire area, inclusive of Petergof, as the Narvskii Gate region, and I will adopt this usage unless otherwise specifically noted.

37. The population of the Nevskii district increased by 57.8% over the decade. Ibid. The area along the Shlissel'burg road was beyond the administrative limits of the city, but colloquially the entire area was known as the Nevskii region. I will follow this usage and refer loosely to the entire region.

38. Ibid.

39. Martov, *Zapiski Sotsial Demokrata*, p. 278.

40. Ibid., p. 279.

41. Garvi, *Zapiski Sotsial Demokrata*, p. 8.

42. Martov, *Zapiski Sotsial Demokrata*, pp. 279–80.

43. Paialin, *Zavod i. Lenina*, pp. 41–42; M. Rozanov, *Obukhovtsy*, p. 81.

44. See, for example, Buiko, *Put' rabochego*, p. 15; *Ist. Put. zavoda*, pp. 68–69; Rozanov, *Obukhovtsy*, p. 47.

45. For further discussion of the complexity and mutuality of this relationship, see Zelnik, "Russian Workers and the Revolutionary Movement," esp. pp. 226–34.

46. Sviatlovskii, "Na zare Rossiiskoi sotsial-demokratii," p. 144.

47. In 1892, for example, the Smolensk school for workers in the Nevskii district attracted about 1,000 students and turned away almost as many applicants. Volk, "Prosveshchenie i shkola," pp. 678–79.

48. Essential to the study of this period is Wildman, *The Making of a Workers' Revolution;* see also Harding, ed., *Marxism in Russia: Key Documents,* pp. 121–221, for a sampling of such leaflets. "On Agitation" is reprinted on pp. 192–205.

49. A. Sil'vin wrote revealingly, for example, that a group of workers from the Nevskii factory who were studying in a circle with Lenin failed to alert him of the dissatisfaction which was about to result in the December 1894 riot at their factory. When asked by Lenin why they hadn't informed the SDs of the mounting tension, they responded that "the movement at first had to go deeper, and only later become wider." Commented Sil'vin: "Yet again it was confirmed that our circle workers were far from the mass." Sil'vin, *Vospominaniia,* vol. 1, p. 125.

50. Martov, *Zapiski Sotsial Demokrata,* p. 263.

51. Biographical information on Zhukov, Babushkin, Zinov'ev, and other worker participants in the Union of Struggle may be found in Kutsentov, *Deiateli;* for Shotman see his *Zapiski starogo bol'shevika,* pp. 4–7 and 14–28. See also Zelnik, *A Radical Worker.*

52. Sil'vin, *Vospominaniia,* vol. 1, p. 128.

53. Martov, *Zapiski Sotsial Demokrata,* p. 278.

54. *Vospominaniia Ivana Vasil'evicha Babushkina,* pp. 29–30.

55. Kutsentov, *Deiateli,* pp. 72–73.

56. Wildman, *The Making of a Workers' Revolution,* ch. 3; Harding, *Marxism in Russia,* introduction.

57. For a discussion of these strikes see Surh, *1905 in St. Petersburg,* pp. 53–65.

58. Takhtarev, *Rabochee dvizhenie v Peterburge,* p. 72.

59. *Nashe vremia,* no. 2 (1898), pp. 34–36. As translated by Jonathan Frankel in *Vladimir Akimov on the Dilemmas of Russian Marxism, 1895–1903,* p. 268.

60. Zelnik, "Russian Bebels," pp. 273–74.

61. This period in the history of Russian Social Democracy has been examined closely by a number of scholars; see especially Haimson, *The Russian Marxists and the Origins of Bolshevism,* and Wildman, *The Making of a Workers' Revolution.*

62. *Rabochee dvizhenie v Rossii v XIX veke,* ed. Pankratova, Ivanov, et al., vol. IV, pt. 2, pp. 260–63.

63. Sablinsky, *The Road to Bloody Sunday,* pp. 26–27.

64. Zelnik, *A Radical Worker,* p. 152. See also the comments of Lydia Dan regarding the police presence in working-class districts in the early twentieth century. Haimson, *The Making of Three Russian Revolutionaries,* pp. 153–54.

65. My discussion of *Rabochaia mysl'* relies heavily on Wildman, *The Making of a Workers' Revolution;* see especially ch. 5. See also the remarks of B—v', "Peterburgskoe dvizhenie," *Rabochee delo,* no. 6 (April 1900), pp. 31–33.

66. Wildman, *The Making of a Workers' Revolution,* p. 135.

67. Wildman notes the considerable pride that this format elicited among Petersburg workers. Ibid., p. 129. On this point see also *Rabochaia mysl',* no. 5 (January 1899), p. 1.

68. B—v', "Peterburgskoe dvizhenie," *Rabochee delo,* no. 6 (April 1900), pp. 28–34. An understanding of the politics of the St. Petersburg labor movement in terms of this polarity, however, has retained a tenacious hold over latter-day historians. For one example see Smith, *Red Petrograd,* pp. 14–23, 190–200.

69. B—v', "Peterburgskoe dvizhenie," *Rabochee delo,* no. 6 (April 1900), p. 30.

70. Writing in the April 1900 issue of *Rabochee delo,* B—v' argued that "the ever-increasing number of politically mature workers suggests that in the not too distant future, the St. Petersburg workers movement will take the form of a mass struggle of the proletariat for political and economic liberation," p. 34.

3. The Emerging Crisis, 1900–1904

1. Balabanov, "Promyshlennost' Rossii v nachale XX veka," pp. 64–65; Bovykin, "Dinamika promyshlennogo proizvodstva," pp. 29–30; Gatrell, *The Tsarist Economy,*

pp. 167–73. For recent research concerning the economic situation of peasant Russia in the late Imperial period see Kingston-Mann and Mixter, *Peasant Economy*.

2. For a report on the impact of peasants on labor conditions in Petersburg see *Rabochee delo*, nos. 4–5 (Sentiabr'-Dekabr' 1899), p. 93; on worsening conditions in the factories generally, see ibid., p. 95.

3. For general discussions of the crisis, see Bovykin, "Dinamika promyshlennogo proizvodstva," pp. 20–52; Iakovlev, *Ekonomicheskie krizisy v Rossii*, pp. 250–308; Gatrell, *The Tsarist Economy*, pp. 167–84.

4. Iakovlev, *Ekonomicheskie krizisy v Rossii*, p. 269, 272.

5. Korol'chuk and Sokolova, *Khronika revoliutsionnogo rabochego dvizheniia v Peterburge*, p. 317.

6. Iakovlev, *Ekonomicheskie krizisy v Rossii*, p. 272.

7. Diakin, *Germanskie kapitaly v Rossii*, p. 89.

8. "Monopolii v metalloobrabatyvaiushchei promyshlennosti" in *Materialy po istorii SSSR*, p. 276; Roosa, "The Association of Industry and Trade," pp. 23–24.

9. Pogrebinskii, "Komitet po zheleznodorozhnym zakazam," pp. 233–36.

10. For a detailed discussion of these financial operations, particularly as they pertained to the Nevskii and Aleksandrovsk works in Petersburg, see Gindin, "Anti-krizisnoe finansirovanie," pp. 105–49.

11. Vanag and Tomsinskii, *Ekonomicheskoe razvitie Rossii*, pp. 25–26.

12. For a general discussion of these financial operations, see McKay, *Pioneers for Profit*, pp. 225–30.

13. Kruze, "Promyshlennoe razvitie," p. 17.

14. This turn to the domestic market may be seen in the increasing share of output of the machine-construction industry going toward the production of agricultural machinery. See Bovykin, "Dinamika promyshlennogo proizvodstva," p. 48.

15. Commenting on the depression in the Russian mining industry, a British paper noted that one of the principal reasons for the current difficulties was that "most of the large works live chiefly by Government orders, which are given not to the best and cheapest but to those who have influence. Most of the works are badly organized and not run on proper commercial lines, and many even of the largest undertakings are on anything but a sound basis." *Commercial Intelligence*, vol. VIII, no. 212 (November 13, 1902), p. 5. That such conditions pertained in many Petersburg metalworking plants is suggested by the observation of one employee at Putilov: "The factory was supported by state orders and, I believe, subsidies. The structures it manufactured were heavy and awkward, since it was advantageous to sell off as much of its own rolled products as possible. That is why all private orders were almost always outbid by the Petersburg Metals Factory." Teplov, *Zapiski Putilovtsa*, p. 10.

16. The textile strikes of early May are discussed in Iukhneva, "Nakanune Ob-ukhovskoi oborony," pp. 57–67.

17. For a careful reconstruction and analysis of these events see Surh, *1905 in St. Petersburg*, pp. 87–98.

18. Rozanov, *Obukhovtsy*, pp. 78–79.

19. Shotman, "Zapiski starogo bol'shevika," p. 146. The twenty-year-old Shotman, then a joiner at the factory, earned with overtime up to 100 rubles a month, a quite substantial sum for the time.

20. Rozanov, *Obukhovtsy*, p. 77.

21. Shotman, *Zapiski starogo bol'shevika*, p. 33.

22. See ch 2., Working-Class Districts in the 1890s.

23. The demands, reported with some variations, may be found in: *Rabochaia mysl'*, no. 12 (July 1901), pp. 9–11; Rozanov, *Obukhovtsy*, p. 131; A. B., *Obukhovskaia oborona*, pp. 14–17. The sources differ on the exact number of worker deputies.

24. *Obukhovtsy: Maiskiia volneniia na Obukhovskom zavode*, p. 16.

25. A. B., *Obukhovskaia oborona*, pp. 17–18.

26. Rozanov, *Obukhovtsy*, p. 139.

27. *Iskra*, no. 19 (April 1, 1902), p. 5. I have been unable to find further information on the work of these committees. Given that similar investigations were conducted at the behest of Naval Ministry officials at the Baltic factory in 1901 and that similar reforms were enacted at both Baltic and Obukhov in 1905–1906, it may be the case that these committees did indeed function and that they developed both the data and the managerial approaches that informed the reforms subsequently introduced.

28. Rozanov, *Obukhovtsy*, pp. 142–45; A. B., *Obukhovskaia oborona*, p. 18–19.

29. Blek, "Usloviia truda rabochikh," pp. 65, 69–70; extracts from Chikolev's report are reprinted on pp. 70–73.

30. Ratnik's report is contained in ibid., pp. 74–85.

31. Ibid., p. 79. Timofeev wrote: "A good worker, used to carrying out responsible work, will agree to take up worse, more simple work only with great sorrow even if it pays the same; still less will he agree to take on the responsibilities of a common laborer." Timofeev, *Chem zhivet zavodskii rabochii*, p. 8. See also pp. 87–88 on the great affront to worker dignity that a loss of employment entailed.

32. Syromiatnikova, "Rabochee dvizhenie," p. 66.

33. Ibid., p. 62.

34. Ibid., p. 63.

35. In addition to the reports of Chikolev, Ratnik, and Mirskii, several other reports circulated in the Ministries of Finance and Internal Affairs. For a discussion of these other reports see Vovchik, *Politika tsarizma po rabochemu voprosu*, pp. 77–93.

36. Syromiatnikova, "Rabochee dvizhenie," p. 66.

37. Ibid., pp. 61–66.

38. Ibid,. p. 62.

39. For a discussion of this ill-fated experiment, see Schneiderman, *Sergei Zubatov and Revolutionary Marxism.*

40. Blek, "Usloviia truda rabochikh," pp. 74–77.

41. Ibid., p. 79.

42. Ibid., p. 84.

43. Ibid., pp. 77–78.

44. Ibid., p. 78.

45. In a memorandum written to the Minister of the Navy in November 1905, Chikolev noted that the 1901 reports had been read with interest within the Naval Ministry, but that the MVD had then blocked further investigations on the grounds that the "workers' question" was within its (the MVD's) competence and that investigations could agitate workers. LGIA, f. 1349, op. 1, d. 1698, ll. 11–12.

46. von Laue, "Tsarist Labor Policy, 1895–1903," pp. 142–43; and Vovchik, *Politika tsarizma po rabochemu voprosu*, pp. 94–98.

47. On the early history of the Society, which secured formal recognition from the government in 1897, see ch. 1, The Entrepreneurial Elite.

48. TsGIA, f. 150, op. 1, d. 481, ll. 16–20.

49. Livshin, *Monopolii v ekonomike Rossii*, p. 412.

50. Pankratova, *Fabzavkomy v Rossii*, pp. 80–81.

51. TsGIA, f. 150, op. 1, d. 481, ll. 16–20.

52. Pankratova, *Fabzavkomy v Rossii*, p. 81.

53. For a detailed discussion of the development of the higher technical schools see Balzer, "Educating Engineers"; on the discipline of economics see Guroff, "The Legacy of Russian Economic Education," pp. 273, 274–45.

54. Balzer, "Educating Engineers," p. 369, 401.

55. For a rich and fascinating account of a different generation of engineers see Fenin, *Coal and Politics.* Fenin was educated at the St. Petersburg Mining Institute in the 1880s and spent his subsequent career working in the Donets Basin. His memoir

illustrates the values that animated the "men of the eighties": a lifelong thirst for "practical," "invigorating," and "constructive" work, and a "realistic" vision of Russia's future which eschewed the "wishful thinking" and "political illusions" that enthralled most of the intelligentsia, ch. 1, passim; see also pp. 85–86, 106.

56. The first Social Democratic student organization in St. Petersburg arose in October 1902 at the Polytechnic Institute; on the eve of the 1905 Revolution, this Institute had one of the largest SD student organizations in the capital. Gusiatnikov, *Revoliutsionnoe studencheskoe dvizhenie*, pp. 107, 112.

57. See, for example, Balzer, "Educating Engineers," p. 414, and Malinin, "O sushchestvuiushchem predlozhenii i sprose v promyshlennosti na inzhenernyi trud," pp. 339–45.

58. Bailes, *Technology and Society*, pp. 29–30.

59. Balzer, "Educating Engineers," p. 411.

60. On the early roots of the technocratic views of some engineers see Rieber, "The Formation of La Grande Société des chemins," esp. pp. 384–85; see also Balzer's discussion of the Pentagonal Society, pp. 134–53. According to Balzer the most "technocratic" of the Pentagonal Society members was V. L. Kirpichev, a man who would play a critical role in the development of polytechnic education.

61. The following description is drawn from an article on the early history of the Union of Engineers written by one of its participants. Kirpichnikov, "Iz proshlago Obshchestva Tekhnologov," pp. 789–94. Unfortunately, Kirpichnikov did not identify the members of this group.

62. Ibid., pp. 789–90.

63. *Vestnik obshchestva tekhnologov*, no. 3 (March 1905), p. 116. Emphasis in original.

64. Already at a regular meeting of the Moscow Polytechnic Society in October 1895, A. P. Gavrilenko, a professor at Moscow's Higher Technical School, read a paper on the new wage systems currently being developed in the West, among them Taylor's piece-rate system. Some years later, Gavrilenko would publish Henry Gantt's lecture to the American Society of Mechanical Engineers on further refinements in incentive wage systems. Gantt, "Sistema premii dlia oplaty truda v promyshlennykh predpriiatiiakh," *Biulleteni politekhnicheskogo obshchestva*, no. 2 (1903), pp. 175–79. In footnotes on pp. 175 and 176 Gavrilenko refers to his earlier paper, which was published in ibid., no. 6 (1895–96).

65. For a hagiographic rendering of Taylor's life see Copley, *Frederick W. Taylor, Father of Scientific Management*. The first comprehensive articulation of the ideas of scientific management came in 1903 with the publication of Taylor's *Shop Management*. "The Art of Cutting Metals" (1906), *The Principles of Scientific Management* (1911), and Taylor's testimony before the Special Committee of the House of Representatives (1912) constitute the essential exposition of Taylor's ideas. The major works are collected in F. W. Taylor, *Scientific Management, Comprising Shop Management, The Principles of Scientific Management, and Testimony Before the Special House Committee*, New York: Harper and Brothers, 1947. Useful analyses of Taylorism may be found in Braverman, *Labor and Monopoly Capitalism*, especially chs. 4–5; Noble, *America by Design*, especially ch. 10; and Montgomery, *Workers' Control in America*, especially chs. 2, 4, 5.

66. See his *Testimony*, 1947 edition, p. 30. See also *Shop Management*, 1947 edition, pp. 130–31.

67. Wrote Taylor: "A careful analysis had demonstrated the fact that when workmen are herded together in gangs, each man in the gang becomes far less efficient than when his personal ambition is stimulated; that when men work in gangs, their individual efficiency falls almost invariably down to or below the level of the worst man in the gang; and that they are all pulled down instead of being elevated by being herded together." *Principles*, 1947 edition, p. 73.

68. One of Taylor's most detailed studies—taking more than twenty years to complete—concerned the analysis of metal-cutting tools and the determination of the

proper driving speed, feed, and depth of cut. With the aid of Carl Barth, slide rules were developed which quickly manipulated the twelve variables which Taylor found to be involved in each metal-cutting problem. *Shop Management,* 1947 edition, pp. 178–80. The determination of these aspects of work had, of course, rested with the skilled metalworker. Taylor's work on the "art" of metal cutting thus provides one of the clearest examples of the divorce of conception and execution in the labor process.

69. This phrase is borrowed from Maier, "Between Taylorism and Technocracy," p. 30.

70. Fractional strife was particularly intense in the capital. The *Iskra* group, which began its life here with a bitter fight with the remnants of the Union of Struggle, proved unable to send a "rock-hard" Iskrist in the name of the Petersburg Committee to the Second Congress of the RSDRP in the summer of 1903, and then experienced bruising battles between Mensheviks and Bolsheviks in the aftermath of that fateful congress. See *Peterburgskii Komitet RSDRP, Protokoly i materialy,* pp. 12–122 passim.

71. Lepeshinskii, "Poputchiki proletariata," p. 178.

72. Somov, "Iz istorii sotsialdemokraticheskago dvizheniia," p. 25.

73. As quoted in Surh, "Petersburg's First Mass Labor Organization," pp. 412–13.

74. Somov, "Iz istorii sotsialdemokraticheskago dvizheniia," p. 25.

75. Garvi, *Vospominaniia sotsialdemokrata,* pp. 440–41, as translated in Schwarz, *The Russian Revolution of 1905,* p. 57.

76. My remarks on the influence of "society's" forms of protest on the labor movement derive from the insightful paper of Gerald Surh, "Sources of Working Class Consciousness in St. Petersburg, 1905" presented at the Midwest Slavic Conference, University of Wisconsin, Madison, April 1986.

4. Labor-Management Conflict in the Revolution of 1905

1. On tsarist policy in the Far East, see Geyer, *Russian Imperialism,* ch. 9.

2. See ch. 3, Prescriptions for Change, for Mirskii's views on the worker queston.

3. Galai, *The Liberation Movement in Russia.*

4. LGIA, f. 1267, op. 1, d. 992, ll. 6–8. See also Smolin, "Bor'ba Peterburgskikh rabochikh za 8-chasovoi den'," p. 115.

5. On the history of the Assembly, see Sablinsky, *The Road to Bloody Sunday;* Schwarz, *The Russian Revolution of 1905,* especially Appendix 4; and Surh, "Petersburg's First Mass Labor Organization."

6. There are no detailed data on the social composition of the Assembly; the surviving evidence on this question is fragmentary and largely impressionistic. Fedor Bulkin, a Menshevik activist in the Petersburg Metalworkers' Union and its first historian, states that metalworkers were numerically the largest group in the Assembly. Bulkin, *Na zare,* p. 102. The Narvskii district, composed primarily of Putilov workers, was the largest and most important branch. The leadership core of the Assembly was drawn from among the skilled, literate, well-off, and somewhat older strata of the work force: among Gapon's closest associates were printers, weavers, and skilled metalworkers. But it has typically been assumed that the mass consisted of extremely "backward" elements, the classically downtrodden "gray" type who at this juncture remained devoutly religious and fundamentally monarchist. However, as Surh has argued, while such workers undoubtedly joined the Assembly and constituted a significant portion of it, there were other, "less backward" elements who longed to join in an organization which would permit them to express their concerns. Surh concurs with the judgment of one Bolshevik observer: "It's not the gray masses that join Zubatovist societies, but workers interested in knowledge and the labor movement; the workers who join these societies have an awakening desire for something better but are not yet conscious of the full class character of their interests." See the discussion in Surh, "Petersburg's First Mass Labor Organization," pp. 436–41;

quote is on p. 438. Such an assessment builds logically on the remarks of one observer in April 1900, quoted above, who maintained that by the turn of the century a significant "intermediate" layer of politically developed workers had emerged, which stood in between the "conscious" revolutionaries and the "backward" mass and which was growing rapidly with each passing year. See B—v', "Peterburgskoe dvizhenie," pp. 28–33. As the Gapon organization moved in an increasingly political direction, it seems reasonable to posit that growing numbers from this "intermediate" layer were drawn in.

7. Sablinsky, *The Road to Bloody Sunday*, pp. 111, 144.

8. On the building momentum of the strike see Surh, *1905 in St. Petersburg*, pp. 155–67.

9. Somov, "Iz istorii sotsialdemokraticheskago dvizheniia," p. 33.

10. For a translation of the petition, see Harcave, *The Russian Revolution of 1905*, pp. 285–89.

11. The estimates of the number of dead and wounded varied widely and remain obscure to this day. By official count there were 130 dead, but this failed to include those who were not admitted to hospital. The Soviet historian V. I. Nevskii estimated 150–200 dead and 450–800 wounded. Sablinsky considers these latter figures too high. *The Road to Bloody Sunday*, pp. 266–67. Surh estimates that about 1,000 were killed or injured. *1905 in St. Petersburg*, p. 165.

12. Important recent studies of the Revolution of 1905 include Ascher, *The Revolution of 1905, Russia in Disarray*; Verner, *The Crisis of Russian Autocracy, Nicholas II and the 1905 Revolution*; Engelstein, *Moscow, 1905, Working Class Organizations and Political Conflict*; Bushnell, *Mutiny amid Repression: Russian Soldiers in the Revolution of 1905–1906*; Shanin, *Russia, 1905–07, Revolution as a Moment of Truth*.

13. For an exhaustive statistical discussion of the changing dynamics of metalworker protest between 1905–1907 and 1912–1914, as well as the distinctive features of this protest as compared to that of other segments of the working class in Petersburg and elsewhere, see Haimson and Tilly, eds., *Strikes, Wars, and Revolutions*, chs. 6, 16.

14. According to Bulkin, these factories were the two most active during 1905: Putilov struck eight times for a total of 63 days and Nevskii struck six times for a total number of 110 days. Semenov, "Metallisty v revoliutsii 1905–1907 gg.," p. 30.

15. Other large plants working primarily for the state or owned by the state were also notable for their activism (e.g., Franco-Russian, St. Petersburg Metals, St. Petersburg Freight Car, and the Sestroretsk Arms factory).

16. I use the broad definitions of the Nevskii (inclusive of the Shlissel'burg road), and Narvskii (inclusive of Peterhof) regions in my discussion. The Putilov factory was located in the Peterhof subdistrict; Obukhov, Nevskii Shipbuilding, and Aleksandrovsk were on the Shlissel'burg road. See Surh, diss., Table 24 on p. 210.

17. My analysis is based on demands presented by workers at the Putilov, Izhorsk, Franco-Russian, Sestroretsk, Aleksandrovsk Engineering, and Baltic plants. See *NPRR*, pp. 12–13 and 190–91; *Peterburgskie bol'sheviki*, pp. 140–41, 164–66, and 167–69; and L'vovich, "Trebovaniia rabochikh," pp. 86–87.

18. *NPRR*, pp. 12 and 135.

19. *Peterburgskie bol'sheviki*, p. 168.

20. Ibid., pp. 169–70. See also the grievances of Nevskii workers in regard to their supervisory personnel. Paialin, *Zavod i. Lenina*, p. 113. The charges leveled by the Aleksandrovtsy and others prefigure the dominant concerns articulated by metalworkers in the conciliation boards in early 1917. See Hogan, "Conciliation Boards in Revolutionary Petrograd."

21. *NPRR*, p. 191.

22. For one poignant description of workers' simple yet profound search for justice and retribution see Somov, "Iz istorii sotsialdemokraticheskago dvizheniia," pp. 34–45.

23. L'vovich, "Trebovaniia rabochikh," pp. 87–88. Similarly, the St. Petersburg *gradonachal'nik* wrote to General Vlas'ev of the Obukhov factory in August 1904 regarding worker dissatisfaction which in his judgment bore an "exclusively economic character" and which was the product of an exhausting amount of overtime work, the lack of correspondence between the intensity of labor and the earnings of workers, and the "unjust and often brutal" dealings of supervisory personnel with workers. LGIA, f. 1267, op. 1, d. 992, ll. 6–7.

24. Mikhailov, "1905 god na Izhorskom zavode," *Krasnaia letopis'*, nos. 5–6 (44–45), 1931, pp. 244–45; *NPRR*, pp. 38–39; and L'vovich, "Trebovaniia rabochikh," pp. 87–88.

25. Smolin, "Pervaia russkaia revoliutsiia," p. 285.

26. Balabanov, *Ot 1905 k 1917*, pp. 30–33; Okun', *Putilovets*, p. 64; Smolin, "Pervaia russkaia revoliutsiia," p. 285.

27. Kats and Milonov, *1905*, pp. 146–47.

28. Romanov, "Peterburgskaia krupnaia burzhuaziia," pp. 50- 53.

29. See Rieber, *Merchants and Entrepreneurs*, generally on these differences; on Petersburg employers in particular in early 1905 see pp. 345–47. For an examination of the various memoranda sent to Kokovtsov, as well as an argument which too easily joins the position of the Petersburg industrialists with those of others in this "heroic" period of bourgeois liberalism, see Menashe, "Industrialists in Politics," pp. 352–68.

30. The Liubimov Commission was constituted in late 1903 to discuss the application of the recently enacted law on elders to naval factories and port facilities as well as other labor legislation. Its sessions were suspended with the outbreak of war in early 1904. L'vovich, "Trebovaniia rabochikh," p. 88, note 2.

31. Ibid., pp. 92–93.

32. The exact composition of the conference is unknown.

33. Ibid., pp. 90–92.

34. As we will observe here and elsewhere, the employers' search for a unified response to labor's demands would be a long and difficult one. Despite employer agreements and "conventions," and despite militant rhetoric, concessions were made over the course of 1905. For a brief discussion of the economic gains made by metalworkers in 1905, see Bulkin, *Na zare*, pp. 113–14; for an examination of aggregate data on strike outcomes contained in Factory Inspectorate reports see Haimson and Tilly, eds., *Strikes, Wars, and Revolutions*, Table 7, p. 125.

35. Shuster, *Peterburgskie rabochie*, pp. 96–98; Smolin, "Pervaia russkaia revoliutsiia," pp. 276–77.

36. Kats and Milonov, *1905*, p. 163.

37. My discussion is largely based on Schwarz, *The Russian Revolution of 1905*, pp. 75–128; Surh, *1905 in St. Petersburg*, pp. 204–18; and Nevskii, "Vybory v kommissiiu senatora Shidlovskogo," pp. 78–90. According to the plan put forward by the government, workers at individual factories were to elect electors; the electors were then to gather in nine groups defined by industrial branch and in a second round of elections choose deputies to the commission.

38. For statements sent by workers of the Baltic and St. Petersburg Freight Car factories see Bulkin, *Na zare*, p. 110.

39. Compare, for example, the 19 demands presented by Izhorsk workers on January 7 and the list of 25 demands developed as a "nakaz" for Izhorsk deputies to convey to Shidlovskii. Respectively, *Peterburgskie bol'sheviki*, pp. 144–45, and Mikhailov, "1905 god na Izhorskom zavode," 3 (48), 1932, pp. 207–9.

40. Writes Solomon Schwarz: "January 9 had stirred up all the workers in Petersburg and not only in Petersburg, but it had had no organizational consequences whatsoever. It was the campaign around the elections to the Shidlovskii Commission that brought home to the workers the advantages of organized unity and representation. Oversimplifying a little, one might say that January 9 had an immense propa-

ganda value in revolutionizing the masses; and the campaign, though incomparably lower in political resonance, a great organizational value." Schwarz, *The Russian Revolution of 1905*, pp. 122–23 for the quote; see pp. 122–28 generally.

41. Surh calculates the number of metalworker electors as 195, or just under half of the total number of 417 electors. Surh, diss., pp. 331–32.

42. Shuster, *Peterburgskie rabochie*, p. 100.

43. The factory inspectorate noted over 20 wheelbarrow incidents, excluding failed attempts or threats of such actions, in the first 18 days of March. Shuster, *Petersburgskie rabochie*, pp. 119–20. See also Paialin, *Zavod i. Lenina*, p. 136, for a discussion of the situation at the Nevskii factory.

44. *NPRR*, p. 221.

45. TsGIA, f. 150, op. 1, d. 484, ll. 3–4. The document is reproduced in Bulkin, *Na zare*, in a footnote on pp. 77–78.

46. Balabanov, *Ob"edinennyi kapital*, p. 18.

47. One notes in this regard Glezmer's statement to the State Council in 1910: "I was the first . . . to say, 'the later the better,' and I do not renounce my words." Gosudarstvennyi Sovet, *Stenograficheskii otchet'*, sessiia V, zasedanie 45, col. 2780.

48. Romanov, *Rabochii vopros*, p. 62.

49. *Sbornik programm politicheskikh partii v Rossii*, vol. 5, p. 43.

50. Romanov, "Peterburgskaia krupnaia burzhuaziia," pp. 50- 53.

51. For the cover letter sent to Kokovstov on May 12 which laid out the views of the Society in general see Romanov, *Rabochii vopros*, pp. 52–63; for critiques of the various proposals, see pp. 72–92; 99–109; 174–93.

52. Ibid., pp. 58–59, 83–84.

53. Ibid., pp. 62–63.

54. By "corporatist" I have in mind a political economy which rejects a liberal conception polity—most especially the role of elective representative institutions and the formal separation of such institutions from the economy—as well as the sort of polity built on the prerogatives traditionally exercised by career bureaucrats serving as agents of an "above-class" monarchy or autocracy. A corporatist polity instead looks toward a distribution of power through bargaining among major organized social interests conducted under the auspices of an allegedly impartial state. Essential to this polity is the enhanced productivity of an "organized" economy, for social conflict is to be transcended and powerful interests "harmonized" by means of the constantly expanding productive capacities of the nation. Given, then, the centrality of key economic interests, the corporative state tends to fuse economics and politics. These thoughts draw primarily on the work of Charles Maier, who discusses the emergence of a corporatist politics in response to the great dislocations brought about by World War I in Germany, Italy, and France. See especially the introduction to his *Recasting Bourgeois Europe*.

55. In the view of one historian, for example, acute conflict over the shortening of the workday provided the fundamental reason for the employers' demonstrative withdrawal from the Kokovtsov Commission on the pretext of the Tsushima defeat. Romanov, *Rabochii vopros*, pp. xii-xiii.

56. Organized by zemstvo activists and professional groups, banquets were to commemorate the 40th anniversary of the judicial reforms and serve as a means by which oppositional politics might be pressed forward.

57. The reflections of engineer Fenin on the liberation movement and the Revolution of 1905 are in sharp contrast with the views articulated by many Petersburg engineers of the day. A self-proclaimed "man of the eighties," Fenin had little use for the oppositional politics pursued by the leaders of the Petersburg branch of the Engineers' Union. See Fenin, *Coal and Politics*, pp. 136–37 and ch. 8 passim.

58. Kirpichnikov, "L. I. Lutugin i Soiuz Soiuzov," pp. 134–46.

59. Kirpichev served as the first director of the Khar'kov Technical Institute, and

then as the first director of the Kiev Polytechnic Institute. Dismissed from this latter position in 1902 by Plehve because of his sympathy for the student movement, Kirpichev was given a professorship at the St. Petersburg Polytechnic Institute by Witte. See Balzer, "Educating Engineers," pp. 145–49. On the early history of the union, see Kirpichnikov, "Iz proshlago Obshchestva Tekhnologov," pp. 792–93; *Pravo*, no. 11 (March 20, 1905), cols. 834–35.

60. Open registration for membership in the union was held, while the Bureau elected at the December meeting was recognized as the union's executive organ.

61. The "Note" was eventually signed by over 800 engineers from across the Empire, as well as a number of technical societies, including the Moscow branch of the Union of Engineers, which sent a telegram in the name of 132 of its members. *Pravo*, no. 11 (March 20, 1905), col. 836. It was published in several newspapers and presented to Witte on January 23 by a 9-man delegation. It may be found in ibid., no. 4 (January 30, 1905), cols. 265–68. See also Cherevanin, "Dvizhenie intelligentsii," pp. 160, 173–75.

62. *Pravo*, no. 11 (March 20, 1905), cols. 837–39, and no. 14 (April 10, 1905), cols. 1111–12. See also Kirpichnikov, "L. I. Lutugin i Soiuz Soiuzov," p. 138.

63. For a discussion of the Union of Engineers in the early months of the revolution and its activities surrounding the Shidlovskii campaign, see Sanders, *The Union of Unions*, pp. 435–56.

64. *Pravo*, no. 11 (March 20, 1905), col. 840, and no. 20 (April 22, 1905), cols. 1666–74; Sanders, *The Union of Unions*, pp. 471–83.

65. Mikhailov, "1905 god na Izhorskom zavode," *Krasnaia letopis'*, 3 (48), 1932, pp. 189–210 passim. Unfortunately, Mikhailov excerpts the "Note" rather than presenting it as a whole. The document, as excerpted, repeatedly speaks about the position and attitudes of both foremen and department heads, thereby blurring the distinctions between these levels of supervisory personnel.

66. Ibid., p. 190.

67. Ibid., pp. 191–92.

68. Ibid., p. 190.

69. Ibid., p. 191.

70. Ibid., pp. 209–10.

71. For further illustrations of this point see the discussion in ch. 5, Sorting Things Out at the State Plants, on developments at the Baltic and Obukhov factories in late December and early January.

72. Mikhailov, "1905 god na Izhorskom zavode," no. 5–6 (44–45), 1931, pp. 253–54. A similar "cap" on piece-rate earnings was also removed at the Aleksandrovsk factory. *Rus'*, no. 35 (February 2, 1905), p. 2. Many other secondary demands also called attention to problems in the work process, e.g., Putilov workers demanded "timely issue of goods and materials in the shop," while Baltic workers insisted that they be asked to work on only one machine tool at a time. *NPRR*, p. 197; L'vovich, "Trebovaniia rabochikh," pp. 87–88.

73. In response to the suggestion that two commissions be established at the Izhorsk factory, Gross's immediate superior at the Naval Ministry wrote: "In other words, Messrs. foremen want to run the factory. But this is impossible to permit. The director of the factory, when he recognizes the need, can gather foremen for joint discussions both about questions of internal order as well as about technical [questions], but in [these discussions] the opinion of foremen may have only consultative force. The decision of a question one way or another must depend solely on the director of the factory, who alone is responsible for it." Mikhailov, "1905 god na Izhorskom zavode," no. 3 (48), 1932, p. 192.

74. Ibid., pp. 194–98. For Mikhailov, writing on these events in the early 1930s, the differences between Gross and his technical-engineering personnel reflected a

conflict being played out generally in Russian industry between two different paths of capitalist development: the "conservative" or "Prussian" path represented by men like Gross, and the "progressive" or "American" path represented by more enlightened entrepreneurs and engineers. Writes Mikhailov: "The entire position of the engineering-technical personnel may be expressed in the following formula: destroy the feudal vestiges in production, utilize capitalist technology to the maximum, be able to exploit workers wisely and advantageously"; p. 192 for the quote, pp. 192–94 for the argument generally.

75. For a discussion of the relationship between domestic and foreign policy, as well as the impact of the war and revolution on Russian finances, see Geyer, *Russian Imperialism*, ch. 10.

76. For one account of the central importance of the "days of meetings" see Grinevich, "Ocherk razvitiia professional'nago dvizheniia," pp. 229–30. See also Smolin, "Pervaia russkaia revoliutsiia," pp. 310–11.

77. Workers at this plant still referred to their factory by the name of one of its former owners, P. V. Semiannikov; hence they continued to refer to themselves as Semiannikovtsy.

78. On this latter point see Paialin, *Zavod i. Lenina*, pp. 74–78.

79. For some recent discussions of *tsekhovshchina* or craft consciousness and the related phenomenon of factory and district patriotism see Bonnell, *Roots of Rebellion*, especially pp. 143–51, and Smith, "Craft Consciousness, Class Consciousness," pp. 33–58. I will return to the debate over this issue below.

80. On these efforts at Nevskii Shipbuilding, see Paialin, *Zavod i. Lenina*, pp. 128–29, and Tsytsarin, "Vospominaniia metallista," pp. 39–40. Obukhovtsy also sought to form a union in October and tried again in November. See Bulkin, *Na zare*, p. 128.

81. While the earliest origins of the metalworkers' union were to be found in the Nevskii district, an effort to organize primarily metalworkers into an association conceived as an all-workers' union was made in the spring of 1905 by the worker Smesov; like the early attempts in the Nevskii district, the Smesov union in fact rested on a single factory—Siemens-Halske. See Bulkin, "Smesovshchina."

82. Shuster, *Peterburgskie rabochie*, pp. 126–27; *RDVL*, pp. 283–84.

83. For a more detailed discussion of the October strike see Surh, *1905 in St. Petersburg*, ch. 7.

84. *Peterburgskie bol'sheviki*, pp. 334–35.

85. Apparently this decision was accepted by the director of the factory. See *VPSO*, p. 349. One assumes that management's willingness to suspend work had to do with the curtailment of orders; work force cuts at Obukhov were already projected in June. See Shuster, *Peterburgskie rabochie*, p. 135.

86. *VPSO*, p. 350.

87. Ibid., pp. 349–50. The different emphases of the two documents, particularly the modest political content of the first set of demands as well as the call for a nine-hour day, *may* reflect the influence of a broader and less militant stratum of workers on the Nevskii Strike Committee.

88. Ibid., p. 347.

89. My description of the October strike is drawn from the following: Smolin, "Pervaia russkaia revoliutsiia," pp. 313–15; Grinevich, "Ocherk razvitiia professional'nago dvizheniia," pp. 228–31; *VPSO*, pp. 21–36, 339–99, passim; *Peterburgskie bol'sheviki*. See also the special supplement to *Pravo*, no. 45–46 (November 20, 1905), which provided a detailed chronology of the development of the strike in Petersburg, Moscow, and other urban centers.

90. Smolin, "Pervaia russkaia revoliutsiia," pp. 316, 318; Semenov, "Metallisty v revoliutsii 1905–1907," p. 26; Kudelli and Shidlovskii, *1905*, p. 79. See also Surh's account, *1905 in St. Petersburg*, pp. 328–35.

91. In the second half of November, of a total of 562 deputies, 351 were from metalworking factories. Kudelli and Shidlovskii, *1905*, pp. 9–10. For Surh's assessment of the role of metalworkers in the Soviet, see *1905 in St. Petersburg*, p. 358.

92. Mehlinger and Thompson, *Count Witte and the Tsarist Government in the 1905 Revolution*, p. 27.

93. The Manifesto is translated in Harcave, *The Russian Revolution of 1905*, pp. 195–96.

94. Two principal documentary collections for the October-December period paint a picture of repeated meetings and spontaneous work stoppages for all sorts of reasons. See *Peterburgskie bol'sheviki*, pp. 348–432 and 500–38, passim; and *VPR*, pp. 345–525, passim.

95. The Black Hundreds were proto-fascist bands of the extreme patriotic Right. For one report among many on the arming of workers, see *Peterburgskie bol'sheviki*, pp. 513–14.

96. The Semiannikovtsy were the first to introduce the eight-hour day; they were followed on October 27–28 by most other factories in the Nevskii district. On October 29, the Soviet issued a directive calling on all workers to implement the eight-hour day beginning on October 31. Smolin, "Pervaia russkaia revoliutsiia," pp. 336–37.

97. TsGIA, f. 150, op. 1, d. 654, l. 21; LGIA, f. 1304, op. 1, d. 2691, l. 164. This *delo* contains numerous reports concerning the decline of foremen's authority at the Baltic factory in the last months of 1905.

98. In the latter part of 1905, some 50 engineers were fired. In a bold move, the Engineers' Union placed these positions under boycott. With time, however, the boycott collapsed. *Trud inzhenera i tekhnikov*, no. 7 (August 16, 1906), p. 273. See also Mikhailov, "1905 god na Izhorskom zavode," *Krasnaia letopis'*, 3 (48), 1932, pp. 194–98.

99. As we have seen above, engineers at the Izhorsk works argued for a gradual reduction of the workday to eight hours in conjunction with technological modernization of the shops. Similarly, the All-Russian Delegate Congress of Engineers and Technicians of All Specialties, meeting in late April, called for a progressive reduction of the workday to eight hours.

100. While sidestepping the issue of the feasibility of immediately introducing the eight-hour day, an editorial in the November issue of the *Vestnik obshchestva tekhnologov* took the employers to task for their refusal to negotiate with workers and to talk through with them the many factors influencing the length of the workday, no. 11 (November 1905), pp. 475–76.

101. Thus, for example, following the arrest of Khrustalev-Nosar', the union sent an open letter of protest to the government; the union subsequently offered its premises to the Soviet in the wake of the December 3 arrests; and it came out in favor of the December political strike. Cherevanin, "Dvizhenie intelligentsii," pp. 200–1; Kirpichnikov, "L. I. Lutugin i Soiuz Soiuzov," p. 144.

102. *Novaia zhizn'*, no. 11 (November 12, 1905), as reprinted in *Peterburgskie bol'sheviki*, pp. 350–51.

103. See ch. 5, Defending the Interests of Heavy Industry.

104. Again, metalworkers played a crucial role in the decision to protest the actions of the autocracy. See the discussion in Surh, *1905 in St. Petersburg*, pp. 356–67. For figures on factories striking on November 2, see *VPR*, pp. 360–61.

105. Smolin, "Pervaia russkaia revoliutsiia," pp. 352–53; Petrov, *Progressivnaia ekonomicheskaia partiia*, p. 36; Livshits, "Bor'ba za 8-chasovoi rabochii den'," pp. 131–35.

106. As will be seen repeatedly below, the Petersburg Society of Mill and Factory Owners worried constantly about securing the support of the state-owned plants in regard to labor policy and went to great lengths to bring about a coordinated response to labor protest.

107. For the Soviet's declaration see *Peterburgskie bol'sheviki*, pp. 50–51.

108. The erosion of constituted authority was not only reflected in physical assaults

on foremen or in what one observer called the "strike epidemic" of late 1905. (Maevskii, "Massovoe dvizhenie v 1904 po 1907 gg.," p. 109.) Snatches of conversation recorded by A. Buzinov, a rather "backward" metalworker from the Nevskii district at the outset of the 1905 Revolution, suggest other aspects of the changing attitudes of workers toward managerial authority, as well as their own sense of self-worth. One exchange reveals the perception that it was not only, and not so much, the worker who was dependent on the boss, but rather "the boss who kicks the bucket without my hands." Buzinov also noted that if a worker needed something, he would now (after the experiences of 1905) no longer run to the office of the foreman, but rather think out the problem himself or turn to his comrades. Still elsewhere, he reported a conversation which calls attention to a particular worker who didn't have the proper attitude toward an engineer, suggesting that the next thing he would do "is doff his cap, as if to some sort of blood relative." Buzinov, *Za Nevskoi zastavoi*, pp. 65, 104. See also the editor's introduction, pp. 3–4.

109. For a brief discussion of the repression at St. Petersburg factories in December 1905 and January 1906, see *IRL*, vol. 1, pp. 303–4.

5. Rethinking Labor Relations "From Above"

1. On this period in general see Bushnell, *Mutiny amid Repression;* Geyer, *Russian Imperialism;* Mehlinger and Thompson, *Count Witte and the Tsarist Government in the 1905 Revolution;* and Wcislo, *Reforming Rural Russia.*

2. *Peterburgskie bol'sheviki*, p. 521. See Gross's remarks to his workers on December 2, 1905. Mikhailov, "1905 god na Izhorskom zavode," *Krasnaia letopis'*, nos. 1–2/46–47 (1932), p. 247.

3. For the situation at Izhorsk, see Mikhailov, "1905 god na Izhorskom zavode," *Krasnaia letopis'*, nos. 1–2 (1932), pp. 239–40; Surh, *1905 in St. Petersburg*, p. 315; *Rabochii po metallu* no. 2 (September 22, 1906), pp. 6–7.

4. I have been unable to determine the exact reasons or the exact dates for these important personnel changes. Veshkurtsev was acting director no later than October 19; Shemanov replaced Vlas'ev no later than October 29. Ratnik was apparently promoted within the Naval Ministry and appears in 1909 as the chairman of the board of directors of the Baltic works. Gross remained as director of the Izhorsk works.

5. My discussion of the reforms at the Obukhov factory is drawn from two reports, one written in April 1906 and entitled "A Memorandum of the Work of the Commission on Questions Regarding the Regulation of Labor-Management Relations at the Obukhov Steel Factory" and the second written in April 1908, which reviewed the 1906 reforms as well as several changes made in 1907, entitled "The System of Paying Workers Employed at Obukhov Steel Factory." The first report (LGIA, f. 1267, op. 1, d. 1701, ll. 92–103ob.) was appended to the second (ll. 76–90). In neither case is the authorship known. Marginalia appear on the 1906 report and may be the comments of the author of the later study. My discussion of the Baltic factory is based on a variety of documents preserved in LGIA, f. 1304, op. 1, d. 2691. Among the most interesting materials here are the responses of foremen to a questionnaire about wage incentive schemes, minutes from staff meetings concerning diverse aspects of factory reorganization, and two reports on "American" premium systems (ll. 74–75, 76–100). These archival materials are discussed in greater detail in my dissertation, see esp. ch. 4.

6. LGIA, f. 1267, op. 1, d. 1701, l. 93.

7. Ibid., ll. 93, 103.

8. See discussion in ch. 4, Defining the Role of Engineers, and Mikhailov, "1905 god na Izhorskom zavode," *Krasnaia letopis'*, nos. 5–6 (1931), pp. 253–54.

9. LGIA, f. 1267, op. 1, d. 1701, l. 94.

10. Ibid., l. 96ob.

11. Ibid., l. 96.

12. Ibid., l. 78.

13. Ibid., ll. 95–96ob., 98ob.

14. Ibid., ll. 98ob., 102ob.-103.

15. Ibid., ll. 76–90, passim; quote is on l. 99. For a discussion of the various wage systems which illustrates how each sought to "work" on the worker, see Krzhizhanovskii, "Kriticheskii obzor sovremennykh sistem oplaty truda," *Inzhener,* 1911, no. 10 (October), pp. 306–29, and no. 11 (November), pp. 361–71.

16. LGIA, f. 1304, op. 1, d. 2691, ll. 76–86, 153.

17. Ibid., ll. 78, 80–84.

18. Ibid., l. 201; *Rabochii po metallu,* no. 15 (June 13, 1907), p. 14, reported the introduction of the "American" system of computation at Baltic. No further information was provided, simply that cards which recorded the work of each hour were now in use and piece pay (*shtuchnaia plata*) had been curtailed on Saturdays. See also Balabanov, *Ot 1905 k 1917,* p. 67.

19. LGIA, f. 1304, op. 1, d. 57, ll. 48–56.

20. Reformers seemed to believe they could eliminate the very desire for shorter hours by changes in wage policy. "Under day pay, workers willingly argued for half-days because they would get a full day's pay. Now [1908] attempts to reduce the workday are not noted. It is even possible to think that if there was some need to increase the workday, then this would not meet any great opposition from the side of workers," ibid., f. 1267, op. 1, d. 1701, l. 80.

21. For example, marginalia on the April 1906 report concerning the Obukhov factory stated that almost all those working on the reforms and the institution of the "new life" at the factory were senior technologists. The author was an assistant manager at the time and was only asked to attend two sessions. At both sessions, he "heard almost nothing but the two voices of V. [sic] V. Poliakov and V. N. Seleznev" (f. 1267, op. 1, d. 1701, ll. 103–103ob.). R. V. Poliakov was a noted exponent of Taylorist ideas; Seleznev, according to a report in the no. 7 (June 2, 1906) edition of *Vpered,* was known to workers as an "eradicator of 'sedition' and the introducer of the so-called 'American system.'" At Baltic, Director Veshkurtsov had his managers and shop personnel submit written opinions on a number of questions regarding wage policy. The nineteen reports that are preserved reflect a wide diversity of views, ibid., f. 1304, op. 1, d. 2691.

22. Ibid., ll. 162–63, 164–66, 168–70.

23. Ibid., ll. 153–54.

24. Director Veshkurtsov ordered this change on January 26, 1906. Other attempts to instill greater order and bring about greater efficiency in factory operations were reflected in directives regarding a reorganization of the instrument shop, the elaboration of new controls over fuel expenditures, and changes in commercial procedures having to do with the receipt of orders. Ibid., ll. 59, 61, 205, 206, 212, 214.

25. Ibid., ll. 167–72, 179–80.

26. The summary of the answers submitted by shop personnel to the director's questionnaire regarding wage policy revealed not only significant differences of opinion on almost all points, but also an underlying confusion on the part of some staff as to what the proposed changes in the wage structure entailed. For example, eight were in favor, eight opposed to the creation of a rates bureau; three stated a rates bureau should be located in each shop. Ibid., ll. 156–61.

27. Ibid., ll. 113–14, 149.

28. For one such statement see ibid., l. 108.

29. Ibid., f. 1267, op. 1, d. 1701, l. 78.

30. Ibid., f. 1304, op. 1, d. 2691, l. 154.

31. For a fascinating discussion, and a useful comparative perspective, on the differing ways in which the needs of a particular local community or the universalistic

claims of the state might be served by industrial development, see Smith, *Harpers Ferry Armory and the New Technology*.

32. These remarks, dated May 21, 1905, were apparently made in response to some of the points raised by the Liubimov Commission in early April. LGIA, f. 1304, op. 1, d. 3910, ll. 62–66.

33. Ibid., ll. 63, 65.

34. Izhorsk engineers in 1905 and Baltic staff in 1906 had been implicitly critical of the technical competence of their managing directors; the former wanted a commission to study the technical needs of their factory, the latter sought to establish the position of Chief Engineer. Mikhailov, "1905 god na Izhorskom zavode," *Krasnaia letopis'*, 3 (48) (1932), p. 192; f. 1304, op. 1, d. 2691, ll. 167–68.

35. It may be that the reformers' stress on the social benefits to be derived from the new "systems" won the initial acceptance of more conservative staff to experiments with a new wage policy. For the appeal of "progressive" schemes promising an end to labor-management conflict could be explained not only by the "logic" of technical rationality, but also by the concerns of those managers who were focused on issues of social control and frightened by the "anarchy" bubbling up from below. It may also have been the case that the promise of labor peace and the emergence of a strategy that could satisfy worker demands for higher wages and shorter hours prompted high officials in the Naval Ministry to support the methods of the reformers in much the same spirit as Ratnik had taken up the task years before.

36. Despite the authorization of enormous sums for the reconstruction of the fleet by the Tsar in 1907, the Naval Ministry did not receive adequate funds for the reequipping of its Admiralty, Obukhov, or Izhorsk facilities until 1910. See Shatsillo, *Russkii imperializm*, p. 218.

37. "Amerikanka" and "ekonomiia" were the slang terms used by workers to characterize all manner of wage incentive systems and speed-up schemes.

38. Chermenskii, *Burzhuaziia i tsarizm*, pp. 183–90. See also Emmons, *The Formation of Political Parties*, pp. 134–36; and Rieber, *Merchants and Entrepreneurs*, pp. 350–53. The complete program of the party and its first "appeal" may be found in *Sbornik programm politicheskikh partii*, vol. 5, St. Petersburg, 1906, pp. 33–46.

39. Advocacy of at least some form of worker participation in the Duma was fully consistent with the employers' contention going into the October events that political discontent lay at the heart of labor protest. Thus at the August 9, 1905, session of the council of the Petersburg Industrial Society members expressed dissatisfaction with the proposed Duma and felt that workers remained completely without political rights: "such a situation cannot but reflect extremely disadvantageously on the restoration of normal industrial life." TsGIA, f. 150, op. 1, d. 50, l. 124. But according to Rieber, the Society subsequently backed away from a position guaranteeing worker representation. See Rieber, *Merchants and Entrepreneurs*, p. 349.

40. *Sbornik programm politicheskikh partii*, pp. 37–38.

41. Ibid., pp. 43–44.

42. Ibid., pp. 33–34.

43. Quoted in Menashe, "Industrialists in Politics," p. 367.

44. Quoted material in Chermenskii, p. 187. Excerpts from Tripolitov's speech may also be found in Reikhardt, "Partiinye gruppirovki i 'predstavitel'stvo interesov' krupnogo kapitala," pp. 24–25. See also Rieber, *Merchants and Entrepreneurs*, pp. 350–51.

45. The Union of October 17 or Octobrist Party linked moderate zemstvo activists led by Dmitrii Shipov with some Muscovite commercial-industrial interests led by Alexander Guchkov. The party was to the right of the Constitutional Democratic or Kadet Party, which was centrally influenced by Pavel Miliukov. One activist in the Petersburg Industrial Society, M. N. Tripolitov, remarked in October 1905, that

Miliukov specifically eschewed "Manchesterism" and sought to distance his party from the interests of industry. Emmons, *The Formation of Political Parties*, p. 134.

46. See the annual report for 1905 of the PSMFO. TsGIA, f. 150, op. 1, d. 51, l. 45.

47. The Association of Trade and Industry—the most important of these "representative" organizations—was founded in 1906. While based in St. Petersburg and involving many leading representatives of the St. Petersburg metalworking industry, the Association and the PSMFO were not synonymous and their policies and practices should not be confused. The leaders of the Association—N. S. Avdakov and V. V. Zhukovskii—were not Petersburg men. The former represented Southern coal mining interests; the latter, Polish heavy industry. See Roosa, "'United' Russian Industry," p. 423.

48. I thank Reginald Zelnik for stressing the importance of this point.

49. For a discussion of the views of the Association of Trade and Industry in the inter-revolutionary period that is suggestive of some of these same issues see Roosa, "Russian Industrialists and State Socialism," pp. 395–417, and "Russian Industrialists Look to the Future," pp. 198–218. Roosa also finds some evidence of a corporatist politics. See the latter essay, pp. 212–13.

50. Early in the second week of November, a massive lockout was imposed which threw some 100,000 workers, mostly metalworkers, onto the street.

51. See ch. 4, The Bending of the Autocracy; Balabanov, *Ob"edinennyi kapital*, pp. 28–29.

52. The committee consisted of B. B. Gerberts, A. F. German of the Atlas factory, M. I. Gol'dberg, V. A. Lomov, N. N. Struk, L. I. Shpergaze of the Erikson factory.

53. TsGIA, f. 150, op. 1, d. 3, l. 50a—s.

54. The evidence is not clear on this point: it seems that there were conflicting opinions on the question of organization by region or by industrial branch; perhaps too, differences had to do with the greater sense of urgency with which metalworking industrialists wished to proceed.

55. Ibid., l. 75.

56. A June 19 circular to the metalworking group stressed the "urgent" need to proceed with the organization of an Engineering Section; a meeting for June 21 was set. Ibid., ll. 112, 130, 131.

57. Ibid., d. 660, l. 162; ibid., d. 654, ll. 8–9, 20, and 24; Balabanov, *Ob"edinennyi kapital*, pp. 29–31. The first Bulletin covered the week of November 20–25, 1905.

58. See ch. 6, Strike Conflict in the Summer of 1906.

59. Shatilova, "Burzhuaziia v bor'be," pp. 136–37.

60. The December legislation legalized peaceful strikes for economic purposes, but retained criminal penalties for politically motivated strikes and for the use of violence against individuals or property. Strikes remained prohibited in factories having particular state or social importance.

61. TsGIA, f. 150, op. 1, d. 51, l. 66.

62. Ibid., l. 26 and d. 3, l. 50e; *Sbornik programm politicheskikh partii*, p. 44.

63. See a report of the PSMFO dated December 14, 1906, on proposed changes in the contract of hire. TsGIA, f. 150, op. 1, d. 496, ll. 73–81; see also d. 493, l.9–11 for the argument that the new legislation should pertain equally to state and private factories.

64. See, for example, a suit brought by the Langenzipen factory. Ibid., d. 660, ll. 8–10.

65. On the conflicts within the government over the regulation of labor relations see Bonnell, *Roots of Rebellion*, pp. 274–80.

6. The Changing Nature of Metalworker Activism in 1906–1907

1. In the workers' curia, elections occurred on consecutive Sundays through March; the urban curia voted on March 20.

2. On the rather minimal party involvement in this movement, and on its non-fractional nature, see the comments of Voitinskii, *Peterburgskii sovet bezrabotnykh*, pp. 4–5, and Garvi, *Zapiski Sotsial Demokrata*, p. 86. Malyshev's tendentious pamphlet, on the other hand, claims the primacy of the Bolsheviks throughout the movement of the unemployed. Malyshev, *Unemployed Councils in St. Petersburg in 1906*.

3. Malyshev, *Unemployed Councils in St. Petersburg in 1906*, pp. 15–16; *Prizyv*, no. 59 (April 18, 1906), p. 1; Voitinskii, *Peterburgskii sovet bezrabotnykh*, pp. 4–5, 7–9; and *Rech'*, no. 31 (April 25, 1906), p. 4. See also the report of the St. Petersburg Council of the Unemployed on its activities through May in *Vpered*, no. 5 (May 31, 1906), as reprinted in *VPRMS*, pp. 231–34.

4. According to the subsequent recollections of the principle organizer of the Council of the Unemployed, Vladimir Voitinskii, the capital's press inflated the number of jobless in the winter months of 1906. Voitinskii, *Peterburgskii sovet bezrabotnykh*, pp. 11–12.

5. Malyshev, *Unemployed Councils in St. Petersburg in 1906*, pp. 21–26; Voitinskii, *Peterburgskii sovet bezrabotnykh*, pp. 13–15. See also *VPRMS*, pp. 232–33.

6. *VPRMS*, p. 232. Reporting on several immediate measures recommended by the city duma's commission on the unemployed, *Rech'* noted that these steps were required not only out of "philanthropic [considerations], but also out of considerations of social order"; no. 56 (April 23, 1906), p. 5.

7. "Dnevnik A. A. Polovtseva (15 Sept. 1905–10 Aug. 1906; 5 March–2 May 1908)," p. 116. I am grateful to Frank Wcislo for pointing this material out to me.

8. *Prizyv*, no. 54 (April 12, 1906), p. 1. Or elsewhere: "But you yourselves know, comrades, how well the city takes into consideration our worker needs. Bosses [Khoziaeva]-capitalists, who control city business, will not lift a finger. . . . " Ibid., p. 1.

9. The phrase comes from Voitinskii, *Peterburgskii sovet bezrabotnykh*, p. 18.

10. The unemployed were to be exempted from paying certain local rates; unredeemed property in municipal pawnshops was not to be sold before June 21; fines for arrears on interest were to be canceled and payment of interest suspended for three months; monies were to be released for food, rent, and to underwrite interest payments at private pawnshops. Malyshev, *Unemployed Councils in St. Petersburg in 1906*, p. 27.

11. *Prizyv*, no. 54 (April 12, 1906), p. 2.

12. Ibid.

13. *Rech'*, no. 31 (March 25, 1906), p. 4.

14. *VPRMS*, p. 234.

15. Estimates varied significantly and over time, with figures running from 13,000 to over 40,000. *Prizyv*, no. 13 (January 27, 1906), p. 3, and no. 22 (February 5, 1906), p. 2, reported 35,000 unemployed in January, falling to 20,000 in early February. *Rus'*—as cited in *VPRIA*, pp. 986–87, note 76—reported 22,500 in February; *Rech'*, no. 56 (April 23, 1906), p. 5, citing an April 20 report of the Duma's Commission on Unemployment, stated that currently the number of unemployed with families equaled 32,250 but that the figure was expected to rise to 43,650. It is equally difficult to define the number of unemployed metalworkers. Semenov-Bulkin variously estimated the number of Petersburg metalworkers as a whole in 1906 between 75,000 and 79,000. See his *Na zare*, pp. 130, 304. Using these numbers as a rough basis for calculation, unemployment in the metalworking industry was running somewhere between 10%, according to the lowest estimates, and 32% at the highest. Semenov [Bulkin], "Metallisty v revoliutsii 1905–1907 gg.," p. 40. Bulkin himself gives the figures as 20%. *Na zare*, p. 130. To my knowledge, no comprehensive analysis was ever made of this registration data. Besides the gross figures, I have only found data on the Gorodskoi, Moskovskii, and Vyborgskii districts.

16. Voitinskii, *Peterburgskii sovet bezrabotnykh*, pp. 29–31; *Vestnik zhizni*, no. 6 (May 5, 1906), pp. 51–52; *Volna*, no. 13 (May 10, 1906), p. 2.

17. According to Voitinskii, the May 1906 registration indicated that 75–80% of the unemployed were thrown out of the factories during the November lockout and subsequent "cleansing," ibid., p. 2. According to a report in February, the state plants were firing workers under 22, especially single men, as they were considered the chief culprits in the strikes and unrest. Older men with families remained. *Prizyv*, no. 22 (February 5, 1906), p. 2.

18. Voitinskii, *Peterburgskii sovet bezrabotnykh*, p. 8. The labor press routinely reported contributions from the factories; for just one example see *Prizyv*, no. 48 (April 6, 1906), p. 2.

19. Voitinskii, *Peterburgskii sovet bezrabotnykh*, pp. 11–13, 65–66, 83–86; Malyshev, *Unemployed Councils in St. Petersburg in 1906*, pp. 28–31; *Prizyv*, no. 48 (April 6, 1906), p. 1, no. 54 (April 12, 1906), p. 2, and no. 59 (April 18, 1906), p. 1.

20. *Volna*, no. 13 (May 10, 1906), p. 2; Kleinbort, *Obrazovanie*, no. 4 (1906), pp. 99–100.

21. Social fear was still an operative factor at this juncture and was reflected in the panicked response of several town councillors. On June 12, the Council of the Unemployed carried out a 75-person march on city hall in order to learn whether the city fathers intended to keep the promises made at the April 12 meeting. The plan was to divide the marchers in half, with each column simultaneously entering duma chambers by a different door. The delegates agreed to announce that they meant to do no violence; they had simply come to determine whether they would receive work. Clearly frightened by the "invasion" of the unemployed and unconvinced by their assurances, someone called the *gradonachal'nik*, who in turn quickly had the city hall surrounded by police and cossacks. When others sought the removal of the police and called the *gradonachal'nik* to this end, it transpired that he had been told that a bunch of unemployed workers had invaded the duma chambers and threatened the dumtsy with stakes and other weapons. When this became known to the workers, they gathered up several umbrellas and canes they happened to be carrying with them and proffered them to the city fathers. Thus "disarmed," they tried again to talk with the councillors. *Rech'*, no. 98 (June 13, 1906), p. 6, and Malyshev, *Unemployed Councils in St. Petersburg in 1906*, pp. 42–43.

22. On these further allocations and on the beginnings of public works over the summer see Voitinskii, *Peterburgskii sovet bezrabotnykh*, pp. 54–57, 65, and Malyshev, *Unemployed Councils in St. Petersburg in 1906*, p. 48.

23. For the bitter reaction of the Council for the Unemployed to this decision, see *VPROD*, pp. 88–89. See also Kleinbort, *Obrazovanie*, no. 4 (1906), pp. 105–7.

24. Voitinskii, *Peterburgskii sovet bezrabotnykh*, pp. 112, 116.

25. Wrote Voitinskii: "The pliability of the city administration in regard to the demands of the unemployed was a consequence of the lack of faith of the bourgeoisie in the final suppression of the revolution. In the beginning of 1906 [July-?] after the dispersal of the State Duma, this faith appeared. City dumas everywhere ceased their concessions to the unemployed; the Petersburg city duma from the fall of 1906 shifted from a defensive position to an offensive [one], trying to take back from the unemployed that which had been given to them earlier." Ibid., pp. 60–61.

26. As we have seen, wage reform began at the state plants in the first part of 1906. See ch. 8 for a detailed discussion of these and other changes in private industry.

27. On the changing composition of the unemployed movement and the ways in which it was related to alterations in the work process, as well as the argument that many workers now "bought into" the interpretation of their bosses about the causes of unemployment, see Voitinskii, *Peterburgskii sovet bezrabotnykh*, pp. 109–10. See also *Trud*, no. 16 (August 1907), p. 12.

28. This violence would include the murder of two engineers who supervised public works projects in May 1907. For a discussion of this incident see Voitinskii, *Peterburgskii sovet bezrabotnykh*, pp. 122–27.

29. For a discussion of "partisan" activities in the Nevskii district in the fall of 1906 see Buzinov, *Za Nevskoi zastavoi*, pp. 115–20.

30. As regards this illustration of factory patriotism see the comments of Petr Garvi, a Menshevik organizer in Nevskii district in 1906–1907, *Zapiski Sotsial Demokrata*, p. 88. By most accounts, "factory patriotism" in these years was expressed most strongly in the Nevskii district; it will be discussed in greater detail below. I would simply add here that Voitinskii noted that the Council of the Unemployed was strongest in the Vyborg district, but played only "an auxiliary role along with the parties" in the Nevskii district (*Peterburgskii sovet bezrabotnykh*, p. 67).

31. For a poignant description of the devastating effects of long-term unemployment and the hopelessness which accompanied it, as well as a painful discussion of the degeneration of the organized movement of the unemployed, see Voitinskii, *Peterburgskii sovet bezrabotnykh*, pp. 92–96, 109–11. See also 1909 survey, pp. 117–18.

32. For brief reference to these efforts in 1905 see ch. 4, The Bending of the Autocracy; for somewhat greater detail see Bulkin, *Na zare*, pp. 120–29, and 1909 survey, pp. 22–28. Bonnell argues that the failure of Petersburg metalworkers to unionize in 1905 can be largely explained by the importance of factory-based organizations to these workers. See Bonnell, *Roots of Rebellion*, pp. 143–51, esp. p. 147.

33. These were among the various interpretations offered as to why Petersburg metalworkers were so late in developing their union. See, for example, Riazanov, "Pochemu tak pozdno organizovalsia v Peterburge soiuz rabochikh po metallu?" Special Supplement to *Professional'nyi soiuz*, nos. 20/21 (June 22, 1906), pp. 8–11.

34. These were Social Democrats or Social Revolutionaries working directly in the labor movement within Russia, in distinction to emigre socialist intellectuals.

35. On the work of the Central Bureau generally in this period, see Grinevich "Ocherk razvitiia professional'nogo dvizheniia v S.-Peterburge," pp. 245–52, and Bonnell, pp. 180–83; on the particularly important role of the Central Bureau in the organization of the Metalworkers' Union, see Bulkin *Na zare*, p. 130–31.

36. Bulkin, *Na zare*, pp. 131–33; *Professional'noi Soiuz*, no. 13 (March 13, 1906), p. 4; *Prizyv*, no. 58 (April 16, 1906), p. 2.

37. Bulkin, *Na zare*, p. 133.

38. Separate craft unions joined electric lighting workers, gold and silver workers, tinsmiths, blacksmiths, carriage workers, watchmakers, dockworkers, pipe layers, and pattern makers. The Woodworkers' Union recruited in some of the major metalworking plants. Ibid., pp. 142, 286.

39. 1909 survey, pp. 29–30; special supplement to *Professional'nyi souiz*, no. 20/21 (June 22, 1906), pp. 18–20.

40. 1909 survey, pp. 30–31; Bulkin, *Na zare*, p. 139.

41. Bulkin, *Na zare*, p. 152, states, without providing any evidence for the figure, that 16% of Petersburg metalworkers were organized and compares this rate to that of the Petersburg printers. See also the table compiled by Bonnell, *Roots of Rebellion*, p. 208, on the percentage of unionized workers in various Petersburg industries in 1906–1907.

42. It is interesting to note, moreover, the representativeness of the district organizational bureaus. Least representative were the bureaus in Nevskii and Narvskii districts: in the former, six representatives each from the "big three" factories formed the 18-member bureau, while in the latter, the bureau was built on two representatives from each shop at Putilov, plus two representatives from each of three smaller factories in the district. In short, the "giants" of the Nevskii and Narvskii districts completely dominated the local organizational bureaus. In contrast, however, Vyborg's bureau had representatives from 17 factories, while the Petersburg branch had 15 representatives from eight factories (six from the St. Petersburg Iron-Rolling [Zhelezoprokatnyi] Factory). See the special supplement to *Professional'nyi souiz*, no. 20/21 (June 22, 1906), pp. 30–32.

43. See Ibid., p. 31. See also Bulkin, *Na zare*, p. 187.

44. 1909 survey, p. 48. Discussing the Nevskii district in 1906, Garvi wrote: "Factory patriotism played a major role in the revolutionary demonstrations of workers, and among the Obukhovtsy it was especially strong." Garvi, *Zapiski Sotsial Demokrata*, p. 40.

45. According to union sources, these funds were often built on the basis of existing *lampadnye kassy* (that is, funds to buy oil for the icon lamps that hung in the shops). The implication was that this was an extremely "primitive" institutional base on which to build assistance for the unemployed. 1909 survey, p. 28.

46. This discussion relies heavily on Bulkin, *Na zare*, p. 145. The quoted phrase is his. Garvi also notes "turf struggles" between the Council of the Unemployed and other working-class organizations, *Zapiski Sotsial Demokrata*, pp. 89–90.

47. 1909 survey, pp. 30–31. For a discussion of these strikes, see ch. 6, Strike Conflict in the Summer of 1906.

48. 1909 survey, pp. 29–51, esp. pp. 34–38; Bulkin, *Na zare*, esp. pp. 130–35, 139–44, 148–49, 187–88.

49. 1909 survey, p. 30. Emphasis in original.

50. Ibid., pp. 38–40. Between February and May 1907, activists worked hard to resolve these organizational difficulties. And while new "instructions" were finally ratified which augmented the authority of the center and circumscribed the power of the district locals, nonetheless the union historians continued to call attention to the problems of "factory patriotism." The "instructions" are reprinted in Bulkin, *Na zare*, pp. 497–503. For continuing laments on factory patriotism, see the 1909 survey, p. 47.

51. See ch. 2, Working-Class Districts in the 1890s.

52. Garvi, *Zapiski Sotsial Demokrata*, p. 10.

53. Ibid., p. 67.

54. On this painful clash between "fathers and sons" see ibid., pp. 59–62.

55. Thus contrary to Bonnell, who finds the roots of a viable and potentially reformist trade unionism in the 1906–1907 period, I would stress the typically nominal commitment of metalworkers of various type to the project of trade unionism, as well as the persistent sense of union weakness on the part of its leaderhsip. As I will argue in chs. 9 and 10, the union was not only dogged by crucial problems at the grass roots, but undermined by the intransigent positions of employers and the state. See Bonnell, *Roots of Rebellion*, pp. 194–95, 233–34, 272–73, 289, 440–41.

56. Smolin, "Pervaia russkaia revoliutsiia," pp. 381–83.

57. *Prizyv*, no. 62 (April 21, 1906), p. 2; TsGIA, f. 150, op. 1, d. 654, l. 94 and d. 654, l. 69. As we will observe below, such incidents figured importantly in the strikes at mid-sized machine-construction factories in the summer of 1906.

58. *VPRMS*, pp. 228–29. But other considerably more violent and less "therapeutic" actions were taken against Black Hundreds which, among other things, deeply alarmed leading Mensheviks. See Garvi, *Zapiski Sotsial Demokrata*, pp. 92–95, but especially p. 94.

59. Here I would like to acknowledge my debt to Tim Mixter, with whom I talked about notions of "workers' turf."

60. The factories were the Erikson Telephone Factory, the Atlas Engineering Works, the Lemmerikh Engineering Factory, Langenzipen, and the Kreiton Shipyards in the Okhta region.

61. This statement requires some qualification as regards the Atlas strike. On the morning of June 17, 1906, before work, workers met to discuss the upcoming trial of the St. Petersburg Soviet deputies and to elect representatives for meetings with the Duma fraction, following which the administration announced that workers would be docked for the late start. Four workers who were particularly agitated by this action were sacked by management. Two days later, workers used wheelbarrows to remove a senior worker and a clerk whom they believed responsible for the denunciation and

subsequent dismissal of their comrades. Management immediately fired five workers directly involved in the incident and announced dismissal within two weeks for the remaining workers. At a citywide delegate meeting of the Metalworkers' Union, the conflict was judged to turn on issues of basic civil rights, in that management encroached on labor's right to elect representatives for conversations with the Duma fraction and then refused to negotiate through the union. However, the demands presented by Atlas workers to the administration did not explicitly address these issues of civil rights. See *Golos truda*, no. 13 (July 4, 1906), p. 3; *Rabochii po metallu*, no. 1 (August 30, 1906), pp. 6–7; TsGIA, f. 150, op. 1, d. 655, l. 16a; and the discussion in Garvi, *Zapiski Sotsial Demokrata*, pp. 46–52. It is worth noting that this union meeting was reported on July 4, that is, before the dispersal of the Duma. At this juncture both factions of Social Democracy were hotly debating what labor's attitude toward the Duma should be; for the Mensheviks, defense of the Duma and "bourgeois" civil rights more generally was the central issue. Ultimately, what may be most interesting in this strike is the way in which Menshevik union leaders were focused on "high" politics, while Atlas workers were more concerned to pursue demands which reflected politics at the point of production. See ch. 6, Social Democracy and the Dilemmas of "Bourgeois" Revolution in Russia.

62. For accounts of the conflict at Erikson see *Prizyv*, no. 62 (April 21, 1906), p. 2; *Rabochii po metallu*, no. 3 (October 10, 1906), p. 6; TsGIA, f. 150, op. 1, d. 655, ll. 31–40, 121, in part reprinted in *VPRMS*, pp. 289–91. On the Atlas strike, see *Rabochii po metallu*, no. 1 (August 30, 1906), pp. 6–7; *Golos truda*, no. 13 (July 4, 1906), p. 3; TsGIA, f. 150, op. 1, d. 655, ll. 12–16a, in part reprinted in *VPRMS*, pp. 276–77.

63. TsGIA, f. 150, op. 1, d. 655, ll. 32–34.

64. *VPRMS*, p. 290.

65. *VPRMS*, pp. 276–77; TsGIA, f. 150, op. 1, d. 655, 16a. While the lack of archival material prevents a detailed discussion of the underlying determinants of the Atlas strike, evidence from a later period leaves little doubt that the Atlas management was in the midst of a major reorganization of accounting procedures, and perhaps production processes, at the time of the strike. In a special lecture series sponsored by the Society of Technologists in the spring of 1912, A. F. German reported on the implementation of accounting and organizational reforms at his factory. By May 1906, a new "cheque system" to monitor and control costs on time, labor, and materials developed by the Berlin firm of L. Lowe had been adopted. The various demands raised by workers in the summer of 1906, then, were most probably designed to counteract the effects of such managerial initiatives. See "Organizatsiia zavodoupravleniia," special supplement to *Vestnik obshchestva tekhnologov*, pp. 30–49.

66. TsGIA, f.150, op. 1, d. 655, ll. 18–21, in part reprinted in *VPRMS*, pp. 283–84; *Rabochii po metallu*, no. 2 (September 22, 1906), pp. 6–7, and no. 3 (October 10, 1906), p. 7.

67. *Golos truda*, no. 15 (July 6, 1906), p. 3; *Rabochii po metallu*, no. 1 (August 30, 1906), p. 6; and TsGIA, f.150, op. 1, d. 655, l. 24, reprinted in *VPRMS*, pp. 266–67.

68. TsGIA, f. 150, op. 1, d. 655, ll. 29–30, reprinted in *VPRMS*, p. 285.

69. Work paid by the hour, rather than by the day, permitted employers to calculate wages more exactly in relationship to the time actually expended. Hourly pay therefore discouraged workers from lateness in the morning and after lunch and, it was hoped, provided a disincentive to demands for a reduction in the length of the workday. See ch. 5, Sorting Things Out at the State Plants, for a discussion of wage reform at the state plants.

70. *Rabochii po metallu*, no. 2 (September 22, 1906), pp. 6–7.

71. It is well to remember that these organizations were only just in the process of formation. The PSMFO submitted statutes for registration with the *gradonachal'nik* on June 27, 1906; one object of its August 19 memorandum to Stolypin was to protest the delay in the legalization of the Society, a process which should have been com-

pleted within a month's time. Organizers for the Metalworkers' Union submitted statutes for registration on April 11; the founding congress of the union occurred on April 30, 1906.

72. *VPRMS*, p. 295.

73. It is also worth noting that Atlas workers resolved not to disperse to the countryside, not to take jobs elsewhere, and not to drink alcoholic beverages for the duration of the strike. *Golos truda*, no. 16 (July 7, 1906), p. 4.

74. See the August 19, 1906, memorandum of the PSMFO to Stolypin in *VPRMS*, pp. 291–95.

75. An appellate brief filed by the Langenzipen company on August 22, 1906, regarding a case first heard in the lower courts on November 28, 1905, argued: "The contract of hire obligates the worker to fulfill the work and those orders which are given by the owner or his deputy in regard to that work. The factory is the property of the owner-employer and only he or his deputy has the right to realize the right of property, which also entails the right of executive direction [*rasporiazheniia*]. In view of this, the employer is free to hire and fire whom he pleases, without asking the permission of workers about this: if workers demand the dismissal of a foreman, then they appropriate for themselves the alien right of executive direction and this is nothing other than an encroachment on the right of property of another person, which is an action clearly contrary to the law." TsGIA, f. 150, op. 1, d. 660, l. 10.

76. Again, the August 19, 1906, memorandum to Stolypin is richly illustrative of employer attitudes at this juncture. *VPRMS*, pp. 291–95.

77. Ibid.

78. Ibid., p. 294.

79. Ibid., p. 295.

80. Ibid., p. 267.

81. In the appellate suit brought by the Langenzipen firm in August 1906 and noted above, management argued on the basis of point 4, article 105 of the *Ustav o promyshlennosti* that because of the "insolence and bad conduct of the worker" [*derzost' i durnoe povedenie rabochago*], the personnel and/or property of the factory had been endangered and therefore the employer had the right to dismiss the worker immediately without two weeks' notification and payment of wages. The brief asserted that the conflict involved the workers and foreman of the instrument shop alone. Workers in other shops had no cause to demand the foreman's dismissal; the fact that they did so indicated the existence of "agitation" and "worker organization." Further, "these organizations" were directly interested in expanding an issue that concerned only a small group of workers to the workers of the entire factory and in so doing pursued "general political interests" and not the interests of the narrower group. See TsGIA, f. 150, op. 1, d. 660, ll. 8–11. The issue thus appeared to be organization per se; and the very demand to remove the foreman was judged to constitute insolence on the part of workers. Moreover, it should be noted, employers relied in their argumentation on an archaic statute ("insolence and bad conduct of the worker"), on a point of law that far more readily mirrored the relations of social deference than contractual relations built on social equality.

82. *VPRMS*, p. 294–95.

83. TsGIA, f.150, op. 1, d. 655, ll. 12–14.

84. Ibid.

85. Ibid., ll. 89, 90.

86. *Rabochii po metallu*, no. 2 (September 22, 1906), pp. 3–4.

87. Garvi, *Zapiski Sotsial Demokrata*, p. 46.

88. *Rabochii po metallu*, no. 1 (August 30, 1906), p. 6.

89. Bulkin, *Na zare*, p. 184.

90. See the discussion in Garvi, *Zapiski Sotsial Demokrata*, pp. 47–52, and in particular the resolution of Vyborg Mensheviks noted on pp. 51–52; Bulkin, *Na zare*, p. 184,

on the weakness of local union leadership in the 1906 strikes more generally; and ch. 6, Social Democracy and the Dilemmas of "Bourgeois" Revolution in Russia, for an analysis of the party-fractional issues at hand.

91. On strike outcomes, see my dissertation, pp. 365–67.

92. On Lenin's rethinking of the role of the peasantry, see Shanin, *Russia, 1905–07*, vol. 2, pp. 148–51.

93. My discussion relies generally on Harding, ed., *Marxism in Russia, Key Documents 1879–1906*, pp. 32–38; Liebman, *Leninism under Lenin*, pp. 42–109; Service, *Lenin: A Political Life. The Strength of Contradiction*, pp. 122–74; Elwood, *Resolutions and Decisions*, pp. 89–107; Shanin, *Russia, 1905–07*, vol. 2, chs. 4–6.

94. Kol'tsov, "Rabochie v 1905–1907 gg.," pp. 265–66. According to Keep, in St. Petersburg, out of a total of 271 qualified factories, 133 boycotted the elections completely. See Keep, "Russian Social Democracy and the First State Duma," p. 185.

95. Emmons, *The Formation of Political Parties*, pp. 286–92; and Schapiro, *The Communist Party of the Soviet Union*, pp. 83–85.

96. Emmons, *The Formation of Political Parties*, pp. 286–88.

97. This phrase is Emmons', ibid., p. 286.

98. See the comments from the Semiannikov factory in *Novaia gazeta*, November 19, 1906.

99. My thinking on these issues has been influenced by the thoughtful essay of Ira Katznelson, "Working-Class Formation."

100. Emmons, *The Formation of Political Parties*, pp. 353–65.

101. For a general discussion, see Liebman, *Leninism under Lenin*, pp. 69–73; Getzler, *Martov, A Political Biography*, esp. p. 115; and Shuster, *Peterburgskie rabochie*, pp. 231–35. For Lenin's attitudes at this juncture and the positions taken by the Petersburg Committee in May, see *VPRMS*, pp. 217–18, 220–22; *Peterburgskii komitet RSDRP, Protokoly i materialy*, pp. 226–29; Lenin, *Collected Works*, vol. 10, pp. 483–84, 500–4. For one statement of the exceptional bitterness of the fractional strife, see Garvi, *Zapiski Sotsial Demokrata*, pp. 22–38.

102. For an excellent discussion of the general disarray of the revolutionary parties in the period surrounding the dissolution of the first Duma, see Bushnell, *Mutiny amid Repression*, pp. 206–21. For Martov's recognition that Petersburg workers blamed the Menshevik Central Committee for the failed general strike, see *ODR*, vol. 3, p. 625. For the Petersburg Committee's post mortem on the strike see *VPRMS*, pp. 287–89.

103. "Liquidators" was the pejorative term used by Lenin to describe those Mensheviks who allegedly advocated work in the open legal labor movement at the expense of the illegal underground party.

104. Garvi, *Zapiski Sotsial Demokrata*, pp. 104–16. For a brief discussion of Martov's views in this period see Getzler, *Martov, A Political Biography*, pp. 115–17.

105. Garvi, *Zapiski Sotsial Demokrata*, p. 104.

106. Israel Getzler, Martov's biographer, captures an essential moment which sheds as much light on the psychology of Menshevism as on its theoretical dispositions. His description is worth quoting at length. "Equipped with a false passport and full of hopes and anxieties, he [Martov] crossed the border in the third week of October 1905 and arrived in Vilno, where he found the station crowded with Jewish refugees who had escaped from the pogroms of Bialystok, Zhitomir, and Minsk, as well as the areas of Kharkov and Kherson. The long-awaited revolution showed to Martov its ugly face of elemental pogromist violence. It reminded him of the pogrom of 1881, and of the old Jew in the train from Odessa to Petersburg: 'the same dim eyes, the same submission to fate and the same story . . . of a human whirlwind which burst over peacefully sleeping people and cast them into an abyss of filth and blood.' 'That memento,' Martov remembered, 'rang cruelly in my ears and shook me deeply, when, full of trepidation, I crossed the threshold of the renewed homeland, dying to draw in the air of the "days of freedom."' It kept him awake all night on his way to Petersburg.

Perhaps it reminded him that even if the tsar should fall, the Russia of the muzhik and the pogrom was still distant by more than one revolution from the construction of a socialist order" (*Martov, A Political Biography*, pp. 109–10). See also note 58 above, regarding Menshevik attitudes toward the purge of Black Hundreds from the factories. Resolutions condemning "exes" and other "partisan" activities were passed at the Fourth (Unity) Congress in April 1906. See Elwood, *Resolutions and Decisions*, pp. 99–100.

107. Garvi, *Zapiski Sotsial Demokrata*, p. 104.

108. Garvi seemed aware that these boundaries were problematic for many workers. See Ibid., pp. 51, 111.

109. *Rabochii po metallu*, no. 8 (January 28, 1907), p. 1.

110. For Lenin's analysis of the elections see *Collected Works*, vol. 12, pp. 62–69, 70–74, 86–92.

111. Martov, "Ianvarskie vybory po rabochei kurii v gorode Peterburge," esp. pp. 74–78. Martov's choice of "seredniak" to describe an average worker posited in a quite literal sense the relationship of this worker to the land (i.e., the primary meaning of "seredniak" is middle peasant).

112. In the absence of data on skill levels and *stazh* at state factories for 1906—I am aware of such data only for the Baltic works at the *beginning* of 1906 (see Rashin, *Formirovanie*, p. 503)—it is impossible to draw such conclusions; but even if such data were available the attempt to relate politics to social origins would be no less reductionist. On recent Western efforts to interpret the results of these elections see Rice, "'Land and Freedom' in the Factories of Petersburg," pp. 87–107, and Melancon, "The Socialist Revolutionaries from 1902 and 1907," esp. 35–48. See also the important unpublished paper by Peter Holquist on the workers' elections in Petersburg. I am indebted to Holquist for sharing his insightful essay with me. (Holquist, "The Course of the Second Duma Elections in the Workers' Curiias of St. Petersburg.") On other efforts to tease out of thin and scattered data a relationship between politics, party affiliation, and social origin, see Perrie, "The Social Composition and Structure of the Socialist-Revolutionary Party before 1917," esp. p. 241, and Lane, *The Roots of Russian Communism*, esp. p. 37.

113. Again, see the discussion in Holquist on the reasons why the structure of the electoral process precludes the determination of party affiliation of workers.

114. These issues will be examined in ch. 9.

115. Minin, "O rabote v Vyborskom raione"), pp. 23–24; *Listovki Peterburgskikh Bol'shevikov*, vol. 1 (1902–1907), pp. 514–15; and *VPRII*, p. 118.

7. Financiers, Employers, and Engineers

1. On the politics of rural Russia and the Third of June system, see Wcislo, *Reforming Rural Russia*, Manning, *The Crisis of the Old Order in Russia*, Haimson, ed., *The Politics of Rural Russia*, and Hosking, *The Russian Constitutional Experiment*.

2. On the fascination with Taylor and Ford, "Amerikanizm," and technocratic utopias, see, for example, Smith, "Taylorism Rules OK?"; Rogger, "*Amerikanizm* and the Economic Development of Russia," esp. pp. 410ff; and Stites, *Revolutionary Dreams*, esp. ch. 7. See also Bailes, *Technology and Society*, esp. chs. 1–2. On general problems of technocracy and professional expertise see Maier, "Between Taylorism and Technocracy," and Haskell, ed., *The Authority of Experts*, especially the essays by Haskell and Larson. I am indebted to Esther Kingston-Mann for sharing with me her many insights concerning the notion of a culture of modernization in Imperial Russia. For her published remarks on this problem see "Marxism and Russian Rural Development," esp. pp. 737–38 and 751–52; see also "In Search of the True West," pp. 23–49.

3. On the relationship of the banks to heavy industry, as well as on the concentration of the commercial banking system, see especially Gindin and Shepelev,

"Bankovskie monopolii." See also Gindin, *Russkie kommercheskie banki,* pp. 155ff. For a brief summary of these issues in English see Portal, "The Industrialization of Russia," pp. 847–51.

4. As noted in ch. 3, the number of joint-stock companies in the Petersburg metalworking industry increased from nineteen to forty-two between 1900 and 1913. On the growth of joint-stock corporations generally over the 1904–1914 period see Shepelev, *Tsarizm i burzhuaziia,* p. 196.

5. Bovykin and Shatsillo, "Lichnye unii," p. 59.

6. On the growth of foreign capital in Russian industry in general and by sector between 1880–1915 see MacKay, *Pioneers for Profit,* Table 4, p. 29, and Table 7, p. 33; on the process of financial reorganization and the role of the big banks see ibid., pp. 225–41. See also Gindin and Shepelev, "Bankovskie monopolii," passim, and Bovykin and Shatsillo, "Lichnye unii," pp. 55–74. Soviet literature on these subjects is substantial and in large measure centers on a debate concerning the emergence of "state monopoly capitalism" and the degree to which the autocracy was subordinated to the dictates of "finance capital" on the eve of the war. For the relevant citations to Soviet literature and a brief discussion of these issues see Rieber, *Merchants and Entrepreneurs,* pp. 364–71, esp. note 78, p. 365.

7. Rieber, *Merchants and Entrepreneurs,* p. 366. See Wcislo, *Reforming Rural Russia,* ch. 4, for a discussion of the political values and attitudes that Witte brought to his governmental service in the decade prior to the first revolution.

8. While several of the factories controlled by Putilov and Vyshnegradskii routinely participated in the work of the PSMFO, available evidence suggests that these men were not personally involved in this association.

9. This discussion draws on Shepelev, *Tsarizm i burzhuaziia,* esp. chs. 3 and 4; Roosa, "Russian Industrialists and State Socialism" and "'United' Russian Industry"; and Rieber, *Merchants and Entrepreneurs,* pp. 364–71.

10. According to one estimate, by 1905 over three-quarters of the total production of the machine-construction and metalworking industry of the Northern and Baltic region came from state orders. Shepelev, *Tsarism i burzhuaziia,* p. 249.

11. Shepelev, *Tsarizm i burzhuaziia,* p. 230; see also the proceedings of the 1908 conference held to discuss the needs of the Empire's heavy industry. *Stenogrammy soveshchaniia o polozhenii metallurgicheskoi i mashinostroitel'noi promyshlennosti, Mai 1908,* St. Petersburg, 1908, pp. 30–50.

12. These investigations have been published as "Monopolii v metalloobrabatyvaiushchei promyshlennosti i tsarizm v nachale XX v.," pp. 269–368; see also Livshin, "K voprosu o voenno-promyshlennykh monopoliiakh," p. 56.

13. See the discussion in Manning, *The Crisis of the Old Order in Russia,* pp. 359–65; see also Diakin, "Iz istorii ekonomicheskoi politiki tsarizma," pp. 47–49; and Shepelev, *Tsarizm i burzhuaziia,* p. 194–96.

14. It may be noted here that such leading members of the capital's entrepreneurial elite as A. I. Putilov, E. L. Nobel, and B. A. Efron were active in the Association of Industry and Trade.

15. Goldberg, "The Association of Industry and Trade, 1906–1917," pp. 45–46.

16. As quoted in Roosa, "Russian Industrialists and State Socialism," p. 413. For a general summary of the complaints of big business on the eve of the war see ibid., pp. 412–13.

17. Rieber, *Merchants and Entrepreneurs,* p. 249.

18. LGIA, f. 1357, op. 3, d. 6b, ll. 349, 350.

19. L'vovich, "Trebovaniia rabochikh," p. 90.

20. TsGIA, f. 150, op. 2, d. 70, ll. 1–8. Its work completed, the Pankov Commission apparently suspended its sessions in mid-1908. But in light of all the many changes taking place in shop floor practice, and in the context of intense strike protest in the prewar period, the commission reconvened in August 1913, to review and update the

contractual documents governing metalworking plants, and in the hope of bringing about greater uniformity in the conditions pertaining at private and state-owned plants. The commission was ultimately able to issue a revised set of "Rules of Hiring" and "Rules of Internal Order" in March 1914. Ibid., d. 70, ll. 64–66, 67–82, and d. 74, ll. 6–7, 43.

21. For a more detailed discussion of this directive and its implementation, see ch. 8, Reforms on the Shop Floor.

22. Livshin, *Monopolii v ekonomike Rossii*, p. 405.

23. The documents variously refer to this as an "inquiry" or "mediation" office.

24. Obshchestvo zavodchikov i fabrikantov, *1907-i god.: Otchet i prilozheniia*, p. 11.

25. Balabanov, *Ob"edinennyi kapital*, p. 42.

26. LGIA, f. 1258, op. 2, d. 245, ll. 287, 301–21, 327–28.

27. Members included P. A. Bartmer of the Nobel factory, A. A. Bachmanov of Lessner, V. V. Diufur of Westinghouse, I. P. Pankov of St. Petersburg Metals, and L. I. Shpergaze of Erikson. These factories had all engaged in various types of work process rationalization. Lessner, Nobel, St. Petersburg Metals, and Erikson were all situated in Vyborg district and would ultimately form a core group within the PSMFO that aggressively imposed a lockout in the spring of 1914.

28. TsGIA, f. 150, op. 2, d. 71, l. 12.

29. Ibid., l. 8.

30. Ibid., l. 9.

31. Ibid., l. 6.

32. Ibid., ll. 6, 8–11.

33. Ibid., ll. 8–11.

34. These data sheets were simple and convenient, humorously modern in a way. Eighteen questions were posed describing the type of worker unrest. The employer was instructed "to underline the phrases and words which express the picture of the day's events. Fold the sheet and send it with a one-kopeck stamp not later than 6 p.m." (Ibid., op. 1, d. 663, ll. 42, 44; d. 667, l. 6). In 1913, new information blanks were introduced: Orange Card A for the outbreak of a strike; Yellow Card B for reportage on the course of the strike; and Green Card C for the end of the strike (ibid., op. 1, d. 668, ll. 108–11).

35. Ibid., op. 1, d. 654, ll. 20, 24; d. 60, ll. 12–13.

36. Two thousand copies were printed and distributed, with the expectation that further editions would be issued in the future. *1907-i god.: Otchet i prilozheniia*, pp. 10–11.

37. TsGIA, op. 2, d. 70, ll. 44–63.

38. Other publishing efforts included V. V. Groman, *Materialy k voprosu o merakh bor'by s zabastovkami* (St. Petersburg, 1914); a long report entitled "Procedures for the Annulment of the Contract of Hire According to Foreign Legislation" (ibid., op. 1, d. 671, ll. 14–29); and a short report issued by the Inquiry Office in 1913 which reviewed the resolutions of the PSMFO since 1905 in regard to the suppression of the strike movement (ibid., op. 1, d. 660, ll. 161–62).

39. Ibid., op. 1, d. 51, l. 230. The committee was composed of representatives from industry and legal advisors, and its tasks included assistance in the discussion of legislative projects, the development of guidelines for Society members concerning newly issued legislation or governmental directives, assistance in court cases that had a "principled" significance, legal aid to members, and the coordination and regulation of various policies and practices. Ibid., op. 1, d. 661, l. 15.

40. See ch. 4, Defining the Role of Engineers.

41. Quoted in Balzer, "Educating Engineers," p. 441.

42. Ibid., p. 417.

43. See, for example, the proceedings of the Fifth All-Russian Congress of Electri-

cal Engineers in nos. 4 and 5, 1909, of *Elektrichestvo;* Shirman, "K polozheniiu 'tekhnika' voobshche i 'inzhenera' v chastnosti," pp. 238–50.

44. Russak, "Ob odnom iz voprosov," p. 6.
45. Geints', "Sistema Teilora," pp. 828–29.
46. Engel'meier, "V zashchitu obshchikh idei v tekhnike," p. 96.
47. Russak, "Ob odnom iz voprosov," p. 7.
48. Ibid., p. 8.
49. Engel'meier, "V zashchitu obshchikh idei v tekhnike," p. 97.
50. Ibid.
51. Ivanov, "O prichinakh malogo sprosa," p. 458.
52. "Znachenie sistemy Teilora," *Fabrichno-zavodskoe delo,* no. 1, 1913, pp. 16–17, reprinted from *Utro·Rossii.*
53. Considerably more sophisticated and ultimately more insidious investigations into the psyche of the worker were under way in the laboratories of such applied psychologists as Hugo Munsterberg. His work, as well as that of many others, would seek to unlock the secrets of human motivation and the links between physiology, psychology, and "optimal" labor productivity. These researches would lie at the foundation of such venerable set pieces of the modern industrial landscape as "human relations" and "human resources" departments. Chapters of Munsterberg's *Psychologie und Wirtschaftsleben* were translated into Russian in 1914, alongside an essay by M. Aronov on industrial rationalization. See the collection edited by the "Legal Marxist" M. Tugan-Baranovskii, entitled *Novyia idei v ekonomike,* Sb. 3 (St. Petersburg, 1914).
54. "Khronometrazh ili rabochii trud po formule i sekundomeru," *Fabrichnoe-zavodskoe delo,* no. 1, 1913, p. 15.
55. Poliakov, *Nastoiashchee polozhenie voprosa o primenenii sistemy Teilora,* p. 41.
56. Netyska, "Neskol'ko slov," p. 436.
57. *Promyshlennost' i torgovlia,* no. 1, 1913, p. 15, as quoted in Livshin, *Monopolii v ekonomike Rossii,* p. 406.
58. Illustrative of this popularization was the publication in 1913–14 of the journal *Fabrichno-zavodskoe delo,* which encouraged factory reorganization in general and propagated Taylorism in particular. See also my dissertation, pp. 81–84.
59. Geints', "Sistema Teilora," p. 825.
60. Ibid., p. 820.
61. Aronov, "Organizatsiia predpriiatii," p. 215.
62. Sharpant'e, "Organizatsiia liteinoi masterskoi," *ZIRTO,* 1911, no. 1, p. 1, and no. 2, p. 63. Writing in 1910, another engineer commented on the recent "epidemic" of rates bureaus; as he saw it, such bureaus had become the "alpha and omega for many major bosses of native manufacturing, their own sort of idée fixe." Filippov, "Iz poezdki po nekotorym avstriiskim i angliiskim zavodam," p. 487.
63. Krzhizhanovskii, "Kriticheskii obzor," p. 307.
64. To cite only a few examples, see "A," "Raspredelitel'nyi biuro, ego organizatsiia i funktsii," pp. 95–99, translated from the English; Pankin, "Organizatsiia i ustroistvo instrumental'nogo otdela," *ZIRTO,* 1912, no. 1, pp. 1–16, and no. 5, pp. 163–76; Sharpant'e, "Organizatsiia liteinoi masterskoi," *ZIRTO,* 1911, no. 1, pp. 1–12, no. 2, pp. 52–68, and no. 4, pp. 125–42; Sharpant'e, "Vedenie fabrichnoi otchetnosti po Lilienthal'iu," *ZIRTO,* 1911, no. 11, pp. 377–86, and no. 12, pp. 425–34; "Organizatsiia zavodskogo predpriiatiia," *Dvigatel',* 1911, no. 12, pp. 178–82, no. 13, pp. 195–98, and no. 15, pp. 220–24; and "Organizatsiia zavodoupravleniia," special supplement to *Vestnik obshchestva tekhnologov,* pp. 1–49.
65. Reflective of the growing propagation of these ideas was the work of N. F. Charnovskii. In the academic year 1909–10, Charnovskii taught a course on "The Organization of Metalworking Factories" at the Imperial Technical Institute and also

at a commercial institute. These lectures were published in the *Biulletini politekhnicheskogo obshchestva* between 1909 and 1911 and then issued in a separate edition in 1911. Imbued with the ideas of the scientific management movement, Charnovskii provided a detailed description of the organization of metalworking factories from their initial conception to questions of site selection, plant layout, equipment acquisition, the organization of managerial and business procedures, and the selection of wage systems. Drawing extensively from German and American sources, the course introduced engineering and accounting students to the leading ideas of the factory reform movement. Technical students, then, imbibed these ideas in the classroom as well as in the library. Charnovskii, "Organizatsiia promyshlennykh predpriiatii po obrabotke metallov," *Biulleteni politekhnicheskogo obshchestva*, 1909, no. 6, pp. 436–41, 1910, no. 1, pp. 51–72, no. 2, pp. 98–108, no. 5, pp. 227–73, and 1911, no. 4, pp. 297–322; and his *Organizatsiia promyshlennykh predpriiatii po obrabotke metallov* (Moscow, 1911).

66. "Organizatsiia zavodoupravleniia," special supplement to *Vestnik obshchestva tekhnologov*, p. 3.

67. Pankin, "Organizatsiia i ustroistvo instrumental'nogo otdela," p. 168. See also Dmokhovskii, "Tsentral'nyia instrumental'nyia otdeleniia," pp. 56–57.

68. See, for example, Salamatin, *Nauchnoe rukovodstvo rabotami*, pp. 5–8, 18, and Levenstern, *Nauchnyia osnovy zavodoupravleniia*, pp. 1–11, passim.

69. Poliakov and Khmelev, *Konsul'tatsionnoe biuro*, p. 6.

70. Aronov, "Ob"edinennye kapitalisty i Tret'ia Gosudarstvennaia Duma," pp. 373–80.

71. Grinevitskii's important essay, dated October 24, 1914, and entitled "Tekhniko-obshchestvennyia zadachi v sfere promyshlennosti i tekhniki v sviazi s voinoi," was first printed in *Biulleteni politekhnicheskago obshchestva*, 1914, no. 11, pp. 583–99, and reprinted in *Vestnik inzhenerov*, vol. 1, no. 1, 1915, pp. 8–14. Specific reference is to the initial publication, p. 590.

72. For recent discussions of the middle class see Clowes et al., eds., *Between Tsar and People*.

73. See Montgomery, *Fall of the House of Labor*, ch. 5, passim, for a discussion of the American experience.

8. Rationalizing the Metalworking Industry

1. On the electro-technical industry see Diakin, *Germanskie kapitaly*, p. 138.

2. On changes in the structure of the metalworking and machine construction industries between 1900 and 1908 see Bovykin, "Dinamika promyshlennogo pro-izvodstva," Tables 9 and 10, p. 48. On the transportation sector, see Il'inskii and Ivanitskii, *Ocherk istorii russkoi paravozostroitel'noi i vagonostroitel'noi promyshlennosti*, p. 99.

3. On rearmament policies see especially Shatsillo, *Rossiia pered pervoi mirovoi voinoi*, and *Russkii imperializm*. See also the important work of Peter Gatrell on the impact of state investment, particularly via huge defense expenditures, on heavy industrial development, "Industrial Expansion in Tsarist Russia," and "After Tsushima." On the interrelationship between rearmament and foreign policy see Geyer, *Russian Imperialism*, pp. 255–92.

4. Kruze, "Promyshlennoe razvitie," p. 18; Rozenfel'd and Klimenko, *Istoriia mashinostroeniia SSSR*, p. 88.

5. For all-Russian data on shifts in the number of workers and total output in the various sub-divisions of the metalworking industry between 1900 and 1908 see Sovet s"ezdov, *Statisticheskii ezhegodnik na 1914 g.*, pp. 262–63.

6. Rozenfel'd and Klimenko, *Istoriia mashinostroeniia SSSR*, p. 92, and the further discussion on pp. 93–94. See also Il'inskii and Ivanitskii, *Ocherk istorii russkoi*

paravozostroitel'noi i vagonostroitel'noi promyshlennosti, p. 99, for reference to the modernization of equipment in the locomotive engine construction sector.

7. *Vestnik finansov, promyshlennosti i torgovli,* 1915, no. 19, p. 265.

8. *Edinstvo,* no. 8 (August 10, 1909), p. 3.

9. *Nash put',* no. 10 (December 3, 1910), p. 15, and no. 15 (March 30, 1911), p. 13.

10. *Metallist,* no. 6 (30) (August 10, 1913), p. 7; *Kuznets,* no. 8 (March 3, 1908), p. 5; Kruze, "Promychlennoe razvite," vol. 3, p. 22.

11. LGIA, f. 1206, op. 1, d. 227, ll. 22, 41, 63; see Table 8.5.

12. *Metallist,* no. 6 (30) (August 10, 1913), p. 7; see Table 8.5.

13. On the latter point see Diakin, *Germanskie kapitaly,* p. 139. More generally, see *Nasha zaria,* no. 9–10 (1911), pp. 49–50, and *Rabochii po metallu,* no. 21 (September 24, 1907), p. 13.

14. "Izhorskii Zavod," *Voennaia entsiklopediia,* vol. 10, pp. 570–71; Zav'ialov, *Istoriia Izhorskogo zavoda,* p. 318.

15. Rozanov, *Obukhovtsy,* pp. 283–84.

16. *Edinstvo,* no. 10 (November 22, 1909), pp. 4–5. A discussion of the Nevskii-Putilov agreement may be found in Bovykin, "Banki i voennaia promyshlennost'," p. 101.

17. Okun, *Putilovets,* pp. 154–60; Zhukovskii, "Ekonomicheskoe razvitie," pp. 157–67; Kruze, "Promyshlennoe razvitie," pp. 20–21; *Ist. Put. zavoda,* pp. 357–59. See also Bovykin, "Banki i voennaia promyshlennost'." Sources conflict as to the exact sums expended on this enormous expansion and retooling.

18. While the utilization of mass production techniques by the prewar period should not be exaggerated, nonetheless plants like Aivaz, Semenov, and Atlas employed such processes. See "Organizatsiia zavodoupravleniia," special supplement, *Vestnik obshchestva tekhnologov,* no. 11, 1912, pp. 10–15, 31; *Novaia rabochaia gazeta,* no. 27 (August 8, 1913), p. 3; see also Rozenfel'd and Klimenko, *Istoriia mashinostroeniia SSSR,* pp. 97–102, 111.

19. 1909 survey, p. 108; Bulkin, *Na zare,* p. 229.

20. *Kuznets,* no. 8 (March 3, 1908), p. 5.

21. 1909 survey, pp. 126–27.

22. See ch. 6, Mobilizing the Jobless.

23. *Vestnik rabochikh po obrabotke metalla,* no. 2 (June 5, 1908), p. 10, no. 3 (n.d.), p. 11; *Edinstvo,* no. 4 (April 23, 1909), p. 19, no. 9 (September 18, 1909), p. 13, no. 10 (October 22, 1909), p. 15; *Nash put',* no. 3 (June 25, 1910), p. 12, and no. 6 (August 30, 1910), p. 12; Bulkin, *Na zare,* p. 390.

24. *Edinstvo,* no. 11 (December 1, 1909), p. 14, and no. 16 (April 1, 1910), p. 17; *Nash put',* no. 3 (June 25, 1910), p. 4.

25. *Metallist,* no. 2 (26) (May 22, 1913), p. 4.

26. *Edinstvo,* no. 8 (August 10, 1909), p. 2.

27. At these 38 plants, work force size had been cut by 7% over the previous year and a half. *Edinstvo,* no. 9 (September 18, 1909), pp. 7–8.

28. Montgomery writes of the comparable process in the United States: "Skilled workers in large enterprises did not disappear, but most of them ceased to be production workers. Their tasks became ancillary—setup, troubleshooting, toolmaking, model making—while the actual production was increasingly carried out by specialized operatives." *The Fall of the House of Labor,* p. 215.

29. See discussion of the Plotnikov Commission, ch. 7.

30. Managers at state-owned plants faced particular pressure: in conjunction with the multimillion-ruble program to reconstruct the fleet, these facilities came under the intense scrutiny of the Duma as well as a variety of bureaucratic agencies. By late 1908 and early 1909, the state's naval installations in Petersburg had been directed to tighten substantially their accounting and reporting practices in order to bring them in line with the principles of commercial accountability, that is, to make these plants respon-

sible for their own profit and loss. And while the Tsar had authorized the program of naval reconstruction in the summer of 1907, the enormity of the changes that had occurred in naval technology, as well as the backwardness of extant facilities, required a comprehensive modernization of the equipment and processes employed at the state's factories which stretched out for several years. Sums in excess of 30 million gold rubles were expended on the naval factories from the state treasury alone over the 1908–1913 period, a figure which excluded additional sums from the reserve capital, profits, etc. of these plants. Soviet researchers have done considerable work on these issues. The literature is extensive, but see especially Shatsillo, *Russkii imperializm*, particularly ch. 5; Polikarpov, "Iz istorii voennoi promyshlennosti," pp. 150–51, and more generally his "O 'kommercheskom' upravlenii gosudarstvennoi promyshlennost'iu," pp. 48–61, for an interesting discussion of the limits of "capitalistic" accounting at the state plants.

31. See, for example, Vebner, "Kak uznat' deistvitel'niu stoimost' proizvodstva," *Kommercheskii deiatel'*, 1910, no. 2/3, pp. 1–7; no. 4, pp. 12–21; no. 5/6 pp. 10–14; and no. 7/8, pp. 9–12; "Organizatsiia zavodoupravleniia," special supplement to *Vestnik obshchestva tekhnologov*, pp. 1–49; Sharpant'e, "Vedenie fabrichnoi otchetnosti (po Lilental'iu)," *ZIRTO*, 1911, no. 11, pp. 377–86, and no. 12, pp. 425–32.

32. Nicholas Hans has estimated that in 1908 some 40,000 pupils attended 160 commercial schools, by 1911 this had risen to 202 commercial schools with an enrollment of 46,764, and by 1917 some 60,000 students attended 250 commercial schools. See his *The History of Russian Educational Policy*, p. 210. As noted above, the number of engineers and engineering schools increased significantly.

33. Suggestive of the growing importance and professionalization of accounting was the opening of the First All-Russian Congress of Accountants in Moscow in June 1909 and the appearance of specialized periodical publications serving this field. See, for example, the following headings in the subject index to *Bibliografiia periodicheskikh izdanii Rossii, 1909–1916* (Leningrad, 1961) vol. 4: "Accounting and Bookkeeping," "Office Equipment," "Commercial Education," and "Stenography," pp. 14, 19, and 30. See also Galagan', *Osnovnye momenty v razvitii schetnoi idei*, pp. 29–30.

34. 1909 survey, p. 13.

35. At a special lecture series sponsored by the Society of Technologists in the fall of 1912, A. F. German of the Atlas factory and I. A. Semenov of the Semenov factory discussed the various systems in place at their respective firms; my discussion is based on the published remarks of the two men found in "Organizatsiia zavodoupravleniia," special supplement to *Vestnik obshchestva tekhnologov*, pp. 1–18, 30–49. Further information on the Semenov factory may be found in *Fabrichno-zavodskoe delo*, no. 1 (1913), pp. 14–16.

36. Ibid., p. 30.

37. Ibid., p. 5.

38. See ch. 5, Sorting Things Out at the State Plants.

39. LGIA, f. 1440, op. 8, d. 183, l. 24.

40. Ibid., l. 40.

41. Ibid., ll. 40–41.

42. Union sources not only noted this aspect of wage reduction, but observed as well that earlier it was often the case that a night shift worked an hour less than the day crew but were paid at the full rate; now, as had happened at St. Petersburg Metals, workers were paid for the hours worked. 1909 survey, p. 108, fn. 1.

43. By June 1908, the metalworkers' press was reporting that a majority of plants had shifted to hourly based wages. *Vestnik rabochikh po obrabotke metalla*, no. 2 (June 5, 1908), pp. 6, 11; no. 3 (n.d.), p. 10. See also ibid., no. 1 (May 15, 1908), p. 18, for a discussion of a general meeting of the union on May 4, 1908, which listened to a report by Chirkin on hourly wages as a prelude to other, more refined wage systems.

44. *Vestnik rabochikh po obrabotke metalla*, no. 2 (June 5, 1908), p. 2.

45. For reports on discussions within the union, see *Rabochii po metallu*, no. 15 (June 13, 1907), p. 14; *Vestnik rabochikh po obrabotke metalla*, no. 1 (May 15, 1908), p. 18; *Edinstvo*, no. 7 (July 10, 1909), p. 10, no. 13 (January 25, 1910), p. 9. For analyses of the "American system" in the labor press see "Amerikanskaia sistema," *Rabochii po metallu*, no. 20 (September 5, 1907), pp. 3–4; "Chto daet rabochim 'Amerikanskaia sistema'?" *Vestnik rabochikh po obrabotke metalla*, no. 2 (June 5, 1908), pp. 9–10; and V. T., "Kak organizovan nadzor za rabotoi v amerikanskoi masterskoi," *Nash put'*, no. 4 (July 15, 1910), pp. 5–6.

46. *Rabochii po metallu*, no. 15 (June 13, 1907), p. 14; no. 18 (July 26, 1907), p. 8; no. 23 (October 25, 1907), p. 13; *Edinstvo*, no. 2 (March 5, 1909), p. 15; no. 3 (March 19, 1909), p. 14; no. 6 (June 15, 1909), p. 16; no. 8 (August 10, 1909), p. 2; LGIA, f. 1267, op. 1, d. 1701, ll. 76–90, 92–103ob.; Paialin, *Zavod i. Lenina*, p. 258; special supplement to *Vestnik obshchestva tekhnologov*, pp. 1–18, 30–49; *Nash put'*, no. 14 (March 4, 1911), p. 13; *Edinstvo*, no. 7 (August 10, 1909), p. 14; *Metallist*, no. 12 (36) (December 5, 1913), p. 14. Commenting generally on the intensification of work, one observer noted: "But the most significant [method] is the manipulation of wages. Everywhere one can see a transfer to more 'modern' systems of pay, from day to piece, from piece to American, from simple American to complex American (with premiums on premiums), with the common task of awarding premiums for speed and intense work." Velox, "Nachalo kontsa," *Nasha zaria*, nos. 8–9 (August-September 1910), p. 19.

47. A survey conducted by the Metalworkers' Union in 1909 noted simply that "a whole series of attempts were made to transfer to the American system in the 1907–08 period," while a 1907 report in a newsletter of Moscow-area employers remarked on the broad usage of piece rate wages by the hour, with a premium fixed for rapid work in St. Petersburg metalworking plants. See the 1909 survey, p. 108; *Obshchestvo zavodchikov i fabrikantov Moskovskogo promyshlennogo raiona. Biulleten' rabochego dvizheniia*, no. 1 (May 30–July 1, 1907), p. 4.

48. Filippov, "Iz poezdki po nekotorym avstriiskim i angliiskim zavodam," *Vestnik obshchestva tekhnologov*, p. 487; *Edinstvo*, no. 16 (April 1, 1910), p. 22; *Metallist*, no. 13 (April 7, 1912), p. 16; *Nadezhda*, no. 1 (July 31, 1908), p. 13; special supplement to *Vestnik obshchestva tekhnologov*, p. 5.

49. *Metallist*, no. 8 (45) (June 13, 1914), p. 6.

50. *Edinstvo*, no. 2 (March 5, 1909), p. 14.

51. By 1911 the union seemed especially concerned about these order sheets. Viewing them as a clever method to get around the law, one detailed article on the subject discussed how employers could more easily cut rates by this method: rates were set individually, hence undermining collective solidarity in protesting any change in rates, while at the same time fostering uncomradely competition among individual workers. See "Zaplatite, skol'ko pozhelaete," *Metallist*, no. 7 (December 30, 1911), pp. 4–7; see also "Iz zhizni i deiatel'nosti O-va," *Metallist*, no. 11 (February 23, 1912), p. 10.

52. *Vestnik rabochikh po obrabotke metalla*, no. 2 (June 5, 1908), p. 2; *Rabochii po metallu*, no. 17 (July 12, 1907), p. 14, no. 18 (July 26, 1907), p. 15; *Pravda*, no. 165 (November 10, 1912), p. 10; *Nadezhda*, no. 2 (September 28, 1908), p. 19; *Nash put'*, no. 14 (March 4, 1911), p. 13; *Edinstvo*, no. 16 (April 1, 1910), p. 22; special supplement to *Vestnik obshchestva tekhnologov*, pp. 10–15, 31.

53. LGIA, f. 1258, op. 2, d. 245, l. 358.

54. TsGIA, f. 150, op. 2, d. 67, l. 27.

55. *Edinstvo*, no. 3 (March 19, 1909), p. 10; *Metallist*, no. 7 (December 30, 1911), pp. 5–7, no. 9 (January 26, 1912), p. 9, no. 11 (February 23, 1912), p. 10.

56. Okun, *Putilovets*, pp. 179–83; *Ist. Put. zavoda*, p. 365.

57. 1909 survey, p. 122.

58. TsGAOR, f. 111, op. 5, d. 454, 1913, ll. 237, 241; LGIA, f. 1267, op. 15, d. 78, l. 135. A detailed description of various time clock systems current in the West and

complete with pictures is preserved in the Obukhov *fond* at LGIA (f.1267, op. 1, d. 2348). Discussing the need for tighter accounting methods in March 1913, the director of Obukhov specifically noted that time clocks had the advantage of (a) recording the work force more quickly and accurately, and (b) controlling the admittance and discharge of workers from the plant. LGIA, f. 1267, op. 1, d. 2348, ll. 14–18.

59. *Edinstvo*, no. 2 (March 5, 1909), p. 14, and no. 7 (July 10, 1909), p. 14; *Pravda*, no. 98 (August 23, 1912), p. 11; *Novaia rabochaia gazeta*, no. 29 (September 11, 1913), p. 4; *Metallist*, no. 6 (December 17, 1911), p. 12, and no. 11 (February 23, 1912), p. 9.

60. *Edinstvo*, no. 2 (March 5, 1909), pp. 12, 13, 14, no. 8 (August 10, 1909), p. 13, no. 15 (March 12, 1910), p. 13, no. 16 (April 1, 1910), p. 17; *Nash put'*, no. 7 (September 20, 1910), p. 14, and no. 10 (December 3, 1910), p. 14; *Metallist*, no. 19 (September 1, 1912), p. 14.

61. Balabanov, *Ot 1905 k 1917*, p. 65; Kir'ianov, *Zhiznennyi uroven' rabochikh Rossii*, pp. 136–39.

62. *Vestnik rabochikh po obrabotke metalla*, no. 1 (May 15, 1908), p. 21; *Nash put'*, no. 4 (July 15, 1910), p. 13. At a meeting of the Textile Section of the PSMFO in December 1907, the fact that metalworking factories used fines more frequently than textile mills was noted. TsGIA, f. 150, op. 1, d. 51, l. 235.

63. TsGIA, f. 150, op. 2, d. 70. l. 5.

64. *Metallist*, no. 24 (December 14, 1912), p. 8.

65. *Edinstvo*, no. 9 (September 18, 1909), p. 8, no. 16 (April 1, 1910), p. 10; *Nash put'*, no. 14 (March 4, 1911), p. 1.

66. *Vestnik zhizni*, no. 6 (May 23, 1906), p. 52; *Luch'*, no. 74 (December 13, 1912), p. 4; *Volna*, no. 11 (May 23, 1906), p. 4.

67. *Rabochii po metallu*, nos. 10–11 (March 15, 1907), p. 10; *Kuznets*, nos. 3–4 (December 20, 1907), pp. 14–15.

68. Time studies conducted at the Aleksandrovsk engine repair factory of the Nizhegorodskii railroad in 1907 led to a more refined division of labor and, in turn, to a substantial reduction in the time required to repair locomotives. Petrochenko and Kuznetsova, *Organizatsiia i normirovanie truda v promyshlennosti SSSR*, pp. 11–12.

69. *Fabrichno-zavodskoe delo*, 1913, no. 1, p. 15.

70. *Edinstvo*, no. 2 (March 5, 1909), p. 13.

71. *Metallist*, no. 9 (January 26, 1912), p. 14; *Edinstvo*, no. 16 (April 1, 1910), p. 22.

72. See ch. 10, Strike Activism and Its Consequences, for discussion of this strike.

73. Haimson and Tilly, eds., *Strikes, Wars, and Revolutions*, pp. 396–97.

9. The Uneven Struggle in the Years before Lena

1. For a brief discussion of the rising cost of living, see 1909 survey, pp. 111–12. For some statistics on suicide see *Pravda*, no. 4 (April 26, 1912), pp. 2–3; for a discussion of deaths due to alcoholism see ibid., no. 20 (May 23, 1912), p. 6; on the high incidence of epidemic disease in the capital, see Bater, *St. Petersburg, Industrialization and Change*, pp. 349–53.

2. These unemployment figures must be taken with great caution. Bulkin provides the figures of 20% unemployed for 1906; 10–15% for 1908–09, and 6–7% for 1910. *Na zare*, pp. 130, 229. The 1909 survey, p. 108, estimated that 20–25,000 metalworkers were jobless in 1907–08. Using Bulkin's estimate of 66,000 metalworkers in St. Petersburg in 1908 (*Na zare*, p. 304), 30–38% would be unemployed. A study of 8 major metalworking plants in 1907 revealed a 36% cut in work force size. *Kuznets*, no. 8 (March 3, 1908), p. 5.

3. Figures are for subgroup VIIIa and VIIIb respectively. Rashin, *Formirovanie rabochego klassa Rossii*, pp. 53–54.

4. Bulkin, *Na zare*, pp. 384–88; 1909 survey, p. 110. According to one recent Soviet work, "the real wage of workers in the metal factories of the capital in the period

under examination [1908–1913] does not have a clearly expressed tendency to change: in one case it grew, in another it remained at the same level or even fell somewhat." *Istoriia rabochego klassa SSSR* (series title), *Rabochii klass Rossii 1907-fevral' 1917 g.* (volume title), pp. 90–91.

5. 1909 survey, p. 108.

6. Ibid., pp. 108–9.

7. *Edinstvo*, no. 8 (August 10, 1909), p. 13.

8. Ibid., no. 16 (April 1, 1910), p. 17.

9. Ibid., no. 8 (August 10, 1909), p. 12.

10. Ibid., no. 1 (February 10, 1909), p. 20.

11. *Metallist*, no. 5 (November 26, 1911), p. 11.

12. 1909 survey, p. 122.

13. *Kuznets*, nos. 3–4 (December 20, 1907), pp. 14–15.

14. 1909 survey, pp. 121–22.

15. *Rabochii po metallu*, no. 14 (May 9, 1907), p. 15; *Edinstvo*, no. 2 (March 3, 1909), pp. 12, 13; 1909 survey, p. 121.

16. 1909 survey, p. 108.

17. *Edinstvo*, no. 11 (December 1, 1909), p. 14.

18. Ibid., no. 15 (March 12, 1910), p. 13.

19. *Zvezda*, no. 12 (March 5, 1911), p. 20.

20. *Zvezda*, no. 13 (49) (March 1, 1912), pp. 19–20.

21. *Nash put'*, no. 3 (June 25, 1910), p. 12.

22. Ibid., no. 20 (August 11, 1911), p. 13; *Metallist*, no. 4 (November 10, 1911), p. 11.

23. *Luch'*, no. 69 (December 7, 1912), p. 4.

24. *Zvezda*, no. 5 (January 13, 1911), p. 19.

25. *Rabochii po metallu*, no. 21 (September 24, 1907), p. 15; *Nadezhda*, no. 1 (July 31, 1908), p. 13, and no. 3 (October 31, 1908), p. 14; *Edinstvo*, no. 8 (August 10, 1909), p. 12; and *Metallist*, no. 9 (January 26, 1912), p. 15.

26. *Kuznets*, nos. 5–6 (January 19, 1908), p. 26; *Edinstvo*, no. 14 (February 16, 1910), p. 16; *Kuznets*, nos. 3–4 (December 20, 1907), p. 15.

27. *Edinstvo*, no. 5 (May 26, 1909), p. 14; *Nadezhda*, no. 1 (July 31, 1908), p. 12.

28. For the resolution, see *Nash put'*, no. 9 (November 7, 1910), p. 11; see also Bulkin, *Na zare*, p. 297. On the closing off of opportunities for upward mobility, see *Rabochii po metallu*, no. 18 (July 26, 1907), pp. 3–4.

29. *Rabochii po metallu*, no. 20 (September 5, 1907), pp. 12–13.

30. *Edinstvo*, no. 11 (December 1, 1909), p. 12.

31. *Kuznets*, nos. 3–4 (December 20, 1907), p. 16; Paialin, *Zavod i. Lenina*, p. 255. For an insightful discussion of the American experience with workplace rationalization, and particularly the unsettling sense of constant change felt by workers, see Montgomery, *The Fall of the House of Labor*, especially ch. 5.

32. *Vestnik rabochikh po obrabotke metalla*, no. 1 (May 15, 1908), p. 18. See also ibid., no. 2 (June 5, 1908), p. 2, quoted in ch. 8, Reforms on the Shop Floor.

33. *Nevskii vestnik*, no. 2 (December 10, 1906), p. 10.

34. *Kuznets*, no. 7 (February 14, 1908), p. 3.

35. 1909 survey, p. 110.

36. Ibid., p. 118.

37. In a June 1911 article which largely concerned trade union organizing and strike tactics, one can glimpse the chasm which opened up between workers and the intelligentsia in the aftermath of 1905. Wrote one activist: "strikers know perfectly well that in the present time the collections once made in support of strikes among 'the sympathetic' intelligentsia are now a matter of the distant past and that the only thing one can count on are collections among workers." Chatskii, "Ocherednyia zadachi," *Nash put'*, no. 18 (June 17, 1911), p. 7.

38. Although closed numerous times and appearing under various names, the

journal of the Petersburg Metalworkers' Union was one of the few trade union publications able to come out with a fair degree of regularity. While its *tirazh* fell during the most intense period of reaction, workers nonetheless passed single copies along to comrades and read the paper collectively. The metalworkers' press was one important source through which labor imbibed a discourse of class.

39. On this point see "Kto vinovat?" *Edinstvo*, no. 12 (December 21, 1909), pp. 2–3, or "Za soiuznoe delo!" *Metallist*, no. 8 (January 13, 1912), pp. 3–4.

40. It is interesting to note the contrast between the front and back pages of the metalworkers' press. The first few pages regularly carried articles about the European labor movement and its leaders, worker legislation at home and abroad, coverage of the various social congresses, and a host of rather academic discussions: on Tolstoy's death, on the Emancipation of 1861, and on municipal government. The back pages published worker correspondence that was closely tied to local issues and life on the shop floor. Even dedicated union literati seemed one step removed from working class life; in a certain sense, workers seemed to appropriate the back pages of the paper as their own. For a specific complaint coming out of a general meeting of members in the Vyborg and Petersburg branch of the union concerning the failure of the editorial board to pay sufficient attention to correspondence from the factories, see "Iz zhizni i deiatel'nosti O-va," *Metallist*, no. 7 (December 30, 1911), p. 9.

41. *Rabochii po metallu*, no. 15 (June 13, 1907), pp. 3, 4; *Zvezda*, no. 9 (45) (February 12, 1912), p. 18; *Kuznets*, no. 2 (May 25, 1907), p. 3.

42. *Nadezhda*, no. 2 (August 28, 1908), p. 19.

43. *Zvezda*, no. 7 (43) (February 4, 1912), p. 20.

44. *Kuznets*, nos. 3–4 (December 20, 1907), p. 15.

45. *Nash put'*, no. 10 (December 3, 1910), p. 15.

46. *Vestnik rabochii po obrabotke metalla*, no. 1 (May 15, 1908), pp. 20–21.

47. *Kuznets*, nos. 3–4 (December 20, 1907), p. 16. See also "'Amerikanskaia' sistema," *Rabochii po metallu*, no. 20 (September 5, 1907), p. 4.

48. *Zvezda*, no. 15 (51) (March 8, 1912), p. 25.

49. *Kuznets*, nos. 5–6 (January 19, 1908), pp. 26, 27; *Edinstvo*, no. 15 (March 12, 1910).

50. *Edinstvo*, no. 5 (May 26, 1909), pp. 13–14; no. 11 (December 1, 1908), p. 11; no. 13 (January 25, 1910), pp. 5–6; and no. 15 (March 12, 1910), p. 3.

51. Kir'ianov, "Ob oblike rabochego klassa Rossii," in *Rossiiskii proletariat*, p. 121.

52. Batrak, "Uroki," *Metallist*, no. 19 (September 1, 1912), p. 5, emphasis in original.

53. *Edinstvo*, no. 1 (February 10, 1909), p. 14.

54. Bulkin, *Na zare*, p. 304.

55. *Nash put'*, no. 9 (November 7, 1910). Further confirmation of this problem can be found in *Metallist*, no. 2 (October 13, 1911), pp. 2–3.

56. See Bulkin, *Na zare*, pp. 314–15. For a more detailed discussion of figures on membership, dues payment, length of stay in the union, attendance at union meetings, and so on, see my dissertation, esp. pp. 305–17.

57. See, for example, *Rabochii po metallu*, no. 21 (September 24, 1907), pp. 2–3, 7.

58. *Nadezhda*, no. 3 (October 31, 1908), p. 11; *Rabochii po metallu*, no. 18 (July 26, 1907), p. 6.

59. For a general lament on the indifference of the rank and file and the isolation of the union from its mass base, see Chatskii, "Ocherednyia zadachi," *Nash put'*, no. 18 (June 17, 1911), esp. p. 4.

60. For a sampling of this debate, see Batrak, "Chto delat'?" *Metallist*, no. 3 (October 27, 1911), pp. 2–5; A. V., "Chto delat'?" *Metallist*, no. 4 (November 10, 1911), pp. 3–5, and no. 5 (November 26, 1911), pp. 3–5; S. P—skii, "K voprosy 'Chto delat'?" *Metallist*, no. 11 (February 23, 1912), pp. 4–5; V—', "Opiat' o tom zhe . . . ," *Metallist*, no. 13 (April 7, 1912), pp. 4–5; G. A., "Eshche o tom, chto delat'," *Metallist*, no. 6 (December 17, 1911), p. 10.

61. Chatskii, "Ocherednyia zadachi," *Nash put'*, no. 18 (June 17, 1911), pp. 6–7.

62. Ibid., p. 7.

63. Ibid.

64. "Soiuz i ditsiplina," *Nash put'*, no. 8 (October 14, 1910), p. 5.

65. *Metallist*, no. 8 (January 13, 1912), p. 3.

66. Ibid., p. 4.

67. So wrote one activist in regard to the "American System." See "'Amerikanskaia' sistema," *Rabochii po metallu*, no. 20 (September 5, 1907), p. 3.

68. Recall the September 1906 resolution of the union stating that it would only offer material aid to strikes when it was informed of the causes, judged the issues worthy of struggle, and itself took on strike leadership.

69. Chatskii, "Ocherednyia zadachi," *Nash put'*, no. 18 (June 17, 1911), p. 7.

70. A. V., "Chto delat'?" *Metallist*, no. 5 (November 26, 1911), p. 5. On the "principled" nature of the strike conflicts in 1906 see ch. 6, Strike Conflict in the Summer of 1906.

71. Ibid., p. 5.

72. Ibid.

73. In January 1912, one union activist wrote that "over the course of the past several years the capitalists have not slumbered—they intensively built their employer organizations so as to oppose their workers with a united force of all capitalists in the metalworking industry. And they were able to do a great deal during this time." *Metallist*, no. 8 (January 13, 1912), p. 3.

74. Velox argued that "the organization of modern processes of production left little place for a direct struggle against the increasing intensity [of labor] and workers more readily resorted to other means of reducing the norms of exploitation, like increasing wages or lessening the work day." "Nachalo kontsa," *Nasha zaria*, nos. 8–9 (1910), p. 19.

75. See, for example, V—', "Opiat' o tom zhe . . . " *Metallist*, no. 13 (April 7, 1912), p. 4.

76. For a sampling of this literature, see "Amerikanskaia sistema," *Rabochii po metallu*, no. 20 (September 5, 1907), pp. 3–4; "Chto daet rabochim 'Amerikanskaia sistema'?" *Vestnik rabochikh po obrabotke metalla*, no. 2 (June 5, 1908), pp. 9–10; Batrak, "K voprosu ob Amerikanskoi sisteme," *Metallist*, no. 8 (January 13, 1912), p. 7; Astrov, "Amerikanskaia plata," *Metallist*, no. 9 (January 26, 1912), pp. 7–9.

77. Said Chirkin, an active member of the board, the union was doing nothing but compiling reports on insurance, mutual aid, trusts, and so on. Now, he insisted, "when the capitalists are introducing more modern machines . . . we need studies of the changes in the intensity and productivity of labor." *Edinstvo*, no. 3 (March 19, 1909), p. 7. See also *Edinstvo*, no. 7 (July 10, 1909), p. 10, which reports on the formation of a commission to study these and other issues; apparently, however, the first meeting was poorly attended, although a plan of work was outlined. A report in *Edinstvo*, no. 13 (January 25, 1910), p. 9, notes that this commission never got off the ground and never accomplished anything. Chirkin, it may be added, had sounded the alarm earlier, calling attention to the shift from day to hourly based pay in 1908 as a first step to the introduction of the "American system." *Vestnik rabochikh po obrabotke metalla*, no. 1 (May 15, 1908), p. 18.

78. S. P—skii, "Amerikanskaia sistema rabot i usloviia truda," *Metallist*, no. 6 (December 17, 1911), p. 7.

79. This ambivalence will be discussed in greater detail below.

80. S. P—skii, "Amerikanskaia sistema rabot i usloviia truda," *Metallist*, no. 6 (December 17, 1911), p. 6. But other activists were clearly more hostile to the American system and argued against the position advanced by S. P—skii. See Astrov, "Amerikanskaia plata," *Metallist*, no. 9 (January 26, 1912), p. 9, and Batrak, "K voprosy ob Amerikanskoi sisteme," *Metallist*, no. 8 (January 13, 1912), pp. 6–7.

81. S. P—skii, "Amerikanskaia sistema rabot i usloviia truda," *Metallist*, no. 6 (December 17, 1911), p. 7.

82. S. P—skii, "K voprosy 'Chto delat'?" *Metallist*, no. 11 (February 23, 1912), p. 5.

83. A. V., "Chto delat'?" *Metallist*, no. 4 (November 10, 1911), p. 5.

84. "Iz zhizni i deiatel'nosti O-va," *Metallist*, no. 6 (December 17, 1911), p. 9.

85. On December 10, the board resolved to bring this question up for detailed discussion at the next regular meeting of the members of the Petersburg and Vyborg branches. "Iz zhizni i deiatel'nosti O-va," *Metallist*, no. 9 (January 26, 1912), p. 9. Whether such a discussion occurred is not known.

86. *Metallist*, no. 11 (February 23, 1912), pp. 8–9.

87. *Kuznets*, no. 7 (February 14, 1908), p. 3.

88. *Edinstvo*, no. 1 (February 10, 1909), p. 15.

89. Ibid., no. 17 (April 29, 1910), pp. 3–4; *Nash put'*, no. 3 (June 25, 1910), pp. 3–4.

90. Smolin, "Iz zhizni professional'nykh soiuzov," *Vozrozhdenie*, no. 6 (1910), p. 68.

91. Mitrevich, "Vospominaniia o rabochem revoliutsionnom dvizhenii," *Proletarskaia revoliutsiia*, no. 4, 1922, pp. 219–20.

92. A. V., "Chto delat'?" *Metallist*, no. 4 (November 10, 1911), p. 4. On the petition campaign see Swain, *Russian Social Democracy and the Legal Labour Movement*, pp. 119–23.

10. Labor and Management in Conflict, 1912–1914

1. Although a modest increase in strike activism could be noted since 1910, and although a bitterly contested strike over fine whistles and bells had occurred during February 1912 at Putilov, nonetheless it is fair to say the strike movement only "took off" after the Lena protests.

2. *Rabochee dvizhenie v Petrograde*, p. 31.

3. McKean provides estimates on the number of strikers in St. Petersburg for the Lena protests: his own estimate of 72,395; a police estimate of 140,000; and the socialist press estimate at 200,000. For May Day, the figures are, respectively, 63,436; 150,000; and 200,000. *St. Petersburg Between the Revolutions*, p. 495.

4. According to an agreement reached in January 1908, member firms pledged to impose fines on workers who were absent due to political holidays or demonstrations. Bulkin, *Na zare*, p. 171.

5. This account is drawn from Dmitriev, "Pervoe maia i Petersburgskoe obshchestvo zavodchikov i fabrikantov," pp. 64–78; Balabanov, *Ot 1905 k 1917*, pp. 198–203; and Kruze, *Peterburgskie rabochie*, pp. 248–58, passim.

6. Quoted in Balabanov, *Ot 1905 k 1917*, p. 198.

7. Kruze, *Peterburgskie rabochie*, pp. 257–58.

8. For the 1905 agreement see Balabanov, *Ob"edinennyi kapital*, p. 18, and discussion in ch. 4, The Shidlovskii Commission, Labor Mobilization, and Employer Politics; for the 1912 Convention see *Rabochee dvizhenie v Petrograde*, pp. 58–60.

9. In the context of reviving labor activism in the 1910–1912 period, many metalworkers sought to utilize the 1903 law on elders for the purpose of forming factory-level organizations. In late March or early April 1912, the PSMFO specifically directed its members to oppose this initiative and hence to refuse workers the right to elect factory elders. *Metallist*, no. 13 (April 7, 1913), pp. 6–7.

10. TsGIA, f. 150, op. 1, d. 58, l. 68.

11. Voting in the PSMFO was determined by the number of workers employed at a given firm. By March 1, 1913, 151 firms employing 98,264 workers belonged to the Society. Of these, 65 factories or 56.3% of the workers employed by members had accepted the Convention in full, 6 factories or 7.4% of the workers had accepted with certain conditions, and 5 factories or 5.1% of the workers had accepted the Convention

without agreeing to the financial guarantees. Therefore, 76 factories employing 68.8% of the work force of member firms had accepted some form of the Convention. The other 75 firms employing 31.1% of the workers of member firms had either not responded, responded indefinitely, or refused. These data suggest that the larger factories had been primarily responsible for ratification. TsGIA, f. 150, op. 1, d. 58, l. 68; see also Kruze, *Peterburgskie rabochie*, p. 258.

12. TsGIA, f. 150, op. 1, d. 58, l. 36.

13. Kruze, *Peterburgskie rabochie*, p. 258. I have been unable to determine whether the election of Nobel to replace Glezmer was in any substantial way related to the conflicts within the PSMFO in the spring of 1912.

14. For a partial listing of these strikes see *Rabochee dvizhenie v Petrograde*, pp. 554–56.

15. On May 10, a strike broke out at Siemens-Halske which lasted until early August; on May 3, a strike began at Erikson which lasted until the end of June.

16. *Nevskii golos*, no. 6 (July 5, 1912), p. 4; Bulkin, *Na zare*, p. 14; *Pravda*, no. 71 (July 21, 1912), pp. 2–3. See also *Rabochii po metallu*, no. 15 (June 13, 1907), p. 14; *Nadezhda*, no. 2 (September 28, 1908), p. 19; *Vestnik rabochikh po obrabotke metalla*, no. 2 (June 5, 1908), pp. 11–12; and *Edinstvo*, no. 16 (April 1, 1910), p. 17, for a steady stream of worker commentary on the various ways in which wage policy and wage rates had been altered at Siemens-Halske.

17. *Pravda*, no. 18 (May 20, 1912), p. 11.

18. Metalworkers at other factories organized collections to support the striking Siemenstsy; it may well be that workers were expressing their support not only over the issue of May Day, but also with efforts to block recent managerial initiatives.

19. Balabanov, *Ot 1905 k 1917*, p. 179.

20. TsGIA, f. 150, op. 1, d. 58, l. 36; Balabanov, *Ot 1905 k 1917*, pp. 179, 217–18.

21. The following analysis of strike demands is taken from *Pravda*, no. 16 (April 11, 1912), p. 11; no. 20 (May 23, 1912), pp. 10–11; no. 21 (May 24, 1912), p. 10; no. 22 (May 25, 1912), p. 10; no. 28 (June 1, 1912), p. 10; *Rabochee dvizhenie v Petrograde*, pp. 50–51, 55; *Nevskii golos*, no. 2 (May 23, 1912), p. 4; *Metallist*, no. 15 (June 1, 1912), pp. 13–14; no. 17 (July 6, 1912), p. 13; no. 22 (October 26, 1912), pp. 11–12; Okun', *Putilovets*, pp. 174–75.

22. On the March 1908 circular, see ch. 8, Reforms on the Shop Floor.

23. *Metallist*, no. 13 (April 7, 1912), p. 16.

24. Ibid.

25. Ibid., no. 19 (September 1, 1912), p. 13.

26. Closed on February 29 but again functioning by mid-March, the union counted 2,100 members by July. *Zvezda*, no. 13 (49) (March 1, 1912), p. 18; Bulkin, *Na zare*, pp. 244–46; and *Metallist*, no. 17 (July 6, 1912), p. 16.

27. Bulkin reported that the union was involved in a mere 4 of 70 metalworker strikes in 1912. *Na zare*, pp. 402–3.

28. Swain has argued that the fortunes of the Metalworkers' Union were largely reversed over the course of 1909 by hard-working, mostly Menshevik *praktiki*, and that they were able to stabilize and then expand membership. See his *Russian Social Democracy and the Legal Labour Movement*, especially ch. 2. As the debate over "What is to be done?" evidences, however, all was not well in the union in the years immediately preceding the Lena demonstrations. Activists had failed to secure solid ties to individual factories and to the rank and file; moreover, membership was exceedingly "soft," averaging around 3,500 or less nominal membership from 1910 to mid-1912. See above, Table 9.1, for membership figures. As was common across industrialized Europe in the 1910s, labor insurgency was very often factory based, and very often developed in specific reaction to reformist or bureaucratic trade unionism. For one example among many, see Comfort, *Revolutionary Hamburg*.

29. The union was again closed in August.

30. *Metallist*, no. 15 (June 1, 1912), p. 2. See also Ezhov, "Ot stikhiinosti k organizatsii," *Nevskii golos*, no. 1 (May 20, 1912), p. 2.

31. *Metallist*, no. 13 (April 7, 1912), pp. 6–7, and no. 16 (June 15, 1912), p. 1–2.

32. Bulkin, *Na zare*, pp. 249–50; see also *Metallist*, no. 4 (28) (August 3, 1913), p. 5, for an assessment of developments within the union since 1912. Reported the *Biulleten'* of the Moscow Society of Mill and Factory Owners in reference to strikes in the first half of 1912: "Almost all of the Petersburg strikes proceeded under the leadership of a strike committee; local strike committees were also elected at several individual factories." *Obshchestvo zavodchikov i fabrikantov Moskovskogo promyshlennogo raiona. Biulleten' rabochego dvizheniia*, no. 16 (January–May 1912), p. 13.

33. *Metallist*, no. 19 (September 1, 1912), pp. 11–12, and no. 23 (November 10, 1912), p. 14. It is worth noting as well that in the hands of primarily Menshevik journalists, *Metallist* chronicled the drift and uncertain leadership characteristic of union activists over the course of 1912. Until April 1912, *Metallist* carried a debate about union reform; with the increase in strike activism in the spring, the paper shifted to a more aggressive assertion of the need of metalworkers for a union, and most especially the need to give the spontaneous strike wave organization and direction. By early fall, neither reform nor an aggressive assertion of the need for trade unionism played such a prominent role; instead, the paper carried a variety of articles on the economic conjuncture, the Duma elections, Western trade unionism, statistics on strikes, and so on. The direction of the journal remained sophisticated, aimed at "conscious" workers; it was considerably less preoccupied with developing the organ as an agitational weapon and remained at a distance from day-to-day life. From the autumn, correspondence from the factories fell off, reflecting declining worker interest in union affairs. The October 26 issue featured a request on page one from the editor asking workers to send reports from the factories about conditions. At the same time, the editor sought guidance from readers as to how the journal might be improved. These observations are based on *Metallist*, nos. 8–24, 1912.

34. For one example of this position see Ezhov, "Ot stikhiinosti k organizatsii," *Nevskii golos*, no. 1 (May 20, 1912), p. 2.

35. *Luch'*, no. 53 (November 17, 1912), p. 1.

36. See especially "Economic and Political Strikes" and "The Revolutionary Upswing" in Lenin, *Collected Works*, vol. 18, pp. 83–90, 102–109.

37. Ibid., p. 106, emphasis in original.

38. Ibid., emphasis in original.

39. Ibid., p. 104, emphasis in original.

40. Ibid., p. 106. For a discussion of the petition campaign see Swain, *Russian Social Democracy and the Legal Labour Movement*, pp. 119–23.

41. Lenin, *Collected Works*, vol. 18, p. 89; see also N. Skopin [Zinov'ev], "'Ekonomika' i 'politika,'" *Nevskaia zvezda*, no. 11 (June 3, 1912), pp. 1–3, and Iu. G. [Kamenev], "Politicheskaia stachka v Rossii," in *Nevskaia zvezda*, no. 14, (June 24, 1912), 1912, pp. 5–8, for a sampling of other Bolshevik writing on this theme.

42. Lenin, *Collected Works*, vol. 18, pp. 116–17.

43. On the cultural-educational tasks to be performed by a trade union, see *Metallist*, no. 16 (June 15, 1912), pp. 1–2.

44. See pp. 159–67 on the August Conference in Elwood, *Resolutions and Decisions*.

45. Lenin, *Collected Works*, vol. 18, pp. 17–21; see the resolutions of the Prague Conference in January 1912, in Elwood, *Resolutions and Decisions*, pp. 146–57.

46. Lenin, *Collected Works*, vol. 18, p. 85 and p. 474.

47. For another discussion of these issues, see Haimson and Tilly, eds., *Strikes, Wars, and Revolutions*, pp. 26–28. It also seems important to note that however much Lenin was bent on formalizing the break within Russian Social Democracy, splitting

the SD Duma delegation, and fanning the flames of factionalism with his often indiscriminate labeling of SD opponents as "liquidators," and however much these internecine battles alienated workers, nonetheless real differences in the analysis of major issues separated Lenin from his Menshevik counterparts. Said differently, Lenin was not simply pursuing a particular polemical course in order to secure his dictatorial hold over the party, but rather was engaged in a substantive debate over the nature of the contemporary political situation and the role of labor in it. Both Swain, *Russian Social Democracy and the Legal Labour Movement*, and McKean emphasize the often distasteful manner in which Lenin conducted the fractional fight in the inter-revolutionary period, sometimes underestimating in my judgment the substantive issues at stake. McKean writes: "There did exist genuine differences of approach to the election campaign between Bolsheviks and Mensheviks. These, however, were deliberately exacerbated by the Bolsheviks' leader for his own sectarian purposes." *St. Petersburg Between the Revolutions*, p. 131.

48. According to McKean, contemporaries estimated that only about one-fifth to one-third of qualified electors voted. He goes on to present detailed findings on a number of particular metalworking plants which confirm worker indifference to the process. *St. Petersburg Between the Revolutions*, pp. 134–35.

49. *Rabochee dvizhenie v Petrograde*, pp. 64–71.

50. *Pravda*, no. 20 (May 23, 1912), pp. 1–2; L. M., "Bor'ba obshchestvennykh sil v 1913 godu," *Nasha zaria*, no. 1 (1913), pp. 95–100. For the classic discussion of these issues see Haimson, "The Problem of Social Stability in Urban Russia," pt. 1, esp. pp. 630–31.

51. For statistical confirmation of this pattern see Haimson and Tilly, eds., *Strikes, Wars, and Revolutions*, p. 396.

52. TsGIA, f. 150, op. 1, d. 667, ll. 170–73; Badayev, *Bolsheviks in the Tsarist Duma*, pp. 82–84. For a detailed if tendentious discussion of the strike see Lur'e, *Sto dva dnia geroicheskoi zabastovki*.

53. Fixed capital grew from 1.65 to 4.0 million rubles between 1911 and 1914. See Table 8.5 above. See also *Edinstvo*, no. 9 (September 18, 1909), pp. 7–8, and Haimson and Tilly, eds., *Strikes, Wars, and Revolutions*, pp. 391–92.

54. Suggestive of the larger patterns structuring the development of the industry, as well as the forward perspectives of the Lessner management, was the launching of a new venture in September 1912 which brought together the principles of the Nobel and Lessner factories under the auspices of one of the St. Petersburg banking consortiums. Bachmanov and Plotnikov, both from Lessner and both key figures in the Uchetno-ssudnyi Bank, joined with E. L. Nobel to form Noblessner, an undertaking destined to build a major ship-construction facility in Revel and win significant contracts from the Naval Ministry for work on submarines in the immediate prewar period. Like Bachmanov and Plotnikov, Nobel played a critical leadership role in the PSMFO. And like the Lessner factories, Nobel's operations had grown considerably over the past several years, while a variety of organizational changes at shop level had taken place. On the agreements between Lessner and Nobel see Bovykin, "Banki i voennaia promyshlennost'," especially pp. 124–26.

55. *Rabochaia pravda*, no. 1 (July 13, 1913), p. 3.

56. Arutiunov, *Rabochee dvizhenie v Rossii*, p. 279; TsGIA, f. 150, op. 1, d. 667, ll. 170–72.

57. Sovet s"ezdov, *Fabrichno-zavodskiia predpriiatiia Rossiiskoi imperii*, no. 1592 (b); Kruze, *Peterburgskie rabochie*, pp. 156–57, 280; *Novaia rabochaia gazeta*, no. 39 (September 22, 1913), p. 3; *Pravda*, no. 116 (320) (May 22, 1913), p. 5. The figure on union membership comes from Balabanov, *Ot 1905 k 1917*, p. 255. I have been unable to find a second source to confirm this number.

58. Zorin was one of the pseudonyms for Alexei Gastev, in 1913 a metalworker at

Aivaz, later the head of the Central Labor Institute and a popularizer of scientific management in the early Soviet period. On Gastev's early life and views see Beisinger, *Scientific Management*, pp. 25–27. I wish to thank Professor Beisinger for sharing with me an earlier draft of his chapter on pre-revolutionary scientific management in Russia.

59. *Metallist*, no. 13 (37) (December 14, 1913), pp. 2–3.

60. TsGAOR, f. 111, op. 5, d. 454, 1913, l. 5; *Severnaia pravda*, no. 13 (August 17, 1913), p. 1; *Novaia rabochaia gazeta*, no. 37 (September 20, 1913), p. 3; *Pravda truda*, no. 5 (September 15, 1913), p. 3.

61. *Rabochaia pravda*, no. 6 (July 19, 1913), p. 3.

62. *Severnaia pravda*, no. 26 (September 1, 1913), p. 3.

63. The adjusters [*ustanovshchiki*] were described as half-administrators and half-workers by the fitters. Most probably, these were a new breed of troubleshooter, required by management to install, maintain, and adjust the more complex machinery that semiskilled laborers operated.

64. See especially *Pravda truda*, no. 5 (September 15, 1913), p. 3.

65. Despite this, the August 24 issue of *Metallist* carried an article entitled "On Wheelbarrows" which could hardly help the situation. While written by the new Bolshevik chairman of the union, A. S. Kiselev, the article did stress that thanks to the fact that there were "a large number of leading comrades" at Aivaz, the strike was given a more organized character. *Metallist*, no. 7 (31) (August 24, 1913), p. 4.

66. *Pravda truda*, no. 5 (September 15, 1913), p. 3; *Metallist*, no. 6 (30) (August 10, 1913), p. 16, and no. 7 (31) (August 24, 1913), pp. 11, 12; and *Severnaia pravda*, no. 26 (September 1, 1913), p. 3.

67. By early August, a set of demands had been worked out, soon to be supplemented with several additional points. See *Severnaia pravda*, no. 8 (August 10, 1913), p. 3. The demands that were actually negotiated with management in September may be found in *Pravda truda*, no. 2 (September 12, 1913), p. 3.

68. *Pravda truda*, no. 2 (September 12, 1913), p. 3, and no. 5 (September 15, 1913), p. 3.

69. At the April 21, 1913, meeting, a temporary governing board was elected with Bolsheviks winning a majority with 13 out of 26 places. A coalition presidium of three Bolsheviks and two Mensheviks was formed. A permanent board was not elected until the August 25 meeting and was entirely Bolshevik in composition. In the intervening months, the Mensheviks retained control over *Metallist*.

70. Here one can see certain crucial linkages to 1917. As Hasegawa and others have noted, a Bolshevik subelite was extremely important in propelling events forward during the February Revolution; this core of activists was very largely based in the Vyborg metalworking factories. Moreover, the strength Bolsheviks enjoyed in the factory committees in 1917 was foreshadowed in the prewar years by their ability to work effectively at the grass-roots level. See Hasegawa, "The Problem of Power in the February Revolution."

71. For the ways in which conditions continued to change at Aivaz see *Metallist*, no. 12 (36) (December 5, 1913), p. 9, and no. 13 (37) (December 14, 1913), p. 3; *Za pravdu*, no. 46 (November 28, 1913), p. 4; *Put' pravdy*, no. 92 (May 21, 1914), p. 2. One measure of the depth of distress experienced by Aivaz workers by the spring of 1914 is captured in a poem entitled "The Plague." "How is it that at New Aivaz/ without smoke and without gas/ the people are collapsing?/ From "plague" with a scholarly guise/ You become an invalid here working just a year. This scholarly "plague"/ Came to us from afar/ From across the seas./ From America it appeared/ It found a place for itself at Aivaz/ To our grief./ We've been sick for more than a year/ But we haven't dared to cure ourselves/ We're all mute./ And the contagion reigns/ Like a Siberian leprosy/ The 'Taylor' system." *Put' pravdy*, no. 41 (March 20, 1914), p. 3.

72. The course of the strike, as well as the nature of union involvement in it, is treated in greater detail in my dissertation, pp. 484–509.

73. Following a conflict over the rate-setting process at Erikson, for example, management substantially increased supervision, according to workers, placing one foreman over every 20 workers instead of the old ratio of one for every 60–100. *Proletarskaia pravda*, no. 15 (December 24, 1913), p. 4. At Obukhov, workers protested the new punch-in procedures that attended the installation of automatic control clocks. Rozanov, *Obukhovtsy*, pp. 297–99.

74. The *Biulleten'* of the Moscow Society of Mill and Factory Owners, reporting all-Russian data for 1913, found that 34.5% of striking metalworkers demanded polite forms of address and 32.5% sought the removal of managerial personnel. Figures for textile workers were considerably lower, 23.6% and 28.6% respectively. Cited in Balabanov, *Ot 1905 k 1917*, p. 237. See Tables 10.2–10.4 for a further comparison of metalworker and textile worker strikes.

75. *Metallist'*, no. 5 (29) (July 19, 1913), p. 6.

76. Statistics compiled by Balabanov on the outcome of economic strikes for metalworkers in all Russia indicate that metalworkers won just 7.8% of their strikes in 1913, while 29.1% ended in compromise settlements. Employers won fully 63.1% of these conflicts. As we shall see, these outcomes became even less favorable in 1914. Balabanov, *Ot 1905 k 1917*, p. 235. Data are given as the percentage of strike participants.

77. As Haimson's statistical studies reveal, the epicenter of conflict was in the electrical engineering firms of the Vyborg district. Haimson and Tilly, eds., *Strikes, Wars, and Revolutions*, pp. 393–94.

78. For a representative sample of metalworker demands in 1913 see *Pravda*, no. 82 (286) (April 9, 1913), p. 3; no. 107 (311) (May 11, 1913), p. 3; no. 136 (340) (June 15, 1913), p. 3; *Rabochee dvizhenie v Petrograde*, pp. 108–13, 144–45, 166, 117, 199–20. See the discussion in Haimson and Tilly, eds., *Strikes, Wars, and Revolutions*, pp. 396–97.

79. Writing of his impressions of May Day, 1913, the Bolshevik Duma deputy Petrovskii noted that virtually all proletarian Petersburg observed the day; Nevskii Prospekt was filled with workers and students, but almost wholly devoid of "Nevskii ladies and strollers." *Rabochee dvizhenie v Petrograde*, pp. 107–8. See also Appendix I in McKean, *St. Petersburg Between the Revolutions*, which summarizes the political mass strikes of Petersburg workers in the prewar period.

80. See McKean, *St. Petersburg Between the Revolutions*, pp. 260–61. Writes David Montgomery of comparable phenomena in the United States: "[W]orkers soon came to realize that scientific management would not take the form of a visit to the factory by some disciple of Taylor's, after which the firm would be fundamentally reorganized for once and for all. On the contrary, the new managerial techniques meant that work relations were subject to incessant reexamination and reorganization. . . . Dynamism, instability, new orders from on high, and angry disputes over those orders, which usually involved only small isolated groups of workers, were endemic to the new regime." *The Fall of the House of Labor*, p. 249.

81. A. S. Kiselev was born in 1879 and worked as a fitter at the Siemens-Halske plant.

82. *Metallist*, no. 7 (31) (August 24, 1913), p. 4.

83. For the classic discussion of the distance between workers and "society" on the eve of World War I see Haimson, "The Problem of Social Stability in Urban Russia."

84. *Metallist*, no. 13 (37) (December 14, 1913), p. 3.

85. TsGIA, f. 150, op. 1, d. 58, ll. 7–8.

86. Ibid., l. 8.

87. Ibid., l. 106.

88. Ibid., op. 1, d. 660, ll. 145–48, 159–60.

89. Ibid., op. 2, d. 72, ll. 56–57.

90. Ibid., l. 55; op. 1, d. 660, l. 174.

91. Ibid., op. 1, d. 660, l. 172; op. 2, d. 72, ll. 55–56.

92. Ibid., op. 2, d. 75, ll. 1, 4–6; op. 2, d. 72, l. 56.

93. Ibid., op. 1, d. 660, l. 172; op. 2, d. 72, ll. 55–58.

94. Ibid., op. 2, d. 72, ll. 55–58.

95. Ibid., op. 1, d. 660, l. 173.

96. Ibid., op. 1, d. 58, ll. 2–4.

97. Ibid., op. 1, d. 667, ll. 531–33.

98. Ibid., op. 2, d. 72. l. 56; op. 2, d. 75, l. 5.

99. Here I refer to the provisions of the 1912 Convention, which growing numbers of employers had ratified by 1913.

100. So forceful was this rebuff, the PSMFO believed that any future effort by the union in this regard must be seen as an action undertaken for "purely demonstrative effect." Ibid., op. 2, d. 72, l. 55.

101. Bulkin, "Raskol fraktsii i zadachi rabochikh," *Nasha zaria*, no. 6 (1914), p. 45.

102. Quote from Rikitin, "Rabochaia massa i rabochaia intelligentsiia," *Nasha zaria*, no. 9 (1913), p. 57. For other examples of this line of argumentation see V. Sh—r', "Nashe professional'noe dvizhenie za dva poslednikh goda," *Bor'ba*, nos. 1, 2, 3, 4 (1914); Bulkin, "Raskol fraktsii i zadachi rabochikh," and "Rabochaia samodeitel'nost' i rabochaia demagogiia," *Nasha zaria*, no. 3 (1914).

103. For a discussion of population growth and demographic change in St. Petersburg by the prewar period see Bater, *St. Petersburg, Industrialization and Change*, pp. 308–21.

104. See ch. 9, Problems and Patterns of Union Development.

105. That those with a significant *stazh* in industry played an important role in the strikes was reflected in the many demands which sought the return of conditions that had pertained earlier.

106. Sh—r', "Nashe professional'noe dvizhenie za dva poslednikh goda," no. 4, p. 23. See also ibid., no. 2, p. 13.

107. *Nasha zaria*, no. 6 (1914).

108. Commenting specifically on the importance of factory strike committees to St. Petersburg metalworkers, Sh—r' remarked that their direct solicitation of funds through the labor press had generated some 12,000 rubles in support of four strikes, a sum almost as large as the yearly income of the union. Sh—r', "Nashe professional'noe dvizhenie za dva poslednikh goda," no. 3, p. 16.

109. For Martov's views see "Bor'ba obshchestvennykh sil v 1913 gody," *Nasha zaria*, no. 1 (1914), pp. 95–100.

110. Lenin, *Collected Works*, vol. 20, pp. 209–12. See G. Z. [G. Zinov'ev], "Poslednyi lokaut' i teoriia 'stachechnago azart,'" *Prosveshchenie*, no. 4 (April 1914), pp. 94–96. See also Ol'minskii, "Ia vas arestuiu," *Prosveshchenie*, no. 2 (February 1913), pp. 40–49, for an interesting argument concerning yet another way in which "economics" and "politics" were intertwined.

111. TsGIA, f. 150, op. 1, d. 60, l. 179.

112. *Rabochee dvizhenie v Petrograde*, pp. 162–73.

113. I base this statement on a reading of the labor and socialist press for the first six months of 1914, as well as on the documents for 1914 in *Rabochee dvizhenie v Petrograde*.

114. Haimson, "The Problem of Social Stability in Urban Russia."

115. *Rabochee dvizhenie v Petrograde*, pp. 566–68, carries the basic chronology of the strikes and demonstrations; for the *gradonachal'nik*'s order see pp. 161–62.

116. Meeting on March 26, members of the Engineering Section reviewed with considerable satisfaction the results of their united effort. One noted that the closure had made a "strong impression" on workers; and a resolution passed by this meeting

stressed the "harmonious" way in which the lockout had been conducted and the "excellent results" that had been achieved. The resolution, adopted unanimously, also stated that those present had agreed to employ lockouts in response to all strikes which might arise prior to May 1. TsGIA, f. 150, op. 1, d. 668, l. 179.

117. Ibid., op. 2, d. 72, l. 35. For just one of the many debates during the spring of 1914 on collective lockouts see ibid., ll. 78–80.

118. The eight factories were Nobel, St. Petersburg Metals, Baranovskii, b. Parviainen, Struck, Lessner, Erikson, and Phoenix.

119. According to records of the Engineering Section of the PSMFO concerning the 42,686 metalworkers employed by their member firms, between October 1913 and March 1914 these workers conducted 234 economic and political strikes, involving 194,681 strikers, and causing 220,688 lost man/days. Ibid., op. 1, d. 665, ll. 159–61, 163, 165, 167.

Epilogue

1. McKean, *St. Petersburg Between the Revolutions*, makes this argument; see p. 189.

2. See, for example, V. V., "Novyi moment' evoliutsii kapitalisticheskoi organizatsii proizvodstva," *Vestnik Evpopy*, no. 3 (1913), pp. 288–310; Belorussov, "Sistema Teilora vo Frantsii," *Russkiia Vedomosti*, no. 40 (February 17, 1913), pp. 5–6; Severianin, "Po povodu sistemy Teilora," ibid., no. 57 (March 9, 1913), p. 6; "Intensifikatsiia proizvodstva i sistema Teilora," ibid., no. 63 (March 16, 1913), p. 6; "Chelovek ili mashina?" *Pravda*, no. 64 (268) (March 17, 1913), pp. 2–3; A. Glotov, "Amerikanskaia vydumka," ibid., no. 65 (269) (March 19, 1913), p. 1; "O sisteme Teilora," ibid., no. 87 (291) (April 14, 1913), p. 5; A. Shliapnikov, "Amerikanskaia potogonnyia sistemy," *Metallist*, no. 10 (34) (October 25, 1913), pp. 3–5, and no. 11 (35) (November 16, 1913), pp. 6–8. *Fabrichno-zavodskoe delo*, a journal launched in 1913 to popularize scientific management, often reprinted articles on Taylorism from other periodicals; as such it reflects well the diversity of opinion on this subject. A useful if incomplete bibliography of works on scientific management in the late Imperial and early Soviet period is Ermanskii, comp., *Ukazatel' knig i statei po voprosam nauchnoi organizatsii truda.*

3. Nik. Gimmer' (Sukhanov), "O 'sisteme Teilora,'" *Russkoe bogatstvo*, no. 11 (1913), pp. 132–54; Lenin, "The Taylor System—Man's Enslavement by the Machine," *Collected Works*, vol. 20, pp. 152–54; see also his "Immediate Tasks of the Soviet Government," *Collected Works*, vol. 27, esp. pp. 257–59. For a similar assessment of this aspect of Leninism, see Smith, "Taylorism Rules OK?"

4. Just these trends were influencing metalworkers from Glasgow to Turin and would contribute substantially to the reconstitution of bourgeois power in Europe after the war. While the literature on these issues is vast, see especially Landes, *The Unbound Prometheus*, for the manifold changes brought about by the second industrial revolution, and Maier, *Recasting Bourgeois Europe*. On the particularities of metalworkers and their industry, see Haimson and Tilly, eds., *Strikes, Wars, and Revolutions*, esp. Part III.

SELECTED BIBLIOGRAPHY

Archival Materials

Tsentral'nyi Gosudarstvennyi Istoricheskii Arkhiv (TsGIA).

  fond 150, Peterburgskoe obshchestvo zavodchikov i fabrikantov.

    op. 1, d. 3. Materials concerning the reorganization of the St. Petersburg Industrial Society (April 1905 to July 1907).

    op. 1, d. 51. Journal of the sessions of the PSMFO (1906–1908).

    op. 1, d. 58. Journal of the sessions of the council of the PSMFO and general meetings (1913–1914).

    op. 1, d. 60. Journal of the sessions of the council of the PSMFO and general meetings (March 1914 to December 1915).

    op. 1, d. 61. Various materials concerning working conditions (March 1914 to November 1916).

    op. 1, d. 654. Materials regarding the registration of strikes (1905–1907).

    op. 1, d. 655. Materials concerning strikes (1906–1908).

    op. 1, d. 658. Information regarding the number of workers employed in St. Petersburg, and materials regarding strikes (1904–1906).

    op. 1, d. 660. Materials concerning measures against the strike movement (March 1907 to May 1909).

    op. 1, d. 661. Information regarding trade unions and the strike movement (June 1907 to November 1914).

    op. 1, d. 663. Correspondence with individual factory owners in regard to strikes, with worker demands appended (July 1907 to September 1911).

    op. 1, d. 667. Materials concerning the strike movement in St. Petersburg (January 1913 to April 1914).

    op. 1, d. 668. Journal of the sessions of the council of the Engineering Section, with correspondence from individual factory owners in regard to strikes (September 1913 to August 1914).

    op. 1, d. 671. Journal of the sessions of the Special Conference on the prevention of strikes, with appended materials (April 1914 to December 1915).

    op. 2, d. 67. Various circulars to members.

    op. 2, d. 70. Materials gathered by the Engineering Section in regard to hiring, rates books, rules of internal order (1908–1914).

    op. 2, d. 71. Materials from the Plotnikov Commission regarding skilled labor shortages (December 1911 to November 1913).

    op. 2, d. 72. Journal of the sessions of the Engineering Section (1914).

    op. 2, d. 74. Materials from the Commission on the development of uniform rules for internal order and the regulation of wages (1913–1915).

    op. 2, d. 75. Materials from the Special Commission on measures to prevent strikes (1913–1916).

    op. 2, d. 76. Materials gathered by the Engineering Section in regard to the length of the workday (1914).

    op. 2, d. 77. Various materials from the Engineering Section (1914–1915).

    op. 2, d. 78. Rules of internal order from the Obukhov Factory (1914).

Leningradskii Gosudarstvennyi Istoricheskii Arkhiv (LGIA).

  fond 1206, Tovarishchestvo Petrogradskogo vagonostroitel'nogo zavoda.

    op. 1, d. 277. Protocols of the meetings of the Board of Directors (1907).

  fond 1258, Akts. Obshchestvo mashinostroitel'nogo zavoda "Liudvig Nobel."

op. 2, d. 245. Various correspondence (1908–1910).

fond 1264, Akts. Obshchestvo mekhanicheskogo i liteinogo zavoda (b. "Vulkan").

op. 1, d. 74. Conciliation board documents (1917).

fond 1267, Obukhovskii staleliteinyi zavod.

op. 1, d. 1701. Materials regarding the managerial structure of the factory (1909).

op. 1, d. 2348. Materials regarding automatic time-clock systems.

op. 15, d. 78. Reports on strikes and worker demands.

fond 1304, Baltiiskii sudostroitel'nyi i mekhanicheskii zavod.

op. 1, d. 57. Various materials regarding working conditions (1901–1911).

op. 1, d. 2691. Various materials in regard to the reorganization of wage systems, personnel changes, accounting procedures (October 1905 to April 1906).

op. 1, d. 3667. Conciliation board documents (May to August 1917).

op. 1, d. 3668. Conciliation board documents (May to June 1917).

fond 1357, Akts. Obshchestvo "Kompaniia Petrogradskogo metallicheskogo zavoda."

op. 3, d. 66. Various circulars from the PSMFO.

fond 1440, Obshchestvo Franko-Russkikh zavodov.

op. 8, d. 7. Petitions from employees and workers (1896- 1917).

op. 8, d. 128. Political arrest of workers; worker demands (1905–1909).

op. 8, d. 137. Various circulars from the PSMFO.

op. 8, d. 182. Various circulars from the PSMFO (1907).

op. 8, d. 183. Various circulars from the PSMFO (1907- 1908).

op. 8, d. 341. Strike movement at the factory (1912–1913).

Tsentral'nyi Gosudarstvennyi Voenno-istoricheskii Arkhiv (TsGVIA).

fond 13251, Tsentral'nyi voenno-promyshlennyi komitet.

op. 11, d. 2. Report on the Petrograd Metalworkers' Union (1916).

Tsentral'nyi Gosudarstvennyi Arkhiv Oktiabr'skoi Revoliutsii (TsGAOR).

fond DP, Departament politsii.

IV d-vo, d. 347/1911. Report concerning the St. Petersburg labor movement written by agent V. A. D'iachenko.

IV d-vo, d. 119, ch. 43/1908. Reports concerning the St. Petersburg labor movement (1908).

fond 111, Peterburgskoe okhrannoe otdelenie.

op. 5, d. 454, 1913. Agent reports concerning the St. Petersburg labor movement.

Contemporary Newspapers and Journals

Biulleten' rabochego dvizheniia.

Biulleteni kruzhka tekhnologov Moskovskogo raiona.

Biulleteni politekhnicheskogo obshchestva.

Bor'ba.

Dvigatel'.

Edinstvo.

Elektrichestvo.

Fabrichno-zavodskoe delo.

Golos truda.

Gornyi zhurnal.

Inzhener.

Iskra.

Izvestiia obshchego biuro soveshchatel'nykh s"ezdov.

Izvestiia obshchestva dlia sodeistviia uluchsheniiu i razvitiiu manufakturnoi promyshlennosti.

Izvestiia obshchestva gornykh inzhenerov.

Kommercheskii deiatel'.

Kuznets.

Luch.

Metallist.
Nadezhda.
Nash put'.
Nasha zaria.
Nevskaia zvezda.
Nevskii golos.
Novaia gazeta.
Novaia rabochaia gazeta.
Obrazovanie.
Obshchestvo zavodchikov i fabrikantov Moskovskogo promyshlennogo raiona.
Otkliki.
Pravda. Title varies: *Rabochaia pravda, Severnaia pravda, Pravda truda, Za pravdu, Pro-*
    letarskaia pravda, Put' pravdy, Rabochii, Trudovaia pravda.
Pravo.
Prizyv.
Professional'nyi soiuz.
Promyshlennost' i torgovlia.
Prosveshchenie.
Rabochaia mysl'.
Rabochee delo.
Rabochee slovo.
Rabochii po metallu. Rech'.
Rus'.
Russkiia vedomosti.
Sovremennik.
Sovremennyi mir.
Tekhnicheskii vestnik.
Tekhnicheskoe i kommercheskoe obrazovanie.
Tekhniko-promyshlennyi vestnik.
Torgovo-promyshlennaia gazeta.
Trud.
Trud tekhnika.
Trud inzhenera i tekhnika.
Vestnik Evropy.
Vestnik finansov, promyshlennosti i torgovli.
Vestnik inzhenerov.
Vestnik obshchestva tekhnologov.
Vestnik politekhnicheskogo obshchestva.
Vestnik rabochikh po obrabotke metalla.
Vestnik zhizni.
Volna.
Vozrozhdenie.
Vpered.
Vsemirnoe tekhnicheskoe obozrenie.
Zapiski imperatorskogo Russkogo tekhnicheskogo obshchestva.
Zaria.
Zhivaia zhizn'.
Zhurnal obshchestva Sibirskikh inzhenerov.
Zvezda.

Contemporary Works, Documents, Memoirs, and Statistical Materials

A. "Raspredelitel'nyi biuro, ego organizatsiia i funktsii." *Zapiski imperatorskogo
    russkogo tekhnicheskogo obshchestva*, 1913, no. 4, pp. 95–99.

A. B. "Chto delat'?" *Metallist*, no. 4 (November 10, 1911), pp. 3- 5; no. 5 (November 26, 1911), pp. 3–5.

A. B. "Noveishie metody organizatsii proizvodstva v krupnoi promyshlennosti." *Kommercheskii deiatel'*, 1910, nos. 2–3, pp. 13–16.

A. G. "Prostaia sistema ucheta stoimosti zavodskikh rabot." *Biulleteni politekhnicheskogo obshchestva*, 1908, no. 2, pp. 89–93.

Abrosimov, V. "K itogam rabochego dvizheniia 1912 goda." *Nasha zaria*, 1913, no. 2, pp. 28–29.

Akademiia nauk SSSR. Institut istorii. *Materialy po istorii SSSR*, vol. 6: *Dokumenty po istorii monopolisticheskogo kapitalizma v Rossii*. Moscow, 1959.

Aleksinskii, G. "Po vsem pravilam nauka." *Sovremennik*, no. 6 (June 1913), pp. 280–92.

"Amerikanskaia sistema." *Rabochii po metallu*, no. 20 (September 5, 1907), pp. 3–4.

Aronov, M. "Neskol'ko slov ob 'amerikanskoi' sisteme organizatsii predpriiatii." *Zapiski imperatorskogo russkogo tekhnicheskogo obshchestva*, 1912, no. 3, pp. 112–15.

———. "Organizatsiia predpriiatii." *Zapiski imperatorskogo russkogo tekhnicheskogo obshchestva*, 1913, nos. 8–9, pp. 204–15.

———. "Printsipy nauchnoi organizatsii zavodov po Teiloru." *Zapiski imperatorskogo russkogo tekhnicheskogo obshchestva*, 1912, no. 5, pp. 178–88, and nos. 6–7, pp. 234–42.

———. "V chem sushchnost' nauchnoi organizatsii predpriiatii?" *Izvestiia obshchestva gornykh inzhenerov*, 1913, no. 2, pp. 3- 13.

———. "Ob"edinennye kapitalisty i Tret'ia Gosudarstvennaia Duma." *Zapiski imperatorskogo russkogo tekhnicheskogo obshchestva*, no. 11, 1912, pp. 373–80.

Astrov. "Amerikanskaia plata." *Metallist*, no. 9 (January 26, 1912), pp. 7–9.

B-v'. "Peterburgskoe dvizhenie i prakticheskie zadachi sotsial- demokratii." *Rabochee delo*, no. 6 (April 1900), pp. 28–34.

Badayev, A. *The Bolsheviks in the Tsarist Duma*. N.p.: Proletarian Publishers, n.d.

Balabanov, M. "Promyshlennost' Rossii v nachale XX veka." *Obshchestvennoe dvizhenie v Rossii v nachale XX-go veka*, v. 1, pp. 39–87.

Batrak. "Chto delat'?" *Metallist*, no. 3 (October 27, 1911), pp. 2–5.

———. "K voprosu ob Amerikanskoi sisteme." *Metallist*, no. 8 (January 13, 1912), p. 7.

Beliaeva, L. N., Zinov'ev, M. K., and Nikofonov, M. M. *Bibliografiia periodicheskikh izdanii Rossii 1901–1916*, 4 vols. Leningrad, 1958–1961.

Belorussov. "'Sistema Tailora' vo Frantsii." *Russkiia vedomosti*, no. 40 (February 17, 1913), pp. 5–6.

Bernshtein-Kogan, S. *Chislennost', sostav i polozhenie peterburgskikh rabochikh*. St. Petersburg, 1910.

"Blagonadezhnost' prezhde vsego." *Trud tekhnika*, no. 10 (March 24, 1907), pp. 9–10.

Blek, A. L., comp. "Protiv zabastovok na zavodakh morskogo vedomstva." *Arkhiv istorii truda v Rossii*, 1921, no. 1, pp. 113–15.

Buiko, A. M. *Put' rabochego: Zapiski starogo Bol'shevika*. Moscow, 1924.

Bulkin, Fedor A. (Semenov). "Ekonomicheskaia bor'ba rabochikh metallistov v 1905–1906 gg." *Trud v Rossii*, 1925, no. 1, pp. 3–12.

———. "Ekonomicheskoe polozhenie rabochikh metallistov do 1905 goda." *Arkhiv istorii truda v Rossii*, kn. 9 (1923), pp. 77–98.

———. "Metallisty v revoliutsii 1905–1907 gg." *Proletariat v revoliutsii 1905–1907 gg.* Moscow-Leningrad, 1930, pp. 1–48.

———. *Na zare profdvizheniia. Istoriia Peterburgskogo soiuza metallistov, 1906–1914*. Leningrad-Moscow, 1924.

———. "Rabochaia samodeiatel'nost' i rabochaia demagogiia." *Nasha zaria*, 1913, no. 3, pp. 55–64.

———. "Raskol' fraktsii i zadachi rabochikh." *Nasha zaria*, 1914, no. 6, pp. 42–51.

———. "Smesovshchina." *Trud v Rossii*, 1925, no. 1, pp. 153–70.

————. *Soiuz metallistov i departament politsii.* Leningrad, 1923.

————. *Soiuz metallistov, 1906–1918.* Moscow, 1926.

————. *V bor'be za soiuz metallistov.* Leningrad, 1926.

Butakov, I. N. "Neskol'ko zamechanii k stat'e I. Ia. E: 'Po povodu stat'i inzh. P. P. Ritsuioni.'" *Vestnik obshchestva tekhnologov,* no. 9 (May 1, 1914), pp. 356–61.

Bykov, A. N. *Fabrichnoe zakonodatel'stvo i razvitie ego v Rossii.* St. Petersburg, 1909.

Charnovskii, N. F. *Organizatsiia promyshlennykh predpriiatii po obrabotke metallov.* Moscow, 1911.

————. "Organizatsiia promyshlennykh predpriiatii po obrabotke metallov." *Biulleteni politekhnicheskogo obshchestva,* 1909, no. 6, pp. 436–41; 1910, no. 1, pp. 51–72; 1910, no. 2, pp. 98–108; 1910, no. 5, pp. 227–73; 1911, no. 4, pp. 297–322.

Chatskii, Ia. "Ocherednyia zadachi." *Nash put',* no. 18 (June 17, 1911), pp. 3–8.

"Chelovek ili mashina?" *Pravda,* no. 64 (268) (March 17, 1913), pp. 2–3.

Cherevanin, N. "Dvizhenie intelligentsii." *Obshchestvennoe dvizhenie v Rossii v nachale XX-go veka,* v. 2, pt. 2, pp. 146–202.

"Chto daet rabochim 'Amerikanskaia sistema'?" *Vestnik rabochikh po obrabotke metalla,* no. 2 (June 5, 1908), pp. 9–10.

Curriculum vitae zavodchika i fabrikanta F. K. San'-Galli. St. Petersburg, 1903.

Dembovskii, K. "Tekhnicheskii progress v russkoi promyshlennosti." *Vestnik finansov, promyshlennosti i torgovli,* 1925, no. 15, pp. 56–61.

Dimer', Gugo (Hugo Diemer). "Administrativnaia i tekhnicheskaia organizatsiia." *Kommercheskii deiatel',* 1913, no. 3, Prilozhenie, pp. 1–8; 1913, no. 9, Prilozhenie, pp. 9–16; 1913, nos. 11–2, Prilozhenie, pp. 17–24.

Dinamika Rossiiskoi i Sovetskoi promyshlennosti v sviazi s razvitiem narodnogo khoziaistva za sorok let (1887–1926): Svod statisticheskikh dannykh po fabrichno-zavodskoi promyshlennosti. V. A. Bazarov et al., eds. 5 chasti. Moscow- Leningrad, 1929–1930.

Dmokhovskii, V. "Tsentral'nyia instrumental'nyia otdeleniia." *Inzhener* 32, no. 1, 1913, pp. 14–19, and no. 2, pp. 50–57.

"Dnevnik A. A. Polovtseva (15 Sept. 1905–10 Aug. 1906; 5 March–2 May 1908)." *Krasnyi arkhiv* 4 (1923), pp. 63–128.

Dnevnik 1-go Vserossiiskogo s"ezda bukhgalterov v Moskve. Moscow, 1909.

Elwood, R. C. *Resolutions and Decisions of the Communist Party of the Soviet Union,* vol. 1: *The Russian Social Democratic Labour Party, 1898–October 1917.* Toronto: University of Toronto Press, 1974.

Emerson, G. "Dvenadtsat' printsipov povysheniia produktivnosti i organizatsiia, sposobstvuiushchaia ikh primeneniiu." *Kommercheskii deiatel',* 1912, no. 1, pp. 17–24; 1912, no. 2, pp. 25–32; 1912, no. 4, pp. 33–40; 1912, nos. 5–6, pp. 41–56.

Engel'meier, P. "V zashchitu obshchikh idei v tekhnike." *Vestnik Inzhenerov,* no. 3 (February 1, 1915), pp. 96–100.

Entsiklopedicheskii slovar' t-va Br. A. I. Granat i Ko. 7th rev. ed. Moscow, vols. 1–55, 57–58, 1910–1948.

Ermanskii, A. "Soiuzy rabotodatelei." *Sovremennyi mir,* 1909, no. 12 (December), pp. 25–45.

Ermanskii, O. A., comp. *Ukazatel' knig i statei po voprosam nauchnoi organizatsii truda.* Moscow, 1921.

Fenin, Aleksandr I. *Coal and Politics in Late Imperial Russia, Memoirs of a Russian Mining Engineer,* Translated by Alexandre Fediaevsky, edited by Susan P. McCaffray. De Kalb: Northern Illinois University Press, 1990.

Filippov, L. "Iz poezdki po nekotorym avstriiskim i angliiskim zavodam." *Vestnik obshchestva tekhnologov,* 1911, no. 1, pp. 1- 15; 1911, no. 11, pp. 487–96; 1913, no. 19, pp. 621–28; 1913, no. 24, pp. 825–37.

Filippovich, A. A. *Polozhenie po upravleniiu i otchetnosti metallurgicheskikh, mekhanicheskikh i sudostroitel'nykh zavodov akts. predpriiatii.* St. Petersburg, 1913.

Galagan', A. *Osnovnye momenty v razvitii schetnoi idei.* Moscow, 1914.

Gantt, G. I. "Sistema premii dlia oplaty truda v promyshlennikh predpriiatiiakh." *Biulleteni politekhnicheskogo obshchestva*, 1903, no. 2, pp. 175–79.

Gar-vi, N. "Nachalo lokautnoi epidemii." *Nasha zaria*, 1913, no. 2, pp. 19–25.

Garvi, P. A. *Zapiski Sotsial Demokrata (1906–1921)*. Newtonville, MA: Oriental Research Partners, 1982.

Geints', S. F. "Sdel'naia tsena, kak chislovoe vyrazhenie funktsional'noi formuly." *Biulleteni politekhnicheskogo obshchestva*, 1913, no. 3, pp. 153–60.

———. "Sistema Teilora i nauka ob upravlenii predpriiatiiami." *Vestnik obshchestva tekhnologov*, no. 22 (October 15, 1914), pp. 818–28.

———. "Sistematicheskaia (desiatichnaia) numeratsiiu chertezhei." *Biulleteni politekhnicheskogo obshchestva*, 1913, no. 3, pp. 382–90.

Glotov, A. "Amerikanskaia vydumka." *Pravda*, no. 65 (269) (March 19, 1913), p. 1.

Golubev, I. "Vospominaniia o peterburgskom professional'nom soiuze metallistov, 1907–1908." *Krasnaia letopis'*, no. 8, 1923, pp. 234–36.

Gorbunov, I. "Rabochii vopros v postanovke ego rabochimi vo vremia stachek v period vremeni s 1896–1909 g. vkliuchitel'no." *Vestnik obshchestva tekhnologov*, 1910, no. 7, pp. 344–48; 1910, no. 8, pp. 371–75; 1911, no. 7, pp. 285–93; 1911, no. S, pp. 324–38.

Gosudarstvennyi Sovet, *Stenograficheskii otchet*, sessiia V, zasedanie 45.

Grinevich, V. [M. G. Kogan]. "Ocherk razvitiia professional'nogo dvizheniia v S.-Peterburge." *Obrazovanie*, 1906, no. 8, pp. 209–26; no. 9, pp. 226–55; no. 10, pp. 109–28.

Grinevitskii, V. I. "Tekhniko-obshchestvennyia zadachi v sfere promyshlennosti i tekhniki v sviazi s voinoi." *Biulleteni Politekhnicheskago obshchestva*, no. 11, 1914, pp. 583–99.

Groman, V. V. *Materialy k voprosu o merakh bor'by s zabastovkami*. St. Petersburg, 1914.

———. *Sbornik postanovlenii Glavnogo po fabrichnym i gornozavodskim delam prisutstviia za 1899 po 1914 g*. Petrograd, 1915.

Gurevich, A. *Vserossiiskii soiuz rabochikh metallistov v rezoliutsiiakh i postanovleniiakh s"ezdov, konferentsii i plenumov TsK*. Moscow, 1928.

Gushka, A. O. *Predstavitel'nyia organizatsii torgovo- promyshlennogo klassa v Rossii*. St. Petersburg, 1912.

Gvozdev, S. *Zapiski fabrichnogo inspektora, iz nabliudenii i praktiki v period 1894–1908 gg*. Moscow-Leningrad (1911), 1925.

"Intensifikatsiia proizvodstva i sistema Teilora." *Russkiia vedomosti*, no. 63 (March 16, 1913), p. 6.

Ivanov, E. P. "O prichinakh malogo sprosa na trud inzhenerov promyshlennykh predpriiatiiakh." *Zhurnal obshchestva Sibirskikh inzhenerov*, 1910, no. 10, pp. 450–62.

Kamenev, Iu. G. "Politicheskaia stachka v Rossii." *Nevskaia zvezda*, no. 14 (June 24, 1912).

Kanatchikov, S. *Iz istorii moego bytiia*. Moscow-Leningrad, 1929.

Khatavner, I. "Sposoby proizvodstva rabot na zavodakh (O nauchnom vedenii proizvodstva rabot)." *Vsemirnoe tekhnicheskoe obozrenie*, 1914, no. 6, pp. 129–30.

Khmylev, I. "K voprosu o sovremennom polozhenii reorganizatsii mekhanicheskikh zavodov i masterskikh v Rossii." *Biulleteni kruzhka tekhnologov Moskovskogo raiona*, 1913–1914, no. 8, pp. 22–29.

Kir'ianov, Iu. I., and Pronina, P. V. *Oblik proletariata Rossii. Bibliografiia*. Moscow, 1967.

Kirpichnikov, S. D. "Iz proshlago Obshchestva Tekhnologov (k istorii Soiuza Inzhenerov)." *Trud inzhenera i tekhnika*, no. 21 (November 13, 1906), pp. 739–94.

———. "L. I. Lutugin i Soiuz Soiuzov." *Byloe*, no. 6 (34), 1925, pp. 134–46.

Kleinbort, L. "Khronika russkoi zhizni." *Obrazovanie*, no. 4, 1906, pp. 98–118.

Kolokol'nikov, P. N. (Dmitriev, K.). *Professional'noe dvizhenie i soiuzy v Rossii*. St. Petersburg, 1909.

Kol'tsov, D. "Rabochie v 1905–1907 gg." *Obshchestvennoe dvizhenie v Rossii v nachale XX-go veka*, v. 2, pt. 1, pp. 185–341.
"Kombinirovaniia sistema bonov i premei." *Zapiski imperatorskogo russkogo tekhnicheskogo obshchestva*, 1912, no. 10, pp. 303–7.
Kropotkin, Peter. *Memoirs of a Revolutionist*, New York, Grove Press, 1986.
Krzhizhanovskii, V. M. "Kriticheskii obzor sovremennykh sistem oplaty truda masterovykh i rabochikh." *Inzhener*, 1911, no. 10 (October), pp. 306–29; 1911, no. 11 (November), pp. 361–71.
Kudelli, P. F., and Shidlovskii, G. L., comps. *1905. Vospominaniia chlenov St. Petersburgskogo Soveta Rabochikh Deputatov*. Leningrad, 1926.
Ladyzhenskii, I. A. "Znachenie kommercheskikh i sotsial'no- ekonomicheskikh nauk dlia inzhenerov v Rossii i vzgliad na tot zhe vopros v Germanii." *Inzhener*, 1909, no. 7 (July), pp. 224- 30.
Larskii, I. "Nauchnyi kapitalizm." *Sovremennyi mir*, 1913, no. 5, pp. 235–50.
Lenin, V. I. *Collected Works*. Moscow: Foreign Languages Publishing House, 1962–1964.
Lepeshinskii, P. O. "Poputchiki proletariata v period staroi 'Iskry.'" *Proletarskaia revoliutsiia* 2 (14), 1923, pp. 167–95.
Levenson, L. "Tekhnicheskaia organizatsiia amerikanskikh mashinostroitel'nykh zavodov." *Zapiski imperatorskogo russkogo tekhnicheskogo obshchestva*, 1912, no. 12, pp. 417–27.
Levenstern, L. *Nauchnyia osnovy zavodoupravleniia. Skhema nauchnoi organizatsii zavoda*. St. Petersburg, 1913.
Levitskii, M., comp. *Putilovskii staleliteinyi, zhelezodelatel'nyi i mekhanicheskii zavod*. Kronshtadt, 1898.
Lisovskii, N. M., comp. *Rabochie v voennom vedomstve (Po povodu 'Trudov' Vysochaishe uchrezhdennoi kommissii po uluchsheniiu byta rabochikh voennogo vedomstva)*. St. Petersburg, 1906.
Listovki Peterburgskikh Bol'shevikov, vol. 1 (1902–1907), vol. 2 (1907–1917). Leningrad, 1939.
Lobach-Zhuchenko, B. "K voprosu o letnei praktike studentov- tekhnologov." *Vestnik obshchestva tekhnologov*, 1912, no. 2, pp. 52–53.
Lur'e, E. "K kharakteristike soiuzov rabotodatelei v Rossii." *Vestnik Evropy*, 1911, no. 12, pp. 308–21.
———. *Organizatsiia i organizatsii torgovo-promyshlennykh interesov v Rossii*. St. Petersburg, 1913.
Maevskii, E. "Massovoe dvizhenie v 1904 po 1907 gg." *Obshchestvennoe dvizhenie v Rossii v nachale XX-go veka*, vol. 2, pt. 1, pp. 34–185.
Malinin, V. F. "O suschestvuiushchem predlozhenii i sprose v promyshlennosti na inzhenernyi trud." *Biulleteni politekhnicheskogo obshchestva*, 1903, no. 4, pp. 339–45.
Malinovskii, A. A. (Bogdanov, A.). *Mezhdu chelovekom i mashiniu (o Teilore)*. St. Petersburg, 1913.
Malyshev, S. *The Unemployed Councils in St. Petersburg in 1906*. N.p.: Proletarian Publishers, 1931(?).
Marshan, G. "Registratsiia, klassifikatsiia i khranenie dokumentov v krupnykh uchrezhdeniiakh." *Izvestiia obshchego biuro soveshchatel'nykh s"ezdov*, 1912, no. 4, pp. 349–54.
Martov, Iu. "Ianvarskie vybory po rabochei kurii v gorode Peterburge." *Otkliki*, no. 2 (April 1907), pp. 65–78.
———. *Zapiski Sotsial-Demokrata*. Berlin, 1922: reprinted Cambridge: Oriental Research Partners, 1975.
Materialy k voprosu o merakh bor'by s zabastovkami. St. Petersburg, 1914.
Materialy po rabochemu voprosu. Predvaritel'nye proekty po peresmotru rabochego

zakonodatel'stva, vyrabotannye Ministerstvom torgovli i promyshlennosti v soveshchanii 15–21 aprelia 1906 pod d.s.s. M. M. Fedorov. St. Petersburg, 1906.

Mezhenko, Iu. A. *Russkaia tekhnicheskaia periodika, 1800–1916.* Moscow, 1916, 1955.

Mikulin, A. A. "Tekhnika ili rutina rukovodit' nashei promyshlennost'iu." *Biulleteni politekhnicheskogo obshchestva,* 1905, no. 3, pp. 200–2.

Minin, M. "O rabote v Vyborskom raione." *Otkliki,* no. 2 (April 1907), pp. 18–27.

Mitrevich, A. "Vospominaniia o rabochem revoliutsionnom dvizhenii." *Proletarskaia revoliutsiia,* 1922, no. 4, pp. 199- 241.

———. "Zametki po rabochemu dvizheniiu ot 1912 goda." *Proletarskaia revoliutsiia,* 1922, no. 4, pp. 241–45.

Munsterberg, Hugo. *Psychology and Industrial Efficiency.* Boston and New York: Houghton Mifflin Co., 1913.

Nachalo pervoi russkoi revoliutsii. Ianvar'-mart 1905 g. Edited by N. S. Trusova et al. Moscow, 1955. [A volume in the series *Revoliutsiia 1905–1907 gg. v Rossii. Dokumenty i materialy.*]

Netyska, M. "Neskol'ko slov po povodu upravleniia mekhanicheskami zavodami." *Biulleteni politekhnicheskogo obshchestva,* 1910, no. 7, pp. 436–61.

———. *Po povody upravleniia mekhanicheskami zavodami i rabochiia otchetnost'.* Moscow, 1911.

"O sisteme Teilora." *Pravda,* no. 87 (291) (April 14, 1913), p. 5.

Obshchestvennoe dvizhenie v Rossii v nachale XX-go veka. Edited by L. Martov, P. Maslov, and A. Potresov. 4 vols. St. Petersburg, 1909–1914.

Obshchestvo zavodchikov i fabrikantov. *Materialy po rabochemu voprosy.* Moscow, 1910.

———. *1907-i god. Otchet i prilozheniia.* St. Petersburg, 1908.

———. *O prave zavodoupravleniia nemedlenno razschitat' rabochikh, uchastvuiushchikh v zabastovke.* St. Petersburg, 1911.

Obukhovtsy: Maiskiia volneniia na Obukhovskom zavode, n.p. 1901.

Okun', S. B., comp. *Putilovets v trekh revoliutsiiakh.* Leningrad, 1933.

Ol'minskii, M. "Ia vas arestuiu." *Prosveshchenie,* no. 2 (February 1913), pp. 40–49.

"Opyt primeneniia sistemy Teilora k ustanovleniiu rastsenik na odnom iz Germanskikh zavodov." *Zapiski imperatorskogo russkogo tekhnicheskogo obshchestva,* 1911, nos. 8–9, pp. 315–23.

"Organizatsiia amerikanskikh mashinostroitel'nykh zavodov. Translated by R. Poliakov. *Izvestiia obshchestva dlia sodeistviia uluchsheniiu i razvitiiu manufakturnoi promyshlennosti,* 1907, no. 3, pp. 119–38; 1907, no. 4, pp. 177–94; 1907, no. 5, pp. 233–42; 1907, no. 6, pp. 260–73.

"Organizatsiia zavodoupravleniia. Special supplement to *Vestnik obshchestva tekhnologov,* 1912, no. 11, pp. 1–49.

"Organizatsiia zavodskogo predpriiatiia." *Dvigatel',* 1911, no. 12, pp. 178–82; 1911, no. 13, pp. 195–8; 1911, no. 15, pp. 220–4.

P. "Nauchnaia sistema ekspluatatsii." *Metallist,* no. 10 (February 11, 1912), pp. 5–6.

Pankin, A. V. "Novyia sistemy zarabotnoi platy i sravnenie ikh sushchestvuiushchimi sistemami oplaty truda na mekhanicheskikh zavodakh." *Zapiski imperatorskogo russkogo tekhnicheskogo obshchestva,* 1911, no. 1, pp. 17–24.

———. "Organizatsiia i ustroistvo instrumental'nogo otdela i magazina na zavode." *Zapiski imperatorskogo russkogo tekhnicheskogo obshchestva,* 1912, no. 1, pp. 1–16; 1912, no. 5, pp. 163–76.

———. "Organizatsiia promyshlennykh predpriiatii i sistema zarabotnoi platy po V. Teiloru." *Zapiski imperatorskogo russkogo tekhnicheskogo obshchestva,* 1909, no. 2, pp. 71–77.

———. "Organizatsiia tekhnicheskoi raboty i tekhnicheskogo nadzora v masterskoi po Tailoru." *Zapiski imperatorskogo russkogo tekhnicheskogo obshchestva,* 1909, no. 3, pp. 106–14.

———. "Osnovnye printsipy organizatsii vysshego tekhnicheskogo obrazovaniia." *Zapiski imperatorskogo russkogo tekhnicheskogo obshchestva,* 1911, no. 5, pp. 161–74.

Parkgorst, F. N. *Ot direktora-rasporiaditelia i do rassyk'nogo . . . : Opyt pis'mennoi instruktsii dlia sluzhashchikh promyshlennykh predpriiatii.* Translated by A. V. Pankin and L. A. Levenstern. Petrograd, 1916.

———. *Prakticheskie priemy reorganizatsii promyshlennykh predpriiatii.* Translated by A. V. Pankin and L. A. Levenstern. St. Petersburg, 1914.

Peterburgskie bol'sheviki v period pod"ema pervoi russkoi revolutsii 1905–1907 gg. Sbornik dokumentov i materialov. Leningrad, 1955.

Peterburgskii komitet RSDRP, Protokoly i materialy zasedanii Iiul' 1902–Fevral' 1917. Leningrad, 1986.

Petrov, M. A. *Progresivnaia ekonomicheskaia partiia. Organizatsiia i partiia Peterburgskikh fabrikantov i zavodchikov.* St. Petersburg, 1906.

———. "Soiuz Rossiiskikh kapitalistov." *Vestnik zhizni,* no. 11 (September 26, 1906), pp. 31–43.

Piletskii, Ia. "Prisposoblenie i otbor sovremennykh rabochikh." *Zapiski imperatorskogo russkogo tekhnicheskogo obshchestva,* 1914, no. 2, pp. 35–45.

Plekhanov, G. *Russkii rabochii v revoliutsionnom dvizhenii (po lichnym vospominaniiam).* Geneva, 1892.

Poliakov, R. V. "Fabrichno-zavodskaia promyshlennost' v Amerike." *Izvestiia obshchestva dlia sodeistviia uluchsheniiu i razvitiiu manufakturnoi promyshlennosti,* 1905, nos. 7–8; 1906, nos. 1–3.

———. "Mashina-orudie, kak faktor sotsial'nogo progressa." *Biulleteni politekhnicheskogo obshchestva,* 1907, no. 4, pp. 216–22.

———. *Nastoiashchee polozhenie voprosa o primenenii sistemy Teilora.* Moscow, 1914.

Poliakov, R. V., and Khmelev, I. A. *Konsul'tatsionnoe biuro po oborudovaniiu i organizatsii mekhanicheskikh zavodov i masterskikh.* Moscow, 1914.

"Premirovochnaia sistema voznagrazhdeniia truda." *Vestnik obshchestva tekhnologov,* 1906, no. 4, pp. 189–94.

Prokopovich, S. "Sistema Teilora." *Russkiia vedomosti,* no. 95 (April 25, 1913), pp. 3–4.

P—skii, S. "Amerikanskaia sistema rabot i usloviia truda." *Metallist,* no. 6 (December 17, 1911), pp. 5–7.

———. "Chto delat'?" *Metallist,* no. 11 (February 23, 1912), pp. 4–5; no. 13 (April 7, 1912), pp. 4–5.

Putilovtsy v 1905 godu: Sbornik vospominaniia rabochikh. Edited by B. Pozern. Leningrad, 1931.

Rabochee dvizhenie v Petrograde v 1912–1914 gg.: dokumenty i materialy. Edited by Iu. I. Korablev. Leningrad, 1958.

Rabochee dvizhenie v Rossii v 1901–1904 gg. Sbornik dokumentov. Edited by L. M. Ivanov. Leningrad, 1975.

Rabochee dvizhenie v Rossii v XIX veke. Sbornik dokumentov i materialov. Edited by A. M. Pankratova, L. M. Ivanov et al. 4 vols. Moscow-Leningrad, 1950–64.

Rabochii vopros v komissii V. N. Kokovtsova v 1905 g. Edited by B. A. Romanov. Moscow, 1926.

Rakitin, G. "Rabochaia massa i rabochaia intelligentsiia." *Nasha zaria,* 1913, no. 9, pp. 52–60.

"Ratsional'naia organizatsiia zavodskogo predpriiatiia." *Tekhniko-promyshlennyi vestnik,* 1911, no. 7 (July), pp. 9–12; 1911, no. 8 (August), pp. 8–10; 1911, nos. 9–10 (September–October), pp. 14–16.

Rech' predsedatelia obshchestva zavodchikov i fabrikantov, chlena Gosudarstvennogo Soveta, S. P. Glezmera, v zasedanii Gosudarstvennogo Soveta, 7-go maia 1910 g. St. Petersburg, 1910.

Rech' predsedatelia obshchestva zavodchikov i fabrikantov, chlena Gosudarstvennogo Soveta,

S. P. Glezmera, v zasedanii Gosudarstvennogo Soveta, 20-go aprelia 1912 g. St. Petersburg, 1912.

Revoliutsionnoe dvizhenie v Rossii vesnoi i letom 1905 g., Aprel'-sentiabr'. Chast' pervaia. Edited by N. S. Trusova et al. Moscow, 1957. [A volume in the series *Revoliutsiia 1905- 1907 gg. v Rossii. Dokumenty i materialy.*]

Riazanov, N. "Pochemu tak pozdno organizovalsia v Peterburge soiuz rabochikh po metallu?" *Professional'nyi soiuz*, nos. 20- 21 (June 22, 1906), p. 10.

Russak, I. "Ob odnom iz voprosov etiki inzhenerov." *Biulleteni kruzhka tekhnologov Moskovskogo raiona*, no. 4, noiabr' 1913- 1914, pp. 6–12.

Russia. Ministerstvo finansov i ministerstvo torgovli i promyshlennosti. *Spisok fabrik i zavodov Rossii 1910 g.* Moscow, St. Petersburg, Warsaw, n.d.

———. Ministerstvo torgovli i promyshlennosti. Otdel promyshlennosti. *Svod otchetov fabrichnykh inspektorov za 1909, 1910, 1911, 1912, 1913, 1914.* St. Petersburg, 1910–1915.

———. Ministerstvo torgovli i promyshlennosti. Otdel promyshlennosti. *Spisok fabrik i zavodov evropeiskoi Rossii.* St. Petersburg, 1903.

———. Tsentral'noe statisticheskoe upravlenie. *Trudy.* Vols. 1–35. Moscow, 1917–1926.

Rytel', S. V. "Sistema poshtuchnoi platy." *Vestnik obshchestva tekhnologov*, 1911, no. 11, pp. 438–40.

Salamatin, V. P. *Nauchnoe rukovodstvo rabotami.* Moscow, 1912.

Sbornik programm politicheskikh partii v Rossii, vol. 5. St. Petersburg, 1906.

Severianin. "Po povodu sistemy Teilora." *Russkiia vedomosti*, no. 57 (March 9, 1913), p. 6.

Sh—r', V. "Nashe professional'noe dvizhenie za dva poslednikh goda." *Bor'ba*, nos. 1, 2, 3, 4, 1914.

Sharpant'e, S. "Organizatsiia liteinoi masterskoi." *Zapiski imperatorskogo russkogo tekhnicheskogo obshchestva*, 1911, no. 1, pp. 1–12; 1911, no. 2, pp. 52–68; 1911, no. 4, pp. 125–42.

———. "Primenenie schetnoi lineiki k opredeleniiu shtuchnykh tsen v liteinykh masterskikh." *Zapiski imperatorskogo russkogo tekhnicheskogo obshchestva*, 1913, no. 4, pp. 103–7.

———. "Uspekhi Teilora v oblasti fabrichnoi organizatsii." *Zapiski imperatorskogo russkogo tekhnicheskogo obshchestva*, 1912, nos. 8–9, pp. 270–73.

———. "Vedenie fabrichnoi otchetnosti (po Lilienthal'iu)." *Zapiski imperatorskogo russkogo tekhnicheskogo obshchestva*, 1911, no. 11, pp. 377–86; 1911, no. 12, pp. 425–34.

Shirman, M. "K polozheniiu 'tekhnika' voobshche i 'inzhenera' v chastnosti." *Vestnik obshchestva tekhnologov*, 1911, no. 6, pp. 238–50.

Shliapnikov, A. "Amerikanskaia potogonnyia sistemy—'rabota na premiiu' i 'khronometrazh.'" *Metallist*, no. 10 (34) (October 25, 1913), pp. 3–5; no. 11 (35) (November 16, 1913), pp. 6–8.

———. *Tarifnyi dogovor, zakliuchennyi mezhdu petrogradskim soiuzom rabochikh metallistov i obshchestvom zavodchikov i fabrikantov s dopolneniiami i raz"iaseniiami.* Petrograd, 19–.

Shotman, A. *Zapiski starogo bol'shevika.* Leningrad, 1963.

———. "Zapiski starogo bol'shevika." *Proletarskaia revoliutsiia*, no. 9, 1922, pp. 138–53; no. 11, 1922, pp. 92–115.

Shuvalov, P. S. "Iz bor'ba za khleb i voliu." *Krasnaia letopis'*, no. 5, 1923, pp. 268–84.

Sil'vin, M. A. "V dni 'Soiuza bor'by za osvobozhdenie rabochego klassa.'" *Vospominaniia o Vladimire Il'iche Lenine*, vol. 1. Moscow, 1956, pp. 122–29.

"Sistema Teilora." *Russkiia vedomosti*, no. 58 (March 10, 1913), p. 5.

"Sluzhashchie v nashikh promyshlennykh zavedeniiakh v otnoshenii poddanstva, iazyka i obrazovaniia." *Vestnik finansov, promyshlennosti i torgovli*, 1904, no. 51, pp. 477–86.

Smidt', K. "Prakticheskiia ukazaniia po voprosu o zavodskoi kal'kuliatsii." *Vestnik obshchestva tekhnologov,* 1910, no. 7, pp. 339–44.

Smolin, G. "Iz zhizni professional'nykh soiuzov." *Vozrozhdenie,* no. 6, 1910, pp. 63–72; no. 7, 1910, pp. 64–69.

Soiuz rabochikh po metallu, St. Petersburg. *Materialy ob ekonomicheskom polozhenii i professional'noi organizatsii peterburgskikh rabochikh po metallu.* St. Petersburg, 1909.

Sokolov, B. "Shtuchnaia plata v metalloobrabatyvaiushchei promyshlennosti." *Tekhnicheskii vestnik,* 1910, no. 1 (November), pp. 1–4; 1910, no. 2 (December), pp. 30–33.

Somov, S. I. "Iz istorii sotsialdemokraticheskogo dvizheniia v Peterburge v 1905 godu." *Byloe,* 4 (16) April 1907, pp. 22–55; 5 (17) May 1907, pp. 153–78.

Sovet s"ezdov predstavitelei promyshlennosti i torgovli. *Fabrichno-zavodskaia predpriiatiia Rossiiskoi imperii.* St. Petersburg, 1914.

———. *Statisticheskii ezhegodnik na 1914 g.* St. Petersburg, 1914.

"Statistika neschastnykh sluchaev s rabochimi v promyshlennykh zavedeniiakh podchinennykh nadzoru inspektsii." *Vestnik finansov, promyshlennosti i torgovli,* no. 41 (October 10, 1910), pp. 69–70.

"Statistika neschastnykh sluchaev s rabochimi v promyshlennykh zavedeniiakh za 1901 g." *Vestnik finansov, promyshlennosti i torgovli,* no. 49 (December 7, 1903), pp. 394–403.

Stenogrammy soveshchaniia o polozhenii metallurgicheskoi i mashinostroitel'noi promyshlennosti, mai 1908. St. Petersburg 1908.

Stepanov, G. P. *Raschet i tablitsy dlia opredeleniia vremeni i zarabotnoi platy masterovogo pri obrabotke predmetov na stankakh po metallu.* Tambov, 1914.

Sukhanov, N. N. [N. Gimmer]. "O 'sisteme Teilora.'" *Russkoe bogatstvo,* no. 11, 1913, pp. 132–54.

Svirskii, A. I. *Zapiski rabochego.* Moscow-Leningrad, 1925.

Takhtarev, K. M. *Rabochee dvizhenie v Peterburge (1893–1901 gg.)* Leningrad, 1924.

Teilor, F. V. (F. W. Taylor). "Ob iskusstve obrabotki metallov rezaniem." Translated by R. Poliakov. *Biulleteni politekhnicheskogo obshchestva,* 1907, no. 7, pp. 371–83; no. 8, pp. 415–38.

———. "Organizatsiia promyshlennykh predpriiatii." *Biulleteni politekhnicheskogo obshchestva,* 1906, no. 3, pp. 89–113; 1906, no. 4, pp. 141–64.

———. *Scientific Management, Comprising Shop Management, The Principles of Scientific Management, and Testimony Before the Special House Committee.* New York: Harper and Brothers Publishers, 1947.

"Tekhnicheskoe obrazovanie i idealy amerikanskikh inzhenerov." *Elektrichestvo,* 1909, no. 2, pp. 81–85.

Teplov, A. *Zapiski Putilovtsa: Vospominaniia 1891–1905.* St. Petersburg, 1908.

Timofeev, P. G. *Chem zhivet zavodskii rabochii.* St. Petersburg, 1906.

"Trudy piatogo vserossiiskogo elektrotekhnicheskogo s"ezda." *Elektrichestvo,* 1909, no. 4, pp. 39–55; 1909, no. 5, pp. 25- 27.

"Tsarizm v bor'be s rabochim dvizheniem v gody pod"ema." Introduced by M. Lur'e. *Krasnyi arkhiv,* no. 74 (1937), pp. 37- 65.

Tsizarevich, E. P. "Glavneishie iz novykh sposobov voznagrazhdeniia za trud." *Izvestiia obshchego biuro soveshchatel'nykh s"ezdov,* 1913, no. 6, pp. 461–74.

Tsyperovich, G. "Ob"edinennyi kapital i organizovannyi trud." *Obrazovanie,* 1908, no. 6, pp. 1–30.

Tsytsarin, V. "Vospominaniia metallista." *Vestnik truda,* no. 12 (December 1925), pp. 34–40.

Tugan'-Baranovskii, M. I., ed. *Novyia idei v ekonomike.* St. Petersburg, 1914.

V. T. "Kak organizovan nadzor za rabotoi v amerikanskoi masterskoi." *Nash put',* no. 4 (July 15, 1910), pp. 5–6.

V. V. "Novyi moment evoliutsii kapitalisticheskoi organizatsii proizvodstva." *Vestnik Evropy,* no. 3, 1913, pp. 288–310.

Varzar, V. E. *Statisticheskiia svedeniia o stachkakh rabochikh na fabrikakh i zavodakh za 1895–1905.* St. Petersburg, 1905.

———. *Statistiki stachek rabochikh na fabrikakh i zavodakh za 1905.* St. Petersburg, 1908.

———. *Statistiki stachek rabochikh na fabrikakh i zavodakh za 1905–1908.* St. Petersburg, 1908–1910.

Vasil'evich, V. "Dogovor naima i zabastovki." *Obrazovanie,* 1906, no. 5, pp. 156–69.

Vebner, F. "Kak uznat' deistvitel'nuiu stoimost' proizvodstva." *Kommercheskii deiatel',* 1910, nos. 2–3, pp. 1–7; 1910, no. 4, pp. 12–21; 1910, nos. 5–6, pp. 10–14; 1910, nos. 7-S, pp. 9- 12.

Velox. "Nachalo kontsa." *Nasha zaria,* 1910, nos. 8–9 (August- September), pp. 5–21.

Ves' Peterburg; adresnaia i spravochnaia kniga. St. Petersburg, 1901, 1908, 1910, 1914.

Voennaia entsiklopediia, 18 vols. St. Petersburg, 1911–1915.

Voitinskii, I. S. *Stachka, i rabochii dogovor po russkomu pravu.* St. Petersburg, 1911.

Voitinskii, Vladimir S. *Peterburgskii sovet bezrabotnykh, 1906- 1907,* Russian Institute Occasional Papers, Russian Institute, Columbia University, New York, 1969.

Vospominaniia Ivana Vasil'evicha Babushkina, 1893–1900 gg. Moscow, 1955.

Vserossiiskaia politicheskaia stachka v oktiabre 1905 g. Chast' pervaia. Edited by L. M. Ivanov et al. Moscow-Leningrad, 1955. [A volume in the series *Revoliutsiia 1905–1907 gg. v Rossii. Dokumenty i materialy.*]

Vtoroi period revoliutsii, 1906–1907 gg. Chast' pervaia. Ianvar'- aprel' 1906 g. Moscow, 1961. [A volume in the series *Revoliutsiia 1905–1907 gg. v Rossii. Dokumenty i materialy.*]

Vtoroi period revoliutsii, 1906–1907 gg. Chast' vtoraia. Mai- sentiabr' 1906 g. Tom 1. Moscow, 1961. [A volume in the series *Revoliutsiia 1905–1907 gg. v Rossii. Dokumenty i materialy.*]

Vtoroi period revoliutsii, 1906–1907 gg. Oktiabr'-dekabr' 1906 g. Moscow, 1963. [A volume in the series *Revoliutsiia 1905–1907 gg. v Rossii. Dokumenty i materialy.*]

Vtoroi period revoliutsii, 1906–1907 gg. Ianvar'-iiun' 1907 g. Edited by N. S. Trusova et al. Moscow, 1963. [A volume in the series *Revoliutsiia 1905–1907 gg. v Rossii. Dokumenty i materialy.*]

Vysshii pod"em revoliutsii 1905–1907 gg. Vooruzhennye vosstaniia. Noiabr'-dekabr' 1905 g. Chast' pervaia. Edited by A. L. Sidorov et al. Moscow, 1955. [A volume in the series *Revoliutsiia 1905–1907 gg. v Rossii. Dokumenty i materialy.*]

Za Nevskoi zastavoi: Zapiski rabochego Alekseia Buzinova. Moscow- Leningrad, 1930.

Zheleznov, V. "Eksperimental'noe izuchenie truda." *Russkiia vedomosti,* no. 258 (November 8, 1913), pp. 2–3.

(Zinov'ev), G. Z. "Poslednii lokaut i teoriia 'stachechnago azarta.'" *Prosveshchenie,* no. 4 (April 1914), pp. 94–96.

Secondary Works

Ainzaft, S. *Professional'noe dvizhenie v Rossii v 1905–1907 gg.* Edited and prefaced by Iu. Milonov. Moscow, 1925.

Anskii, A. "Sotsial-demokraticheskaia fraktsiia 3-i Gosudarstvennoi dumy i professional'nye soiuzy." *Krasnaia letopis',* 1929, no. 3 (30), pp. 245–60.

Arskii, P. "Epokha reaktsii v Petrograde, 1907–1910 gg." *Krasnaia letopis',* 1923, no. 9, pp. 63–106.

Arutiunov, G. A. *Rabochee dvizhenie v Rossii v period novogo revoliutsionnogo pod"ema, 1910–1914 gg.* Moscow, 1975.

Ascher, Abraham. *The Revolution of 1905, Russia in Disarray.* Stanford: Stanford University Press, 1988.

Bailes, Kendall E. "Alexei Gastev and the Soviet Controversy over Taylorism, 1918–1924." *Soviet Studies* 29 (July 1977), pp. 373- 94.

——. *Technology and Society under Lenin and Stalin*. Princeton: Princeton University Press, 1978.

Balabanov, M. S. *Ob"edinennyi kapital protiv rabochikh, 1905–1917 gg*. Leningrad, 1930.

——. *Ot 1905 k 1917, Massovoe rabochee dvizhenie*. Moscow- Leningrad, 1927.

——. *Rabochee dvizhenie v Rossii v gody pod"ema*. Leningrad, 1927.

Balzer, Harley David. "Educating Engineers: Economic Politics and Technical Training in Tsarist Russia." Ph.D. dissertation, University of Pennsylvania, 1980.

Bater, James H. *St. Petersburg: Industrialization and Change*. London: Edward Arnold, 1976.

Beisinger, Mark. *Scientific Management, Socialist Discipline, and Soviet Power*. Cambridge: Harvard University Press, 1988.

Beskrovnyi, L. G. "Proizvodstvo vooruzheniia i boepripasov dlia armii v Rossii, 1898–1917." *Istoricheskie zapiski*, no. 99, 1977, pp. 88–139.

——. *Armiia i flot Rossii v nachale XX v*. Moscow, 1986.

Blek, A. L. "Iz praktiki predvaritel'nogo obsledovaniia zavodskikh arkhivov." *Arkhiv istorii truda v Rossii*, 1921, no. 1, pp. 116–21.

——. "Usloviia truda rabochikh na peterburgskikh zavodakh po dannym 1901 g." *Arkhiv istorii truda v Rossii*, 1921, no. 2, pp. 65–85.

Bogdanov, F. A. "Deviatisotye gody." *O revoliutsionnom proshlom Peterburgskogo metallicheskogo zavoda, 1958–1905: Sbornik*. Leningrad, 1926.

Bonnell, Victoria E. "Radical Politics and Organized Labor in Pre-Revolutionary Moscow, 1905–1917." *Journal of Social History* 12 (Winter 1978), pp. 282–300.

——. *Roots of Rebellion*. Berkeley: University of California Press, 1983.

Bovykin, V. I. "Banki i voennaia promyshlennost' Rossii nakanune pervoi mirovoi voiny." *Istoricheskie zapiski*, no. 64 (1959), pp. 82–135.

——. "Dinamika promyshlennogo proizvodstva v Rossii (1896- 1910)." *Istoriia SSSR*, no. 3 (May-June 1983), pp. 20–52.

Bovykin, V. I., and Shatsillo, K. F. "Lichnye unii v tiazheloi promyshlennosti Rossii nakanune pervoi mirovoi voiny." *Vestnik Moskovskogo universiteta*, 1962, no. 1, pp. 55–74.

Bovykin, V. I., and Tarnovskii, K. N. "Kontsentratsiia proizvodstva i razvitie monopolii v metalloobrabatyvaiushchei promyshlennosti Rossii." *Voprosy istorii*, 1957, no. 2, pp. 19- 31.

Braverman, Harry. *Labor and Monopoly Capital, The Degradation of Work in the Twentieth Century*. New York and London: Monthly Review Press, 1974.

Brody, David. *Steelworkers in America: The Non-Union Era*. New York: Harper Torchbooks, 1969; originally published by Harvard University Press, 1960.

Brusianin, V. "Chernaia sotnaia na fabrikakh i zavodakh Peterburga v gody reaktsii." *Krasnaia letopis'*, 1929, no. 1 (28), pp. 154–81; 1929, no. 2 (29), pp. 151–72.

Burawoy, Michael. *The Politics of Production*. London: Verso, 1985.

Burstein, Abraham C. "Iron and Steel in Russia, 1861–1913." Ph.D. dissertation, New School for Social Research, 1963.

Bushnell, John. *Mutiny amid Repression: Russian Soldiers in the Revolution of 1905–1906*. Bloomington: Indiana University Press, 1985.

Chermenskii, E. D. *Burzhuaziia i tsarizm v pervoi russkoi revoliutsii*. Moscow, 1970.

Clowes, Edith W., Kassow, Samuel D., and West, James L., eds. *Between Tsar and People: Educated Society and the Quest for Public Identity in Late Imperial Russia*. Princeton: Princeton University Press, 1991.

Comfort, Richard A. *Revolutionary Hamburg, Labor Politics in the Early Weimar Regime*. Stanford: Stanford University Press, 1966.

Copley, Frank Barkley. *Frederick W. Taylor, Father of Scientific Management*. 2 vols. New York: Harper and Brothers, 1923.

Crisp, Olga. *Studies in the Russian Economy before 1914*. London: Macmillan, 1976.

Davidenko, A. I. "K voprosu o chislennosti i sostave proletariata Peterburga v nachale XX veka." *Istoriia rabochego klassa Leningrada*, vol. 2, pp. 92–112. V. A. Ovsiakin, ed. in chief. Leningrad, 1963.

Devinat, Paul. *Scientific Management in Europe*. International Labour Office, Studies and Reports, Series B, no. 17. Geneva, 1927.

Diakin, V. S. *Germanskie kapitaly v Rossii (Elektroindustriia i elektricheskii transport)*. Leningrad, 1971.

———. "Iz istorii ekonomicheskoi politiki tsarizma v 1907–1914 gg." *Istoricheskie zapiski*, no. 109, 1983, pp. 25–63.

Dmitriev, N. "Pervoe maia i Peterburgskoe obshchestvo zavodchikov i fabrikantov, 1907–1914 gg." *Krasnaia letopis'*, 1926, no. 2 (17), pp. 51–81.

Emmons, Terence. *The Formation of Political Parties and the First National Elections in Russia*. Cambridge: Harvard University Press, 1983.

Engelstein, Laura. *Moscow, 1905, Working Class Organizations and Political Conflict*. Stanford: Stanford University Press, 1982.

Ermanskii, O. A. *Nauchnaia organizatsiia truda i proizvodstva i sistema Teilora*. Moscow, 1922.

Feldman, Gerald. "Socio-economic Structures in the Industrial Sector and Revolutionary Potentialities, 1917–1922." *Revolutionary Situations in Europe, 1917–1922*, pp. 160–68. Edited by C. Bertrand. Montreal: Inter-university Centre for European Studies, 1977.

Fitch, John. *The Steel Workers*. The Pittsburgh Survey. Edited by Paul U. Kellogg. New York: Charities Publication Comm., 1911.

Frankel, Jonathan, editor. *Vladimir Akimov on the Dilemmas of Russian Marxism, 1895–1903*. Cambridge: Cambridge University Press, 1969.

Galai, Shmuel. *The Liberation Movement in Russia, 1900–1905*. Cambridge: Cambridge University Press, 1973.

Gatrell, Peter. "After Tsushima: Economic and Administrative Aspects of Russian Naval Rearmament, 1905–1913." *Economic History Review*, 2nd ser., XLIII, 2 (1990), pp. 255–70.

———. "Industrial Expansion in Tsarist Russia, 1908–1914." *Economic History Review*, 2nd ser., XXXV, 1 (1982).

———. *The Tsarist Economy, 1850–1917*. New York: St. Martin's Press, 1986.

Geary, Dick. "Radicalism and the Workers: Metalworkers and the Revolution, 1914–1923." *Society and Politics in Wilhelmine Germany*, pp. 267–86. Edited by Richard J. Evans. London: Croom Helm, 1978.

Gerbach, V. V., et al. *Rabochie-Baltiitsy v trekh revoliutsiiakh*. Leningrad, 1959.

Gerschenkron, Alexander. "Problems and Patterns of Russian Economic Development." *The Structure of Russian History*, pp. 282–308. Edited by Michael Cherniavsky. New York: Random House, 1970.

Getzler, Israel. *Martov, A Political Biography of a Russian Social Democrat*. Cambridge: Cambridge University Press, 1967.

Geyer, Dietrich. *Russian Imperialism, The Interaction of Domestic and Foreign Policy, 1860–1914*. Leamington Spa: Berg, 1987.

Gindin, I. F. "Antikrizisnoe finansirovanie predpriiatii tiazheloi promyshlennosti (konets XIX–nachalo XX v.)." *Istoricheskie zapiski*, no. 105, 1980, pp. 105–49.

———. "O nekotorykh osobennostiakh ekonomicheskoi i sotsial'noi struktury rossiiskogo kapitalizma v nachale XX v." *Istoriia SSSR*, 1966, no. 3, pp. 48–66.

———. "Russkaia burzhuaziia v period kapitalizma, ee razvitie i osobennosti." *Istoriia SSSR*, 1963, no. 2, pp. 57–80; 1963, no. 3, pp. 37–60.

———. *Russkie kommercheskie banki*. Moscow, 1948.

Gindin, I. F., and Shepelev, L. E. "Bankovskie monopolii v Rossii nakanune Velikoi Oktiabr'skoi sotsialisticheskoi revoliutsii." *Istoricheskie zapiski*, no. 66, 1960, pp. 20–95.

Goldberg, Carl Allen. "The Association of Industry and Trade, 1906–1917: The Successes and Failures of Russia's Organized Businessmen." Ph.D. dissertation, University of Michigan, 1974.

Goldstein, Edward Ralph. "Military Aspects of Russian Industrialization: The Defense Industries, 1890–1917." Ph.D. dissertation, Case Western Reserve University, 1971.

Gordon, M. "Dvizheniia na Putilovskom zavode v 1901–1917 gg." *Arkhiv istorii truda v Rossii,* kn. 11–12 (1924), pp. 132–48.

———. "Rabochie na Obukhovskom staleliteinom zavode." *Arkhiv istorii truda v Rossii,* kn. 9 (1923), pp. 54–76.

Groh, Dieter. "Intensification of Work and Industrial Conflict in Germany, 1896–1914." *Politics and Society* 8 (1978), pp. 349–97.

Gudvan, A. "K istorii zakona 4 marta 1906 g." *Vestnik truda,* 1924, no. 7 (44), pp. 242–52.

Guroff, Gregory. "The Legacy of Russian Economic Education, The St. Petersburg Polytechnicum." *Russian Review* 31 (July 1972), pp. 272–81.

Gusiatnikov, P. S. *Revoliutsionnoe studencheskoe dvizhenie v Rossii, 1899–1907.* Moscow, 1971.

H.D. "Bor'ba za 8-chasovoi rabochii den' v Peterburge v 1905 gody: Na Franko-russkom zavode v 1905 g." *Krasnaia letopis',* 1925, no. 4 (15), pp. 130–35.

Haber, Samuel. *Efficiency and Uplift, Scientific Management in the Progressive Era, 1890–1920.* Chicago: University of Chicago Press, 1964.

Haimson, Leopold. "Introduction: The Russian Landed Nobility and the System of the Third of June." *The Politics of Rural Russia, 1905–1917,* pp. 1–29. Edited by Leopold Haimson. Bloomington: Indiana University Press, 1979.

———. "The Problem of Social Stability in Urban Russia, 1905- 1917." *Slavic Review* 23 (December 1964), pp. 619–42, and 24 (March 1965), pp. 1–22.

———. *The Russian Marxists and the Origins of Bolshevism.* Boston: Beacon Press, 1955.

Haimson, Leopold, in collaboration with Ziva Galili y Garcia and Richard Wortman. *The Making of Three Russian Revolutionaries, Voices from the Menshevik Past.* Cambridge: Cambridge University Press, 1987.

Haimson, Leopold, and Tilly, Charles, eds. *Strikes, Wars, and Revolutions in an International Perspective. Strike Waves in the Late Nineteenth and Early Twentieth Centuries.* Cambridge: Cambridge University Press, 1989.

Halsey, F. A. "The Premium Plan of Paying for Labor." *Transactions of the American Society of Mechanical Engineers,* 22 (1891), pp. 755–80.

Hans, Nicholas. *The History of Russian Educational Policy, 1701- 1917.* New York: Russell and Russell, 1964.

Harcave, Sidney. *The Russian Revolution of 1905.* London: Collier Books, 1970.

Harding, Neil. ed. *Marxism in Russia: Key Documents 1879–1906.* Cambridge: Cambridge University Press, 1983.

Hasegawa, Tsuyoshi. "The Problem of Power in the February Revolution of 1917 in Russia. *Canadian Slavonic Papers* 14, no. 4 (Winter 1972), pp. 611–33.

Haskell, Thomas L., ed. *The Authority of Experts, Studies in History and Theory.* Bloomington: Indiana University Press, 1984.

Hogan, Heather. "Conciliation Boards in Revolutionary Petrograd: Aspects of the Crisis of Labor-Management Relations in Russia." *Russian History* 9, pt. 1 (1982), pp. 49–66.

———. "Industrial Rationalization and the Roots of Labor Militance in the St. Petersburg Metal Working Industry, 1901–1914." *Russian Review* 42, no. 1 (April 1983), pp. 163–90.

———. "Labor and Management in Conflict: The St. Petersburg Metal Working Industry, 1900–1914." Ph.D. dissertation, University of Michigan, 1981.

———. "Scientific Management and the Changing Nature of Work in the St. Petersburg Metal Working Industry, 1900–1914." L. Haimson and C. Tilly, eds. *Strikes, Wars and Revolutions in an International Perspective.* Cambridge: Cambridge University Press, 1989, pp. 356–79.

———. "The Origins of the Scientific Mangement Movement in Russia." M. Dubovsky, ed., *Technological Change and Workers' Movements.* Beverly Hills: Sage Publications, 1985, pp. 77–99.

Holquist, Peter. "The Course of the Second Duma Elections in the Workers' Curiias of St. Petersburg." Unpublished paper, Columbia University, 1988.

Iakovlev, A. F. *Ekonomicheskie krizisy v Rossii.* Moscow, 1955.

Iakovlev, N. "Aprel'sko-maiskie dni 1912 goda v Peterburge." *Krasnaia letopis',* 1925, no. 3 (14), pp. 224–49.

Il'inskii, D. P., and Ivanitskii, V. P. *Ocherk istorii russkoi paravozostroitel'noi i vagonostroitel'noi promyshlennosti.* Moscow, 1929.

Il'in-Zhenevskii, A. F. "Kogda i kak nachal svoe sushchestvovanie Putilovskii zavod." *Krasnaia letopis',* 1929, no. 4 (31), pp. 190–206.

———. "Putilovskii zavod, S-Peterburgskii kazennyi chugunnoliteinyi zavod." *Krasnaia letopis',* 1930, no. 3 (36), pp. 192–222; no. 4 (37), pp. 157–95; no. 5 (38), pp. 144–63.

Istoriia rabochego klassa SSSR. Rabochii klass Rossii 1907-fevral' 1917 g.. Moscow: Nauka, 1982.

Istoriia rabochikh Leningrada. Tom pervyi. 1703-fevral' 1917. Leningrad, 1972.

Iukhneva, N. V. *Etnicheskii sostav i etnosotsial'naia struktura naseleniia Peterburga. Vtoraia polovina XIX-nachalo XX veka. Statisticheskii analiz.* Leningrad, 1984.

———. "Nakanune Obukhovskoi oborony (Pervomaiskaia stachka v Peterburge v 1901 godu)." *Vestnik Leningradskogo universiteta* 16, no. 2, 1961, pp. 57–67.

Ivanov, L. M. "Samoderzhavie, burzhuaziia i rabochie (k voprosu ob ideologicheskom vliianii na proletariat)." *Voprosy istorii,* 1971, no. 1, pp. 81–96.

Ivanov, L. M., ed. *Rabochii klass i rabochee dvizhenie v Rossii, 1861–1917.* Moscow, 1966.

Ivanov, L. M., et al., eds. *Bol'shevistskaia pechat' i rabochii klass Rossii v gody revoliutsionnogo pod"ema, 1910–1914.* Moscow, 1965.

———. *Rossiiskii proletariat: oblik, bor'ba, gegemoniia.* Moscow, 1970.

Johnson, Robert Eugene. *Peasant and Proletarian: The Working Class of Moscow in the Late Nineteenth Century.* New Brunswick: Rutgers University Press, 1979.

Kantor, R., comp. "Pervye shagi legalizovannogo profesional'nogo dvizheniia v Rossii." *Arkhiv istorii truda v Rossii,* kn. 2 (1921), pp. 108–23.

Kats, N. I. "Professional'nye soiuzy Peterburga v gody reaktsii, 1907–1910 gg." *Istoriia rabochego klassa Leningrada,* vol. 2, pp. 132–55. V. A. Ovsiakin, ed. in chief. Leningrad, 1963.

Kats, N. I., and Milonov, Iu., comps. *1905, Materialy i dokumenty: Professional'noe dvizhenie.* Moscow-Leningrad, 1926.

Katznelson, Ira. "Working-Class Formation: Constructing Cases and Comparisons." *Working-Class Formation: Nineteenth-Century Patterns in Western Europe and the United States,* edited by Ira Katznelson and Aristide R. Zolberg. Princeton: Princeton University Press, 1986.

Keep, J. L. H. "Russian Social Democracy and the First State Duma." *Slavonic and East European Review* 34, no. 82 (December 1955), pp. 180–99.

Khromov, P. A. Ekonomicheskoe razvitie Rossii v XIX-XX vekakh. Moscow, 1950.

King, Victoria. "The emergence of the St. Petersburg industrialist community, 1870–1905. The origins and early years of the St. Petersburg Society of Manufacturers." Ph.D. dissertation, University of California, Berkeley, 1982.

Kingston-Mann, Esther. "In Search of the True West: Western Economic Models and Russian Rural Development." *Journal of Historical Sociology* 3, no. 1 (March 1990), pp. 23–49.

———. "Marxism and Russian Rural Development: Problems of Evidence, Experience and Culture." *American Historical Review* 86, no. 4 (October 1981), pp. 731–52.

Kingston-Mann, Esther and Mixter, Timothy, eds. *Peasant Economy, Culture, and Politics of European Russia, 1800–1921.* Princeton: Princeton University Press, 1991.

Kireev, N. V. "Promyshlennost'." *Ocherki istorii Leningrada,* vol. 2, pp. 75–125. Edited by V. M. Kochakov et al. 4 vols. Moscow- Leningrad, 1955–1964.

Kir'ianov, Iu. I. "Ekonomicheskoe polozhenie rabochego klassa Rossii nakanune revoliutsii 1905–1907 gg." *Istoricheskie zapiski,* no. 98 (1977), pp. 147–89.

———. "Ob oblike rabochego klassa Rossii." *Rossiiskii proletariat: oblik, bor'ba, gegemoniia,* pp. 100–40. Edited by L. M. Ivanov et al. Moscow, 1970.

———. *Zhiznennyi uroven' rabochikh Rossii.* Moscow, 1979.

Kniazev, V. A. "Nikolai Petrovich." *Vospominaniia o Vladimire Il'iche Lenine.* Moscow, 1956.

Koenker, Diane. *Moscow Workers and the 1917 Revolution.* Princeton: Princeton University Press, 1981.

———. "Urban Families, Working Class Youth Groups, and the 1917 Revolution in Moscow." *The Family in Imperial Russia,* pp. 280–304. Edited by David L. Ransel. Urbana: University of Illinois Press, 1978.

Kolpenskii, V. "Fabrichno-zavodskie volneniia i fabrichnoe zakonodatel'stvo." *Arkhiv istorii truda v Rossii,* kn. 2 (1921), pp. 37–43.

Komissiia po izucheniiu istorii professional'nogo dvizheniia v Rossii. *Materialy po istorii professional'nogo dvizheniia v Peterburge za 1905–1907 gg.* Leningrad, 1926.

———. *Materialy po istorii professional'nogo dvizheniia v Rossii.* 4 vols. Moscow, 1924–1925.

Korol'chuk, E. A. "Ob osobennostiakh ekspluatatsii i stachechnoi bor'by peterburgskogo proletariata, 70–90-e gody XIX v." *Istoricheskie zapiski,* no. 89, 1972, pp. 134–86.

Korol'chuk, E. A., and Sokolova, E. *Khronika revoliutsionnogo rabochego dvizheniia v Peterburge.* Leningrad, 1940.

Kruze, E. E. "Antirabochaia politika monopolii." *Bol'shevistskaia pechat' i rabochii klassa Rossii v gody revoliutsionnogo pod"ema, 1910–1914,* pp. 389–400. Edited by L. M. Ivanov et al. Moscow, 1965.

———. "Gody novogo revoliutsionnogo pod"ema v Peterburge." *Ocherki istorii Leningrada,* vol. 3, pp. 460–531. Edited by V. M. Kochakov et al. 4 vols. Moscow-Leningrad, 1955–1964.

———. *Peterburgskie rabochie v 1912–1914 godakh.* Leningrad- Moscow, 1961.

———. "Promyshlennoe razvitie Peterburga v 1890-kh–1914 gg." *Ocherki istorii Leningrada,* vol. 3, pp. 9–60. Edited by V. M. Kochakov et al. 4 vols. Moscow-Leningrad, 1955–1964.

Kruze, E. E., and Kutsentov, D. G. "Naselenie Peterburga." *Ocherki istorii Leningrada,* vol. 3, pp. 104–46. Edited by V. M. Kochakov et al. 4 vols. Moscow-Leningrad, 1955–1964.

Kutsentov, D. G. *Deiateli Peterburgskogo Soiuza bor'by za osvobozhdenie rabochego klassa, Kratkie biograficheskie ocherki.* Moscow, 1962.

———. "Naselenie Peterburga. Polozhenie Peterburgskikh rabochikh." *Ocherki istorii Leningrada,* vol. 2, pp. 170–230. Edited by V. M. Kochakov et al. 4 vols. Moscow-Leningrad, 1955–1964.

Kuznetsov, K. A., et al., eds. *Baltiiskii sudostroitel'nyi, 1856- 1917: Ocherk istorii Baltiiskogo sudostroitel'nogo zavoda im. S. Ordzhonikidze.* Leningrad, 1970.

Landes, David S. *The Unbound Prometheus, Technological Change and Industrial Development in Western Europe from 1750 to the Present.* Cambridge: Cambridge University Press, 1969.

Lane, David. *The Roots of Russian Communism.* University Park: Pennsylvania State University Press, 1968.

Leningrad. Istoriko-geograficheskii atlas. Moscow, 1977.

Levin, Sh. M. "Obshchestvennoe dvizhenie v Peterburge na rubezhe 60–70-kh i v 70-kh godakh. Bor'ba peterburgskikh rabochikh v 70-x godakh." *Ocherki istorii Leningrada*, vol. 2. Edited by V. M. Kochakov et al. 4 vols. Moscow-Leningrad, 1955–1964.

Liebman, Marcel. *Leninism Under Lenin.* London: Merlin Press, 1975.

Livshin, Ia. I. "K voprosu o voenno-promyshlennykh monopoliiakh v Rossii v nachale XX v. (po materialam senatskikh revizii)." *Voprosy istorii*, 1957, no. 7, pp. 55–70.

———. *Monopolii v ekonomike Rossii.* Moscow, 1961.

———. "'Predstavitel'nyi' organizatsii krupnoi burzhuazii v Rossii v kontse XIX-nachale XX vv." *Istoriia SSSR*, 1959, no. 2, pp. 95–117.

Livshits, S. "Bor'ba za 8-chasovoi rabochii den' v Peterburge v 1905 godu: Na S.-Peterburgskom vagonostroitel'nom zavode v oktiabre-noiabre 1905 g." *Krasnaia letopis'*, 1925, no. 4 (15), pp. 116–30.

Lur'e, M. L. *Sto dva dnia geroicheskoi zabastovki.* Leningrad, 1938.

L'vovich, A. "Trebovaniia rabochikh Baltiiskogo i drugikh morskikh zavodov v ianvarskie dni 1905 godu." *Arkhiv istorii truda v Rossii*, kn. 4 (1) (1922), pp. 85–96.

McDaniel, Tim. *Autocracy, Capitalism, and Revolution in Russia.* Berkeley: University of California Press, 1988.

McKay, John P. *Pioneers for Profit: Foreign Entrepreneurship and Russian Industrialization, 1885–1913.* Chicago: University of Chicago Press, 1970.

McKean, Robert B. *St. Petersburg Between the Revolutions: Workers and Revolutionaries, June 1907-February 1917.* New Haven: Yale University Press, 1990.

McKinsey, Pamela Sears. "From City Workers to Peasantry: The Beginnings of the Russian Movement 'To the People.'" *Slavic Review* 38, no. 4 (December 1979), pp. 629–49.

Maier, C. S. "Between Taylorism and Technocracy." *Journal of Contemporary History* 5 (1970), pp. 27–61.

———. *Recasting Bourgeois Europe.* Princeton: Princeton University Press, 1975.

Mandel, David. *Petrograd Workers and the Fall of the Old Regime.* London: Macmillan, 1983.

Manning, Roberta. *The Crisis of the Old Order in Russia: Government and Gentry.* Princeton: Princeton University Press, 1982.

Mazdorov, V. A. *Istoriia razvitiia bugalterskogo ucheti v SSSR.* Moscow, 1972.

Meerson, G. "Promyshlennaia depressiia v Rossii, 1906–1909 gg." *Vestnik kommunisticheskoi akademii*, 1924, no. 9, pp. 147–74.

Mehlinger, Howard D., and Thompson, John M. *Count Witte and the Tsarist Government in the 1905 Revolution.* Bloomington: Indiana University Press, 1972.

Melancon, Michael. "The Socialist Revolutionaries from 1902 and 1907: Peasant and Workers' Party." *Russian History* 12, no. 1 (spring 1985), pp. 2–47.

Menashe, Louis. "Industrialists in Politics: Russia in 1905." *Government and Opposition* 3 (1968), pp. 352–68.

Mikhailov, M. M. "1905 god na Izhorskom zavode." *Krasnaia letopis'*, 1931, nos. 5–6 (44–45), pp. 241–65; 1932, nos. 1–2 (46–47), pp. 226–48; 1932, no. 3 (48), pp. 189–210.

Mitel'man, M., Glebov, B., and Ul'ianskii, A. *Istoriia Putilovskogo zavoda.* Moscow, 1939, 1941, 1961.

Montgomery, David. *Fall of the House of Labor.* Cambridge: Cambridge University Press, 1987.

———. *Workers' Control in America.* Cambridge: Cambridge University Press, 1979.

Murzintseva, S. V. "Bor'ba rabochikh voennykh predpriiatii Peterburga v 1910–1914 gg." *Vestnik Leningradskogo universiteta*, 1967, no. 14, pp. 63–75.

———. "Iz istorii ekonomicheskogo polozheniia rabochikh na predpriiatiiakh voennogo i morskogo vedomst v 1907–1914 gg. v Peterburge." *Uchenye zapiski LGU,* no. 270 (1959), pp. 217–41.

Netesin, Iu. N. "K voprosu o sotsial'no-ekonomicheskikh korniakh i osobennostiakh 'rabochei aristokratii' v Rossii." *Bol'shevistskaia pechat' i rabochii klass Rossii v gody revoliutsionnogo pod"ema, 1910–1914,* pp. 192–211. Edited by L. M. Ivanov et al. Moscow, 1965.

Nevskii, V. "Ianvarskie dni v Peterburge v 1905 godu." *Krasnaia letopis',* 1922, no. 1, pp. 13–74.

―――. "Vybory v kommissiiu senatora Shidlovskogo (1905 g.)." *Arkhiv istorii truda v Rossii,* kn. 3, 1922, pp. 78–90.

Nikolaev, S. "Iz revoliutsionnogo proshlogo Nevskogo sudostroitel'nogo i mekhanicheskogo zavoda." *Krasnaia letopis',* 1925, no. 1 (12), pp. 67–74.

Noble, David F. *America by Design: Science, Technology, and the Rise of Corporate Capitalism.* New York: Alfred A. Knopf, 1979.

Ocherki istorii Leningrada, vol. 2: *Period kapitalizma. Vtoraia polovina XIX veka.* Moscow-Leningrad, 1957. Vol. 3: *Period imperializma i burzhuazno-demokraticheskikh revoliutsii. 1895- 1917 gg.* Edited by B. M. Kochakov et al. Moscow-Leningrad, 1956.

Ocherki po istorii ekonomiki i klassovykh otnoshenii. Sbornik statei. Moscow-Leningrad, 1964.

O revoliutsionnom proshlom Peterburgskogo metallicheskogo zavoda, 1886–1905. Sbornik. Leningrad, 1926.

Paialin, N. P. "Zavod b. Semiannikova." *Krasnaia letopis',* published in eleven installments from 1930, no. 1, to 1931, nos. 5–6 (44–45).

―――. *Zavod imeni Lenina, 1857–1918.* Moscow-Leningrad, 1933.

Palat, M. K. "Labour Legislation and Reform in Russia, 1905- 1914." D. Phil., Oxford, 1973.

Pankratova, A. *Fabzavkomy v Rossii v bor'be za sotsialisticheskuiu fabriku.* Moscow, 1912.

Pavlovskaia, A. A., and Kureev, N. V. "Gody reaktsii v Peterburge." *Ocherki istorii Leningrada,* vol. 3, pp. 410- 59. Edited by V. M. Kochakov et al. 4 vols. Moscow-Leningrad, 1955–1964.

Pazhitnov, K. A. *Polozhenie rabochego klassa v Rossii,* vol. 3: *Revoliutsionnyi period s 1905 po 1923 g.* Leningrad, 1924.

Perrie, Maureen. "The Social Composition and Structure of the Socialist-Revolutionary Party Before 1917." *Soviet Studies* 24, no. 2 (October 1972), pp. 223–50.

Petrochenko, P., and Kuznetsova, K. *Organizatsiia i normirovanie truda v promyshlennosti SSSR.* Moscow, 1971.

Pogrebinskii, A. P. "Komitet po zheleznodorozhnym zakazam i ego likvidatsiia v 1914 g." *Istoricheskie zapiski,* no. 83, 1969, pp. 233–43.

Polikarpov, V. V. "Iz istorii voennoi promyshlennosti v Rossii (1906–1916 gg.)." *Istoricheskie zapiski,* no. 104, 1979, pp. 123–67.

―――. "O 'kommercheskom' upravlenii gosudarstvennoi promyshlennost'iu v Rossii nachala XX v." *Vestnik Moskovskogo Universiteta,* Seriia 8, Istoriia, no. 4 (1988), pp. 48–61.

Portal, Roger. "The Industrialization of Russia." *Cambridge Economic History of Europe,* vol. 6, pt. 2. Cambridge, 1965, pp. 801–72.

Pushkareva, I. M. *Rabochee dvizhenie v Rossii v period reaktsii, 1906–1910.* Moscow, 1989.

Rashin, A. G. *Formirovanie rabochego klassa v Rossii.* Moscow, 1958.

―――. *Zhenskii trud v SSSR.* Moscow, 1928.

Reikhardt, V. V. "Partiinye gruppirovki i 'predstavitel'stvo interesov' krupnogo kapitala v 1905–1906 gg." *Krasnaia letopis',* 1930, no. 6 (39), pp. 5–39.

Rice, Christopher. "'Land and Freedom' in the Factories of Petersburg: The SRs and the Workers' Curia Elections to the Second Duma, January 1907." *Soviet Studies* 36, no. 1 (January 1984), pp. 87–107.

————. *Russian Workers and the Socialist-Revolutionary Party Through the Revolution of 1905–07.* New York: St Martin's Press, 1988.

Rieber, Alfred. "The Formation of La Grande Société des chemins de fer russes." *Jahrbucher fur Geschichte Osteuropas* 21, no. 3 (1973), pp. 375–91.

————. *Merchants and Entrepreneurs in Imperial Russia.* Chapel Hill: University of North Carolina Press, 1982.

Rimlinger, Gaston V. "Autocracy and the Factory Order in Early Russian Industrialization." *Journal of Economic History* 20 (March 1960), pp. 67–92.

————. "The Legitimation of Protest: A Comparative Study in Labor History." *Comparative Studies in Society and History* 11 (April 1960), pp. 329–43.

————. "The Management of Labor Protest in Tsarist Russia." *International Review of Social History* 5, pt. 2 (1960), pp. 226–48.

Rogger, Hans. "*Amerikanizm* and the Economic Development of Russia." *Comparative Studies in Society and History* 23, no. 3 (July 1981), pp. 382–420.

Romanov, B. "Peterburgskaia krupnaia burzhuaziia v ianvarskie dni 1905 goda." *Krasnaia letopis'*, 1925, no. 1 (12), pp. 47–56.

————. "Putilovskii zavod v ianvare-avguste 1905 g. v osveshchenii zavodskoi administratsii." *Krasnaia letopis'*, 1925, no. 3 (14), pp. 175–78.

————. *Rabochii vopros v komissii V. N. Kokovtsova v 1905,* Moscow, 1926.

Roosa, Ruth Amende. "The Association of Industry and Trade, 1906- 1914: An Examination of the Economic Views of Organized Industrialists in Pre-Revolutionary Russia." Ph.D. dissertation, Columbia University, 1967.

————. "Russian Industrialists and State Socialism, 1906–1917." *Soviet Studies* 23 (January 1972), pp. 395–417.

————. "Russian Industrialists Look to the Future: Thoughts on Economic Development, 1906–1917." *Essays in Russian and Soviet History in Honor of G. T. Robinson,* pp. 198–218. Edited by John S. Curtiss. New York: Columbia University Press, 1963.

————. "Russian Industrialists, Politics and Labor Reform in 1905." *Russian History* 2, pt. 2 (1975), pp. 124–48.

————. "'United' Russian Industry." *Soviet Studies* 24 (June 1973), pp. 421–25.

————. "Workers' Insurance Legislation and the Role of the Industrialists in the Period of the Third State Duma." *Russian Review* 34 (October 1975), pp. 410–52.

Rosenberg, William G. "Workers and Workers' Control in the Russian Revolution." *History Workshop,* no. 5 (Spring 1978), pp. 89–97.

Rozanov, M. *Obukhovtsy: Istoriia zavoda 'Bol'shevik'.* Leningrad, 1938.

Rozenfel'd, S. Ia., and Klimenko, K. I. *Istoriia mashinostroeniia SSSR.* Moscow, 1961.

Sablinsky, Walter. *The Road to Bloody Sunday.* Princeton: Princeton University Press, 1976.

Sanders, Jonathan E. "The Union of Unions: Political, Economic, Civil, and Human Rights Organizations in the 1905 Russian Revolution." Ph.D. dissertation, Columbia University, 1983.

Schapiro, Leonard. *The Communist Party of the Soviet Union.* New York: Vintage Books, 1960.

Schneiderman, Jeremiah. *Sergei Zubatov and Revolutionary Marxism: The Struggle for the Working Class in Tsarist Russia.* Ithaca, N.Y., 1976.

Schwarz, Solomon M. *The Russian Revolution of 1905.* Chicago: University of Chicago Press, 1967.

Semanov, S. N. *Peterburgskie rabochie nakanune pervoi russkoi revoliutsii.* Moscow-Leningrad, 1966.

————. "Peterburgskie rabochie nakanune pervoi russkoi revoliutsii (chislennost' i sostav)." *Ocherki po istorii ekonomiki i klassovykh otnoshenii v Rossii kontsa XIX-nachala XX veka. Sbornik statei.* Moscow-Leningrad, 1964.

Service, Robert. *Lenin: A Political Life,* vol. 1: *The Strength of Contradiction.* Bloomington: Indiana University Press, 1985.

Sestroretskii instrumental'nyi zavod imeni Voskova. Ocherki, dokumenty, vospominaniia. 1721–1967. Leningrad, 1968.

Shanin, Teodor. *Russia, 1905–07, Revolution as a Moment of Truth,* vol. 2. New Haven: Yale University Press, 1986.

Shatilova, T. "Burzhuaziia v bor'be s zabastovkami v kontse 1905 goda." *Krasnaia letopis',* 1925, no. 4 (15), pp. 126–47.

———. "Rabochee dvizhenie v Peterburge v 1914 g. do voiny." *Krasnaia letopis',* 1927, no. 1 (22), pp. 150–69.

Shatsillo, K. F. "Inostrannyi kapital i voenno-morskie programmy Rossii nakanune pervoi mirovoi voiny." *Istoricheskii zapiski,* no. 69 (1961), pp. 73–100.

———. *Rossiia pered pervoi mirovoi voinoi. Vooruzhennye sily tsarizma v 1905–1914 gg.* Moscow, 1974.

———. *Russkii imperializm i razvitie flota nakanune pervoi mirovoi voiny (1906–1914 gg.).* Moscow, 1968.

Shchap, Z. *Moskovskie metallisty v professional'nykh dvizhenii: Ocherki po istorii Moskovskogo soiuza metallistov.* Moscow, 1927.

Shepelev, L. E. *Tsarizm i burzhuaziia v 1904–1914 gg.* Leningrad, 1987.

Shuster, U. A. *Peterburgskie rabochie v 1905–1907 gg.* Leningrad, 1976.

Sidorov, A. L., ed. *Ob osobennostiakh imperializma v Rossii.* Moscow, 1963.

Smith, Merritt Roe. *Harpers Ferry Armory and the New Technology.* Ithaca: Cornell University Press, 1977.

Smith, Steve. "Craft Consciousness, Class Consciousness: Petrograd, 1917." *History Workshop,* no. 11 (Spring 1981), pp. 33- 56.

———. *Red Petrograd. Revolution in the Factories, 1917–1918.* Cambridge: Cambridge University Press, 1983.

———. "Taylorism Rules OK? Bolshevism, Taylorism and the Technical Intelligentsia in the Soviet Union, 1917–41." *Radical Science Journal* 13 (1983), pp. 3–27.

Smolin, I. S. "Bor'ba Peterburgskikh rabochikh za 8-chasovoi den' v gody pervoi russkoi revoliutsii." *Istoriia rabochego klassa Leningrada,* vyp. 2. Leningrad, 1963.

———. "Pervaia russkaia revoliutsiia v Peterburge." *Ocherki istorii Leningrada,* vol. 3, pp. 223–409. Edited by V. M. Kochakov et al. 4 vols. Moscow-Leningrad, 1955–1964.

Solodnikova, M. "Rabochii v svete statistiki." *Arkhiv istorii truda v Rossii,* kn. 9 (1923), pp. 14–41.

Steinberg, Marc D. *Moral Communities: The Culture of Class Relations in the Russian Printing Industry, 1867–1907.* Berkeley: University of California Press, 1992.

Stepanov, Z. V. *Rabochie Petrograda v period podgotovki i provedeniia Oktiabr'skogo vooruzhennogo dvizheniia.* Moscow- Leningrad, 1965.

Stites, Richard. *Revolutionary Dreams: Utopian Vision and Experimental Life in the Russian Revolution.* New York: Oxford University Press, 1989.

Stolpianskii, P. N. *Zhizn' i byt peterburgskoi fabriki za 210 let ee sushchestvovaniia 1704–1914 gg.* Leningrad, 1925.

Strumilin, S. G. *Problemy ekonomiki truda; ocherki i etiudy.* Moscow, 1925.

Subbotin, Iu. F. "Iz istorii voennoi promyshlennosti Rossii kontsa XIX-nachala XX veka." *Vestnik Leningradskogo universiteta,* 1973, no. 20, pp. 45–51.

———. "K istorii vzaimootnoshenii mezhdu chastnymi i kazennymi predpriiatiiami v voennoi promyshlennosti Rossii kontsa XIX- nachala XX veka." *Vestnik Leningradskogo universiteta,* 1974, no. 14, pp. 35–42.

Surh, Gerald. *1905 in St. Petersburg, Labor, Society and Revolution.* Stanford: Stanford University Press, 1989.

———. "Petersburg's First Mass Labor Organization: The Assembly of Russian Workers and Father Gapon." *Russian Review* 40, no. 3 (July 1981), pp. 241–62; no. 4 (October 1981), pp. 412–41.

———. "Petersburg Workers in 1905: Strikes, Workplace Democracy, and the Revolution." Ph.D. dissertation, University of California, Berkeley, 1979.

———. "Sources of Working Class Consciousness in St. Petersburg, 1905." Paper presented at the Midwest Slavic Conference, University of Wisconsin, Madison, April 1986.

Sviatlovskii, V. "Druz'ia i vragi professional'nogo dvizheniia." *Krasnaia letopis'*, 1923, no. 8, pp. 183–219.

———. "Iz istorii kass i obshchestv vzaimopomoshchi i rabochikh." *Arkhiv istorii truda v Rossii*, kn. 4, pt. 1 (1921), pp. 32–46.

———. "Na zare Rossiiskoi sotsial-demokratii. Epokha 'kruzhkovshchiny' i 'gruppa Brusneva.'" *Byloe*, no. 19, 1922, pp. 139–60.

———. "Pervye konferentsii i s"ezdy professional'nykh soiuzov (1905–1907 gg.)." *Arkhiv istorii truda v Rossii*, kn. 9 (1923), pp. 3–13.

———. "Professional'noe dvizhenie rabochikh v 1905 g." *Krasnaia letopis'*, 1922, nos. 2–3, pp. 165–96.

Swain, Geoffrey. *Russian Social Democracy and the Legal Labour Movement, 1906–1914*. London: Macmillan, 1983.

Syromiatnikova, M., comp. "Rabochee dvizhenie na zavodakh Peterburga v mae 1901 g." *Krasnyi arkhiv*, 3 (76) 1936, pp. 49- 66.

Thompson, C. B. *Scientific Management: A Collection of the More Significant Articles Describing the Taylor System of Management*. Cambridge: Harvard University Press, 1914.

Thompson, E. P. *The Making of the English Working Class*. New York, 1964.

Timoshenko, S. P. "The Development of Engineering Education in Russia." *Russian Review* 15, no. 3 (July 1956), pp. 173–85.

Tiutiukin, S. V. *Iiul'skii politicheskii krizis 1906 g. v Rossii*. Moscow, 1991.

———. "O nekotorykh osobennostiakh 'rabochei aristokratii' v Rossii." *Proletariat Rossii na puti k Oktiabriu 1917 goda (oblik, bor'ba, gegemoniia)*. Materialy k nauchnoi sessii po istorii proletariata, posviashchennoi 50-letiiu Velikogo Oktiabria, 14–17 Noiabria, 1967. Odessa, 1967. Chast' 2, pp. 93–98.

Vanag, N. *Finansovyi kapital v Rossii nakanune mirovoi voiny*. Moscow, 1925.

Vanag, N., and Tomsinskii, S., comps. *Ekonomicheskoe razvitie Rossii, Epokha finansovogo kapitalizma*. Moscow-Leningrad, 1930.

Verner, Andrew M. *The Crisis of Russian Autocracy, Nicholas II and the 1905 Revolution*. Princeton: Princeton University Press, 1990.

Volk, S. S. "Prosveshchenie i shkola." *Ocherki istorii Leningrada*, vol. 2, pp. 663–714. Edited by V. M. Kochakov et al. 4 vols. Moscow-Leningrad, 1955–1964.

von Laue, Theodore H. "Russian Peasants in the Factory, 1892–1904." *Journal of Economic History* 21, no. 1 (March 1961), pp. 61- 80.

———. "Factory Inspection under the Witte System, 1892–1903." *American Slavic and East European Review* 19 (October 1960), pp. 347–62.

———. "Russian Peasants in the Factory, 1892–1904." *Journal of Economic History* 21 (March 1961), pp. 61–80.

———. "Tsarist Labour Policy, 1895–1903." *Journal of Modern History* 34 (June 1962), pp. 135–45.

Vovchik, A. F. *Politika tsarizma po rabochemu voprosu v predrevoliutsionnyi period*. L'vov, 1964.

Wcislo, Francis W. *Reforming Rural Russia. State, Local Society, and National Politics, 1855–1914*. Princeton: Princeton University Press, 1990.

"The Works 'Red Putilovets.' A Short Historical Description." Petrograd, n.d. Typescript held at the Hoover Institution, Stanford, California.

Za 20 let. K dvadtsatiletiiu soiuza metallistov. Sbornik statei. Edited by V. Radinovich. Leningrad, 1926.

Zav'ialov, S. *Istoriia Izhorskogo zavoda.* Moscow, 1934.

———, ed. and trans. *A Radical Worker in Tsarist Russia: The Autobiography of Semën Ivanovich Kanatchikov.* Stanford: Stanford University Press.

Zelnik, Reginald E. *Labor and Society in Tsarist Russia: The Factory Workers of St. Petersburg, 1855–1870.* Stanford: Stanford University Press, 1971.

———. "On the Eve: An Inquiry into the Life Histories and Self-Awareness of Some Russian Industrial Workers, 1870–1905 (*Ocherki*)." Paper presented at the conference on "The Making of the Soviet Working Class." Michigan State University, November 9–11, 1990.

———. "Russian Bebels: An Introduction to the Memoirs of Semen Kanatchikov and Matvei Fisher." *Russian Review* 35, no. 3 (July 1976), pp. 249–89, and 35, no. 4 (October 1976), pp. 417–47.

———. "Russian Workers and the Revolutionary Movement." *Journal of Social History* 6, no. 2 (Winter 1972–1973).

Zhdanov, V. A. *Dovoennaia moshchnost' metallopromyshlennosti i ee znachenie v ekonomike strany.* Moscow-Leningrad, 1925.

Zhukovskii, Ia. "Ekonomicheskoe razvitie Putilovskogo zavoda." *Problemy Marksizma,* 1932, nos. 9–10, pp. 136–67.

INDEX

HEATHER HOGAN is Associate Professor of History at Oberlin College and author of articles on Russian labor history.